THE URBAN IMAGE OF AUGUSTAN ROME

The Urban Image of Augustan Rome examines the idea and experience of the ancient city at a critical moment, when Rome became an Imperial capital. Lacking dignity, unity, and a clear image during the Republic, the urban image of Rome became focused only when the state came under the control of Augustus, the first emperor, who transformed the city physically and conceptually. Intervening in an ad hoc manner, he repaired existing public structures, added numerous new monuments, established municipal offices for urban care, and promoted an enduring aesthetic. Directed by a single vision, the cumulative results were forceful and unified. This book explores for the first time the motives for urban intervention, methods for implementation, and the sociopolitical context of the Augustan period, as well as broader design issues such as formal urban strategies and definitions of urban imagery.

The Urban Image
of Augustan Rome

DIANE FAVRO

University of California, Los Angeles

CAMBRIDGE
UNIVERSITY PRESS

Published by the Press Syndicate of the University of Cambridge
The Pitt Building, Trumpington Street, Cambridge CB2 1RP
40 West 20th Street, New York, NY 10011-4211, USA
10 Stamford Road, Oakleigh, Melbourne 3166, Australia

First published 1996

Printed in the United States of America

Library of Congress Cataloging-in-Publication Data

Favro, Diane G.
    The urban image of Augustan Rome / Diane Favro.
        p.   cm.
    Includes bibliographical references and index.
    ISBN 0-521-45083-7 (hc)
    1. Rome (Italy)—Buildings, structures, etc.   2. City planning
—Italy—Rome—History.   3. Architecture, Roman—Italy—Rome.
4. Augustus, emperor of Rome, 63 B.C.–14 A.D.—Contributions in city
planning.   5. Rome (Italy)—History—To 476.   I. Title.
DG69.F38   1996
937′.06—dc20   96-5565
                                                                CIP

A catalog record for this book is available from the British Library

ISBN 0-521-45083-7 Hardback

To my parents

Because I know that time is always time
And place is always and only place
And what is actual is actual only for one time
And only for one place.

T. S. Eliot, *Ash Wednesday*

CONTENTS

ILLUSTRATIONS

TABLES

PREFACE

With good will one person can enter into
the world of another despite differences
in age, temperament, and culture.

Yi-Fu Tuan, *Topophilia*, 5

Cities evoke strong responses. Each urban environment simultaneously projects hundreds of multifaceted, sometimes contradictory, impressions. A city can be friendly in one context, threatening in another, attractive or unappealing, inspiring or mundane. People respond to and remember the feeling and idea of a city more than its physical layout. The Architect Balkrishna Doshi succinctly articulated this phenomenon: "Forms are not as important as the experience. That is the memory we always carry with us."[1] In any given period, people forge a common conceptual image based upon both physical interaction with an urban environment and shared ideas regarding urban content. It is this complex, experientially based response to cities that interests me.

My fascination with the urban image deepened while studying ancient Rome and teaching in Los Angeles. A sprawling city, Los Angeles lacks not only an obvious urban focus, but also a clear identity. Experienced usually at high speed from an automobile, the city evokes blurred, multivalent memories of great intensity, but of limited clarity. Even logos such as "the Big Orange" have not successfully defined the elusive image of this megalopolis. Rome, too, struggles to shape a clear contemporary identity, laboring under the added burden of innumerable diverse urban images piled up over an extensive history. A walk through this complex cityscape provides fleeting glimpses of different moments in Rome's history. Faced with these two distinctive examples, I began to explore how an urban image is created, promulgated, and transformed. More specifically, I became concerned with modern applications. How might the admired cities of the past inspire today's residents to demand richer experiences and more meaning from their cities? What lessons could they provide modern patrons and designers interested in creating more focused urban images?

Though an evolving construct, the urban image is best analyzed at specific periods and for specific cities. Historically, select cities projected forceful identities, usually by choreographing a positive urban experience. The explication of an individual example reveals the complex factors involved in the creation of a strong urban image, from the rhetoric accompanying patronage to the effective sequencing and distribution of projects, from the judicious use of materials for effect to the ceremonial choreography of urban events and messages. Only by looking at a city in a holistic manner can we understand why patrons and institutions funded urban projects or their choices of building types, materials, and placement. Reflecting specific cultural priorities, the conceptual content interwoven within any urban fabric likewise is in large part time-specific. Most important, examination of a cityscape at a particular period encourages consideration of how contemporary users actually experienced the urban environment. Evaluated together, these issues expand our understanding of cities and city processes. They explain why some urban environments are more memorable than others, why some attempts at formulating an urban image succeed while others fail.

I wrote this book for people interested in cities. Though the temporal range is succinct, the issues and concerns are broad. My wish is that historians, designers, and users of cities will all find parts of interest, while the whole retains its integrity as a period study. The body of the text is framed by recreated experiential walks through the ancient city accessible to general readers. The sections on the historical and cultural context analyze topics of concern to academic specialists. The evaluations of urban components and forms address urban designers and architects. Above all, I hope that the power and excitement of the Augustan example will underscore the importance of human experience and conceptualization in the evaluation of built environments.

I have been helped in this research by many. Above all, Spiro Kostof has taught me that buildings and environments are meaningless without people. His inspiration imbues every page. Through an unstinting belief in the project, valuable criticism, and emotional support, Fikret Yegül enriched the process as well as the product. I owe a debt to many other good friends who shared their ideas, patiently read and reread sections, and provided appreciated encouragement. Special thanks go to William L. MacDonald, Peter Holliday, Dana Cuff, Lionel March, and Murray Milne. Bernard Frischer and Barbara Kellum kindly commented on early versions of this work. I am indebted to Julie Dercle, Jocelyn Gibbs, Linda Hart, and Philip

Hu for their assistance in research, and to Rodica Reif and Ric Abramson for their patience and skill in making the illustrations. Research on the project was made possible through the generous support of the Fulbright Fellowship Program, American Association of University Women, Florida A and M University Fund, and Academic Senate Grants from UCLA. I am especially grateful to Beatrice Rehl who has provided guidance, expertise, and encouragement. She and the entire team at Cambridge University Press, including production editor Ernie Haim and Janet Polata, made the entire process a pleasure.

D.G.F.

CHAPTER ONE

INTRODUCTION
DEFINING AN URBAN IMAGE

A city is like a living thing . . . a united
and continuous whole.

Plutarch, *Moralia* 559

Visitors to a city form an impression of what they have experienced. This mental construct is based upon two reactions. The first and most immediate as observers move through the urban environment is the external physical response registered by the senses – hearing, smell, touch, and above all sight. Second is the internal conceptual reaction determined by culturally conditioned notions of what a city is, does, and means. Together these reactions forge a memorable urban image. According to this definition, an urban image is not a pictorial representation, but the idea of the city produced in the minds of contemporary visitors. Each individual who passes through an urban environment devises a slightly different mental image, yet all visitors in any given period navigate the same physical and cultural environment. As a result, they together formulate a collective urban image sharing the same basic characteristics. Responsive to the physical environment, it is highly visual in nature, yet is also forcefully shaped by such intangibles as urban mood and character. A strong urban image is not reliant solely upon grand individual urban monuments or a comprehensive urban design, but also upon the molding of enriched and interrelated experiences.

Kevin Lynch brought the concept of an urban image to a broad audience with his influential book, *The Image of the City,* of 1960. Studying how city residents conceptualized their urban environments, he discovered that individual, personal ideas and experiences melded to form a common urban image.[1] For study purposes, Lynch defined three components of an environmental image: identity, structure, and meaning. Though he reminded his readers always to consider the three together, his own work focused on the identity and structure of the physical form rather than on

1

conceptual issues. As a result, his presentation was more prescriptive than expository. Such an emphasis is understandable for an investigator operating in the same time period as his subject. The tangible is more immediate and well-defined, and thus demands more attention.[2] In contrast, examinations of past urban environments allow modern researchers sufficient distance for tempered analysis.

In the majority of cities throughout history, urban experiences evolved in an ad hoc manner, with limited purposeful manipulation. The lack of concern with the choreography of experiences and urban meaning resulted in unclear or unmemorable urban ideas. In select instances, however, strong forces attempted to shape a focused, purposeful image. The choreographed experiences, imprinted signs and symbols, and unifying narratives of a few cities from different periods and cultures still have the power to affix in the memory. The attraction of strong historical urban images is heightened in late twentieth-century America, when a lack of positive sensorial stimuli and diffused overall identities have made our cities less than appealing or memorable. Today, we treat our urban environments as disposable because they offer impoverished experiences and devalued content. As a result, tourists flock to urban environments with clear meanings and rich sensorial experiences such as the historic cores of Florence and old Cairo, or such faux historical examples such as Main Street at Disneyland. In a few notable instances, modern cities have consciously labored to recapture the potency of a favored urban image from their past long after the historic physical environment has been lost. For example, the California city of Santa Barbara obsessively and profitably promotes the positively perceived urban image associated with its early days as a Spanish settlement.[3]

Study of the more notable urban images from the past can advance the understanding of how cities become memorable. Historic cities are urban laboratories frozen in time. Isolated from the particular concerns that shaped a historical urban form, modern researchers can bring an objectivity impossible for the study of the environments in which we live. In contrast to open-ended contemporary images, those of the past can be concisely isolated temporally and topically. With hindsight, we can identify succinct periods when an image was formed, and trace the complex factors affecting its evolution. Through the examination of past urban environments, we are reacquainted with the conceptual and experiential aspects that have been lost or minimized over the centuries. For example, the urban images of preindustrial cities are based upon pedestrian experience, allowing researchers to evaluate concerns and responses foreign to generations weaned on vehicular movement. Similarly, the framework for urban patronage has changed radically over the years. The experience of modern cities

Figure 1. Model of Augustan Rome. Photo: J. Laurentius, courtesy the Antikenmuseum, Staatliche Museen Preussicher Kulturbesitz, Berlin.

frequently results from consensus planning involving the input of numerous diverse groups of politicians, users, government agencies, interest groups, designers, and planners. In contrast, some of the most powerful historic urban images were purposeful creations of single autocratic rulers.

Rome at the turn of the millennium presents an intriguing subject for the analysis of an urban image. The city was a true metropolis, comparable in size and complexity to many modern environments (fig. 1). In addition, at this moment in time, Rome came under the leadership of a strong individual. Augustus (63 B.C. – A.D. 14) forged the transition from the Roman Republic to the Roman Empire. An integral part of this change was the recasting of the Republican city on the Tiber River as an Imperial capital. Rome had to convey her importance as both the seat of a great State and the home of a great man. Simply, her image had to outshine those of other cities in the Mediterranean. Along with art, architecture, and literature, Augustus treated the image of Rome as a tool for legitimizing and conveying both Imperial and personal might. Blessed with the advantages of power, wealth, and, above all, time, Augustus manipulated the cityscape to offer dynamic and meaningful sensorial experiences, imbued with directed meaning. In the end, Augustan Rome had a forceful and urban image.

THE ROMAN URBAN IMAGE

Modern observers rely heavily upon words and icons to convey urban meaning. The image of contemporary cities often is encapsulated in logos or slogans created by hired promoters: "The Big Apple" for New York, "The Poinsettia City by the Sea" for my hometown San Buena Ventura. These epithets complement "sound bites," the stock phrases used to describe the condition of particular cities: Los Angeles as "the city in search of a center," Houston as "the city without zoning." Equally potent are select "visual bites," those easily recognizable views repeatedly used in promotional literature such as the silhouette of Hagia Sophia for Istanbul or the Golden Gate Bridge for San Francisco.[4] Popular culture provides additional shared perceptions, revealed in songs ("Chicago"), cinema ("Miami Vice"), and writing (*Slaves of New York*).[5] Significantly, all these modern interpretations are received passively, divorced from the personal experience of a city. All lack direct interaction with an observer.

The Romans likewise described cities verbally. Histories, geographies, letters, and poems all preserve data about the urban environments of antiquity. These texts, however, tend to be largely descriptive or historical in nature. Furthermore, they most frequently focus on the great cities of the Hellenistic East.[6] Such favoring of Greek-based urban images reflects the sense of cultural inferiority that permeated Republican society. In addition, verbal presentations were in themselves privileged, being written by and for the educated.

Because literacy was low in antiquity, the Romans employed other means to convey information about cities to a broader audience. Visual depictions of cityscapes are found in Roman paintings, mosaics, and reliefs.[7] Although rarely accurate portraits of urban form, such pictorial representations do indicate the features and cultural priorities valued by contemporary observers. They succinctly reflect the contemporary perception of individual urban components and their interrelationships, as well as specific physical characteristics such as scale, textures, and colors.[8] For example, the carver of an imperial relief from Avezzano chose to emphasize a town's external wall and gate, its regular plan, and the relationship between the highly for-

Figure 2. Imperial relief showing a walled Roman city, Palazzo Torlonia, Avezzano. Photo: DAIR 79.2757.

mal urban environment and the unstructured countryside (fig. 2).[9] Overall, however, such verbal and visual representations had limited currency. Infrequently replicated or disseminated, they did not coalesce into a collective urban image for any specific city.

In general, the Romans had a much more circumscribed awareness of cities than modern observers. Few had the opportunity to read about other cities or about theories of urban design and meaning. Instead, they relied on first-hand knowledge and awareness. Travel by foot ensured that observers' interaction with urban environments was immediate and personal. Cities had few street names and no addresses; maps were rare.[10] As a result, visitors were forced to conceptualize the placement of urban features and themselves in a relational manner based upon the location of monuments or other notable urban features. In the second century B.C., the playwright Terence has one character give another directions in the city:

SYRUS: You know that colonnade near the meat market, down that way?
DEMEA: Of course I do.
SYRUS: Go straight up the street past it. Then there's a turning going downhill; go straight down and you'll see a temple on this side and next to it that alley –
DEMEA: Which one?
SYRUS: Where there's a big fig tree.
DEMEA: I know
SYRUS: Go on through it.

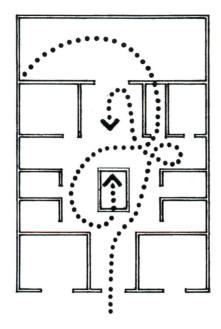 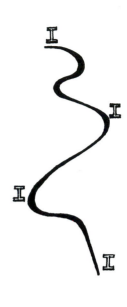

Figure 3. Diagram, movement through a Roman house of memory.

Figure 4. Diagram, urban locations of *imagines*.

DEMEA: (*After some thought*) That alley hasn't got a way through.

SYRUS: So it hasn't. What a fool I am. My mistake. Go back to the colonnade. Yes, this is a much shorter way and less chance of going wrong. Do you know Cratinus' house, that rich fellow's?

DEMEA: Yes.

SYRUS: (*Rapidly*) Go past it, turn left, straight up the street, come to the Temple of Diana, then turn right and before you come to the city gate just by the pond there's a small flour mill and a workshop opposite. . . . That's where he is.[11]

As this example shows, good environmental memories were essential to navigate the convoluted byways of larger cities, and to understand the meaning woven into the urban fabric. For the Romans, the most enduring recollections resulted from the stimulation of as many senses as possible. Movement through a physical environment was one of the most powerful ways to learn and to remember.

The Romans were experienced readers of nonverbal texts. People of all classes read messages embedded in their surroundings.[12] On the most obvious level, artwork conveyed information of diverse types and every level of complexity. Based upon a shared religious pantheon, common ancestry, and familiar iconographic vocabulary, pictorial representations provided legible documents. In effect, the familiar representations in sculptures, coins, and other art forms served as the *lingua franca* of the Roman world (fig. 102).[13] Buildings and cityscapes were likewise texts meant to be read by people of all classes and backgrounds. Unlike artworks, however, these were to be read experientially by moving through, not merely looking at, the environments.[14]

Upperclass Romans received specific training in the reading of physical environments. All educated citizens studied rhetoric in preparation for public careers. As an aid in the memorization of long speeches, teachers of rhetoric instructed orators to fashion environments (*loci*) in their minds and to stock them with memorable objects (*imagines*) representing various concepts (fig. 3).[15] Speakers placed *imagines* so as to reflect the interconnections and hierarchies within the speech being memorized. To recall the text, an orator simply imagined walking through the constructed mental environment "reading" the content-bearing images. He could achieve different effects by varying his path, safe in the knowledge that the relationships between *imagines* remained intact. Familiar with this mnemonic system, learned Romans were predisposed to look for an underlying, coherent narrative in built environments. In the first century A.D., Quintilianus noted that even a cityscape could form a usable *locus* for memorization with buildings, not objects, serving as *imagines* (*Inst.*11.2.21) (fig. 4). By further expansion of scale to a regional or imperial context, an entire city could likewise become a content laden object (*imago*) to be read by knowledgeable observers.

Romans with limited formal education were also expert readers of their surroundings. Oral traditions and daily experience provided ample training in environmental reading. Even more explicitly than rhetoric, story telling relied upon visual images as organizational cues.[16] Familiar locales grounded the storyline in long epics; descriptions of environmental ambience set the tone for events to come. In the real world, observers learned about politics, religion, and cultural norms from the messages conveyed by physical objects. Throughout every Roman city, public as well as private displays of artwork, decorations, and architecture informed the citizenry. Not all conveyers of meaning were iconographical; styles, textures, and materials also carried a content. A sculpture of exotic-colored marble signaled wealth and provoked associations with the country of origin and other works using the same material. Similarly, the experience of moving through different spaces had meaning. Sequences of derelict buildings projected municipal poverty and lack of public pride; clean, safe streets signaled a stable government; juxtapositions of monuments identified telling relationships between patrons; and so on. In particular, ritual events such as parades or contemporaneous celebrations experientially linked together disparate urban sites, embuing them with collective meaning.

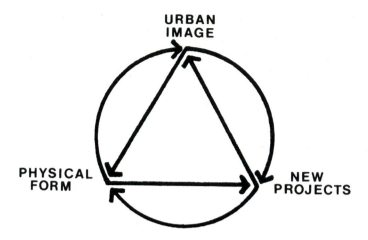

Figure 5. Diagram of codependency.

Bred on an animistic religion, the Romans readily associated spirits with inanimate objects and locations. Interacting on an intimate level, they anthropomorphized physical environments. Each crossroad, natural feature, and significant locale within the city had its own identifiable spirit of place or *genius loci*.[17] These spirits enlivened both visits and memories of urban environments with human characteristics. As a result, a walk through a Roman city was punctuated by encounters with numerous well-known personas. Notably, the collective identification of each *genius loci* helped to leaven variations in the individual interpretation of experiences. The cities of the Roman world likewise had anthropomorphized spirits, though these *genii* were not as specifically defined as those for particular locales.[18]

Essential to understanding Roman urban images is the notion of cities as living entities. In antiquity, as in the present, the metaphor of the "living" city clarifies the conceptual difference between a single building and an urban environment or urban image. Architects and patrons often conceive individual structures as independent works, each with an identifiable, pristine appearance and content. Cities are more complex and organic. With the exception of planned new towns, urban environments result from hundreds of separate decisions made by different agents, at different times. Cumulatively, these isolated transformations create the impression of an independent, living entity that seems to grow and evolve according to its own life cycle. Evolution of the urban image likewise supports the notion that cities are animated. New developments in every sphere – from politics to technology, aesthetics to economics – continuously transform an existing urban image. A codependent cycle results, with each alteration to the physical environment affecting the conceptualization of the city and thus its image;

interpretation of the urban image, in turn, impacts the design, patronage, and meaning of new projects (fig. 5). The experience of a city is also biotic. Every aspect of a city cannot be experienced concurrently, so its identity takes shape after many encounters. Moving through urban environments on different days or years, under different climatic and political situations, observers create an urban image unique to their time and place, yet embodying change. In effect, an urban image lives and evolves in the same manner as a person. Like a human being, it changes form and personality over time, yet retains a unique character. Plutarch in the first century A.D. succinctly captured this aspect of the urban image,

A city, like a living thing, is a united and continuous whole. This does not cease to be itself as it changes in growing older, nor does it become one thing after another with the lapse of time, but is always at one with its former self in feeling and identity. (*Mor. 599*)

Each person reacts differently to different people based upon personalities, backgrounds, education, culture, and sheer chemistry. Similarly, each observer reacts slightly differently to the same urban experience. For ancient urban observers, the range of interpretations was somewhat broader than today due to the greater variations in class and education found within Roman society, and especially to the lack of a homogenizing mass media. The impressions of a Roman city formed by a slave walking barefoot on the rough streets naturally differed significantly from those of an educated senator carried in a litter; similarly diverse were the interpretations of a Greek from an eastern metropolis compared to those of a visitor from a village in the western provinces. Nevertheless, dissimilar reactions shared certain identifiable commonalities. Regardless of status, observers perceived the same interrelationships between individual projects, the same contrasts in scale, the same calibrated viewing angles, and the same manipulated sequencing of spaces in ancient cities. Most important, they evaluated such factors through the same general cultural filter.[19] Of course, investigators in the twentieth century can never fully understand the impact a Roman city had on ancient observers; our cultural and perceptual frameworks are too foreign. Still, generalized reactions can be approximated. The sensorial responses of human observers have not changed dramatically over the centuries and thus can be calibrated.[20] Available physical evidence allows us to identify contrasts and repetitions, the average and the exceptional.

Similarly, sufficient documentation about Roman culture exists to permit reasoned evaluations of the meaning behind urban features. Easiest to trace are the motivations for the patronage of urban projects. Building is a conscious, costly, and enduring act. Requiring wealth and power to be implemented, large-scale urban projects have left both archaeological and written remains documenting their content. For Roman society in particular, urban interventions were often highly politicized. Ancient patrons sought maximum return on their investments by using each structure to convey a desired meaning, as well as serve a specific function. Buildings were tools of self-aggrandizement, political competition, and State glorification. On the most personal level, the form, size, materials, and iconographic programs of private residences overtly communicated the social stature and sensibilities of the occupants.[21] As the standing of certain individuals became inflated in the late Republic, they began to exploit larger and larger projects as transmitters of personal status and propaganda, including cityscapes. Simultaneously, the populace assumed a proprietary relationship to all buildings within the city, and to their encoded messages.

Because the Romans read environments experientially, patrons naturally considered how their urban projects conveyed meaning kinetically and haptically. Like words in a text, buildings do not stand alone, but have to be read as part of a phrase or sentence. Patrons of urban projects exploited a number of diverse design strategies to evoke the desired content and associations. Whenever possible, they tried to site their buildings carefully in relation to extant structures and to each other. Thus, designers were called upon to manipulate urban viewing angles and establish preferable sequences within the cityscape in order to elicit desired reactions.

The complete choreography of projects within a dense cityscape was, of course, impossible. Instead, patrons relied upon the readers of urban environments to create linkages between disparate projects based upon commonalities of form, material, scale, iconography, and, above all, narrative content. Drawing upon a shared heritage of myths, tales, and history, Roman observers associated singular urban projects together within narrative structures. Simply, they imposed familiar stories onto urban environments. Thus, a walk from the Tiber River, up the Scalae Caci, and across the Palatine Hill immediately recalled tales about the life of Romulus. The pedestrian moved from the riverbank where the foundling Romulus washed up on shore, past the Lupercal cave where he was suckled by the she-wolf, and finally came to the rustic hut atop the hill alleged to be his residence (fig. 85). When various urban works shared iconographical programs or physical traits, observers were predisposed to create their own narratives to explain and reenforce such associations.

Observers in the twentieth century do not as readily read meaning in built form, relying instead upon words, numbering, and signage to transmit content. Not only is the experience of a modern city very different from that of an ancient city, but so are the tools and framework for interpretation. Com-

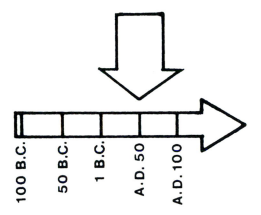

Figure 6. Diagram, time lines.

munication through physical form was natural, easy, and necessary for the Romans. Interwoven with histories, narratives, and propaganda, ancient buildings and urban environments provided enduring and highly visible frameworks for conveying information. Following cultural predispositions, the Romans read this data experientially. Thus, the connection among people, urban environments, and meaning had an immediacy and strength foreign to modern urban observers. The resulting urban images were animated and powerful.

HISTORIOGRAPHY

Analyses of urban experience and imagery have focused on modern and future cities.[22] Investigations of historic urban environments from this perspective are infrequent for all periods, but especially for the classical past.[23] Far removed from the present, the cities of antiquity present obvious problems. The past never preserves as much information as subsequent generations would wish. Furthermore, extant remains convey only part of the picture. Compelled to deal with complex fragmentary evidence, researchers have tended to specialize topically and methodologically. In both instances, this leads to a preferencing of broad diachronic analyses of issues and their development over time.[24] Such an evolutionary approach further precludes the consideration of an urban image. Synchronic overviews of a particular ancient city at a select moment have been rare.[25] The few works examining a city at a particular period usually emphasize political or cultural developments rather than urban form or image (fig. 6).[26] Even when sharpening the temporal focus, urban biographies continue to minimize the importance of the overall cityscape and urban experience.[27]

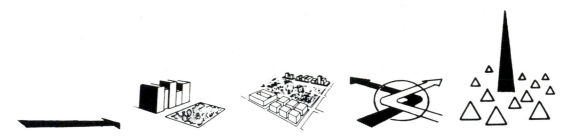

Figure 7. Diagram, five physical elements of urban image as defined by Lynch.

The time is ripe for new experiments. In the second-half of the twentieth century, developments in archaeological and academic research, and in architecture and urban design are provoking interest in the conception and experience of past urban environments. Recent studies of Rome's ancient remains and new excavations have brought to light much new information.[28] The gradual acceptance of interdisciplinary approaches to urban studies is leading to more comprehensive examinations of historic cities.[29] Included among these are full-bodied biographies of cities at specific times.[30] Works by architects and planners on environmental perception likewise are resulting in new approaches and tools for analyzing entire cities at specific periods, rather than segmentally or as long-term incubators of formal and historical topics.[31] Concurrently, the renewed general popularity of ancient architectural elements and topics is stimulating further study of the classical past by practitioners.[32] Most recently, the pervasive impact of critical theory is prompting researchers to consider conceptual aspects of built environments, exploring reception theory, authorship, and collective memory in relation to cities.[33] All these factors collectively support the experiential investigation of ancient cities.

The eugenicist and anthropologist Sir Francis Galton in 1879 gave an initial boost to the study of urban experience. Taking a stroll down Pall Mall in London, he used free association to record both sensorial stimuli and the thoughts they inspired.[34] Almost a century lapsed before this approach became integrated into urban studies. In the interim, interest centered on observers' reactions to individual buildings or contained complexes, rather than the kinetic experience of holistic urban environments. For example, in *Experiencing Architecture* of 1959, Steen Eiler Rasmussen explores the observational criteria for evaluating built form. Analyzing such perceptual stimuli as color, light, texture, sounds, sizes, and spatial properties, Rasmussen broadened the discourse on the experience of built form, yet did not consider how experiential responses related to the city as an independent entity.[35]

Interest in overall urban experience and imagery peaked in the sixties in direct response to contemporary environments. Planners, urban designers, architects, and city dwellers alike felt the cityscapes created in the boom period after World War II lacked the sensorial and conceptual richness of historic urban environments. Anxious to forge a positive bond between urban observers and physical form, they studied past environments and sought ways to apply contemporary perceptual and psychological research to the design of more sensorially and conceptually stimulating cities. In 1960, Lynch gave structure and direction to experiential urban research with *The Image of the City*. Expanding upon Galton's first-hand approach, he moved beyond the observers' immediate reactions to explore the memory of urban components. Lynch questioned the residents of three large American cities about the memorable features in their environments. Based on these interviews, he identified five highly legible urban components ordering observers' mental image of a city – landmarks, nodes, districts, paths, and edges (fig. 7). To gauge the potency or effectiveness of these features, he coined the term "imageability," defined as "the quality in a physical object which gives it a high probability of evoking a strong image in any given observer."[36] Reaction was immediate and positive. Lauded as a major contribution, Lynch's small book succinctly and persuasively articulates a theory of urban experience based upon objective criteria.

While Lynch focused on contemporary cities, other planners and designers considered examples from the past to determine why historic environments provided richer experiences and images than modern cities. This historical focus also reflected an expanded interest in the cultural factors shaping the form, patronage, and content of urban environments. In most cases, authors briefly cited numerous historical examples in relation to design theory, rather than evaluating a single past urban environment in depth. For example, the geographer Yi-Fu Tuan referred to a large number of past cities and world views in his examination of how observers perceive, structure, and evaluate environments.[37] Similarly, Amos Rapoport explored the psychological and cultural factors affecting the interpretation and image of urban environments throughout the world and throughout history.[38]

Significantly, the study of environmental experience, memory, and spatial geography sparked renewed interest in antiquity. Research on these topics immediately led to classical references that, in turn, legitimized and broadened the discourse. Thus, semioticians and colorists investigating the symbolic content of architecture turned to antiquity for potent physical and theoretical examples.[39] Above all, attention focused on the Romans, acknowledged experts at image making, experiential symbolism, and spatial concerns. In particular, the Roman concept of the "spirit of place"

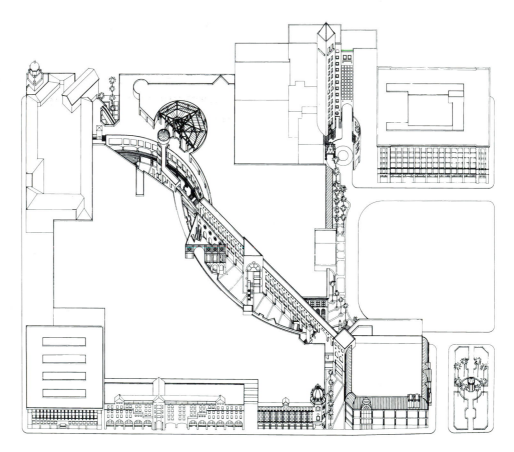

Figure 8. Axonometric drawing of Horton Plaza shopping center, San Diego, Jerde Associates, 1986. Courtesy of Jerde Partnership.

(*genius loci*) attracted several authors interested in the phenomenology of architecture.[40]

Developments in contemporary architecture likewise prompted further study of classical environments and concepts. By the late 1970s, architects throughout the world were embracing Post Modernism. Visually, they exploited references to historic architecture, highlighting reconstituted classical components with a twentieth-century palette. So potent were the conceptual reminders of the past, the Italians dubbed the movement "Memory Architecture." Beyond stimulating remembrance of things past, Post-Modern works addressed the senses, providing sensorially rich experiences in contrast to stark modernist environments. Designers found equal vitality and meaning in the contemporary urban commercial strip, provoking interest in heterogeneous environments past and present.[41] On an urban scale, developers and city promoters of the Reagan/Bush era exploited the economic potential of sensorially complex designs. They created environments aimed to titillate the senses and evoke positive, though unspecific, associations with history.[42] For example, the Jerde Partnership provided the Horton Plaza shopping center in San Diego (1986) with eye-catching recollections of Italian Renaissance plazas, evocative textures, constantly changing views, animated fountains, and diverse historical details (fig. 8). Jerde clearly stated the aim of this project was the creation of a "coherent but eccentrically complex topographic armature," to be read experientially.[43]

The preoccupation with experientially rich environments prompted practitioners to devise ways to place themselves "in" past environments. The townscape consultant Gordon Cullen in 1961 experimented with serial sketches and photographs to recreate the kinesthetic experience of pedestrians in extant and fabricated historical environments (fig. 9).[44] Architect David Macaulay brought a Roman city to life in his accessible and entertaining book, *City: A Story of Roman Planning and Construction* of 1974.[45] Using reconstruction sketches and storytelling, he draws readers into the experience of an ancient urban environment, providing an immediacy and reality lacking in other approaches (fig. 10). The most engaging recreations occur with film. In 1977, the BBC aired the miniseries "I Claudius," directed by Herbert Wise, based upon the book of the same name by Robert Graves. This popular series allowed the general public to simulate the experience of being in Roman buildings and cities.[46] Computer-based recreations offer the most potential for future experiential research. Complex digitized models provide great versatility. Modeled forms can be viewed under different lighting conditions, at different scales and viewing angles, and can be altered as new information becomes available. Most valuable for experiential study is the ability to simulate movement through the modeled environments, allowing kinetic evaluation.[47]

Spurred by popular and professional interest in urban vitality, historians and classicists in the last twenty years likewise began to consider the meaning, experience, and impact of ancient environments.[48] In the provocative book *The Idea of a Town, The Anthropology of Urban Form in Rome, Italy and the Ancient World* of 1976, Joseph Rykwert analyzed the ancient city as a symbolic human construct.[49] A few years later, John Clarke adopted a kinesthetic approach to the study of Roman mosaics *in situ;* more recently, he analyzed the experience of Roman houses to help understand their interior decorative programs and layouts (fig. 11).[50] Bettina Bergmann extended experiential research on domestic environments by applying the Roman environmental mnemonic system and employing computer-generated models.[51] Kevin Lynch's work found admirers among art historians and classicists. Paul Zanker, D. Scagliarini Corlàita, and William L. MacDonald all referenced his work when dealing with Roman environments.[52] MacDonald

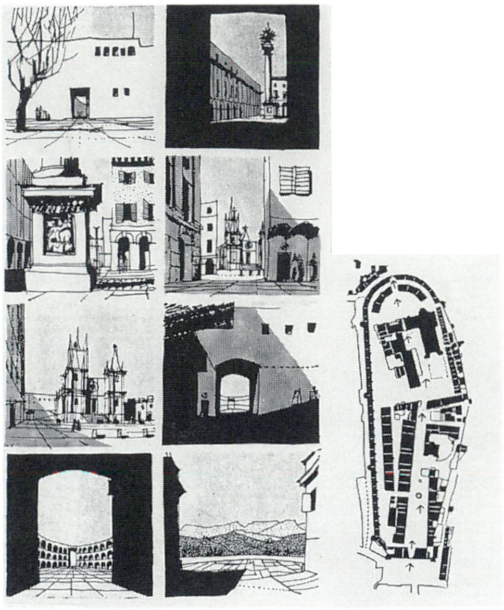

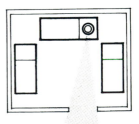

Figure 9. Fictional serial sketches of urban experience from George Cullen, *The Concise Townscape* (London: Architectural Press 1961).

Figure 10. Reconstruction of a Roman city street. Courtesy of David Macaulay, *City: A Story of Roman Planning and Construction* (Boston: Houghton Mifflin 1974).

Figure 11. Diagram, viewing angle in a Roman dining room.

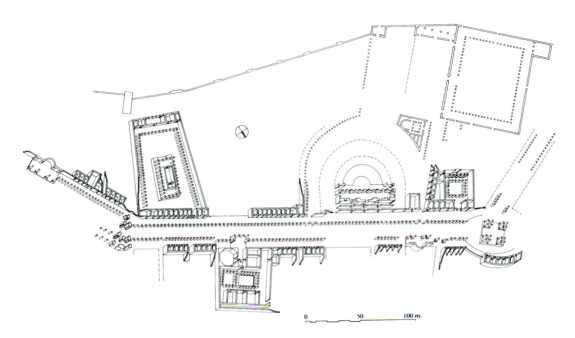

Figure 12. Three-dimensional representation of Palmyra's urban armature. Drawing from MacDonald, *Roman Empire II*, courtesy of Yale University Press.

Figure 13. Axonometric drawing of the Forum Romanum in the second century B.C. Drawing: E. H. Riorden from Stambaugh, *Ancient Roman City,* courtesy Johns Hopkins University Press.
1: Tribunal Aurelium; 2: Regia; 3: Fornix Fabiorum; 4: Temple of Vesta; 5: Atrium Vestae; 6: Temple of Castor and Pollux; 7: Tabernae Veteres; 8: Basilica Sempronia; 9: Temple of Saturn; 10: Basilica Opimia; 11: Temple of Concordia; 12: Basilica Porcia; 13: Curia; 14: Comitium; 15: Rostra; 16: Shrine of Janus; 17: Shrine of Venus Cloacina; 18: Tabernae Novae; 19: Basilica Aemilia.

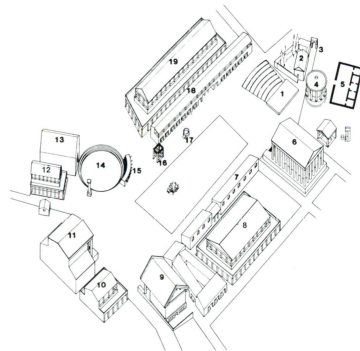

subtitled his second volume on the architecture of the Roman Empire "An Urban Appraisal," published in 1986. In this masterful study of Imperial cities, he transcends the usual preoccupation with formal patterns and individual complexes, considering instead how urban components addressed the sensory and conceptual experience of the moving observer. MacDonald identifies the Roman urban armature as a complex composition of main streets, squares, and essential public buildings sited along primary thoroughfares; together these form what he describes as "the framework for the unmistakable imagery of imperial urbanism" (fig. 12).[53]

The power of the Roman urban experience inspired John E. Stambaugh to investigate "the way in which individuals perceived the physical and social frame of the city in which they lived" in *The Ancient Roman City* of 1988.[54] This book is a useful and enjoyable text on Roman cities, but does not fulfill the stated goal. Stambaugh's presentation is fairly traditional, with chapters describing major urban themes and the formal evolution of Rome and five other cities over their entire histories. His experiential analyses are limited and do not include in depth evaluation of any specific urban image. The tantalizing reconstruction drawings by E. H. Riorden included in Stambaugh's book hint at experiential possibilities (figs. 13 and 77). These axonometric drawings succinctly convey the three-dimensionality of Roman urban spaces, yet the viewing angle is inappropriate for full experiential understanding. Depicted from a bird's-eye perspective, the illustrations show a view rarely possible for ancient observers.

Other authors are experimenting with word pictures to recreate the experience of past environments. Exploring the potent interconnections between the city (*urbs*) and countryside (*rus*), Nicholas Purcell describes a walk from Rome out to the rural surroundings around A.D. 55.[55] He discusses individual structures and views, but emphasizes generalities rather than the specifics of actual sensorial experience. Purcell provides no illustrations. Antonio Varone presents an episodic experience of Pompeii in A.D. 79 by evaluating graffiti from throughout the city. His tour is enlivened with the words of ancient residents, but lacks both a clear physical association with a particular path and illustrations of the actual environments in which the graffiti were placed.[56]

Recent developments in architectural design, environmental research, and historical studies have sharpened the definition of the urban image and revealed the significance of experience and conception in shaping classical cities. The next logical step is to examine specific examples. Such an exploration requires the merging of the soft data necessary for an experiential approach with the hard facts and time constraints essential to an urban biography. To be effective, the chronological focus must be sharp. Even within a single lifetime, the forces affecting memorability and urban narratives can change, as demonstrated by the case study of Rome under the first emperor, Augustus.

EVALUATING THE AUGUSTAN URBAN IMAGE

The Rome of Augustus captivates. Vitruvius writing in this period opens book two of his *De Architectura* with a story about an urban design. Anxious to be employed by Alexander the Great, the architect Dinocrates devised a way to grab attention; he boldly stood in the path of the famous general dressed as the hero Hercules, complete with wreath, lion's skin, club, and oiled body. The ruse worked. Alexander asked him to draw near and explain who he was; Dinocrates replied, "a Macedonian architect, who brings you ideas and designs worthy of your renown." He then presented a flamboyant design showing Mount Athos carved in the shape of a man with a spacious city in his left hand (fig. 14). Alexander criticized the plan, not for its ostentatious design, but because the region could not support a city of the size depicted. Nevertheless, he hired Dinocrates on the spot. Here was a designer able to conceptualize a forceful urban image worthy of a great patron. Dinocrates went on to design many projects for Alexander, including his great eponymous city in Egypt. The story held obvious appeal in the Augustan Age when Rome, too, was being redesigned in the conceptual and physical image of one man.

For modern observers, the attraction of Augustan Rome lies both with the number and quality of urban projects and with the perceived beneficent absolutism of Augustus himself (fig. 15).[57] Hamstrung by the numerous modern restrictions imposed on urban alterations, patrons, planners, and architects today envy the scope and coherence of urban interventions possible under this strong Roman leader.[58] Wielding a singular vision and singular voice, Augustus created a focused urban image. He operated simultaneously on several fronts. In addition to dozens of new buildings and restorations, he instituted programs promoting building maintenance, strong construction, safe streets, and unifying urban rituals. By A.D. 14, his presence dominated every corner of the city, forcefully linking the image of Rome with a single personality.

A plethora of recent studies has expanded knowledge of Augustan aesthetics, artwork, politics, economy, and propaganda, as well as of individual structures, complexes, and building types.[59] Few, however, have evaluated the overall cityscape of Rome.[60] As a result, the urban image of the city under the first emperor remains to be analyzed. Before beginning, several caveats must be made. The first involves temporality. As a living entity, the

Figure 14. Illustration for Vitruvius' story of the city on Mount Athos designed by Dinocrates to impress Alexander the Great. Drawing: Richard H. Abramson after J. B. Fischer von Erlach, *Entwurff einer historischen Architektur* (Vienna 1721), pl. XVIII.

urban image of Augustan Rome was neither monolithic nor static. There was no one, ideal image of the city either physically or conceptually. Always evolving, Rome's urban image projected various emphases during the five decades of the Augustan Age, just as an individual's personality emphasizes different characteristics during various periods in a lifetime. These subperiods cover time segments of varying length, but each is conceptually distinct. Eventually, they coalesced into a unified conception of the city during the entire Augustan Age (fig. 16).

The second caveat relates to experiential analysis. The calibration of sensorial reactions is possible only after careful reconstruction of a past environment. Fortunately, physical data exist for Augustan Rome. Constructed of magnificent hard stones, the remains of numerous public buildings from the period have endured and can be reconstructed. Available topographic information allows large works to be securely placed within the sprawling, urban site.[61] Nevertheless, the picture is not complete. Rome of Augustus

Figure 15. Colossal head of Augustus with Baroque restoration of the hair (H. ca. 1.20 m), Cortile della Pigna, Vatican. Photo: Archivio Fotografico, Musei Vaticani, inv. # 5137.

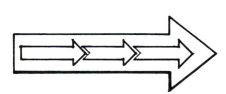

Figure 16. Diagram, subperiods.

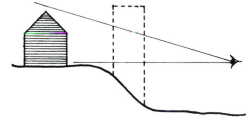

Figure 17. Diagram, temple and view angle.

sheltered one million people and covered approximately 700 hectares (1700 acres). Despite the comparatively abundant material on the Augustan period, the entire ancient cityscape cannot be recreated in full. Large gaps exist both topographically and typologically. Certain sections of the city have not preserved their ancient remains; others have not been comprehensively excavated. Notably, the high water table of the Campus Martius has hindered excavations in this important Augustan district. Furthermore, the impermanence of particular building types naturally affects experiential investigations. Great public monuments of stone and concrete left documentable remains; infill vernacular structures of wattle and daub or mud brick disintegrated.

Based on fragmentary information, analyses of urban experience and conceptual reactions for the Augustan city must be considered provisional and open to repeated reevaluation. For example, initial conclusions about sight lines derived from known archaeological evidence may prove incorrect if future excavations reveal intervening structures blocking the view (fig. 17). New discoveries or interpretations of literary sources may likewise change the shading of how contemporaries envisioned their urban environment. These drawbacks, however, do not diminish the value of attempting experiential analysis as a means to understand the conceptualization and implementation of an ancient urban image.

A third caveat deals with class. For the most part, evidence on the Augustan city is elitist. The preserved remains lead to a reconstructed cityscape filled with great buildings for and by upper class patrons. Similarly, ancient literature in large measure presents an upper class, male interpretation of Augustan Rome. Patricians, the wealthy, the learned, and their concerns dominate; the urban poor, foreigners, and women speak less overtly. Thus, both the physical remains and ancient literature project the voice of power. Yet by listening closely, we can hear the murmurings of the urban "others." An urban image responds to conversations at all levels. Shoddy infill housing, raucous wine shops, dripping laundry, crowding, and rampant crime affect the experience of an ancient city as much as do propagandistic monuments and ritualized events. By definition, vernacular buildings and urban ambience evolve in an ad hoc manner and therefore appear less subject to manipulation. In fact, developments in these areas are often consciously directed. Legislative and administrative directives affect built form and experience by making a city cleaner, safer, and more efficient for all occupants. Furthermore, overall improvements in the functionality of a city in turn enhance the urban ambience and thus the daily life of each occupant.

Caveats aside, there is much to learn from studying the urban image of Augustan Rome. To set the stage, Chapter 2 takes us inside the city for a "first-hand" observation. A reconstructed walk through the city in approximately 52 B.C. recreates the sights, sounds, smells, views, and urban ambience experienced by two fictional pedestrians. The path leads from the urban center to the rural outskirts as the characters hurry to leave the embattled city. The fictionalized experience of spatial relationships, sequencing, and building scale, along with landscaping, colors, textures, art, and such intangibles as conceptual content, safety, and crowding all combine to forge an urban image of the late Republican city. Seeking experiential accuracy, the narrative includes only those urban features actually encountered by the pedestrians; visual impressions beyond their sensorial range are purposely excluded. Chapter 3 considers how significant changes in the traditional political structure during the late Republic prompted new attitudes toward personal and State images, as well as new ideas about patronage. These, in turn, led to a reevaluation of urban forms and experience as effective vehicles for the transmission of propaganda as evidenced by the proliferation of large-scale projects by single patrons. The chapter ends with the planned urban interventions of the Dictator Julius Caesar.

The next three chapters consider the urban image of Augustan Rome, following the Lynchian categories of context, identity, and structure. The emphasis on the overall perception of the city precludes discussion of every Augustan project in the city, or of contemporary issues significant to other inquiries. For example, historically vital changes in the Roman government are considered only in relation to their impact on urban form and imagery; conversely, marginal administrative changes dealing with urban care receive full coverage. Chapter 4 explores the identity of the Augustan city, isolating subperiods based upon shifting political imperatives, motives for patronage, and iconographic associations. Chapter 5 considers the structure of the Augustan urban image, examining the basic architectural and urban design components and their orchestration. Here again Lynch provides a model for analysis with his five urban organizers: landmarks, nodes, districts, paths, and edges. Chapter 6 evaluates the meaning of the Augustan urban image, considering unity, legibility, and endurance. The book ends with a walk through Rome of A.D. 14. Retracing in reverse the path described in Chapter 2, we enter the city with the descendants of the fictional pedestrians. Here the urban image of Augustan Rome congeals. During the six decades intervening between the two walks, the urban environment changed substantially. The imagined pedestrians experience remarkable sensorial and conceptual advances, and the forceful message of a calculating individual. In a single lifetime, Augustus irrevocably transformed the experience of Rome, crafting a cohesive urban image to be admired and emulated for centuries.

CHAPTER TWO

A WALK THROUGH
REPUBLICAN ROME, 52 B.C.

The city was not adorned as the renown of
our empire demand.
Suetonius, *Augustus* 28

Loud creaking drowns out the noise of the crowd seated in the back-to-back theaters. With jumps and moans, the structures begin to move. Screams fill the air. Slowly rotating on pivots, the two theaters turn to face one another (fig. 18). Fear gives way to amazement as gladiators run into the newly formed amphitheater. Gaius Curio nods with satisfaction. Erected for the funeral games honoring his father, the impressive engineering project will bring much glory. The ingenious construction sways the people figuratively as well as literally; it will buy Curio many votes when he becomes tribune. The year is 52 B.C.; the city is Rome (fig. 19).

The theaters of Curio encapsulate the contemporary situation in the premier city of the Roman Republic. At midcentury, Rome is a battleground for political favor. Even minor figures like Curio lead significant skirmishes.[1] Like the theater, the populace turns one way and then another, manipulated by powerful individuals and fascinated by the latest contraption. Writing about Curio's theaters, Pliny marvels at "the madness of a people . . . bold enough to take its place in such treacherous, rickety seats. . . . Here we have the nation that has conquered the earth, . . . swaying on a contraption and applauding its own danger!" (*HN*.118). The residents of Rome know danger well; for them, the rotating theaters pose no more threat than the city's streets.

For the last three decades, internecine conflicts have torn apart families, property, and faith throughout the Italian peninsula. Daily the situation worsens in the city. Riots are common. The delicately balanced triumvirate of Rome's three most powerful men – Crassus, Caesar, and Pompey – collapsed the year before with the death of Crassus. For the greater part of

24

52 B.C., Caesar has been busy north of the Alps combatting the Gauls; Pompey stands alone as consul. Like two hungry dogs, these two powerful men metaphorically circle each other, with large packs at their heels. Everyone is tense. The smell of blood is in the air. Those who can leave the city (fig. 20).

Two figures wrapped in gray woolen cloaks move slowly across the Mons Capitolinus, Rome's smallest and most sacred hill (fig. 21).[2] The taller is a staunch Roman father. He leads his young son just in from the countryside on a last walk through the city, hoping to imprint the power of place upon the youth's memory before leaving the city and Italy for safety. In the uneasy present, they stare sadly at the monuments to Rome's former greatness crowding the Area Capitolina, an artificial platform supporting a paved piazza.[3] Brisk fall winds swirl between altars and bronze plaques, and threaten to ruffle the marble and bronze togas of the commemorative statues. A carved Jupiter placed atop a column ten years earlier still stares eastward where trouble continues to menace the Republic. Nearby, a colossal sculpted Hercules casts a menacing, long shadow and representations of the Egyptian deities Isis and Serapis stand serenely even though their temples have been torn down by the Senate. Maneuvering between the images of heros, Rome's early kings, famous citizens, and various gods, the pedestrians stop before the grand temple dominating the hill.

Before them rises the greatest structure in Rome, the temple of the Capitoline triad: Jupiter Optimus Maximus, Juno, and Minerva. In the limited space of the Area Capitolina, the temple fills the pedestrians' entire cone of vision. For centuries, the structure has reigned supreme over Rome, though its current form reflects a rebuilding by the general Sulla after a devastating fire thirty years before.[4] The inscribed name of Catulus, the proconsul who completed the work, is accentuated by the strong light of Latium. The observers shield their eyes from the glare bouncing off the monumental, white marble columns looted from Greece (fig. 22).[5] When rebuilding the structure, religious restrictions prevented alterations to the foundations; thus, Sulla and Q. Lutatius Catulus extended the building vertically.[6] Craning their necks, the observers see dozens of sculptures atop the great structure and proud eagles supporting the tarnished gilt roof. They strain to see the sculpture group surmounting the temple's pediment. Standing in a quadriga, the mighty Jupiter appears ready to begin a tumultuous gallop across the sky. The older man closes his eyes and makes a silent vow to Jupiter, "May Peace again find a home in Rome before my son returns."

The young figure at his side runs to see the squawking sacred geese and barking guard dogs penned at the side of the Area Capitolina (fig. 23).[7] His father sighs and moves past the smaller temples to Opis and Fides on the

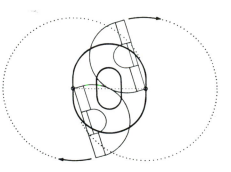

Figure 18. Hypothetical reconstruction of the rotating theaters of Gaius Curio. Drawing: Richard H. Abramson after Landes and Golvin.

Figure 19. Map of Rome in 52 B.C. Drawing: Rodica Reif and Richard H. Abramson. 1: Circus Maximus; 2: Temple of Magna Mater; 3: Temple of Victoria; 4: Temple of Fortuna; 5: Forum Julium; 6: Porta Fontinalis; 7: Temple of Juno Moneta; 8: Temple of Jupiter Optimus Maximus; 9: Temples of Apollo and Bellona(?); 10: Porticus Octaviae; 11: Porticus Philippi; 12: Republican temples (Area Sacra di Largo Argentina); 13: Ovile; 14: Theater of Pompey; 15: Temples in the Forum Holitorium; 16: Temple of Aesculapius; 17: Temples of Fortuna and Mater Matuta (Area Sacra di Sant'Omobono); 18: Temples of Minerva and Diana.

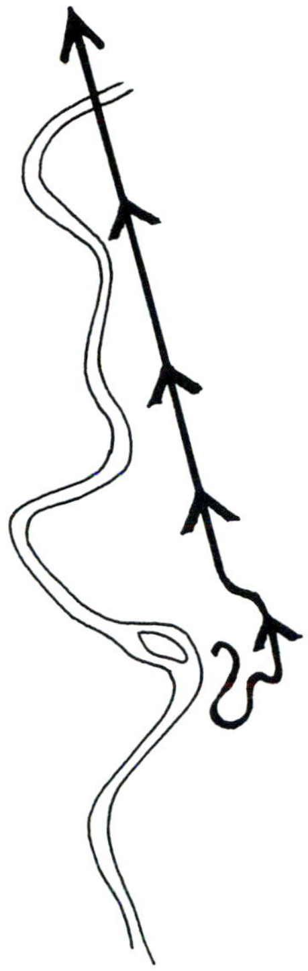

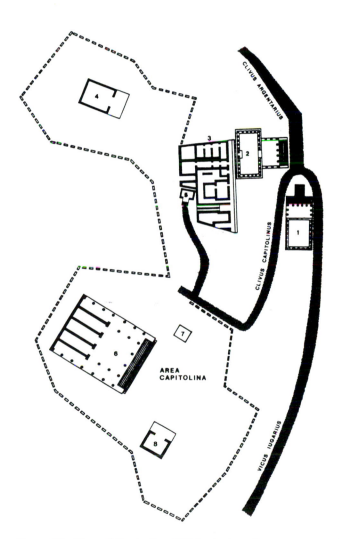

Figure 20. Diagram, walk 1.

Figure 21. Plan of Capitoline Hill in the late first century B.C. Drawing: Rodica Reif.
1: Temple of Saturn; 2: Temple of Concordia; 3: Tabularium; 4: Temple of Juno Moneta;
5: Temple of Vediovis; 6: Temple of Jupiter Optimus Maximus; 7: Temple of Jupiter Tonans;
8: Shrine to Ops(?).

Figure 22. Coin of M. Volteius, 78 B.C., showing the Temple of Jupiter Optimus Maximus. Photo: British Museum, # 3154.

southwest to the edge of the mountain. Below spreads Rome, premier city-state of the federated Republic. Hill after hill, and valley after valley are covered with buildings. The smoke from a hundred thousand wood fires melds with the damp fall air. After the whiteness of the Capitoline temple, everything appears slightly blurred, slightly gray. Cooking fires blacken the structures of wood frame filled with rubble and mud-brick. The plaster covering building exteriors, porous tufa of foundations, and unglazed terra-cotta architectural decorations absorb what little light penetrates the enveloping haze. From atop the hill, even the few accents of white travertine and marble appear dull; the slaves who usually polish the stone have been called to more pressing duties.

Many of the building materials of the Republican city require constant upkeep to maintain a sharp appearance. Recent disruptive events, including fires, floods, and civil unrest, have taken their toll on the city's physical form. Even revered temples show a lack of care. Sacred groves go untended; dried ceremonial garlands hang forlornly between temple columns. Plaster flakes off temple podia. The gods seem to have abandoned Rome.

With each burst of fall wind, the observers on the Capitoline shiver. The father can feel danger exuding from the dense jumble of constructions below. Rome is bulging with people who mistakenly thought they would be safe in the city. Instead, they have aggravated the city's hazards. Rome's recent immigrants push the cost of urban living ever higher. Property owners gouge huge rents for shoddy speculative structures; few undertake repairs. Great profits can be made from speculative urban rentals, yet such invest-

Figure 23. Marble relief showing the Temple of Juno Moneta with geese; second century A.D. Drawing: Richard H. Abramson after Gismondi.

ments are clearly not secure.[8] The swollen populace constantly threatens to explode. Urban residents far exceed the number of jobs available. Hungry and cold, even honorable men become dishonorable. Robbers haunt the narrow muddy streets; loiterers stand at every crossroads anxious to express their frustration.

Rome's inefficient municipal services cannot begin to cope with the tremendous social and physical problems of the city. The water and sewer systems are strained beyond endurance. No police prevent thefts and muggings. Pigs rout through the garbage in the streets.[9] Little attention is paid to civic responsibilities. The public infrastructure decays daily. Property owners neglect their responsibility for the upkeep of public roads. Private citizens spend their funds currying favor from one faction or the other; they have scant resources left to maintain monuments donated in better days. Occupied with street riots and food shortages, the Senate has little time or revenues to lavish on improvements to the urban layout. The city remains a skein of unpaved, unplanned streets.

From their high vantage point thirty meters above the valley floor, the two observers look down on the cityscape. The streets below take on the appearance of rivers. Slow-moving currents of humanity eddy around overloaded carts; progress is slow. Here and there the observers can identify a large retinue of armed slaves and lictors opening a protected pathway for an important magistrate. Soldiers march everywhere.[10] Even from this distance, they notice that several apartment buildings lean precariously. Repeated floods have weakened walls of inexpensive unfired mud-brick or rubble.

The form of individual buildings is further compromised by ramshackle shanties attached like leeches by the poor wherever space allows.

Immediately below the Capitoline Hill to the east come the sounds of construction. Through the overhanging cloud of dust, the elder observer can make out the figures of workers scrambling over two large structures in the revered Forum Romanum. Without a second thought, he identifies the buildings. These are the much talked about basilicas funded by the ambitious general Julius Caesar in an attempt to curry popular favor. Squinting, the observer sees other building activity throughout the Forum as workers labor to repair the fire damage sparked by an angry mob earlier in the year.[11]

Above and beyond the Forum Romanum, the father can just discern the hazy outline of residences on the Fagutal, one of the elevated spurs protruding from the tableland on the eastern side of Rome. Though named after the beech, few trees now grow there.[12] The observer's eyes are immediately drawn to the fresh appearance of the temple to Tellus, restored by the orator Cicero two years before (Cic.QFr.3.1.4; Har.Resp.31). Even from this distance, he can distinguish a change in the housing stock surrounding the temple. Above the crowded apartments of the Subura valley separating the Esquiline from the Oppian stand one- and two-story, single-family homes. He looks intensely to identify the residence of the orator Cicero among the spacious homes of the rich who can afford servants to carry water up from the valleys or from the fountains of the Aqua Tepula to the east. Distanced from the rabble of the city, the well-to-do residents atop the Oppian enjoy the relative quiet of their walled gardens and painted dining rooms.

The homes of senators and wealthy entrepreneurs spread southwest, along the spur of the Velia up to the Palatine Hill. With tall trees and viewing towers, these houses present a pleasing silhouette against the sky. Our observer knows the tranquil picture is misleading. The residences of powerful politicians are often the flashpoints of political conflicts.[13] Furthermore, like all hilltops in the city, the Palatine frequently suffers the wrath of Jupiter. Many times lightning has hit the Temple of Magna Mater prominently sited on the northwestern edge of the hill. Staring southeast at the temple's flank, the cloaked figure on the Capitoline edge observes the poor condition of this peperino and stucco building.

Joined by his son, he squints in a vain attempt to locate the residence of Rome's eponymous founder. For centuries, the Romans have maintained a small, thatch hut on the Palatine commemorating the original residence of Romulus. Below is the Lupercal, a cave on the slope of the Palatine where Romulus and his twin Remus were suckled by a she-wolf (fig. 24).[14] Strain as they might, the father and son cannot catch a glimpse of either sacred spot. The greater height of the Palatine prevents a view of buildings sited

Figure 24. A wall painting depicting the life of Rhea Silvia, mother of Romulus and Remus. The story unfolds before the northwestern corner of the Capitoline Hill, with the Temple of Victoria on the upper right, the she-wolf and twins in the Lupercal at right center, and the personified Tiber River at the bottom. From the House of M. Fabius Secundus, Pompeii. Retouched photo reproduced from E. Pais, *Ancient Legends of Roman History* (London: Swan Sonnenschein 1906), frontispiece.

away from the edge; the multifloored housing and warehouses at the base of the Palatine block the view of the slopes. The father wonders what Romulus would think if he saw Rome now – a bloody, crowded, unkempt panorama.

A shriek of excitement brings the observer to his senses. His young son has located the source of a strange trumpeting noise. Looking down to the southwest, he can see an enormous beast mingling with the cattle on sale in the Forum Boarium by the river. It is an elephant from distant Africa, perhaps one of the twenty that performed in the nearby Circus Maximus at the dedication ceremonies for the Theater of Pompey in 55 B.C.[15] Looking carefully, the two can see one end of the Circus Maximus, just visible to the south beyond the Palatine. Even from their removed perch on the Capitoline, father and son hear the raucous noises of the animals and herders, and catch a whiff of strong, earthy smells from the Forum Boarium. The dust stirred up by the animals, carts, and traders obscures visibility somewhat, but they can identify the rectangular temple to Portunus, god of the port, and the circular shrine to Hercules. The father begins a stylistic discourse, explaining to his son the Greek decorations, form, and marble of the Hercules temple.[16] The young boy yawns with disinterest at the art lesson.

Beyond the Forum Boarium to the south, the narrow strip between the river and the Aventine Hill is tightly packed with shanties, small workshops, and large warehouses (horrea). Little can be seen atop the distant hill itself. Located outside the sacred boundary of the city, the pomerium, this populous zone is filled with hungry, unemployed plebeians. Continuing the lesson in connoisseurship, the father begins to discuss the barely visible temple to Diana on the Aventine. According to tradition, Servius Tullius, sixth king of Rome, persuaded members of the Latin towns to model this shrine on that to Artemis (Diana) at Ephesus. As a result, the structure is more Greek than Italic in form, with columns on all four sides forming a true peristyle.

The sky begins to cloud over. The older observer immediately looks at the turbulent yellow waters of the Tiber.[17] If rains come, the river undoubtedly will flood. Already he can see the barges and other river craft having difficulty maneuvering on the uncompromising waterway. The young boy points to the prow of a large, amazingly stable white trireme directly to the west. His father explains this warship is in reality an island carved in creamy travertine to recall the vessel that brought the healing god Aesculapius to Rome. The great vessel is "moored" to the shore with two stone bridges.

Two other bridges span the Tiber south of the island. Closest to the "ship," the stone and wood Pons Aemilius links the city proper with the right bank. The bustling activities of the Forum Boarium are also serviced by a second bridge, the Pons Sublicius. Following tradition this early, venerated structure is constructed entirely of wood, without even the use of iron pins. As a result, the bridge easily topples with every flood. Even now it is closed to passage; repairs are still underway after the devastating flood of 54 B.C.[18]

Across the river, a dark cloud hovers over buildings occupied by tanning and other polluting industries. The low-lying plain by the river is crowded with warehouses and housing. Noxious fumes and isolation from the city center lower the rents on the right bank. Foreigners favor the Transtiberine zone where, outside the pomerium, they can erect temples to their native deities. At the urging of his son, the father tells of the exotic foreigners and their strange gods, including Yahew, Dea Suriae, Hercules Cubans, and Iovis Heliopolitani. He also points out the new residences of famous citizens. Many wealthy individuals have begun to erect large private estates on the ample open tracts west of the river along the base and slopes of the Janiculum Hill. The land is less expensive than on the left bank and yet offers high visibility. The large villas and gardens developed across the Tiber are easily seen from the left bank, especially from the hilltop residences likewise occupied by the upper class.[19]

A chill now fills the air. The two urban observers must hurry to beat the storm. They turn from the engaging overview of Rome and begin their descent from the Capitoline. The father pushes aside the vendors hawking small garlands, offerings, and religious mementos in the Area Capitolina. He and his son carefully negotiate the Clivus Capitolinus down the slope (fig. 25).[20] Burnished by long use, the dark lava paving stones are slippery under their feet. The street is congested. Stopping to catch their breath on the steep incline, the two observers are immediately jostled by the unceasing street traffic. A slave carrying a large vase jumps to avoid a messenger on horseback; water splashes everywhere. An overfilled cart throws off smelly rubbish as it careens down the Clivus. A whiff of perfume hovers over a curtained litter carried by slaves. A rowdy group of soldiers drunkenly march up the slope singing war songs. Seeking a moment's peace, the father pulls his son inside the portico flanking the street.[21] Respite is not to be found. The portico offers shelter from the fall wind, but little protection from the urban rabble. Whithin the portico, beggars and vendors have staked their territory, mercilessly haranguing all passersby.

For a moment, the father wishes he had chosen to take the internal stairway under the Tabularium. This large building in the low saddle of the hill between the Capitolium and the Arx was constructed by Q. Lutatius Catulus in 78 B.C. to house the state archives. By the small Temple of Vediovis, a doorway in the Tabularium leads to a steep, stone stair descending directly to the Forum Romanum (fig. 26). Even with the noisy jostling on the Clivus Capitolinus, the father knows he has chosen the right path; only a fool would enter a dark, confined space in a city filled with cutthroats and thieves.

As the street begins to level, father and son are able to slow their pace. To their right, they pass at midheight the cella wall and porch columns belonging to the Temple of Saturn.[22] From this height, our observers easily see the terra-cotta upper ornament of the structure, though they cannot discern the temple's broad, old-fashioned profile. Numerous armed guards around the temple attract attention. They protect the state treasury placed in the podium; this stronghold was also the repository for official documents until the construction of the Tabularium. The pedestrians shiver in the cold shadows cast by the hill and buildings. Continuing, they next face the front corner of the temple to Concordia.[23] The poor condition of the shrine, last restored over seventy years earlier, mirrors the decaying state of civil harmony in the 50s B.C. Turning to face the Temple of Concordia, they con-

Figure 25. A view westward from the Forum Romanum up the Clivus Capitolinus. Photo: Fototeca Unione AAR 121.

front the full elevation of the Tabularium. Leaning back, they peer up at rusticated ashlar masonry, arches, and Doric columns. With its modulated play of open and shaded elements, the towering façade recalls the exterior elevations of Roman theaters (fig. 27). Indeed, the Tabularium forms an impressive scenographic backdrop for the Forum Romanum.[24]

The crowds in the street do not allow time for much reverie. Easing out of the main flow of traffic, father and son stand on the edge of the thoroughfare. Running along the base of the Capitoline hill, the Clivus provides an ideal view of the perpendicular area below to the southeast. This is the great Forum Romanum.[25] Literal and symbolic center of Rome, the Forum has a strong spirit of place. In distant times, the kings of Rome reclaimed the low-lying swampland formerly used for burials. For centuries, Romans gathered in this open space to hear speeches, conduct business, as well as to watch gladiatorial contests, state funerals, and other civic performances (fig. 13). Every building commemorates public activities and achievements. Directly below the observers, the speakers' platform, the Rostra, physically and sym-

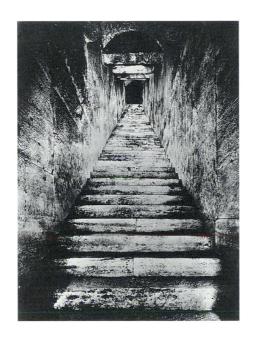

Figure 26. Internal stairs of the Tabularium connecting the Forum Romanum with the Capitoline Hill. Photo: Fototeca Unione AAR 3271.

Figure 27. Exterior of the Tabularium. Photo: Fototeca Unione AAR 141.

bolically elevates public orations. The sanctified plaza directly to the east is the Comitium where crowded public assemblies gather. Adjacent rises the Curia, home to the powerful Senate. The two basilicas under construction are public arenas for courts and business transactions. To the southeast, the Regia contains sacred objects and other ritual paraphernalia; the adjacent Domus Publica houses the high priest, the Pontifex Maximus. Across the road, the shrine of Vesta protects the sacred fire.

The Forum presents an active scene filled with life and potent associations. Looking down from the Clivus Capitolinus, the elder observer considers the parallel between the Forum and the society of Rome. Like Roman citizens, the buildings stand as distinct individuals, related by proximity and common purpose rather than by rigid dictate. The observers' eyes move ceaselessly over the scene; no one structure, object, or action dominates. Attention drifts from the animated action of the crowds in their dusty gray cloaks to the stately repose of the great buildings; from the reflected light on the water in the Lacus Curtius to the sacred fig trees, anomalous touches of greenery in this contrived human environment. Many important monuments, including the shrines of Venus Cloacina and Janus on the north, are too small to stand above the milling crowd. Even the large Temple of Castor and Pollux cannot galvanize visual attention. From the Clivus Capitolinus, the observers look down and across the Forum to the structure's lateral columns and sloping roof.

A thousand sounds rise to the ears of our observers. Workers on the two facing basilicas yell directions, Senators vociferously lobby, beggars moan with outstretched hands, money changers clang their scales, vendors and prostitutes hawk their wares. The idle gather to listen and watch. In part, the crowding in the area around the Lacus Curtius is due to construction work. The crowds that normally gather in the Basilica Sempronia and the old shops before it now loll in the open. They await the completion of the larger, more spectacular Basilica Julia. Hordes have always characterized the Forum. The father recites for his son a passage from a play by Plautus written a century earlier, "for perjurers try the Comitium. Liars and braggarts, by the shrine of Cloacina; rich married wastrels, in stock by the Basilica."[26] If anything, the Forum's population has worsened in the intervening decades. Hired guards or armed slaves accompany everyone who can afford them. The tension is palpable. A single spark will ignite the combustible crowd.

Political rivalries are evident everywhere in the Forum. The blackened architecture left from the fire last January keep in mind the riot at the funeral of the ambitious and popular Clodius. Every day, the supporters of Pompey work the crowd. Those promoting Julius Caesar point repeatedly to the great Basilica Julia on the southwest side of the central open space.

Rumors tell how Caesar used his booty from Gaul to help fund the reconstruction of the Basilica Aemilia as well.[27]

Father and son rejoin the stream of traffic moving along the Clivus Capitolinus and continue northward. At the juncture with the Clivus Argentarius, they look down on the curved steps defining the Comitium. Usually filled with politicians, this open place of assembly is instead bustling with construction workers paid by Faustus Cornelius Sulla, son of the dictator Sulla and son-in-law of Pompey. They labor to restore the adjoining Senate building, another casualty of the recent fire. The dust and commotion obscure the individual monuments around the Comitium. The observers can locate neither the Columna Maenia nor the Lapis Niger, the famous black stone covering the mysterious spot believed by many to be the tomb of Rome's founder, Romulus.

Shuddering at the memory of the riots that defiled the Comitium, the father leads his young son up the Clivus Argentarius on the rise between the Capitoline and the Quirinal. They pass the Basilica Porcia, the ominous state jail known as the Carcer, and the offices of the censors in the Atrium Libertatis. The climb is steep. At the top of the rise, the older observer pauses, panting. The street is flanked on the north by shops and on the south by thick retaining walls holding back the Capitoline. Narrow and crowded, the street is constricted, the air stagnant. Turning back to look at the Forum Romanum, he sees a large open area to the southeast. New construction again signals the hand of Caesar. Two years ago, the general sent instructions from Gaul for the purchase of land for an expansion to the Forum to accommodate public business. Houses and commercial structures are being demolished to make way for an extension to the venerated Forum Romanum. The property alone cost a small fortune, but for Caesar it is a small price to pay to keep his name constantly before the public.[28]

The pedestrians pass through the Porta Fontinalis. Although Rome has long since expanded beyond her decaying fortifications of the third century b.c., traces of this gate remain. The large, pitted blocks of yellowish-gray Grotta Oscura tufa attest to an early date. Passing through the gate, the observers exit the city proper and begin to descend. They step over the garbage in the street and push through the teaming crowds entering Rome. The pair jostle with Greeks, Spaniards, Cilicians, and other foreigners; the jumble of tongues is deafening.[29] At the creak of a wagon, everyone automatically lurches to the side, fearing the heavy load of lumber will topple down the hill. The father again pulls his son into a protective portico.[30] They continue their descent. As the ground levels, the pedestrians remain in the shade of the second-century b.c. portico following the curve of the street toward the west. The presence of tombs lining the roadway confirms they are outside the *pomerium*.[31]

The observers are now on the Via Flaminia.[32] This road cuts a broad swath across the Campus Martius. The great flood plain stretches westward over 1300 meters to the Tiber River.[33] A fluttering of wings draws their attention. A dark flock of birds rises in ominous flight over the Campus. Do they portend imminent conflict? Why else would they circle over the field of the war god Mars? In past times, soldiers gathered in the plain to practice maneuvers in readiness to fight the enemies of the Republic. Now, Romans seem determined to fight Romans.

The sheltering portico ends at the altar to Mars, patron god of the plain. Before the pedestrians, the relentlessly straight Via Flaminia stretches to the horizon. After the narrow, winding streets within the pomerium, the single-mindedness of the Via Flaminia is a relief. Because the plain slopes downward toward the river, the highway acts as a platform, offering a good view of the buildings in the Campus. Each great structure tells a story about one of Rome's great achievers. Directly to the observers' left is the Villa Publica. Here State officers take the census and levy troops, and generals await the celebration of their triumphs. The father stares blankly at the structure. As a youth thirty years earlier, he looked at the same building while the air filled with cries of anguish. In 82 B.C., the general Sulla ordered 4,000 prisoners in the Villa Publica to be summarily massacred. Even the colorful costumes of foreign ambassadors milling around the Villa today cannot erase the painful association.

Beyond the Villa Publica to the west rises the largest structure in the Campus Martius, the impressive Theater of Pompey. Dedicated with tremendous fanfare three years earlier, the structure caused great controversy. Contrary to Republican ideas of propriety, Pompey made his theater permanent. The boastful structure of peperino and red granite stands tall above the plain. The young boy strains to see the building, hoping for a glimpse of exotic animals, but the crowded buildings of the southern Campus do not allow a clear view.[34] The dampness in the air blurs the details; all he can see are a smear of green from the plane trees in the large portico enclosure and a reddish mass towering behind.

Standing at the foot of the Capitoline, the two figures feel as if they are still in the city. The physical form of the southernmost Campus Martius is quite urban. Crowded structures of mud-brick, timber, and rubble fill the area between the Theater of Pompey and the old city wall. At the sound of dripping water, father and son look skyward, but the dark sky has not yet opened. The noise comes from wet laundry hung from a balcony above the highway. As they move northward, the density of construction lessens, easing the transition from the city to the countryside. Marshy and somewhat removed from the urban core, the central Campus is not completely built over. The open plain offers welcome space where citizens can exercise or gather in large groups. On this day, the great Campus seems as inundated with problems as the State. A brackish smell wafts up to the pedestrians. After the recent rains, the low-lying field is dotted with muddy pools. The dampness recalls the disastrous flood two years earlier, when the Tiber was an unwelcome guest in many parts of the city.

Across the plain north of the Villa Publica, the observers can see an enormous rectangular area being prepared for construction. When work begins in earnest, the rectangle will define a permanent enclosure for the voting of the large assemblies. Hoping to capture the interest of his son, the father explains that previously the assemblies met here in a wooden structure known familiarly as the sheepfold or *ovile*. Even without an informational sign, everyone knows the project well. Caesar is the patron. He envisions a structure of unprecedented size and grandeur, with covered booths of marble and a colonnade a mile long. The building will carry his family name, the Saepta Julia.

As they progress ever northward, the observers see another project linked with Caesar. Above the flat plain rises the mountain-shaped tomb to his daughter Julia, wife of Pompey.[35] Two years earlier, in 54 B.C., Julia died in childbirth. In pity for the young woman, the people of Rome buried her in the Campus Martius even though she had not been formally awarded this honor. The Tumulus Juliae marks the spot. The earthen mound keeps the precarious contemporary political situation ever in mind; with Julia's death, the uneasy alliance between Caesar and Pompey is rapidly unravelling.

The rivalry of Rome's ambitious men is further evident to the east. On the slopes of the tableland, the wealthy compete in the creation of elaborate villas and pleasure parks, or *horti*. Inspired by the gardens of Hellenistic rulers in the eastern Mediterranean, Rome's notables rival one another in the size and richness of their private estates. The *horti* of the general L. Licinius Lucullus are particularly notorious.[36] Unable to conquer Pompey in the political arena, he has set out to conquer pleasure. The sumptuous, unproductive gardens provide an appropriate setting. From the Via Flaminia, the observers see a verdant blanket covering the tableland and its slopes.[37] The green-coded area of privilege stands in marked contrast to the buff-colored housing on the Quirinal Hill to the south and the marshy field to the west. The whole zone is a paean to overindulgence, a visible manifestation of hedonistic Eastern ways and the decline of Republican morality.

The Campus Martius itself is a stage for ever greater extravagant displays. The broad flood plain readily accommodates large crowds that gather for games, religious ceremonies, and other performances. For these events, the State erects wooden bleachers and stages. Squinting as they turn to face west, the observers see towering piles of timber, the mute remnants of such temporary structures. A steady stream of people fills the Campus as crowds pour out of the day's attraction, the rotating amphitheater. Patrons like Curio this year and M. Scaurus, stepson of Sulla, six years earlier expended enormous sums on entertainment facilities with a short life.[38] Scaurus' theater was the most extravagant building the city had ever seen. The three-story stage had 360 columns, some as tall as thirty-eight feet. The lowest level was of marble, the next of glass mosaic, and the top of gilded wood. Large paintings, golden cloth, and 3,000 bronze statues further embellished the area.[39]

As they move ever northward, the two pedestrians pass through the landscaped property of Pompey. The consul lavished his war booty on a sumptuous estate at the northern edge of the city. The Horti of Pompey run from the Campus Martius, across the Via Flaminia, and up the slopes of the eastern tableland. In contrast to other parts of Rome, Pompey's *horti* show little sign of neglect. Recently, the general borrowed large sums of cash to cover his projects and dealings in the city.[40] The exotic plants, trained gardeners, and imported statuary for the great park are costly, yet such expenditures are necessary; a man's residence reflects his status. Comparing Pompey's *horti* with those on the hill, the observers acknowledge the general's superiority.

The meticulously tended parkland of Pompey contrasts markedly with the forlorn gardens around the tombs lining the Via Flaminia.[41] Funerary monuments of prominent citizens line the highway. In better days, the father often stopped to read the lengthy inscriptions, holding up the lives of deceased Romans as models for his son. The tombs are no longer ideal exemplars. The disruptive political climate has taken its toll even here. Many tombs are neglected. Stucco crumbles, revealing the brick underneath; funerary gardens are choked with weeds. Furthermore, it is no longer wise to stand exposed on the open highway.

A cold wind races across the broad paved surface of the Via Flaminia. The observers tightly grab their gray woolen cloaks and hurry onward. They find it increasingly difficult to look at the surroundings. Unmaintained, the great highway is riddled with holes. The pedestrians focus their eyes downward. In any case, there are few sights to distract them. Abandoned farm plots now flank the highway. Two hours after leaving the Porta Fontinalis, the pair reach the Mulvian bridge. They turn and look back at Rome. From this location, the great city is identified by a dense brownish haze in the distance. They peer down at the raging Tiber. Swollen from rains upstream, the angry river seems ready to burst its untended banks.

They do not dawdle on the bridge. With a final glance, the two observers bid farewell to the city. Silently, they move on, each mentally reviewing the images of Rome. The metropolis is huge, lively, and dynamic. The city boasts magnificent new buildings such as Pompey's theater and anticipates added grandeur with the completion of the numerous impressive projects of Caesar currently underway. Yet, the overall impression is negative. Images of dereliction, crowding, filth, danger, and disorder overshadow any episodic impact of great structures or civic spaces. Rome is the premier city of an expansive territory, but it cannot claim to possess decorum.

CHAPTER THREE

CONTEXT
THE REPUBLICAN
URBAN IMAGE

They have ordained this city to be most beautiful,
most flourishing, most powerful.
Cicero *In Catilinam* 2.13.29

In 182 B.C., courtiers of Philip V of Macedon spent hours belittling their rivals, the Romans. "Some would jeer at their habits and customs, others at Roman achievements, others at the appearance of the city itself, which was not yet beautified in either its public places or its private districts."[1] This was powerful propaganda. The Romans may have defeated Philip V in war, yet the Macedonians and other peoples in the eastern Mediterranean claimed cultural victory. Residents in Alexandria, Pergamon, Athens, and other Hellenistic cities considered themselves superior in many areas, including urban appearance. From opulent palaces, verdant public parks, and formally ordered districts, they exchanged derogatory descriptions of Rome. Visits to Italy only confirmed the negative image. Every walk though the narrow byways of Republican Rome revealed unsafe streets, poorly maintained public buildings, decaying private structures, and undirected planning. Who could consider the Romans serious contenders for political hegemony when their primary city projected an unimpressive image?

An urban image reflects both the physical and the conceptual status of a specific city. The urban images of allied cities taken together may reflect the status of the group. More commonly, however, the image of the dominant city represents the collective. During the early Republic, Rome was the locus of interaction for a federation of independent city-states. By the third century B.C., the Republic's influence extended beyond the Italian peninsula. Externally, rivals like the Macedonians directed their barbs at Rome, viewed by them as the enemy's capital. Internally, however, Latin members of the Roman alliance still considered the city on the Tiber not as a true capital city, but as the first among equals.

42

The two perceptions of Rome began to coalesce in the late Republic. By the first century B.C., the Romans were acknowledged players on the Mediterranean stage. The poor urban image of their premier city negatively affected the political aspirations of independent Republicans and of the State as a whole. As a result, ambitious citizens vied to place their own stamp on Rome; the greater their individual power, the greater the imprint. Simultaneously, external models sparked emulation. Interacting with other world powers, the Romans could not help but draw unfavorable comparisons between Rome and the strong urban images of contemporary eastern capitals. Faced with positive models and the derision of outside observers, they began to conceive of the city in a different light. Rome was not just the locus of Roman political strength, it was a tangible manifestation of individual and collective power.

Rome lies in an eroded volcanic plateau framed by the Albani Mountains to the south and the Sabatini Mountains to the north.[2] On the east, long fingers of land reach toward the Tiber River forming the Colles Quirinalis and Viminalis, and the Montes Esquilinus and Caelius. Between these projections and the river stand three solitary hills, the Montes Capitolinus, Palatinus, and Aventinus (fig. 19).[3] To the west, the protective rise of the Janiculum and, farther north, the Mon Vaticanus define a plain cut by the meandering Tiber River. At a sharp bend in its course, a solitary island obstructs the brisk flow of water from the northern Apennine mountains to the sea.

By the ninth century B.C., villages appeared atop the protective high points east of the Tiber. Earliest were the settlements on the Palatine and Capitoline overlooking well-traveled communication routes: the pathways running east–west along the valleys crossing the river at the island, and along the Tiber flowing from the Apennines to the Tyrrhenian Sea approximately 26 km southwest of the site. Over the following centuries, these isolated settlements incorporated into a city girded by formidable fortifications.[4] The central meeting point in the valley between the hills was drained by the sixth century B.C. and rapidly developed into the Forum Romanum, the locus of urban public life. To enhance the prestige of this civic center, select commercial undertakings were moved out to secondary fora along the river banks and major roads into the city.[5] Atop the Capitoline hill rose Rome's most important religious buildings, the temples to Jupiter Optimus Maximus and Juno Moneta. Directly south, the Palatine evolved into a residential quarter for those rich enough to own servants and slaves to carry water and provisions up the hill.[6] The valley between the Palatine and Aventine was a natural race track, formalized with construction of the Circus Maximus in the days of Etruscan rule.[7] The Mons Aventinus stood within the city wall, but outside the *pomerium,* Rome's ritualized border.[8] Lacking prestige, the Aventine became a primarily plebeian quarter. In general, however, diversity was the norm in the cityscape, with rich and poor, foreigner and slave living and working in close proximity. Public open space was at a premium within the city walls, so many large civic events took place on the broad, flat plain dedicated to Mars northwest of the city center. Nestled in the curve of the Tiber River, the Campus Martius frequently flooded and thus was not encumbered with permanent structures. Here soldiers conducted maneuvers, assemblies voted, and celebrants gathered. Romans considered the area across the river as less desirable than the left bank; developing under a stigma, the right bank was occupied by workers' quarters, foreigners, and such noxious industries as tanning.

The physical form of Rome suffered significantly during the early decades of the first century B.C. Ever growing, the city on the Tiber had a population numbering several hundred thousand, with construction extending far beyond the confines of the Republican walls.[9] Shanties, tombs, temples, workshops, and residences reached out along the major roads in every direction. Atop the plateaus to the northeast of the city center, the wealthy established large estates and pleasure gardens in overt rivalry with one another. Land costs escalated at a rapid rate. Building occurred haphazardly, with little consideration for the functioning and image of the overall city. Preoccupied with external issues and internecine conflicts, magistrates and private patrons alike ignored pragmatic urban concerns. Rome's sewers, aqueducts, and roads strained under the double burden of overuse and lack of maintenance. In 58 B.C., a sewer contractor feared his work could not support any unusual weight; he forced the patron Marcus Scaurus to post a security when moving heavy marble columns to his house on the Palatine (Pliny *HN*.36.6). Frequent fires and floods also wrecked havoc on the cityscape, devastating large urban tracts in a few hours (cf. Chart 2). Human actions were equally destructive. Agitated by crowding, unemployment, and famine, urban residents often rioted, damaging large segments of the urban fabric.[10] Neglect, lack of planning and maintenance, along with civic unrest, resulted in an unattractive urban appearance.

Observers walking through late Republican Rome were jostled by thousands of city dwellers and thousands of city images. Their primary emotions were fear and confusion. The Romans capably controlled vast holdings and ably negotiated complex treaties, yet their premier city did not reflect these skills or attainments. In fact, the cityscape impugned such achievements. Poorly maintained public spaces and buildings projected an impression of disorganization and decline, and a lack of collective pride. Monuments to individuals embellished the city, yet such self-serving works conveyed rivalry and thus did not foster a unified urban identity. As the Romans expanded their sphere of influence throughout the Mediterranean basin, the negative, unfocused image of their premier city-state became a liability. Simultaneously, the hegemony of strong individuals in Rome fanned the desire to improve the city and set the stage for the creation of an imperial urban experience.

THE URBAN IMAGE OF LATE REPUBLICAN ROME

The evolution of Rome's urban form can be traced in the physical remains; the evolution and impact of the urban image is more difficult to track. Writing in the first century B.C., Cicero repeatedly described the Republican city-state as supremely beautiful.[11] Yet anyone actually moving through Rome at that time had to acknowledge the city as a whole was not physically attractive (fig. 28). Though individual buildings and one or two urban spaces were impressive, the city as a whole did not please the eye, impress, or project a cohesive message. Furthermore, Rome was neither clean nor safe. The same authors who praised the city described the experience of Rome in decidedly negative terms. For example, Cicero portrays the dregs of humanity who occupied the city and Varro records the mugging and murder of a minor official in broad daylight.[12] In effect, late Republican authors sought a definition of urban beauty applicable to the existing condition. Minimizing the physical form as the primary indicator of urban attractiveness, they exploited nontangible characteristics and associations. Republican authors argued that the city's beauty resided not necessarily in the experience or appearance of its physical form, but in its stature, or rather, in the *idea* of Rome.[13]

Roman historians of the first century B.C. affirmed the greatness of the city-state through anachronistic divine associations. Looking to the heavens, they attributed Rome's growth and beauty to divine ordination. After all Romulus, son of a god, founded the city (fig. 24).[14] Writing in the late first century B.C., Vitruvius explains, "It was, therefore, a divine intelligence that placed the city of the Roman people in an excellent and temperate country, so that she might acquire the right to rule over the whole world" (6.1). Imagining the divinely chosen site before development, late Republican authors listed its attributes: good springs, easily protected hills, and ready access to the sea along the Tiber (Livy 5.54.4; Strab.5.3.7; Cic.*Rep*.2.3, 5–6). In turn, this manufactured, idyllic image of early Rome informed ideas about the contemporary city. No matter that the original site was in fact not ideal, with brackish streams, an insalubrious climate, a flood-prone river, and easily assaulted hills, or that the city of the first century B.C. was severely lacking in amenities. Blessed by the gods, Rome had innate beauty.

Figure 28. Reconstruction of a street in Rome. Drawing: Richard H. Abramson.

Discussions of urban aesthetics were limited in antiquity.[15] City planning focused on issues of siting and fortifications on the pragmatic side, and social and moral concepts on the theoretical side. Much lauded works on cities such as the description of Atlantis by Plato or the theories of Hippodamus of Miletus gave primacy to the sociopolitical context; the depictions of urban form were secondary and largely metaphorical.[16] Yet as the Romans came in direct contact with the great cities of the Hellenistic world – Alexandria, Ephesus, Antioch – they grudgingly acknowledged, "the Greeks had the repute of aiming most happily in the founding of cities, in that they aimed at beauty..." (Strab.5.3.8). In ancient art, beauty was equated with organization, or more specifically, with the strict adherence to rules and canons of perfection. Beauty was to be found in the relationships between elements and the whole, not in individual components. Buying wholesale into Greek ideas of abstract beauty, the Romans of the first century B.C. based their connoisseurship in large part on provenance.[17] For his treatise on architecture written in the second half of the century, Vitruvius cited Greek sources to validate his ideas. He defines good architecture as based on order, arrangement, proportion, symmetry, propriety, and economy (1.2.1). Individual buildings in Rome satisfied these criteria for beauty; the city as a whole did not. Rome was unplanned, unordered, and certainly uneconomical in layout.

Following chapters on fundamental architectural principles, Vitruvius delves into urban issues. Rather than general principles of city planning or urban beauty, he focuses on siting, fortifications, and orientation to the winds.[18] According to these criteria, the city on the Tiber again did not fare well. Some authors attempted to explain or excuse Rome's formal inadequacies. Livy writing in the second half of the first century B.C. describes the events following the sack of the city by the Gauls in 390 B.C. Looking at the decimated cityscape, some citizens put forth a bill to relocate to the more attractive and safe Etruscan city of Veii. After a persuasive speech by Camillus emphasizing the powerful *genius loci* of Rome and a favorable omen, the residents agreed to rebuild on the same site. The State offered incentives to promote rapid rebuilding, but provided no comprehensive urban plan or guidelines for implementation.[19] Instead, Livy records the people of Rome "began to rebuild the city without plan of any kind. . . . Such was their haste that they did not take care to lay out the streets since all the boundary distinctions had been lost and they were building *in vacuo*. This is the reason why . . . the appearance of the city resembles one that has been occupied rather than being properly planned" (5.55.1–5). According to this story, circumstances, not planning, shaped the city's form.[20]

An emphasis on events and achievements, rather than formal aesthetics, proved especially useful in exalting Rome. Though they admired Greek art and city planning, the Romans put forth distinctly different criteria for beauty and fame. Vergil, in the late first century B.C., explains:

Let others fashion from bronze more lifelike, breathing images, for so they shall, and evoke living faces from marble. . . . But, Romans, never forget that government is your medium! Be this your art: to practice men in the habit of peace, generosity to the conquered, and firmness against aggressors.[21]

The Romans admired tangible results. They had not set out to conquer the world. Beginning with low expectations, the citizens of the central Italian state were amazed by their own attainments.[22] In the middle of the second century B.C., the Greek historian Polybius marveled, "the Romans in less than fifty-three years have succeeded in subjecting nearly the whole inhabited

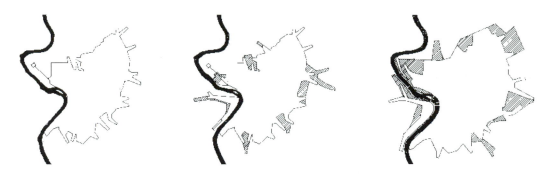

Figure 29. Diagram, three thumbnail maps showing the growth of Rome. Left: Republic, late second century B.C. Middle: Late Republic, mid-first century B.C. Right: Augustan Age, early first century A.D.

world to their sole government – a thing unique in history" (1.1). Having achieved great things, both Rome and the Republic deserved to be described as "most beautiful, most flourishing, most powerful" (Cic.*Cat*.2.13.29). Similarly, the transformation of a cluster of rural huts into the seat of an expansive Republic, though slow by modern standards, seemed phenomenal in antiquity (fig. 29).[23] When citizens focused attention on the premier city-state, they saw not just an urbs with crowded streets and scattered monuments, but a significant urban development. The very existence of a huge metropolis on the banks of the Tiber was a notable achievement; thus, it followed that the city itself had to be considered inherently beautiful.

Rome's own glorious history elevated her stature. The achievements of all famous Romans informed the city's appearance. By the first century B.C., almost every urban corner evoked memories of significant events.[24] The urban fabric served as an historical ledger. With each step, the pedestrian encountered documentation of the city's great residents. Inscriptions, sculptures, paintings, reliefs, and building names all conveyed information about the past. Memories about Romulus or Scipio, or even about contemporaries such as Sulla, stimulated both the intellect and feelings. Cicero has Piso explain, "Whether it is a natural instinct or a mere illusion, I can't say; but one's emotions are more strongly aroused by seeing the places that tradition records to have been the favorite resort of men of note in former days, than by hearing about their deeds or reading their writings."[25] The urban experience was thus highly charged. The power of the place drew upon all past events and past lives; the cumulative effect was conceptually, if not necessarily tangibly, beautiful.

By the second century B.C., artists and philosophers had begun to consider the lay viewers' reception of artworks.[26] This trend resulted in the association of moral characteristics with aesthetic criteria. In a beautiful work, the physical form reflects the moral characteristics appropriate for the subject depicted. Accordingly, the statue of a great man should reveal *decorum* (propriety), *dignitas* (esteem), and *auctoritas* (authority). Likewise, an architectural environment should evoke the associations appropriate for the particular divine or human occupants. Vitruvius directly associates the use, size, decoration, and form of a house with the status of the resident. For example, he argues, "persons of high rank . . . should be provided princely vestibules, lofty halls . . . libraries and basilicas" (6.5.2). Ethical standards for architecture, however, were not adhered to in Rome of the first century B.C. Throughout the city, important deities resided in shabby temples and minor political figures lived in great houses.[27] Furthermore, the overall urban form did not elicit an elevated moral response. Rome had earned *auctoritas* through her illustrious history, yet her indecorous plan and disheveled appearance signaled a lack of propriety.

Capital cities bear a dual charge. They house the state government and at the same time preserve and convey collective memories and aspirations. In several modern capitals, these associations coalesce in a single building or complex. The urban image of Washington, D.C., is embodied in the Mall with its surrounding buildings, the import of London in the Houses of Parliament.[28] Rome harbored the collective memories of the Roman peoples, but was not technically a national capital. Rather, it stood as the premier city among allied city-states. The patrician Senate and various assemblies of the people governed the Republic. The Senate had its own meeting hall, the Curia, but it also met frequently in other buildings throughout the large city. Similarly, the assemblies congregated at different locales; they had no permanent, monumental structure. The heart of the city, the venerated Forum

Figure 30. Helmeted Roma on a South Italian coin from the early second century B.C. (left); Alexandria with turreted crown (Tyche) on a coin of the first-century B.C. Drawing: author.

Romanum, possessed a strong power of place, yet in the Republican period, its collection of buildings did not readily compose a unified portrait (fig. 13). Republican Rome had neither a singular visual symbol nor a cohesive overall program precisely because the Republic itself was multivalent.[29]

The belief in place-specific spirits furthered the heterogeneous image of Rome. The Romans embodied each independent being and place with a *genius,* or guardian spirit, who determined and reflected its unique character.[30] By definition, every spirit of a place, *genius loci,* in the city was particularized. Thus, the city had almost as many *genii locorum* as people, all vying for attention and stature within the cityscape. Rome had its own, all-encompassing city *genius,* yet even this spirit of the city was not singular.[31] The *genius* of Rome represented the collective, and thus reflected the Republic and Roman society rather than the city itself (fig. 30).[32]

A group anxiety pervades the unfocused, often contradictory contemporary urban descriptions of Rome. Attempts to reframe the criteria for urban greatness to favor Rome had limited impact on the world's perception of the city. By the early first century B.C., the Romans wielded control over the whole inhabited world. Their capital had a commanding role on the world stage, but it was not dressed for the part. The inappropriateness of the city's appearance and overall image in relation to its stature was against the perceived order of things. Furthermore, it reflected badly upon the powerful individuals who resided there. Gradually, this disparity became too overt to ignore and a call arose for patrons to fund buildings as, "the renown of our empire demand" (Cic.*Verr.*2.4.68).

CONTEXT FOR CHANGE

Intimate contact with Greek cities affected Roman ideas about urban appearance. As early as the fourth century B.C., the Romans had carried artworks and even architectural elements as booty from Greek cities back to Rome. Though they could not literally transport urban environments, the Romans did transfer concepts of urban imagery. Many had first-hand familiarity with the grand cities of the east.[33] In the second and first centuries B.C., thousands of soldiers, sailors, and merchants traveled widely throughout the Mediterranean. More sedentary Romans knew of great Hellenistic capitals and cities from literary and pictorial descriptions.[34] Even the most uneducated had heard of the lush gardens of Antioch, the grand palaces of Alexandria, and the beautiful siting of Syracuse.[35] Cicero records that when Marcellus captured Syracuse in 211 B.C., he left the city intact believing "it would not tend to the credit of Rome that he should blot out and destroy all this beauty" (*Verr.*2.4.120).

The contrast with Rome was palpable. In 195 B.C., Livy has Cato lament that many Romans praised the ornaments of Corinth and Athens while belittling the terra-cotta antefixes on temples in Rome (34.4.3). Beyond the admirable proportions, decorations, and rich materials of Greek buildings, Roman observers commented on the large scale of eastern projects. Aristotle and other Hellenistic authors had equated largeness with superiority.[36] The Temple of Apollo at Didyma measured approximately 5,668 sq. meters; the largest temple in Rome, that of Jupiter Optimus Maximus, measured approximately 3,339 sq. meters (fig. 31). Equally obvious, Hellenistic cities displayed formal planning, with regularized districts or plans imposed by powerful patrons.

In control for decades, Hellenistic rulers (or dynasties) had the time, motivation, and resources to rebuild entire urban regions and lay out new cities. The Hellenistic city was a vehicle for not only individual or dynastic fame, but also for state propaganda, acculturation, and control. Dynasts viewed opulent capital cities and grand public facilities as a means to unite the diverse populations under their control.[37] The comparative unity of patronage focused the image of these cities. For example, the Ionian city of Pergamon developed over many years, yet the continuing patronage by a primary family, the Attalids, resulted in a scheme notable for its stylistic coherency and directed message (fig. 32). Rome, with her wood and stucco temples embellished with terra-cottas, her confusing skein of streets, and buildings by diverse patrons, could not compare to the unified urban image created by the directed vision of a single dynasty.

The Romans did not hide their envy. They admired both the appearance of Hellenistic cities and the political advantages of focused urban patronage. Cicero tells that earlier Romans decided only three cities in the world could support the dignity and name of an imperial city: Carthage, Corinth, and Capua (Leg.2.32.87). With great determination, they destroyed the first two both politically and physically. By the end of the second century B.C., hardly a vestige of Carthage or Corinth remained to be seen. The Romans chose an alternative solution for Capua, located closer to home in Campania on the Italian coast south of Rome. Rather than razing this Greek-founded city, they deprived the Capuans of their territories and the right to govern. In 63 B.C., Cicero argued against a proposed resettlement; with derision, he stressed the Campanians' arrogance, based in part on pride of the city's arrangement and beauty. Cicero invited his listeners to imagine the Capuans' reaction if their city were augmented: "They will laugh at and despise Rome, planted in mountains and deep valleys, its garrets hanging up aloft, its roads none of the best, by-ways of the narrowest, in comparison with their own Capua" (Leg.2.35.95–6). Cicero's arguments were persua-

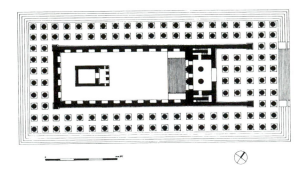

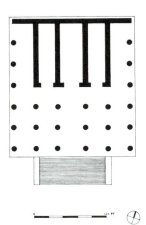

Figure 31. Scale comparison of plans for the temples of Apollo at Didyma (top) and Jupiter Optimus Maximus at Rome. Drawing: Rodica Reif.

Figure 32. Model of ancient Pergamon. Model by H. Schleif, Staatliche Museen zu Berlin, Antiken-Sammlung.37.

sive; Capua was not resettled. However, this city remained a constant visual reminder of Greek superiority in urban aesthetics.

Efforts to improve Rome's urban image coincided with a redirection and intensification of private architectural patronage. The writings of Cicero reflect both the yearning for a less opportunistic climate and the competitive pressures of his own day. He idealizes the past, venerating citizens of the early Republic who exhibited modesty in all things.[38] Such men resided in simple structures and erected buildings for the collective good, not for personal gain. Cicero claims, "The Roman people hate private luxury, they love public magnificence."[39] He explains how private citizens assumed responsibility for impressive public structures in Rome, while erecting modest homes for themselves. In particular, the *mos maiorum,* the customs of the ancestors, exhorted victorious generals to "employ their booty and spoils on monuments to the immortal gods . . . or for the embellishment of Rome."[40] Triumphators dutifully erected numerous victory monuments, primarily in the southwestern Campus Martius near the Porta Triumphalis (cf. fig. 45). By their very nature, however, such works were not primarily for the public's benefit. Victory monuments in Rome were blatant self-promotions championing a general's achievement. Similarly, triumphal parades were both important urban events and the means for generals to advertise their distant achievements (Polyb.6.15.8). Cicero gives a vivid, moralizing description of a triumph:

What . . . is the use of yon chariot, of the generals that walk in chains before it, of the models of [captured] towns, of the gold and the silver, of the lieutenants and the tribunes on horseback, of the shouting of the troops, and of all the pageantry of the show? Vanity, mere vanity I tell you . . . to hunt applause, to drive through the city, to wish to be a gazing-stock. (Cic.*Pis.*60; cf. Livy 37.59.3–5)

Given such evidence in his own day, Cicero acknowledges that the Roman people "have ever been, beyond all nations, seekers after glory and greedy of praise" (*Leg.Man.*19–21). In the hierarchical society of Rome, the desire for glory (*cupido gloriae*) motivated many actions.[41] Military glory and other achievements brought a citizen *auctoritas* and the concomitant elevation in social and political standing.[42]

By the first century B.C., the individual quest for fame dominated and was made possible by the city.[43] Building in Rome brought personal celebrity and prestige.[44] There was a direct positive correlation between individuals who patronized architecture in the city and political success, and a negative correlation between those who did not make notable additions to the city's physical form.[45] A great building project in Rome brought the patron votes, prestige, and enduring remembrance. Conversely, damage to extant structures or neglect brought disrepute.[46] When Gaius Verres misappropriated funds for repairs to the Temple of Castor and Pollux, Cicero ranked the severity of the crime in relation to the building's significance; the temple was not only an historical monument, it stood in the most revered of public places, the Forum Romanum. Cicero exhorted the jury, "think of the Temple of Castor, that famous and glorious memorial of the past, that sanctuary which stands where the eyes of the nation may rest upon it every day" (*Verr.*2.1.129).

Everyone in Rome with the means vied for recognition through increasingly extravagant building projects.[47] The fierce competition compelled patrons to make their structures ever larger and more opulent. Exotic imported materials appeared more and more frequently.[48] In the 70s B.C., Marcus Lepidus used luscious giallo antico for his door sills and Lucullus introduced a black marble to Rome called Lucullean in his honor. When aedile in 58 B.C., Marcus Scaurus imported 360 marble columns to ornament the stage of a temporary theater; after the performances, he moved the columns to his own house (Pliny *HN.*36.4–8). The standards for architectural magnificence constantly escalated. Pliny records that a house considered beautiful in 78 B.C. was not even rated in the top 100 residences 35 years later.[49] Caught up in the frenzy of competition, patrons did not always benefit from such urban investments in fame. They created extravagances that shocked and alienated the public and often overextended themselves financially. Looking back at the excesses of this period, Pliny wondered why sumptuary laws never curbed the use of extravagant marbles (*HN.*36.4–6).

Not surprisingly, reliance on architecture as an indicator of stature soon led to misapplication and devaluation. Patrons increasingly used magnificent buildings to acquire fame, rather than ennobling modest structures by their own renown or achievements. Cicero argues, "a man's dignity may be enhanced by the house he lives in, but not wholly secured by it; the owner should bring honor to his house, not the house to its owner." Yet in the same passage, he describes an imposing house in Rome: "Everyone went to see it, and it was thought to have gained votes for the owner" (*Off.*1.39). The situation extended even outside the city on the Tiber. Cicero tells that the consul Lucius Lucullus was criticized for constructing an ostentatious villa at Tusculum, but he justified his excess by pointing to the showy structures of his two neighbors of lower standing, an equestrian and a freedman; "as their villas also were most luxurious, he thought that he ought to have the same privilege" (*Leg.*3.13).

Buildings in Rome stood as enduring texts, read by generations of urban observers. Blatant advertisements underscored the direct connection between patrons and structures throughout the city. Inscriptions, project names, and programmatic artwork all promoted the donor responsible for each major public building.[50] Among the most explicit were the dedicatory inscriptions on temples, important works in every Roman city. Religious and State restrictions tightly regulated religious patronage. According to tradition, only a magistrate with *imperium* could dedicate a public temple.[51] State projects authorized by the Senate bore the inscription *S.P.Q.R.* (*Senatus Populusque Romanus*), yet frequently also carried the name of the officiating magistrate. For example, the two censors of 179 B.C. contracted for the erection of a large structure in the Forum Romanum. The project came to be called the Basilica Aemilia in honor of the more prominent censor, M. Aemilius Lepidus.[52] Through the original patron, a projects' fame accrued to the donors, descendants, or, more broadly, to the entire family or *gens*. As a result, the condition of a donated structure became an overt barometer of a family's economic and political health. To maintain their prestige, descendants were obliged to keep up the maintenance of "family" buildings virtually in perpetuity. Thus, over the decades, the Aemilii continually repaired the basilica that bore their name, even when doing so strained their resources.

By the first century B.C., Rome's urban fabric showed obvious signs of wear and tear. Private and public custodianship of urban buildings dwindled. Following the internal crises of the Gracchan period (132–121 B.C.), the State increasingly was preoccupied with calamities ranging from internecine conflicts to famine, from external wars to fires. As a result, the government paid little attention to the regular maintenance of the urban infrastructure and public buildings, or even to preserving public holdings. When famine threatened in 93 B.C., the government raised funds to purchase grain by selling valuable properties around the Capitoline (Oros. 5.18). With funds limited, both magistrates and private patrons selectively intervened in the built environment. Lowest priority was given to projects with limited prestige value such as road or sewer repairs. Private maintenance of existing public buildings also declined. In some cases, donor families had died out, leaving no one responsible; in others, they lacked the funds or desire to restore crumbling public structures. Wealthy patrons and magistrates continued to fund new projects, primarily for personal glory, not the betterment of the *res publica*.

The situation was exacerbated by the hegemony of powerful generals who wielded overscaled power and nurtured a global vision from campaigns abroad. In 88 B.C., the general Sulla boldly marched on Rome. Following a bloody civil war, he became dictator in 81 B.C. With a private treasury filled from wars and proscriptions, he planned architectural works appropriate to his elevated status. Sulla's projects in Rome reveal a grandeur of conception

and overt urban monumentality lacking in earlier Republican works. After a
fire in 83 B.C. destroyed the Temple of Jupiter Optimus Maximus on the
Capitoline, Sulla began an extensive rebuilding. He planned to replace the
Etruscan-style structure with a towering marble temple like the Hellenistic
Greek examples he had seen in the east. For this purpose, he imported
gigantic columns from the Olympieion temple at Athens.[53] Because sacro-
sanct parts of the structure could not be altered, the renovation appeared
awkward (fig. 22). After Sulla's death, work on the temple fell to the proconsul Catulus (Cic.*Verr*.2.4.69). He dedicated the temple in 69 B.C., keeping the height envisioned by Sulla, but placing his own name on the building
for all to see (Val.Max.4.4.11).

Catulus also completed the nearby record office, the Tabularium (fig. 27).
No ancient sources connect the Tabularium specifically with Sulla, yet its
scale, prominence, proximity to other Sullan projects, and the involvement
of Catulus all point toward his involvement.[54] The construction of the Tabularium replaced the irregular profile of the saddle on the southeast edge of
the Capitoline hill with a monumental, balanced silhouette. From a rough
tufa base rose several floors with evenly spaced arched openings flanked by
engaged columns.[55] The Tabularium's towering elevation served as a formal
curtain wall defining the northwestern edge of the Forum Romanum. Thus,
the project reflects a concern with the staging of new and existing structures
into a cohesive scheme. Such urban choreography was well known in Hellenistic cities where, as in this instance, it was made possible through individual effort.[56]

In conjunction with the projects on the Capitoline, Sulla began to rework
the Forum Romanum. He rejected the orientation to the cardinal points followed by earlier buildings and positioned his projects northeast/southwest
loosely aligned to the temples of Saturn, Castor and Pollux, and the Basilica
Aemilia. This arrangement placed greater emphasis on the imposing wall of
the Tabularium rising above the Forum.[57] A new paving of Monte Verde
tufa elevated the central open area of the Forum nearly a meter, with the
edges defined by polygonal blocks of selce. In effect, the materials coded different areas, with selce for road surfaces and tufa for area pavements. The
change in level necessitated the reworking of virtually every structure in the
Forum, as well as the roads leading up to the Palatine and Capitoline hills.[58]
The most dramatic alteration was the rebuilding of the Curia Hostilia. Having doubled the number of senators, Sulla of necessity had to enlarge the
Senate house (Pliny *HN*.34.26). Although the reworking of the Curia
overtly expressed oligarchic power, Sulla's cumulative actions confirmed the
possibility of near-absolute individual control. Looking at the rebuilt senate
house, Piso remarked, "[it] seemed smaller since its enlargement," because

the new building could not draw upon the rich power of place developed by the former structure (Cic.*Fin*.5.2). From atop the realigned speaker's platform or Rostra, a sculpted representation of Sulla on horseback oversaw all actions in the Forum.[59]

In addition to transforming the Capitoline and Forum, Sulla funded two temples to Hercules and made improvements in the roads throughout the city.[60] He also enlarged the *pomerium*. A sacred urban border determined by augurs, the *pomerium* imposed religious restrictions against building along its line. By extending the *pomerium,* Sulla released land from this prohibition, thereby transforming undeveloped property near the urban core into marketable real estate.[61]

Collectively, the range and extent of Sullan alterations were made possible by a change in the scale and conceptualization of individual patronage. As Dictator, Sulla was able to make his own expansive interventions at Rome and direct those of others. Holding dictatorial powers in perpetuity, he began to look beyond individual projects to urban environments as conveyors of his elevated personal stature. Such a reconceptualization of urban patronage was directly in line with the examples of Hellenistic dynasts. Despite such changes, Sulla remains in many ways a transitional figure. He gradually restored constitutional government and, following the model of Cincinnatus who set aside the dictatorship in 458 B.C., retired to the countryside in 79 B.C. Ailing health may have prompted his withdrawal; equally possible, the general was not yet willing to threaten the Republic. Sulla's expanded interventions in the cityscape reflect his expanded personal powers and quest for fame, yet simultaneously are in the tradition of earlier magistrates who funded urban projects to enhance the public realm.

Pompey, a precocious general under Sulla, further strained Roman conventions regarding fame and architectural patronage. Whereas Sulla honored the traditional Roman framework for acquiring glory, Pompey simultaneously exploited an eastern Hellenistic model.[62] He took Alexander the Great as his ideal, even adding *magnus* (the Great) to his name when still in his twenties (Plut.*Vit.Pomp*.13). Throughout his career, Pompey flaunted extraordinary commands and powers.[63] Similarly, he spent his booty on architectural projects in Rome notable for their size and form.[64] Conceptually, the general's buildings teetered at the edge of Roman propriety.

Where Sulla focused his attention on the long-venerated *loci* of central Rome, Pompey in contrast located his greatest project in the Campus Martius. This relatively open flood plain north of the city center accommodated large-scale public gatherings outside the *pomerium*. Activities took place on the grassy plain itself or in rickety temporary structures of wood. During his travels in the east, Pompey saw many Greek stone theaters; he was

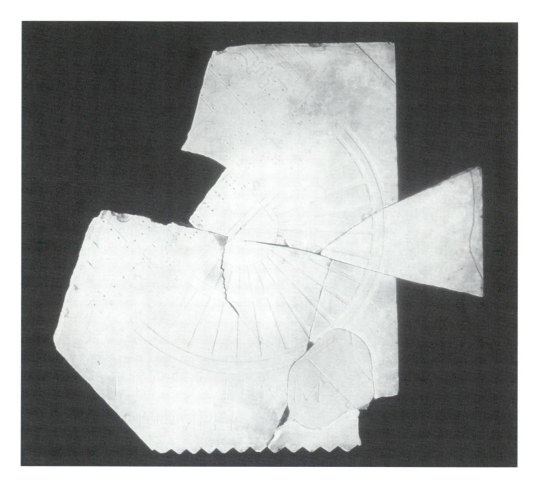

Figure 33. Fragments of the Severan map, the *Forma Urbis Romae,* showing the Theater of Pompey. Photo: Negativo Archivio Fotografico dei Musei Capitolini #X G/31.

impressed. While at Mytilene on Lesbos in 62 B.C., Plutarch tells us the general "was very pleased with the theater . . . and had sketches and plans of it made for him, with the intention of building one like it in Rome, only larger and more magnificent" (*Vit.Pomp.*42). On his return to Rome, Pompey began a stone theater in the central Campus Martius (fig. 33).[65]

Before Pompey, Roman conservatism had prevented the construction of permanent, Greek-style theaters. In 154 B.C., the Senate had objected to construction of a stone auditorium in Rome arguing that such a structure would encourage the people to squander their time at performances and foster sedition.[66] To circumvent conservative reaction, Pompey attached a temple to Venus Victrix atop the theater's cavea, calling the curving seats mere "steps" up to the shrine.[67] Before the battle of Pharsalus, he dreamed of entering his theater to great applause and offering the spoils of war to Venus

Victrix (Plut. *Vit.Pomp*.68; *Vit.Caes*.42). Although much has been made of Pompey's subservient respect for traditional scruples, more should be made of his simple and familiar solution to a problem of individual and urban decorum. Other Italian cities had had permanent theaters for generations.[68] In the Mediterranean basin, civic competition for fame required a city to have facilities for great performances. By playing the champion of conservative communal beliefs Rome had restrained her own *gloria*, and thus that of her great men. Pompey broke these bonds. Although some criticized his transparent justification for construction of a permanent theater, others celebrated Pompey's solution. The large and magnificent structure affirmed the extended scope of Rome's fame and that of the theater's patron.

Like Pompey, the impressive stone theater was called "the great" (Pliny *HN*.7.158). The title was deserved. Seating over 11,000 and elaborately decorated, the theater remained the most important in Rome for centuries.[69] Adjoining the structure stood a spacious, fully enclosed quadriportico with ornamental plantings, displays of art and booty, and a curia for Senate meetings (Prop.2.32.11–16; Pliny *HN*.35.59). The complex provided the general with appropriate environments for both literary and political performances, and highlighted his achievements. For the dedication in 55 B.C., Pompey arranged unprecedented spectacles.[70] The complex brought Pompey renown; simultaneously, the theater basked in the glory of its patron. Among the rich artwork stood statues of the fourteen nations subdued by the military prowess of Pompey.[71]

The reciprocal aggrandizement of building and individual was furthered by Pompey's personal relocation to the Campus Martius. Plutarch tells us that during the construction of "the beautiful and famous theater which is called after him, [Pompey] constructed close by it, like a small boat attached to a big ship, a house for himself which was grander than the one he had before" (*Vit.Pomp*.40–1). Also in the area, the general developed expansive gardens, or *horti*.[72] Though not Rome's first private pleasure park modeled after lush, Hellenistic examples, the large Horti of Pompey were strategically sited. Near to the voting place of the tribal assemblies, these gardens provided the manipulative general with an excellent location for bribery (Plut.*Vit.Pomp*.44). Furthermore, the loose grouping of the *horti*, grand theater, portico, and residence of Pompey evoked memories of Hellenistic palace complexes with their pleasure gardens, opulent residences, sculpture-laden porticos, and nearby theaters all honoring one individual or, rather, one family.[73]

The allusion to a royal enclave reflected the enlarged world view of Romans in the late Republic. Pompey stressed that he alone in Roman history had triumphed over three continents: Europe, Asia, and Africa

(Plut. *Vit.Pomp*.45–6). Yet neither he nor other Romans were quite sure how such achievement fit in the existing Roman context for personal fame. As Leo Braudy has pointed out, "Pompey had the imperialist sensibility before there was an actual Roman Empire," and, indeed, before he knew all the ramifications of such a sensibility.[74] He stood in the awkward position of a man receiving acknowledgment from an audience far broader than that which had established the Roman criteria for success. The uncertainty of this position is reflected in Pompey's approach to architectural patronage. He used his ample booty to build projects in Rome. Following the example of other triumphators, he focused on the Campus Martius, yet built an enclave of unparalleled splendor securely linked to his private residence.

By interrelating public and private projects, Pompey intuitively broadened the relationship between the city and individual patron. In first-century Rome, projects got larger and larger to accommodate the greater and greater status of individuals. As the political framework realigned to handle autocratic power, individual patronage responded in harmony. Generals vying for control made increasingly expansive gestures in the cityscape, internalizing projects to distill the potency of their architectural messages. The groundwork was laid for one individual to take the entire cityscape as a memorial to his fame and mold it into a directed image.

JULIUS CAESAR AND ROME

In comparison to Sulla, Gaius Julius Caesar had a far clearer idea of himself and the propagandistic possibilities of architectural patronage. At first he did not seek, as had Pompey, "extraordinary" advancement through the *cursus honorum*.[75] Working loosely within the system, Caesar honed his political skills. After victories in Spain, the Senate awarded Caesar a triumph in 60 B.C. Anxious to run for the consulship, he declined the honor, for a triumph would have required him to make preparations outside the *pomerium* during the crucial election period.[76] His strategy paid off; Caesar held his first consulship in 59 B.C. When his opponents threw up constitutional obstructions to his proposed land act, he used force to secure passage. With good reason, the Senate feared Caesar's military strength and moved to block his proconsular appointment in the following year. Caesar was prepared. He had forged alliances with the powerful men of his day: Pompey, Crassus, and Cicero. With the first two, he formed a political *amicitia*, the so-called "First Triumvirate." Through this unofficial agreement, Pompey got approval for his settlement of the Near East and support for his veterans; Crassus received financial advantages; and Caesar gained the proconsulship in Cisalpine Gaul and Illyricum for 5 years.

Caesar's military successes in the north and west enhanced his prestige and brought him into conflict with his colleagues. In 54 B.C. came the death of his daughter Julia, wife of Pompey, followed by the death of Crassus. The triumviral alliance shattered. The last years of the decade found Rome submerged in civil chaos promoted by political rivalries and food shortages. Pompey restored order posing as the Senate's champion, and unsuccessfully urged Caesar's recall. In 49 B.C., Caesar was proclaimed triumphator for his victories in Gaul. Again he did not celebrate the honor, this time due to the outbreak of civil war. Early in 49 B.C., Caesar crossed the Rubicon stream separating his province from Italy, and began to march on Rome. Civil war ignited. Within 4 years, Caesar defeated Pompey and settled affairs in the east. Returning to Rome in 45 B.C., the successful general assumed the dictatorship held previously *in absentia*. In 44 B.C., he was named Dictator for life. Unable to accept absolute tyranny, a determined core of Republican aristocrats assassinated Caesar in the Curia at the Theater of Pompey complex on the Ides of March.

From his earliest moments on the public stage, Caesar demonstrated great adeptness at self-promotion. He mesmerized audiences with his oratory and kept himself ever in the mind of Rome's residents even when outside the city. Describing the period of the late 60s, Sallust noted that Caesar "was heavily in debt on account of his eminent generosity in private life and lavish entertainments when in office" (Sall.*Cat*.49.3). While away in Gaul from 58–49 B.C., he crafted his own history, sending back matter-of-fact accounts of his military successes to be read to a rapt urban audience at home. During the period before the fatal crossing of the Rubicon, he also skillfully exploited architectural projects in Rome as a means to gain favor and renown. Even before being awarded a triumph Caesar made urban gestures recalling those of a triumphator. For example, when elected one of the aediles in 65 B.C., he honored his father with elaborate performances including plays and combats with wild beasts and gladiators. In addition, Caesar extended the display of materials for his shows beyond the Forum Romanum, the traditional locus for aediles' displays, up to the Capitoline where triumphal goods were usually exhibited. He not only used the games to commemorate his dead father, he also restored monuments in the Forum Romanum honoring the victories of his great uncle Marius. Such familial associations closely tied all undertakings by the aediles of 65 B.C. to Caesar alone, leading his colleague in office to lament he suffered the same fate as Pollux, whose name was usually dropped when people mentioned the Temple of Castor and Pollux (Suet.*Caes*.10–11).

Though absent from Rome in 54 B.C., Caesar initiated several schemes to aggrandize spaces for public business. Traditionally, the assemblies (*comitia centuriata* and *tiburta*) gathered in a fenced area associated with the Villa Publica in the Campus Martius. Caesar planned to replace the old wooden enclosure, commonly referred to as a sheep pen (*ovile*), with a magnificent marble structure.[77] Around the same time, he empowered his agents to expend large sums purchasing land in the very city center. The proposed undertaking was a much needed extension to the Forum Romanum to accommodate public activities.[78] The project soon changed focus. In 52 B.C., the funeral pyre of P. Clodius set the northwestern Forum ablaze, destroying the Curia Hostilia, Basilica Porcia, and other structures. The son of Sulla hastily erected a new Curia. For his contribution, Caesar replaced the Basilica Sempronia with the grand Basilica Julia, paid for with the spoils of his Gallic campaign. Further changes occurred with a shift in power. Facing Pompey in battle at Pharsalus in 48 B.C., Caesar vowed a temple to Pompey's own patron, Venus Victrix, in return for her support (Serv.*on Aen.*1.720, 7.637). She complied. Victory over Pompey placed Caesar in a superior position in the Roman world. In boastful acknowledgment, he redefined the expansion of the Forum. Caesar now incorporated the promised temple to Venus, acknowledging her as Genetrix, ancestor of the Romans and in particular the Julians, rather than Victrix as she was honored in Pompey's own complex in the Campus Martius. As a result, the project was transformed from a simple extension to the Forum Romanum into a distinct enclosure associated with both public business and the aggrandizement of its patron. As the name implies, the new Forum Julium became, in effect, a heroon to Caesar.[79] The associated rhetoric, however, was more subdued. In 47 B.C., Caesar proclaimed that he had spent his private fortune and borrowed heavily to fund projects, all for the public good (DioCass.42.50).

The following year, Caesar with great fanfare celebrated five triumphs, four in a single month (Suet.*Caes.*37; Chart 6.1). As an official triumphator, he now had the booty and the traditional obligation to erect public buildings. The general acted with characteristic *Caesariana celeritas* (Caesarean swiftness). For the extravagant events associated with the celebrations of 46 B.C., he funded a stadium, a temporary hunting theater, an artificial lake (*naumachia*) for sham naval conflicts, and improvements to the Circus Maximus and Forum Romanum.[80] To add to the celebration, he dedicated the two grand projects underway in Rome's center, the Basilica Julia and the Forum Julium even though neither was complete.

The entertainment projects erected for the triumphs of 46 B.C., had great popular appeal. In the fashion of modern politicians, Caesar wisely targeted his undertakings to favor a specific social group. With Pompey supported by the optimates, Caesar courted the equites and the commons. For example, he gained the favor of the renter class by remitting rents for 1 year during the conflicts of 47 B.C., much to the chagrin of property owners such as Cicero.[81] In addition, Caesar enamored himself to the people through his love of public spectacles; on the eve of crossing the Rubicon, he attended a public presentation and busied himself examining plans for a new gladiatorial school.[82] Large enclosures such as the Saepta Julia and Forum Julium reflect the Dictator's concerted interest in establishing places where his supporters could congregate.

Competition with political rivals fueled Caesar's architectural patronage. The Dictator selected specific projects to outshine those of other prominent citizens. For example, he planned to build a theater, "as Pompey had done" (DioCass.43.49). Caesar placed his structure south of Pompey's, specifically selecting a site closer to the urban center. Furthermore, he redirected worship of Venus away from Pompey's theater to the splendid new temple to Venus Genetrix in the Forum Julium. In 55 B.C., another political contender, Lepidus Aemilius Paullus, began to restore his familial basilica; looking at the Basilica Aemilia a year later, Cicero noted, "Paullus has almost reached the roof of his colonnade in the Forum. . . . It goes without saying that a monument like that will win for him more popularity and glory than anything" (Cic.*Ad Att*.4.17). Shortly after, Caesar began his own Basilica Julia opposite, and in direct competition with, the Basilica Aemilia.[83] Whereas Paullus built his basilica with shops across the façade, Caesar adopted a more refined form, pushing the shops to the rear of the interior. When Paullus ran into financial trouble restoring his namesake basilica in 50 B.C., Caesar bailed him out with 1,500 talents from the Gallic wars.[84] This gesture bought the neutrality of Paullus, if not his direct support, and associated Caesar with the opulent renovated structure. So successful was Caesar in using architecture to gain support, Pompey angrily pointed out that he was spending money far beyond his means. In the end, Caesar bought power cheaply (Plut.*Vit*.*Caes*.5).

To enhance his own fame further, Caesar worked to decrease that of others. After the battle of Thapsus in 46 B.C., he decided to erect a temple honoring Felicitas for her help in the victory. With calculation, he selected the site of the Curia erected by Sulla's son.[85] Dio Cassius succinctly explains why: "the real intention was that the name of Sulla should not be preserved [on the Curia] and that another Senate house, newly constructed, might be named Julian" (44.5). The same year, Caesar manipulated another degradation of an earlier patron. Rome's most important religious building, the Temple of Jupiter Optimus Maximus, bore the name of Sulla's supporter, Catulus. Caesar convinced the Senate to replace Catulus' name with his own, arguing that he had finished the temple and called Catulus to account for embezzling building funds.[86]

Due to Caesar's political success, others erected projects in the city on his behalf. Repeatedly, a fawning Senate awarded the Dictator architectural honors. For example, in 46 B.C., this collective body voted him a house so he would live on State property.[87] As an added distinction, the Senate bestowed the further privilege of erecting a *fastigium* (pediment) on his residence, an architectural form traditionally associated with kings and gods. Cicero respectfully commented, "What greater honor had he obtained than to have a . . . pediment to his house."[88] In addition, Appian notes that "many temples were decreed to him as to a god" (*BCiv*.2.106.443). In 46 B.C., the Senate voted a temple to Libertas to commemorate Caesar's liberation of Rome from the evils of Pompey. The following year it marked his clemency after the Civil War with a temple to Clementia Caesaris, and two years later celebrated the end of conflict with a shrine to Concordia Nova (DioCass.43.44; 44.4, 6).

In his words and actions, Caesar performed for a large audience. Of course, other Romans had made significant conquests outside Italy, but none had so successfully and consciously crafted a directed self-image for external as well as internal consumption. Cleverly written in the third person, his books on the Gallic wars affirm Caesar's ability to stand outside and evaluate his efforts and their impact.[89] Conscious of his image in history as well as the present, Caesar took steps to set his era apart. When named Pontifex Maximus, he completely reformed the calendar establishing a temporal system still in use today.[90] Similarly, he convinced the Senate to place his features on coins minted in Rome and distributed throughout the empire, the first man so honored while alive.[91] Through such maneuvers,

Figure 34. Coin of C. Vibius Pansa, ca. 48 B.C., showing Roma seated on a pile of shields, holding a scepter, with her left foot on the globe. She is being crowned by Victoria, barely visible in the background. Photo: British Museum, # 3983.

Figure 35. Relief found on the Via Cassia near Rome showing Caesar (?) crowned by Victoria with a trophy and prisoners to the right and a globe and Oikoumene or Roma kneeling to the right. A wall under construction is shown at either end. Drawing: Dorothy J. Renshaw.

many Romans began to consider Caesar as not only their representative, but as equivalent to the State. Addressing the general in 46 B.C., Cicero regretfully acknowledged the realities of his day, "I mourn that while the Republic must be immortal, its existence should turn upon the spirit of one man" (*Marcell.*7.22).

During this same period, the Romans began to redefine the city of Rome in more universal terms. As they expanded their sphere of activity to encompass the entire Mediterranean, the Romans gradually outgrew the image of Rome as the first among a federation of city-states. Instead, they perceived of the city on the Tiber in activist terms as representative of a forceful hegemony. In literature of the first century B.C., Rome is not just a city, but conqueror of the world.[92] Exploiting the pun of *urbis* and *orbis*, the Romans united the personified image of Roma and the world globe as depicted on a coin from the 40s B.C. showing Roma crowned by Victoria with her left foot on the globe (fig. 34).[93] The city controlled and represented the Roman world. As a result, her physical form came to be seen as a direct reflection of the State's success.

Drawing on these attitudinal changes, Caesar bonded with Rome in new ways. Like the city he, too, claimed mastery of the world and adopted the same imagery (Cic.*Off.*3.83; Luc.9.20; 8.553). In 46 B.C., the Senate decreed that a bronze statue of Caesar identified as a demigod be mounted upon a likeness of the inhabited world and placed before the Temple of Jupiter on the Capitoline.[94] A relief from the period is believed to show Caesar crowned by Victoria with the world globe at his feet and an amazon figure on his right representing Roma or perhaps Oikoumene, personification of the whole world (fig. 35). Furthermore, Caesar identified with Romulus, who was the city's eponymous founder, first king, and his own distant relative.[95]

Like Romulus, Caesar claimed to be a founder of the city for having saved Rome from siege.[96] Caesar carefully preserved the Lapis Niger, believed by many to be the tomb of Romulus, and planned a new temple honoring Mars, father of Romulus (Festus, *Gloss.Lat.*177). Atop the Collis Quirinalis on the eastern plateau of the city, the Romans worshiped Romulus as Quirinus.[97] Caesar purchased a garden near the Temple of Quirinus, and may have also undertaken repairs to the structure after lightning struck in 47 B.C. Two years later, the Senate chose the Temple of Quirinus to hold a statue of Caesar inscribed by the Senate, "To the unconquered god." At the same time, the Senate placed another image of the Dictator on the Mons Capitolinus beside statues of Romulus and Rome's other venerated kings (Dio-Cass.43.45; Cic.*Att.*12.45; 13.28). The general carefully choreographed events in 45 B.C. to underscore further his association with Romulus. He arranged for the messenger bringing news of his victory at Munda to arrive in Rome on night before the Parilia festival commemorating the founding of the city. As a result, the celebration incorporated the glorification of both Rome's original foundation and its salvation by Caesar (DioCass.43.42; Cic.*Div.*2.98) (Table 6).

The association of Caesar with Romulus/Quirinus tied Caesar simultaneously to specific locations and to the entire city. In addition, the linkage with king Romulus helped Caesar evaluate the political climate. The reaction to monarchy was not positive. In response, the Dictator rejected the crown several times and instead accepted the title *parens patriae* (parent of his country) from the Senate in 44 B.C.[98] This appellation further reenforced the familial relationship between Caesar and the city, as well as the State. As master of the empire, descendant of Romulus, second founder, and parent of the country, the Dictator had an obligation to care for Rome. The city on the Tiber was not just a place to erect individual monuments to self glorification, Rome was in totality a representation of Caesarean power.

An ingratiating Cicero told Caesar only the greatest undertakings could be considered worthy of his stature (Cic.*Marcell.*26). In the mid-40s B.C., however, Rome's physical form did not reflect the grandeur Caesar felt was his due. Caesar was well familiar with Alexandria, Antioch, and other great Hellenistic cities. As military tribune from 81–78 B.C., he toured through the east; in the mid-seventies, he studied at Rhodes. After his campaigns in Gaul and Britain, he again moved through the eastern provinces during the Civil War. Caesar's dissatisfaction with the image of Rome is reflected in contemporary reports that he contemplated moving the seat of government eastward; among the choices brandied about were vanished Troy, mother city of Rome, or the great city of Alexandria in Egypt (Suet.*Caes.*79). The rumors were false. Instead, the Dictator developed elaborate schemes to aggrandize the city on the Tiber. He made no little plans. Suetonius notes that "for the adornment and convenience of the city . . . [Caesar] formed more projects and more extensive ones every day."[99] When stabbed in 44 B.C., Caesar had splendid urban interventions on the drawing boards, including magnificent individual buildings and a grand urban-scale alteration, as well as drafts of legal provisions to improve care of the city's overall fabric.

All patrons faced with a dense urban environment must consider ways to make new projects legible in the cityscape. In Rome of the late Republic, triumphators erected ever larger and more elaborate structures. Caesar followed in this tradition, undertaking projects unique in size, opulence, and, in some cases, in form. His urban complexes were described in superlative terms. The planned Temple of Mars was to be "greater than any in existence" (Suet.*Caes*.44). After the burning of the famous library at Alexandria in 47 B.C., Caesar planned the first public libraries in Rome to be "the greatest possible" (Suet.*Caes*.44; Plut.*Vit.Caes*.49). Large scale signified great status and *auctoritas*. Caesar conceived works of a size equivalent to his perceived stature and power. Plans for the Saepta Julia called for a voting hall with a porticoed perimeter of one mile (Cic.*Att*.4.16). The enormous artificial lake of the Naumachia Caesaris accommodated a naval engagement of 4,000 oarsmen and 1,000 soldiers (App.*BCiv*.2.102). Caesar's planned theater below the Capitoline was to be "of vast size"; Pliny the Elder described the great Circus Maximus as "built by Julius Caesar . . . with nearly three acres of buildings and seats for 250,000" (*HN*.36.102).

Projects by Caesar and his supporters also drew attention for their materials. In the Republican city, the majority of buildings were of mud-brick, rubble-filled timber frame, and tufa with surface decoration of matte terracotta and stucco. As a result, highly polished hard stones were notable. Earlier in the century, builders used strong travertine at points of stress; in the Caesarean period, this creamy white stone appeared increasingly as pavements, podia, and arches. At the same time, the Italian quarries at Luni northeast of Rome gradually began to be exploited. Increased contact with the east, along with growing private fortunes, promoted interest in building with colorful hard stones, especially marbles. With the end of the Civil War, Caesar made plans for the large-scale importation of opulent building materials from throughout the Mediterranean. He devised improvements to the port facilities at Ostia and along the Tiber River and even proposed the legislation of surface traffic within the city. When Caesar's chief engineer Mamurra returned to Rome in 48 B.C., he used his share of the Gallic spoils to build the first house in the city employing marble on a truly lavish scale.[100] Caesar honored his divine ancestress Venus by constructing her temple of solid white marble (Ov.*Ars Am*.1.81). Ancient sources document the use of a particularly remarkable material for the games celebrating Caesar's triumph in 46 B.C. To shelter the spectators, the Dictator erected an awning of pure silk. The temporary covering ran from his residence on the Sacra Via across the whole Forum Romanum and up the Capitoline to the Temple of Jupiter (DioCass.43.24). Pliny described this temporary construction as so remarkable it was "recorded to have been thought more wonderful even than the show of gladiators which [Caesar] gave" (*HN*.19.23).

In form, the projects of Caesar displayed the full stylistic diversity of the period. Vitruvius characterized the admixture of Greek, Hellenistic, and Italic architectural features in late Republican architecture as the *consuetudo italica* ("Italic custom").[101] Given the expansive repertoire of styles and forms from which to draw, the Dictator had no need to create unique building types. He, as other patrons of the first century B.C., selected architectural styles and forms according to the nature and symbolism of each particular project. For example, Pompey experimented with Greek forms in his new stone theater, yet chose an archaic Italic form for his temple to Hercules (Vitr.3.3.5). Caesar picked an Etruscan style tumulus for the tomb of his daughter Julia, wife of Pompey, who died in 54 B.C.[102] For the spectacles associated with his triumph in 46 B.C., he erected a stadium for Greek-style athletics. Despite well-known Italian paradigms, Appian writes that Caesar modeled the new Forum Julium after the squares of the Persians, an affirmation of the contemporary amalgamation, or confusion, of building styles and types.[103]

Rome of the late first century B.C. was filled with decaying structures. Most blatantly obvious to any visitor were the city's important, yet unmaintained, religious buildings. Significantly, Caesar did not establish a program for renovation. Though Pontifex Maximus, or high priest, he can be linked securely only with the restoration of the temple to Jupiter Optimus Maximus. Rome's many other temples remained neglected. His few identifiable reworkings of existing public works were so extensive as to be virtually new buildings.[104] Displaying the mentality of a triumphator, Caesar planned to improve the appearance of his city through the addition of significant new individual monuments commemorating his achievements, not through the improvement of the overall urban image.

To maximize his patronage, Caesar clustered his projects in the Forum Romanum (fig. 36). Individually and collectively, buildings in this important civic location had high visibility.[105] In addition, the Forum was Caesar's home. After becoming Pontifex Maximus in 63 B.C., he took up official residence in the Domus Publica on the southern edge of the Forum. By the triumphal celebrations of 46 B.C., Caesar had significantly transformed the Forum Romanum. The axis running northwest to southeast first emphasized by Sulla was strengthened and clarified. A sparkling new paving covered the central area, laced underground with galleries for use during spectacles.[106] Still under construction, the Basilicae Julia and Aemilia rose in opposition six degrees off parallel. These huge structures reenforced the new axis and blocked views outward to the rest of the city (fig. 37).[107] The central space broadened toward the west to the approximate width of the Tabularium (74 m) rising above the Forum. The most important structure on the primary axis was the new speakers' platform. Caesar relocated the Rostra westward, siting it on the new axis.[108] With a benevolent flourish, he restored statues of Sulla and Pompey atop the Rostra and gave the glory for this act to Mark Antony. Romans entering the Forum from the southwest along the Sacra Via faced this central platform embellished with the prows of captured ships (fig. 38). A fig tree in the hardscape of the Forum acted as a sightline, directing attention upward to the temple to Concordia and the arches of the Tabularium.[109] Pedestrians descending into the Forum from the northeast along the Clivus Argentarius saw the Rostra's flank against the stunning backdrop of the Basilica Julia. By entering from the southwest along the Vicus Jugarius, the angled podium wall of the Temple of Saturn channeled their glance to the Rostra with the Curia Julia beyond.[110]

The Forum Julium to the north presented an even more unified program and design. According to Appian, Caesar created the complex "not for buying or selling, but [as] a meeting place for the transaction of public business . . . where the people assemble to seek justice or to learn the laws" (*BCiv*.2.102). The location was ideal. The complex was adjacent to the Forum Romanum and tangent to the Senate house. In fact, if later versions of the Curia Julia maintained the original configuration, senators could move from inside the Curia directly into the Forum Julium through two rear doors. The rooms lining the western side of the new forum probably housed official archives and paraphernalia for public assemblies, or accommodated diverse senatorial business. The high podium of the Temple of Venus Genetrix served as a speakers' platform. A splashing fountain attracted people of all types.[111]

The enclosed Forum Julium encompassed approximately 12,000 square meters of prime downtown property formerly occupied by housing and shops. To achieve a level surface for the Forum, Caesar's workers removed part of the Collis Latiaris connecting the Capitoline and the Quirinal. At the same time, they demolished the remains of the Republican fortifications running along the top of the spur. Construction on the southwest served as a retaining wall for the Capitoline hill. The row of shops was punctured by two steep stairs leading down into the forum from the Clivus Argentarius. Visitors could also undoubtedly enter from the Campus Martius, though the

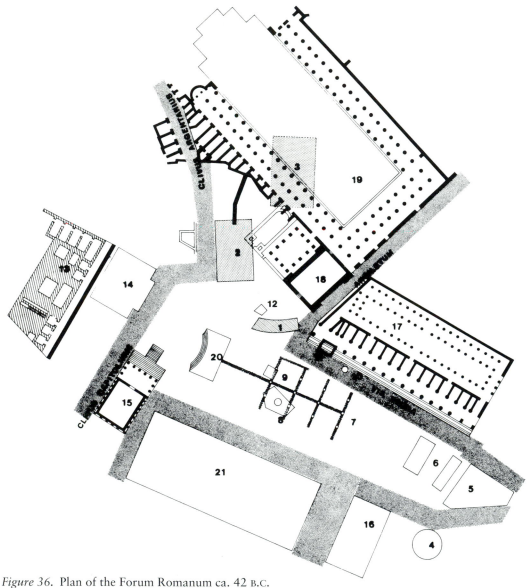

Figure 36. Plan of the Forum Romanum ca. 42 B.C.
Drawing: Rodica Reif. **Preexisting Structures:**
1: Rostra Vetera, removed; 2; Basilica Porcia (?)
removed; 3: Curia Hostilia (?), replaced by Temple
of Felicitas; 4: Temple of Vesta; 5: Regia; 6: Tribunal Aurelium; 7: Underground galleries; 8: Lacus
Curtius; 9: Statue of Marsyas; 10: Shrine of Venus
Cloacina; 11: Temple of Janus Geminus; 12: Lapis
Niger; 13: Tabularium; 14: Temple of Concordia;
15: Temple of Saturn; 16: Temple of Castor and Pollux. **Caesarean Projects:** 17: Basilica Aemilia,
restoration; 18: Curia Julia; 19: Forum Julium;
20: Rostra Julia; 21: Basilica Julia.

Figure 37. Reconstructed view of the central Forum Romanum looking northwest toward the Tabularium. From P. Zanker, *Il Foro Romano*, 20.

exact route remains uncertain. Primary access occurred from the southeast, from the Argiletum or through the Curia Julia itself. Fully self-contained, Caesar's new forum was largely invisible from the Forum Romanum. Even from the higher level of the Clivus Argentarius, pedestrians caught slight glimpses of the large marble temple to Venus and the rectangular forecourt surrounded by porticos with rooms against the slope on the west. Only from an elevated vantage point before the Temple of Juno Moneta on the eastern mound of the Capitoline hill could observers see the introverted complex in a single glance.[112]

Porticoed, rectilinear urban enclosures were familiar to Caesar from Hellenistic market buildings and complexes to ruler cults.[113] His Saepta directly emulated eastern market buildings with porticos surrounding an open rectangular space. His new forum related to Hellenistic temple enclosures, yet with a significant departure. In eastern models, a temple or altar stood in the center of a porticoed rectangular enclosure; with the Forum Julium, the temple stood at one of the short ends, leaving a well-defined open area (fig. 39). This configuration was in line with Italic interpretations. By the late Republic, the Hellenistic quadriportico form had been adapted for the layout of municipal fora (Vitr.5.1.1–2). For example, in the second century B.C., the forum at Pompeii received a unifying portico on three sides, defining a crisp rectangular open space before the temple to Jupiter.[114]

The Forum Julium combined the basic layout of the Italian municipal fora, with the unified program found in enclosures to ruler cults. The use of

Figure 38. Coin of 45 B.C. showing the Rostra decorated with ships' trophies (sometimes identified as a harbor installation). Photo: British Museum, # 4011.

Figure 39. Coin of Trajan showing the Temple of Venus Genetrix and the portico of the Forum Julium and "Appiades" Fountain. Photo: Fototeca Unione AAR 2980.

architecture to promote an individual was fully in accord with earlier commemorative projects in Rome. The isolationism of the new Caesarean project set it apart. The monuments of Republican triumphators stood cheek-by-jowl in the city, with the impression of one memorial competing and counterbalancing those of its neighbors. A project's appearance in the cityscape was paramount. Thus, even though the great theater complex of Pompey had a large internalized court, the external image was of greater importance. Collectively, individual monuments in the Republican city reflected the competitiveness of Roman society and the shared efforts required to make the State successful. In contrast, the Forum Julium enveloped observers in an isolated, all-pervasive message. From within the complex, Romans had little external contact with the rest of the city and the achievements of other citizens. Supported by his divine ancestress, Caesar reigned supreme.

The new Forum Julium was an explicit paean to its patron. The internalized, orthogonal layout of Caesar's project created an oasis of order within the untamed jumble of roads and spaces in the city. Inside the Caesarean environment, all was order, beauty, and opulence. Carefully contrived, the enclosure assumed the characteristics of a theatrical set, with every component interrelated. Throughout, artistic embellishments promoted Caesar and his achievements. Displays included a sculpture of Caesar in cuirass, pearls from the conquest of Britain, and an equestrian statue depicting the Dictator in the guise of Alexander the Great.[115] The formal hieratic layout of the complex focused all attention on the temple facade with its closely spaced columns and lateral stairs (Vitr.3.3.2). The elevated podium was more than a mere speakers' platform, it was a Caesarean stage. When awarded honorary decrees, the Dictator chose to receive the Senate while seated on the podium of the temple to his divine ancestress. Imperiously, he did not rise to greet the august body, but relied on the power of place to justify his seated position.[116] So compelling was the image of the Forum Julium, it even caused the revered Forum Romanum to be renamed. Emphasizing Caesar's role as patron of the Forum, Julium Dio Cassius wrote, "he had himself constructed the forum called after him, and it is distinctly more beautiful than the Roman Forum; yet it had increased the reputation of the other so that the latter was called the Great Forum" (43.22).

Building titles had great importance. By placing their names on structures, important patrons empowered the *genius loci*. Places with powerful associations, in turn, enhanced the status of new donors. Caesar planned for his name to appear in every major locale in the city. Atop the Capitoline, Romans saw a statue of the Dictator with the world at his feet; turning, they read his name emblazoned across the great Temple of Jupiter Optimus Maximus.[117] Ground clearing at the eastern base of the Capitoline provoked city residents to speculate about the shows that might occur in the planned Caesarean theater. Hundreds of citizens frequented the law courts in the Basilica Julia; Senators met in the Curia Julia and conducted other public business in the Forum Julium. In the Campus Martius, members of the assemblies gathered to vote in the Saepta Julia; thousands watched naval engagements in the Naumachia Caesaris and races in the Stadium Caesaris. Across the river, they admired the sprawling Horti Caesaris (Suet.*Caes*.83).

Caesar conceived one project so expansive, it would associate his name with the entire city. Rome was abuzz at the prospect. In early July, 45 B.C., Cicero wrote to Atticus, "I do not understand what the proposals are for improving the city; and I should much like to know" (Cic.*Att*.13.20.1). A week later, Cicero expressed interest in buying some property in the area of the proposed renewal; Capito warned him, "Don't you do it . . . for the law [to alter the city] will be passed: Caesar wants it."[118] In another missive a few days after, Cicero records a further outrage; the planning of the city was to be undertaken by someone who had first set eyes on Rome only two years earlier.[119] Capito described the proposed alteration to Cicero: "the course of the Tiber is to be diverted from the Mulvian bridge along the Vatican hills; the Campus Martius to be built over, and the Vatican plain to be a sort of Campus Martius" (Cic.*Att*.13.33a). Thus, the river was to be straightened, forming a north/south spine running roughly parallel to the ridge of the Janiculum and the Via Lata (fig. 40). The project had two potential benefits. First, the canalizing of the Tiber would limit flooding and improve river traffic. Second, less desirable, unhealthy land on the right bank would become valuable

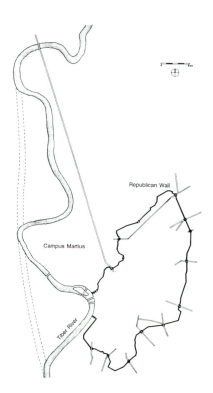

Figure 40. Hypothetical plan of Caesar's proposed straightening of the Tiber River. Drawing: Rodica Reif.

property attached to the city proper, approximately doubling the area for development.[120] The personal advantages for Caesar were obvious: His claim to the title of second founder of Rome would be strengthened and his own land on the former right bank would increase in value.[121]

The political cost of such a project would have been high. The Romans were extremely property-conscious. The proposed reworking would have voided honored property rights, violated sacred plots, and forever changed the personalities of time-honored *genii locorum*. Given these considerations, the credibility of the entire scheme may be questioned. Cicero is the primary source, and he is quoting Capito whom he admits is a "news monger" (*Att.*13.33.4). Conceivably, the project may have been either a rumor set forth to discredit the Dictator or a rhetorical exercise (*suasion*). Even Cicero does not seem overly concerned that the project would come to fruition, though he admits he would be sorry if it did, especially since it would quash one of his real estate deals. His ire focuses on the proposed urban planner: a man without familiarity of the beloved city. Despite these caveats, the urban alteration described by Cicero has a ring of truth about it. The flooding of the Tiber made the city unusable and projected a debased picture of Roman organizational skill. Further, the scheme was in line with other Caesarean plans to improve river transportation. The Dictator proposed to canalize the Tiber south of the city, continuing the work all the way to Terracina.[122]

Equally important, the Tiber transformation conformed to the overscaled undertakings associated with Caesar. According to Plutarch:

His many successes, so far from encouraging him to rest and to enjoy the fruits of all his labors, only served to kindle in him fresh confidence for the future, filling his mind with projects of still greater actions and with a passion for new glory, as though he had run through his stock of the old. (*Vit.Caes.*58.8–10)

For this man, an urban intervention of such scale and hubris was not inconceivable.

Caesar's broadened vision of Rome led him to consider not only great projects in his name, but also how the city functioned. After all, marvelous new structures decrease in meaning if located in an unkempt, inefficient urban environment. Neither Sulla nor Pompey had addressed urban care. Concerned with both external and internal reaction to Rome, Caesar took steps to improve urban life. Intervention was much needed. Despite a decrease in population due to civil conflict, the number of residents in Rome continued to strain the urban infrastructure and municipal services.[123] In 59 B.C., Caesar proposed to move some urban residents to the countryside. Dio Cassius explains, "the swollen population of the city, which was chiefly responsible for frequent rioting, would thus be turned toward labor and agriculture" (38.1). Still, crowding persisted. During the festivities of 46 B.C., hundreds came to the city and lodged "in tents pitched in the streets or along the roads, and the press was often such that many were crushed to death, including two senators" (Suet.*Caes.*39). Faced with volatile urban crowding, Caesar ordered a thorough census, with the count taken not in the usual manner or place, but street by street. Based on the findings, he reduced the number on the dole from 320,000 to 150,000 and raised the number of senators to 900.[124] After resettling 80,000 citizens overseas, he sought to repopulate Rome with more desirable residents by awarding citizenship to doctors and teachers who practiced in Rome, "to make them more desirous of living in the city and to induce others to resort to it" (Suet.*Caes.*42). To curb urban crime and violence, Caesar strengthened some criminal laws and abolished the riot-prone guilds.[125]

In addition, the Dictator drafted a series of laws based on existing provisions for municipal administration. Soon after his death, Mark Antony gathered the incomplete provisions and motioned for their collective passage with little, if any, revision. Known together as the *Lex Julia Municipalis*, these provisions dealt with the management of Rome and other Italian cities.[126] Two sections directly considered the urban fabric. The first carefully reenforced the responsibility of property owners to repair and maintain public streets and footpaths adjacent to their land, and empowered the aediles to intervene in cases of negligence (nos. 20–55).[127] The second section regulated the use of public areas by private individuals in an attempt to prevent unapproved obstructions (nos. 68–82). To ensure effectiveness, Caesar extended jurisdiction of the law beyond the *pomerium* and the Republican wall to the actual edge of urban construction.

The most famous provision of the *Lex Julia Municipalis* dealt with urban traffic. In the first century B.C., Rome's streets were jammed with hundreds of carts bringing in goods for urban consumers and carrying refuse out of the city. Clogged circulation promoted conflicts, impeded State processions, and slowed progress on building projects. Caesar took a dramatic step: he outlawed wheeled traffic within Rome during the daylight hours (nos. 56–67).[128] As specific exceptions, he cited religious and triumphal vehicles, those carrying refuse, and wagons moving building materials for public projects. Though not directly dealing with urban form, this regulation greatly improved Rome's operation and facilitated the construction of public buildings.

Every urban image depends not only on patrons and their projected goals, but on observers of the urban text and their interpretations. Romans of the 40s B.C. could not easily separate Caesar's actions in the city from his political program. Detractors viewed the Dictator's urban undertakings as consistent with what they considered his autocratic political moves. Describing the proposed alteration of the Tiber River, Cicero sarcastically remarked, "[Caesar] thinks it [Rome] too small though it's big enough to hold him!" (*Att*.13.35.1). Discussing the proposed Saepta Julia and its unusual size, Cicero dismissed questions of utility asking, "Now why should we worry ourselves about that?" (*Att*.4.16).

Certainly, the Dictator acted on the edges of acceptability. In the construction of urban projects, he apparently did not hesitate to demolish or move existing structures. For example, to clear land for his proposed theater below the Capitoline, Caesar destroyed not only existing dwellings, but shrines, burning cult statues and appropriating temple treasures.[129] Similarly, he cavalierly moved the sacred altar of the Lacus Curtius in the Forum to allow ample space for his gladiatorial show.[130] Further, Caesar sold public lands, including consecrated lots, an act that strengthened charges against him for taking bribes.[131] Such transgressions were not unique to Caesar. Pompey had defied tradition by building a permanent theater; Verres misappropriated funds for the Temple of Castor and Pollux. Rather, the scale of proposed Caesarean interventions and imperious treatment of private and public property further fanned existing flames of dissatisfaction with the Dictator's role.

Despite the extent and scale of his projects, Caesar did not develop an integrated plan for the entire city. His individual projects, from the reloca-

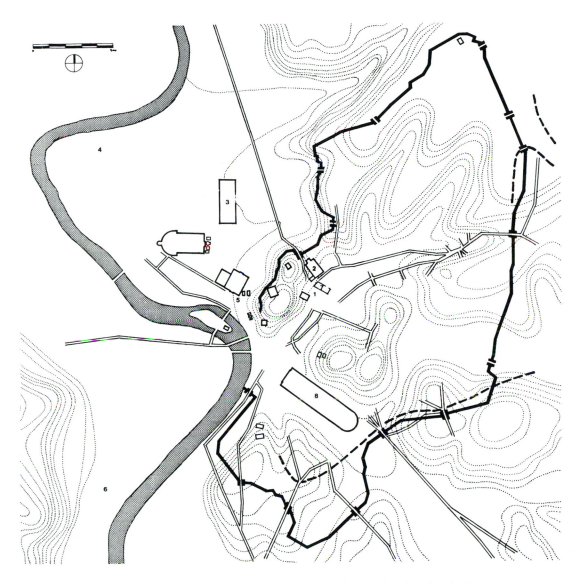

Figure 41. Map of Rome with projects of Caesar. Drawing: Rodica Reif and Richard H. Abramson. **Projects Initiated:** 1: Forum Romanum (see fig. 12); 2: Forum Julium; 3: Saepta Julia; 4: Naumachia Caesaris; 5: Theater near river; 6: Horti Caesaris. **Projects Initiated (location unknown):** Temple of Clementia Caesaris; Tumulus Juliae in Campus Martius; Temporary Stadium in Campus Martius; Hunting theater in Campus Martius. **Restoration Projects:** 7: Basilica Aemilia; 8: Circus Maximus. **Projects Planned:** Alteration to Tiber; Temple to Mars; Temple Libertas; Temple of Concordia Nova.

tion of the Rostra to the proposed alteration of the Tiber, all responded to specific functional and propaganda needs. They were united by patronage, iconography, and program, not by physical planning. Similarly, the Dictator considered problems of the city's infrastructure when compelled by necessity. For example, he dealt with transportation issues in direct response to the difficulties of crowd control during public events, moving building materials, and controlling the city. Caesar did nothing to improve Rome's inadequate water or fire-fighting systems because circumstances had not yet become acute. In short, his approach to urban planning was calculated, yet episodic and ad hoc.

By the mid-first century B.C., the Republic was moving from a class definition of the State to a nationalist one with a single man in control. In response, the Romans tentatively began to redefine Rome as the capital city of an empire, and of the premier citizen. The urban image was important to both. Caesar undertook building projects in Rome early in his career and had numerous large schemes on the drafting boards. The quantity, scale, and broad distribution of his urban undertakings are amazing in themselves; they are doubly so when considering that simultaneously the Dictator was embroiled in major military conquests, complex political intrigues, and ingrained social problems. Following the tradition of Sulla and Pompey, Caesar molded himself into an oversized figure. By 46 B.C., he stood victorious atop the detritus of the Civil War. Cicero wrote, "It is for you and you alone, Gaius Caesar, to reanimate all that you see lying shattered, as was inevitable, by the shock of the war itself" (*Marcell*.23). With purpose, the Dictator began to invigorate the physical form of Rome. He addressed the home audience by building in the tradition of a triumphator. At the same time, Caesar performed for a world audience, planning projects kingly in scale and magnificence. Caesar, as new founder of Rome, envisioned the entire city as a reflection of his *dignitas* (fig. 41).

Comparatively few of Caesar's plans for Rome had been realized when the knives struck on the Ides of March in 44 B.C. The city as a whole remained unappealing, unsafe, unsanitary, undirected, and in many ways unimaginable. Visitors entering on any of the major roads found no memorable monuments to introduce them to the urban text. Only the grand Saepta underway in the northern Campus Martius offered any promise of providing a legible and impressive architectural reading. Not until they entered deep into the heart of the capital did visitors experience the magnificence of the Forum Julium and reworked Forum Romanum. Caesar redefined his role as founder and caretaker of the entire city, yet did not live to focus the impression made by the city. The urban text remained disjointed, episodic, and incomplete. Rome still lacked a focused image.

CHAPTER FOUR

IDENTITY
EVOLVING AUGUSTAN
MOTIVES

> He who takes it upon himself to look after his fellow
> citizens and the city, the empire and Italy and the temples
> of the gods, compels all the world to take an interest.
>
> Horace, *Satire* 1.6.34–7

On March 20, 44 B.C., only a few short days after Caesar's death, Rome honored him with a grand funeral at public expense.[1] From the Dictator's former residence at the Domus Publica, the state-funded funeral cortege slowly moved northeast toward the raised speakers' platform at the opposite end of the Forum Romanum. With great solemnity, magistrates and ex-magistrates carried an ivory couch covered in gold and purple coverlets surmounted by a gilded architectural model. They placed the miniature building atop the Rostra for all to see; it was a replica of Caesar's own temple to Venus Genetrix. Visible inside lay the blood-stained garments worn by the Dictator at his death (Suet.*Caes*.84). Before this effigy, gladiators clanged swords as part of elaborate funeral games. The program next called for the transfer of Caesar's body to a pyre at the Tumulus Juliae in the Campus Martius. Anticipating a great crowd, the organizers urged mourners not to join the main procession, but to take different paths to the burial site.[2]

The elaborateness and conscious choreography of the funeral indicate the direct hand of Caesar. He may have planned the entire event and ordered the gilded shrine in advance. In any case, even this elaborate program proved insufficient. Angered by the assassination, Rome's residents sought ever greater honors for the Dictator. They made various proposals to tie Caesar eternally with potent urban locations. Some mourners wished to erect his pyre at the Temple of Jupiter on the Capitoline. The structure was the religious focal point of Rome and recently restored by Caesar himself. Furthermore, a pyre at this location would mark (or mock) the place where his murderers had recently taken refuge. Other mourners recommended the murder site, the Curia of Pompey, as the most appropriate location for the pyre. Faced with a plethora of suggestions, the people of Rome in a spontaneous gesture of "enthusiastic excess" cremated Julius Caesar in the Forum itself. After the fire died down the Dictator's freedmen collected his bones and placed them in the Tumulus Juliae in the Campus Martius (Tac. *Ann.*1.8; Suet.*Caes.*84.3; DioCass.44.51).

The events confirm Caesar's enduring impact on Rome, even in death. Furthermore, they affirm the continuing Republican perception of the city as independent and introverted. In the first half of the first century B.C., Roman citizens persisted in defining the Republic as a product of isolated, independent agreements between Rome and other cities and states. Similarly, they envisioned the city on the Tiber in a disjointed fashion as composed of distinct *loci* made important by events. When the Dictator's remains were interred, urban residents converged on the Tumulus Juliae from all directions; the specific goal was important, not the relation between urban locations or the overall urban image. Yet the Republic's political expansion had begun to minimize introversion and atomization. More and more Rome was becoming the *theatrum mundi.* Here all events of import occurred, including the killing of the Dictator. The gaze from outside, along with the internal concentration of power, sparked a reevaluation.

The murder of Caesar galvanized the Romans, and set in motion a sequence of events leading to the formation and acknowledgment of the Roman Empire. Attitudes toward the city reflect this process. Over the next five decades, power shifts, social upheavals, and day-to-day pressures all shaped contemporary perceptions of Rome. Any division of this long period is subjective, yet shifts in the city's development and meaning lead to the identification of three distinct phases.[3] In each, the motivations for building in Rome changed and, as a result, so did the types of projects, their distribution, and meaning.

PHASE I, 44–29 B.C.: A CITY OF FRAGMENTS

Shocked by the murder of Caesar, Rome's residents exhibited an outpouring of fealty to the Dictator. Suetonius records that soon after the brutal stabbing in the Curia of Pompey, "It was voted that the hall in which he was slain be walled up, that the Ides of March be called the Day of Parricide, and that a meeting of the Senate should never be called on that day."[4] At the site of the funeral pyre in the Forum Romanum, the people set up first an altar and later a column with an inscription addressing Caesar as *parens patriae,* "parent of his country." Within a few months of the "parricide," they worshiped Caesar as a god and clamored for the construction of a temple in his honor.[5]

In the communal psyche, the martyred Dictator represented peace and Roman sovereignty in the Mediterranean. Milling about the closed door of the Curia of Pompey or making offerings on the altar to the new god in the Forum, the citizenry drew strength from urban places associated with the great man. Aspirants to Caesar's political position likewise sought empowerment through association with the projects and sites in Rome important to the Dictator. Rivalry was keen. Within a few days of the murder, a self-proclaimed relative of Caesar, Amatius, began to erect an altar at the pyre in hopes of being the first to sacrifice there; Mark Antony, general and coconsul with the deceased Dictator, had Amatius summarily put to death without a trial.[6] The most legitimate and direct heir to Caesar was his great-nephew Gaius Octavius, adopted by the Dictator in his last testament. The young Octavius rushed back to Rome from Greece and assumed the name Gaius Julius Caesar Octavianus (Octavian) to acknowledge his inheritance.

Those seeking to fill Caesar's role naturally came into conflict; Rome overflowed with dissent. In late 43 B.C., the three most influential heirs to Caesarean power forged an uneasy alliance. Confirmed by law, the triumvirate of Octavian, Antony, and M. Aemilius Lepidus in effect had autocratic control over the city and State. The *triumvirs* set out to destroy the murderers of Caesar, and their own foes in the process. They ravished the citizenry with terrifying proscriptions, seized property throughout Rome, and taxed all the houses the value of their annual rent, claiming a need for funds to fight the parricides.[7] To assuage the demoralized citizenry, the *triumvirs* affirmed their fealty to Caesar by proposing high-profile architectural projects in Rome. On the first of January, 42 B.C., they instituted a state cult to *Divus Julius* and authorized a magnificent temple on the empowered site of Caesar's funeral pyre in the Forum.

The triumvirate endured for approximately ten years, yet it was a loose alliance at best. The three men never labored in unison to shape a government or an urban image. Problems intensified once Octavian and Antony defeated the murderers of Caesar at Philippi in 42 B.C. Rome again succumbed to internecine violence, with the aspiring caesars employing a carrot-and-stick approach, at one moment seeking the favor of Rome's residents with donatives, at another compelling support by force. In 41 B.C., with Antony abroad, Octavian faced a famine-stricken city divided into unruly factions. The populace attacked his soldiers and set houses afire during inconclusive street battles. Many were left homeless. To provide some stability, the rent of city dwellers was remitted for up to a maximum of 2,000 sesterces.[8]

Under the triumvirate, sweeping gestures related primarily to administration and taxation. The divisiveness of the *triumvirs* precluded a collective urban view or the realization of joint projects. Whereas Caesar had begun to mold a unified urban image in line with his absolutist vision of power, his supporters could not maintain this image when faced with rampant competition and diffused power. Architectural patronage reverted to a fragmented view with individual projects, not the overall cityscape, as the primary conveyor of propaganda.

Despite the individuality of projects erected in Rome in this phase, three unifying subthemes can be identified. The city was more than the administrative center of Roman expansion; Rome was the communal birthplace. The physical place grounded all Romans. During the disruptions of the 40s B.C., patrons anxiously emphasized the theme of continuity. For example, victorious triumphators continued to commemorate their military achievements by building monuments in time-honored locations. A newer theme also came into play. The ineffable power of Caesar reverberated in the cityscape; many sought to give it physical form. Ambitious individuals, including the *triumvirs,* vied to complete the numerous urban projects planned by Caesar. By the late 30s B.C., a third theme became obvious in the new projects of Rome. As Antony began to build a power base in the east, Octavian and his supporters exploited the symbolism of Rome as the focus of Latin heritage. The image of the city, therefore, continually shifted focus from a center of Republican tradition to a physical embodiment of a single individual and back again.

Rome as Traditional Stage for Manubial Building

As battles proliferated in the years after 44 B.C., so did the opportunities for triumphs and related building projects funded from *manubiae* (booty). Rome remained the traditional stage for projects celebrating military successes. Most triumphs recorded during this period can be linked with one or more specific architectural project in Rome (Table 1). Selection of building type and location depended on the personal program of the individual triumphator and his political affiliations. With alliances changing daily, the initial propagandistic programs often had to be redirected. Buildings from this period demonstrate the flexibility (and confusion) of messages conveyed by privately funded monuments. Pointedly, Rome's buildings were multivalent, allowing readers of the architectural text to find sympathetic messages even as the political and environmental context changed.

At the end of 43 B.C., L. Munatius Plancus and the *triumvir* M. Aemilius Lepidus celebrated triumphs shortly before becoming coconsuls. Both supported Antony, yet each desired his own independent fame. They held individual celebrations and erected separate donative buildings. With booty

Table 1. Buildings in Rome Associated with Triumphs, Ovatios, Victories, and Related Events, 44 B.C.–A.D. 14[9]

43 B.C.

    Dec. 29, triumph of L. Munatius Plancus for victory in Gaul

      Reconstructs Temple of Saturn in Forum Romanum

    Dec. 31, M. Aemilius Lepidus celebrates triumph over Spain

      Continues work on Saepta begun by Julius Caesar; dedicated 26 B.C.

42 B.C.

    Cn. Domitius Ahenobarbus saluted as *imperator* after naval victory over Cn. Domitius Calvinus at Brundisium; not awarded triumph

    Oct. 23, Octavian vows temple to Mars at Battle of Philippi against the Tyrannicides

      Mars temple on Capitoline represented on coin in 20 B.C. (uncertain if built); Temple of Mars Ultor in the Forum Augustum; dedicated 2 B.C.

    July 31, P. Vatinius celebrates deferred triumph for victory in Illyria

      No associated buildings in Rome

41 B.C.

    Jan. 1, L. Antonius celebrates triumph for victory in the Alps

      No associated buildings in Rome

40 B.C.

    Autumn, *ovatio* shared by Octavian and Mark Antony: Peace of Brundisium

      No associated buildings in Rome

39 B.C.

    Jan. 1, triumph of L. Marcius Censorinus for victory in Macedonia

      No associated buildings in Rome

    Oct. 25, triumph of C. Asinius Pollio for victory in Parthia

      Rebuilds Atrium Libertatis; completed before 28 B.C.

38 B.C.

    Nov. 27, triumph of P. Ventidius for victory in Parthia/Taurus Mountains

      No associated buildings in Rome

37 B.C.

    Agrippa awarded a triumph for victory in Gaul though does not celebrate

36 B.C.

    July 17, triumph of Cn. Domitius Calvinus for victory in Spain

      Rebuilds Regia in Forum Romanum

    Nov. 13, *Ovatio* of Octavian for victory over Sextus Pompey

      Arch [location unknown] and columna rostrata in Forum Romanum

Table 1. continued

34 B.C.

    June 30, triumph of T. Statilius Taurus for victory in Africa

      Builds stone amphitheater in Campus Martius; dedicated 30 B.C.

    Sept. 3, triumph of C. Sosius for victory in Judea

      Builds Temple of Apollo in southwestern Campus Martius; dedicated ca. 32 B.C.

    Oct. 12, triumph of C. Norbanus Flaccus for victory in Spain

      No associated buildings in Rome

    Unsanctioned triumph of M. Antony in Alexandria for victory in Armenia

33 B.C.

    April 26 (year uncertain), triumph of L. Marcius Philippus for victory in Spain

      Rebuilds Temple of Hercules Musarum in Campus Martius with surrounding Porticus Philippi; dedicated 29 B.C.

    June 1 (year uncertain), triumph of Ap. Claudius Pulcher for victory in Spain

      No associated buildings in Rome

    Dec. 3 (year uncertain), triumph of L. Cornificius for victory in Africa

      Rebuilds Temple of Diana on Aventine

29 B.C.

    Aug. 13–15, triple triumph of Octavian for victory in Dalmatia, Actium, Egypt

      Restores Porticus Octavia; also repairs the Via Flaminia, completed 27 B.C.

      Senate approves arch in Forum Romanum

      Aug. 18, dedicated Temple of Divus Julius

      Aug. 28, Altar of Victoria in Curia Julia

28 B.C.

    May 26, triumph of C. Calvisius Sabinus for victory in Spain

      Rebuilds portion of Via Latina

    July 14, triumph of C. Carrinas for victory in Gaul

      No associated buildings in Rome

    Aug. 15, triumph of L. Autronius Paetus for victory in Africa

      No associated buildings in Rome

    Celebrations for the Battle of Actium

27 B.C.

    Jan. Augustus voted laurels flanking and *Corona civica* above the door of his residence

    July 4, triumph of M. Licinius Crassus for victory in Thrace

      No associated buildings in Rome

Sept. 25, triumph of M. Valerius Messalla Corvinus for victory in Gaul

    Rebuilds segment of Via Latina

26 B.C.

    Jan. 26, triumph of Sex. Appuleius for victory in Spain

        No associated buildings in Rome

    During Cantabrian expedition Augustus vows temple on the Capitoline to Jupiter Tonans; dedicated 22 B.C.

25 B.C.

    Augustus voted triumph for victories in Spain and North Italy; not celebrated[10]

21 B.C.

    Oct. 12, triumph of L. Sempronius Atratinus for victory in Africa

        No associated buildings in Rome

19 B.C.

    Mar. 27, triumph of L. Cornelius Balbus for victory in Africa

        Theater in Campus Martius dedicated 13 B.C.

    Augustus declines triumph for diplomatic success with Parthians

    Oct. 12, Augustus' return to Rome with Parthian standards treated as a triumph

        Arcus Augusti in Forum Romanum

        Altar of Fortuna Redux at Porta Capena

    Agrippa declines triumph for victory in Cantabria

14 B.C.

    Agrippa voted triumph for victory in Pontus; not celebrated

12 B.C.

    Tiberius voted triumph for victory in Pannonia

        Augustus instead grants him "triumphal honors"

        No associated buildings in Rome

11 B.C.

    "Triumphal honors" awarded Drusus for victory in Germania[11]

9 B.C. (date uncertain)

    Ovatio of Tiberius for victories in Dalmatia and Pannonia[12]

8 B.C.

    Augustus declines triumph for victories of Tiberius in Germania

7 B.C.

    Jan. 1, triumph of Tiberius for victory in Germania

        Porticus Liviae with a shrine to Concordia (dedicated at triumph?)

        Rebuilds Temple of Concordia in the Forum Romanum, dedicated Jan. 16, A.D. 10

        Restores Temple of Castor and Pollux; dedicated Aug. 13, A.D. 6

A.D. 9/10

Jan. 16, Tiberius enters Rome triumphant after victory in Pannonia; postpones triumph until 12/13[13]

A.D. 12/13

Oct. 23, triumph of Tiberius for victories in Pannonia and Dalmatia

No associated buildings in Rome

from Gaul, Plancus embellished the venerable, tall Temple of Saturn in the Forum Romanum, restoring the podium in creamy white travertine. The project linked Plancus with the powerful early deity who watched over the Roman treasury. Located on the rise of the Clivus Capitolinus at the northwestern edge of the Forum, the building also related directly to three projects by Caesar: the Basilica, Rostra, and Curia (fig. 36). In the late afternoon, the shadow of the tall temple fell on the Rostra Caesaris embellished with the gilded statues of Plancus' rivals Octavian and Lepidus.[14] Two days after the triumph of Plancus, Lepidus rode through Rome in a triumphal parade of his own commemorating victories in Spain. As his gift to the city, he funded work on the Saepta Julia in the Campus Martius for the voting of the assemblies, a gigantic project begun by Caesar.

Neither triumphator immediately realized his manubial project. During the disruptions of the late 40s and 30s B.C., a shortage of workers, materials, and funds greatly slowed construction in Rome. Nevertheless, residents were well aware of the projects and debated their complex associational meaning. Both Lepidus and Plancus as triumphators exploited a wide range of linkages. The functions of their buildings related to traditional Republican activities, the scale represented the triumphators' lofty self images, and the ties with Caesar added an extra, affirming gloss of importance.

Donors of public buildings in Rome never stood alone. All Romans were aligned through a complex system of interrelated families, patron/client relationships, and personal fealties. Attuned to such connections, urban residents could readily identify changes in the message of a building as reflections of shifts in political alliances. Thus, the physical fabric of Rome, not billboards or television news spots, conveyed important political updates and well as individualized messages. The shifting alliances of the period demonstrate the independence of single donors. Many additions to the city resulted from specifically personal motivations. For example, when awarded a triumph 36 B.C. for successes in Spain, Cn. Domitius Calvinus used only a small part of the gold booty for a triumphal celebration. He spent the greater part on restoring the Regia, a small structure in the Forum Romanum housing sacred objects. Calvinus rebuilt it of solid white marble. He selected this project not only because the Regia had been damaged recently by fire, but because the structure stood near his own house on the Velia. Thus, when complete, the opulent Regia projected its glory onto the entire clan of the patron. Wishing to decorate the building for its dedication, Calvinus asked his friend Octavian to lend some sculptures. When Octavian later asked for their return, Calvinus told him to, "Send some men and take them." To denude a sacred building of art placed by another would be a sacrilege; Octavian was compelled to leave his sculptures as a votive offering.[15] This single story demonstrates the competitiveness of the time and the enduring strength of individual patricians during the period of the triumvirate.

Despite personal gestures in the cityscape, building patronage in Rome, like politics, became increasingly fractionalized into the two camps of Antony and Octavian. New urban projects became associated with one or the other, and frequently, over time, with both. Lepidus constructed the Saepta, but Agrippa added marble ornamentation and artworks, diminishing association of the building with the *triumvir*. Agrippa, general to Octavian, dedicated the building in 26 B.C. and, as Dio Cassius tells us, "named it the Saepta Julia in honor of Augustus" (53.23). The restored Temple of Saturn also may have become tied to Octavian before completion. Plancus left the camp of Antony to join Caesar's adopted son in the late 30s B.C. Octavian later implied the restoration of this great temple was undertaken at his urging (Suet. *Aug.* 29).

Architectural projects from the late 40s B.C. affirm the most important locations for triumphal building in Rome: the Forum Romanum as the political center of the city and the southwest Campus Martius as the traditional area for triumphal display. Of the ten buildings linked with triumphs from the period immediately following the death of Caesar, all but one belong to these zones.[16] In addition to the renovated Temple of Saturn, the Forum received restorations of the Regia and Atrium Libertatis, and a new library. The Campus Martius acquired two quadriporticos, restored temples devoted to Hercules Musarum and Apollo, a repaved highway, and an amphitheater.

The honor of celebrating a triumph was greatly coveted. Octavian was clearly one of the most important men in Rome, yet in the late 40s or early 30s B.C., he had few military successes of his own against foreign enemies. To prevent any diminution of his status, the partisans of Octavian declined earned triumphs and the accompanying responsibility for building in Rome. Among his supporters, Octavian counted those he had elevated to the position of *novus homo,* the first man in a family to reach the Senate, including T. Statilius Taurus and Marcus Agrippa. In 34 B.C., Statilius celebrated a triumph for campaigns in Africa and began a stone amphitheater in the Campus. He was acclaimed *imperator* two additional times, though apparently did not celebrate triumphs.[17] Similarly, Agrippa, another ardent follower of Octavian, was awarded three triumphs, yet declined them all in clear deference to Octavian. For example, in 37 B.C., he refused a triumph to honor his successes in Gaul, "considering it disgraceful for him to make a display when Caesar [Octavian] had fared so poorly [in his own campaigns]."[18]

Octavian himself had garnered victories, but against other Romans. Such conquests naturally could not be celebrated with ostentatious triumphs in Rome. Furthermore, campaigns against fellow Romans usually did not result in substantial booty. When Octavian and Antony defeated the murderers of Caesar at Philippi in 42 B.C., neither celebrated a triumph. Similarly in 36 B.C., after defeating another enemy of Roman stock, Sextus Pompey, the son of Pompey the Great, Octavian could not claim a triumph. Unwilling to forego completely any acknowledgment of these two successes, Caesar's heir exploited a lesser form of triumph called an *ovatio,* in which the victorious general entered Rome on foot or horseback, not in a chariot (Gell.5.6). Like a *triumphator,* Octavian lavished favors upon jubilant urban residents, abolishing all debts to the state, as well as certain taxes.[19] Simultaneously, he accepted several commemoratives, including an honorific column in the Forum Romanum covered with captured ships' beaks and surmounted with a golden statue (DioCass.49.15; App.*BCiv*.5.130). As a further self-promotion, Octavian restored a similar column on the Rostra honoring another naval victory at Mylae, that of Gaius Duilius in 260 B.C. (*CIL* 1².25).

Octavian also used personal vows to associate his military exploits with buildings in Rome. During the heat of battle against Crassus and Brutus at

Figure 42. Coin from Pergamon, 19–18 B.C., showing the Temple of Mars proposed for the Capitoline Hill. Photo: British Museum, # 704.

Figure 43. Model of the Temple of Mars Ultor in the Forum Augustum. Photo: Fototeca Unione AAR 10189.

Philippi, he pledged a temple to Mars. He may have first erected a small Mars shrine on the Capitoline (fig. 42), but ultimately satisfied his vow in full years later with the dedication of the grand temple to Mars Ultor (Mars the Avenger) in 2 B.C. (fig. 43).[20] While fighting Sextus Pompey off Sicily in 36 B.C., Octavian likewise vowed a temple in exchange for divine aid. He satisfied this pledge more quickly, dedicating an elaborate temple complex to Apollo on the Palatine in 28 B.C. (Suet.*Aug.*29; Vell.Pat.2.81.).

Other patrons followed this same route, using vows to justify building in situations where they did not receive a triumph. For example, Cn. Domitius Ahenobarbus won a number of naval victories, but on the side of Caesar's murderer Brutus. As a result, he was not honored with triumphs. To keep his achievements before the people in Rome, he planned a new temple to the sea god Neptune as demonstrated by a coin issued around 42 B.C. depicting the projected structure (fig. 44).[21] Because Ahenobarbus did not receive extensive booty from his campaigns against fellow Romans, he was forced to stall construction until he acquired another source of revenue. After holding the

Figure 44. Coin of 42/41 B.C. showing the Temple of Neptune. Drawing: Dorothy J. Renshaw.

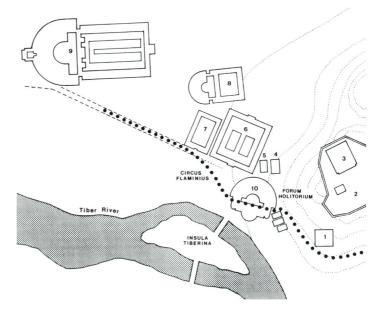

Figure 45. Plan of southwestern Campus Martius showing possible path of a Roman triumph. Drawing: Richard H. Abramson: 1: Area Sacra di Sant'Omobono; 2: Area Capitolina; 3: Temple of Jupiter Optimus Maximus; 4: Temple of Bellona (?); 5: Temple of Apollo; 6: Porticus Octaviae; 7: Porticus Philippi; 8: Theater and Crypta Balbi; 9: Theater of Pompey; 10: Theater of Marcellus.

lucrative governorship of Bithynia in the 30s B.C., he erected a temple to Neptune in the area of the Circus Flaminius.

During the decade following the death of Caesar, Mark Antony had several conquests, yet was not awarded a triumph and the accompanying honor of parading in triumph through Rome. By the mid-30s B.C., he became alienated from Octavian and developed his own power base in the east. After capturing the king of Armenia in 34 B.C., he put on an impressive celebration. Leading the Armenian ruler bound in golden chains, Antony proudly rode a chariot through a great city. The location was Alexandria, not Rome. Back in the city on the Tiber, Romans bridled at the affront.[22]

Personally, Antony showed little regard for the propagandistic importance of building in Rome. He did, however, like Octavian, draw positive

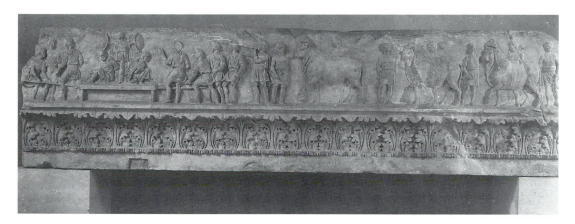

Figure 46. Relief frieze of a triumphal celebration, Temple of Apollo Sosianus. Photo: Negativo Archivio Fotografico dei Musei Capitolini # 2776/S.

publicity from buildings erected by partisans. The same year as the parade in Alexandria, C. Sosius, ardent supporter of Antony, was voted a triumph for defeating the Jews. After the celebrations, Sosius stayed in Rome as agent of Antony and applied his booty to rebuilding an early temple to Apollo. Located in the Forum Holitorium next to that of Bellona, goddess of war, this temple played an important role in all triumphal ceremonies (fig. 45).[23] The project had other obvious associations. Few in Rome could miss the explicit comparison between the structure by a partisan of Antony and the new complex to the same deity begun by Octavian atop the Palatine hill to the southeast. Ultimately, however, the reworked temple in the Forum Holitorium became associated not with Antony, but with his rival. As an ally of Antony, Sosius suffered defeat at Actium in 31 B.C. The magnanimous Octavian allowed him to go free. To honor his new benefactor, Sosius reprogrammed the in-progress Temple of Apollo to exalt Octavian. Thus, the reliefs on the completed building do not depict the Jews over whom Sosius triumphed, but a trophy with northern barbarians, probably commemorating the Illyrian triumph of Octavian in 29 B.C. (fig. 46).[24] The finished temple therefore became a triumphal monument to Octavian.

Throughout the late 30 B.C., Octavian came to dominate Rome. Notable victories against foreign foes gave him the justification and wealth to undertake impressive building projects in the city on the Tiber. After a successful campaign in Dalmatia (35–33 B.C.), he used the *manubiae* to erect or rebuild several buildings, including the Porticus Octavia.[25] By 30 B.C., he had conquered Egypt. This last victory brought Octavian the most praise and the most funds. The extensive wealth flowing into Rome from Egypt caused interest rates to fall and real estate values to rise precipitously (Suet.*Aug.*41). Although only the reworking of the Via Flaminia can be directly associated

Figure 47. Coin of 44/38 B.C. showing the Temple of Jupiter Feretrius. Photo: British Museum, # 4207.

with Egyptian *manubiae,* the treasury of conquered Egypt certainly made possible dozens of new undertakings. Booty from Egypt embellished buildings throughout the city, including the Curia. When Octavian later proclaimed he built the Temple of Mars Ultor and Forum Augustum on private ground purchased *ex manubiis,* he may have been referring to Egyptian funds, an assumption supported by the representation of the Egyptian god Amon in the upper register of the side porticos (fig. 80).[26]

With a single restoration, Octavian confirmed and focused his military successes and his ties to greater Roman imperatives. He completely rebuilt the neglected Temple of Jupiter Feretrius on the Capitoline Hill (fig. 47).[27] Many Romans believed this small structure to be the first temple in Rome, erected by Romulus to mark the site where he had dedicated the original *spolia opima,* the optimum spoils of war. In the following centuries, a military leader who killed a hostile general in single combat was likewise allowed to dedicate trophies in this shrine, though the honor remained rare.[28] Octavian could not claim this privilege himself, yet he could reconstruct the temple erected by Rome's founder. Furthermore, he apparently blocked others from association with this important building. In 28 B.C., M. Licinius Crassus triumphed in Thrace and killed an enemy chieftain with his own hands. He demanded the *spolia opima,* but Octavian rejected this request arguing that because he was only proconsul, not a general in supreme command, he could not be proclaimed *imperator.*[29] Crassus celebrated his triumph a year later, but did not receive the *spolia opima.*

In 29 B.C., Octavian commemorated his Dalmatian campaigns (35–33 B.C.), his victory at the battle of Actium (31 B.C.), and his conquest of Egypt (30 B.C.) with a lavish triple triumph (Suet.*Aug.*22; DioCass.51.21). Over three days in August, all Rome took part in the extravagant event. Drawing upon the *manubiae* of these campaigns, Octavian and his partisans gave existing structures quick facelifts and hurriedly completed projects currently underway. Three days after the triple triumph Octavian dedicated the tem-

Figure 48. Model reconstruction of the Tomb of M. Vergileus Eurysaces, 40–30 B.C. Photo: DAIR 72.2568.

Figure 49. Terra-cotta relief from the Temple of Apollo Palatinus, ca. 28 B.C., depicting Apollo and Hercules in a struggle for the Delphic tripod. Photo: Soprintendenza Archeologica di Roma.

ple in the Forum Romanum to his adoptive, deified father. Also in 29 B.C., he dedicated the Curia Julia with the Chalcidicum honoring the war goddess Minerva. With calculation, these projects emphasized his military successes. In the Curia, Octavian placed a statue and altar of Victoria; on the podium of the new Temple of Divus Julius, he proudly displayed the prows of ships captured at Actium. Tangent to the temple on the south, the Senate and people of Rome dedicated a triumphal arch commemorating the triple triumph.[30] Octavian also took steps to ensure his victories would not fade from memory. In 28 B.C., he celebrated the battle of Actium with gymnastic contests in a temporary wooden stadium in the Campus Martius. The Actian games thereafter were celebrated quinqennially.

Manubial building dominated Rome's cityscape between 44 and 29 B.C. Throughout these years of internecine and external warfare, victorious generals above all others had both the funds and the political motivation to build in the city. They chose high-visibility public structures. The majority of their projects were religious in nature, affirming the close connection between military skill and divine favor. Most frequently, triumphators restored existing shrines, hoping to draw on their potent history. On a practical level, restoration work usually cost far less than new building and could be implemented more quickly. Simple additions could greatly enhance existing structures. For example with the addition of a surrounding portico, an existing shrine became isolated within the cityscape. Enclosures such as the Porticus Octavia provided ideal environments for residents to gather and admire displays of captured goods and art (cf. fig. 76).

In the competitive climate of the late 40s and 30s B.C., personal rivalries and unrest led to exaggerated forms of self-promotion. As Zanker has pointed out, even people with little to gain politically expended large sums on ostentatious displays.[31] On the edge of the city, between the Viae Praenestina and Labicana, a master baker, the freedman M. Vergilius Eurysaces, erected a showy tomb in the 30s B.C. This unique, foursquare monument has carved, tall cylinders like granaries surmounted by ovenlike openings, and figural friezes depicting the bakers' profession. In effect, Eurysaces presented his tomb as a monument celebrating not a military battle, but his victory over slavery and poverty. During the famines and disruptions in Rome, a baker served the state as much as a general and could reveal equal hubris by constructing a permanent monument (fig. 48).[32]

Spurred by individual ambition, the projects from this phase lacked formal unity. Diversity was rampant in all areas, from building techniques and styles, to materials and scale. The temple to Apollo Sosianus had Greek marble and sculptures; that to the same god on the Palatine was embellished with archaizing terra-cotta plaques (fig. 49). In size, projects ran the gamut from the small marble Regia to the large, temporary wooden stadium for the celebrations of 28 B.C. Concentrated in the Campus Martius and Forum Romanum, and united by the theme of Roman victory, these architectural projects affirmed Rome as the traditional center of Roman display. Nevertheless, they remained independent urban expressions. Each was tied to an individual general and a specific battle; each was designed to be seen independent from, not in unison with, its urban neighbors. Overall the complex, intertwined military, political, and personal motivations that generated these structures resulted in multivalent readings. Furthermore, most projects remained incomplete for decades, visually affirming the fractionalization and moral bankruptcy of the Roman state. Pedestrians moving through Rome of 30 B.C. found only one theme repeated with regularity throughout the cityscape: praise of Julius Caesar.

Urban Associations with Julius Caesar

The brutal murder of Caesar created a backlash of popular and military support, culminating with the Dictator's deification. In response, ambitious men competed to complete the urban projects proposed by Caesar. Dio Cassius records that the triumvirs "eagerly did everything which tended to [Caesar's] honor, in expectation of some day being themselves thought worthy of like honors" (47.18). Together, in 42 B.C., they ordered continuation of construction on the Curia Julia and authorized a new temple to Divus Julius in the Forum Romanum. Weakly positioned in relation to Antony and Octavian, the triumvir Lepidus sought affirmation by continuing work on two Caesarean projects, the Saepta Julia and the temple to Felicitas (DioCass.43.1; 44.52; 47.18–19; 51.22; App.*BCiv*.2.148; Vell.Pat. 2.67.4). Other patrons likewise courted political support through architectural associationism. In 39 B.C., Gaius Asinius Pollio, advocate of Antony, realized another of Caesar's projects; he incorporated twin libraries into the rebuilding of the Atrium Libertatis adjacent to the Forum Julium.[33]

As the official blood heir, Octavian had the most immediate claim to Caesar's fame. According to the propaganda of the day, the gods agreed; when he entered Rome following Caesar's death, lightning struck the Tumulus Juliae (Suet.*Aug*.95). After the peace of Brundisium in 40 B.C., Octavian began to call himself *Divi filius* (son of a god).[34] In fulfillment of filial obligations, he assumed responsibility for the urban projects of his adoptive father. Octavian continued work on the Forum Julium, placing a statue of Caesar on display in the center. In the Forum Romanum, he finished the Basilica Julia. To underscore the family tie, Octavian publicly ordered his heirs to carry on if he should die before the Basilica was completed.[35] He

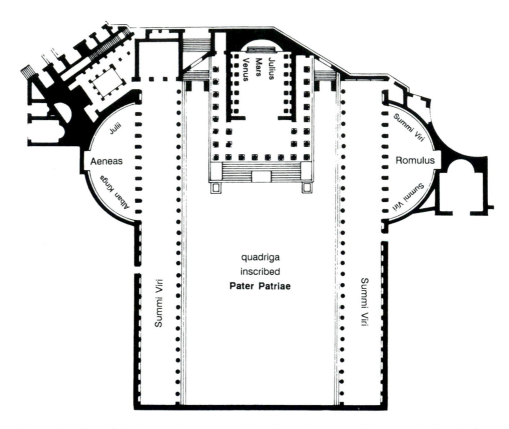

Figure 50. Plan of the Forum Augustum with sculpture locations. Drawing: Rodica Reif.

may also have reworked the nearby Rostra earlier rebuilt by Caesar. A few days after his great triple triumph in 29 B.C., Octavian dedicated the new Temple of Divus Julius. With Antony dead and Lepidus ousted from power, he was the only triumvir left with a claim on the project (DioCass.51.22; *ResG*.19).

Octavian also instituted work on Caesarean projects barely begun or still on the drafting table at the time of the murder. The Dictator had cleared land in the Forum Holitorium for a theater; Octavian initiated actual construction. Not to be outdone by Asinius Pollio, who had funded public libraries, Octavian realized Caesar's proposal for a public book collection. He added Greek and Latin libraries to the portico adjoining the new Temple of Apollo on the Palatine. With the grand Temple of Mars Ultor in the Forum Augustum, Octavian satisfied Caesar's vow to create a temple to Mars "greater than any in existence."[36]

In fact, Octavian may have initially conceived the entire Forum Augustum as an homage to Caesar (fig. 50). Formally, the complex emulated the Forum Julium. Placed tangent and at right angles to Caesar's enclosure, the

Figure 51. Reconstruction drawing, Temple of Mars Ultor in the Forum Augustum. From J. Ward-Perkins, *Roman Imperial Architecture* (Harmondsworth: Penguin Books 1981), fig. 8.

Forum Augustum kept the son forever in proximity to the father. Furthermore, a complicated iconographical program linked the two complexes. The Augustan temple honored Mars Ultor who helped Octavian avenge the murder of Caesar. Equally important, Mars was both the consort of Venus, who was worshiped in the Forum Julium, as well as the father of Romulus, distant ancestor of the Julii. The elaborate sculptural program of the new Augustan forum clarified and celebrated these interconnections. For example, the sculpture group in the temple represented Venus Genetrix, Mars Ultor, and Divus Julius (figs. 51 and 56).[37]

Antony drew upon his close associations with Julius Caesar, but in a decidedly nonarchitectural manner. Immediately after the murder of Caesar, he set himself up as political and personal heir of the Dictator, arguing that the young Octavian was too inexperienced to manage complex affairs (DioCass.44.53). As self-proclaimed executor of Caesar's business, he enacted the incomplete laws drafted by Caesar known collectively as the *Lex Julia Municipalis*. Including provisions regarding urban traffic and the maintenance of public works, these laws were advantageous for the city on a functional level, yet in many ways, they were inconvenient for the urban masses and thus did not enhance Antony's popularity. In contrast to Octavian and other Roman patrons, Antony made little effort to complete the urban projects of Caesar or to script his own statements in the cityscape.

Instead, he sought less tangible manifestations of power, expending his funds to purchase the favor of the legions and potential rivals.[38]

In an obvious effort to offset the growing power base of Octavian, Antony fashioned himself as the caretaker of Caesarion, Caesar's blood son from Cleopatra. At the unsanctioned triumph in Alexandria of 32 B.C., Antony sat on a golden throne next to the Egyptian queen who was dressed as the Egyptian goddess Isis. Around them stood their own three children and Caesarion. Poised as father to this brood, Antony declared *urbi et orbi* that Caesarion was the natural, legitimate son of Julius Caesar, thus implying the youth had a stronger claim as Caesar's heir than Octavian.[39] Cementing his role as paternal overseer, Antony magnanimously divided the eastern territories captured by Roman soldiers among Cleopatra and her offspring.[40]

Throughout the fifteen years following the Dictator's murder, the name of Caesar remained on everyone's lips. His great building schemes began to make their mark in the cityscape, presaging a Rome of great strength and purpose. Seen through the filter of subsequent events, the projects seemed less the self-centered schemes proposed to promote a single individual, and more the manifestation of a belief in Roman tradition, strength, and endurance. For all Rome's problems – unmaintained public buildings, poor sanitation, unsafe streets, unmonumental public centers – the city on the Tiber remained the center of the Roman world and psyche. By not tying in to this imagery, Antony made a significant mistake.

East versus West

Antony's disinterest in Rome sparked immediate and deep offense among city residents. Roman authors carefully recorded his irreverent attitude toward the power of place. Plutarch tells how Antony mistreated the *genius locus* of the important house he purchased in the Campus Martius:

> [Antony's] general reputation was bad enough, but he aroused still more hatred on account of the house in which he lived. It had previously belonged to Pompey the Great, a man who was admired no less for his sobriety and his modest, orderly, and democratic way of life than for the fact of his having earned three triumphs. People were indignant when they saw that this house was . . . filled with actors, jugglers, and drunken parasites. (*Vit.Ant.*21; cf. 10)

Caesar willed his magnificent gardens to the people of Rome, yet Antony cavalierly transferred the artwork displayed there to private venues (Cic.*Phil.*2.42.109). Octavian shrewdly capitalized upon Antony's neglect of Rome's collective image. He himself consistently paid homage to the *genius* of individual places and of the city as a whole. He lavished particular attention on the Forum Romanum, the political center of Rome. By the late 30s B.C., Caesar's legitimate heir could stand in the Forum and in every direction point to impressive architectural gifts he had bestowed upon the city and people (fig. 84). There was no *locus* in Rome where Antony could do the same.

Octavian played upon Antony's apparent lack of concern for the city. In 32 B.C., he illegally acquired the will of his very much alive rival and read it aloud before the Senate. On hearing the contents, the people soon forgot their indignation at the acquisition of the document. The will again confirmed Caesarion as Caesar's heir and bestowed more gifts on Cleopatra. Most shocking of all, Antony requested that at his death his body be carried in state through the Forum in Rome, but then be buried in Alexandria at the side of Cleopatra. These bequests, along with the searing remembrance of the triumph held in Alexandria two years earlier, fueled rumors that Antony planned to give Rome to the Egyptian queen and transfer the seat of Roman power to Alexandria. Dio Cassius records the reaction in Rome: "not only Antony's enemies or those who were not siding with either man, but even his most intimate friends, censured him severely" (50.3–4). Buoyed by the popular reaction to the contents of the will, Octavian declared war nominally on Cleopatra, in reality on Antony. At the Battle of Actium in 31 B.C., he defeated the joint forces of the Egyptian queen and her Roman consort. Both Cleopatra and Antony committed suicide at Alexandria when Octavian arrived the following year. The death of Caesarion followed shortly after.

During these political maneuvers, Octavian styled himself as a distinctly Roman champion, pointing at every opportunity to the decadent, "eastern" actions of his rival. With calculation, he stressed a Republicanism rooted in the Italian peninsula versus the perceived decadent orientalism of Antony. Bemoaning his rival's eastern debauchery and liaison with Cleopatra, Octavian stated, "He has forgotten the dress of his ancestors, and imitates the garb of the barbarians; he lives as the slave of a harlot" (DioCass.50.25.3). Further, Octavian pointed disparagingly to the patron gods of his rival. Antony claimed descent from Hercules and often dressed like the famous hero; he also styled himself as a new Dionysius.[41] In contrast, Octavian overtly revered the gods of the Italian peninsula. Before the battle of Actium, he made special vows to the Capitoline trinity of Rome and to all the gods of Italy. The poet Propertius stressed that Antony instead fought his countrymen under the curse of Rome's founder, Romulus, in his deified form as Quirinus.[42]

Octavian allied himself with one Greek deity, Apollo, but made much of the god's Latin associations. Apollo had served as savior of Aeneas, Trojan ancestor of the Romans and, most directly, of the Julii. This Greek deity represented clarity and reason in contrast to the orgiastic Dionysius and bestial Egyptian divinities believed to be favored by Antony.[43] In effect, Apollo mythologically united the Greek and Roman worlds. Before the time of Octavian, the Romans had not allowed temples to this foreign god within the *pomerium* of Rome. Caesar's heir credited Apollo for his military victories and called himself "shining," an adjective frequently applied to the sun god. Furthermore, he did not deny rumors identifying Apollo as his real father. Aggravated by this posturing, Antony accused Caesar's heir of equating himself with a deity.[44] Octavian certainly provided justification for such an accusation. His ties with Apollo boastfully stood out in the cityscape of Rome. When he erected an arch to his biological father, Octavian did not include a sculpture of C. Octavius, but instead surmounted the structure with a quadriga portraying Apollo and his sister Diana by the sculptor Lysias. The arch to Octavian's fathers spanned the road leading up to the Palatine, perhaps serving as an informal gateway to the new developments atop the hill.[45]

In the 30s B.C., Octavian moved from a *domus* near the Forum Romanum to another on the upscale Palatine, near the hut of Romulus. Soon after, lightning struck the property. Octavian declared the site public property dedicated to Apollo who had aided him in battle against Sextus Pompey in 36 B.C. Thus, he used the lightning to justify both the worship of the foreign god within the *pomerium* and a *locus* adjacent to his own residence. Such a diplomatic and reverential solution was a vast improvement upon Caesar's more cavalier approach to urban interventions. Admiring this pious act, the people of Rome purchased a nearby house for Octavian at public expense.[46]

The complex to Apollo Palatinus included rich materials and a complex iconographical program of artwork.[47] Among the ornate decorations were terra-cotta plaques depicting Apollo in combat with Hercules for the sacred tripod (fig. 49). The divine figures represented the patrons respectively of Octavian and Antony and, in turn, two different attitudes to Rome and the Mediterranean world. Apollo symbolized learning, refinement, and the union of classical Greece with Rome. Hercules stood for brute strength, oriental hedonism, and disinterest in the appearance and propriety of the city on the Tiber.

Octavian demonstrated his concern for Rome not only through grand architectural gestures, but also through a broadened care of the city. With the death of Caesar, plans for improved municipal services and maintenance had been shelved. In the late 30s B.C., Octavian needed popular support in his rivalry against Antony. Improvement of city services and conditions was a sure way to gain popular favor. He entrusted this undertaking to his friend and confidant, the *novus homo* Marus Agrippa.[48] By 33 B.C., Agrippa had already held a string of prestigious positions. He had been urban praetor in 40 B.C., governor of Gaul in the early 30s B.C., and consul in 37 B.C. Furthermore, he had demonstrated his military prowess in numerous battles. Despite his obvious *auctoritas*, Agrippa assumed the relatively low office of aedile in 33 B.C. and on behalf of Octavian curried the favor of the urban masses.

Aediles held responsibility for the *cura urbis,* the care of the city. Unlike previous aediles who ignored the pragmatic duties of the office, Agrippa took the post seriously.[49] Dio Cassius wrote, "Agrippa agreed to be made aedile, and without taking anything from the public treasury repaired all public buildings and all streets, cleaned out the sewers and sailed through them underground to the Tiber" (49.43). Agrippa also reworked Rome's aqueduct system. He repaired existing channels and added two new lines, the Aqua Julia and Aqua Virgo, the latter in part carried on a new bridge, the Pons Agrippae. With a crew of 240 slaves, he increased the volume of water to Rome by approximately 100%.[50] In addition to caring for Rome's infrastructure, Agrippa presented games for 59 days, and lavished gifts on the capital's residents, including rations of olive oil and salt, free barber services, and a year's bathing privileges.[51] Shortly after 33 B.C., the popular support turned in favor of Octavian.

Agrippa also embellished the cityscape with artwork. Such patronage was not unusual. Many others had displayed art in Rome, often creating triumphal displays of manubial artwork. The scale, however, of Agrippa's artistic donatives was phenomenal. He decorated the Saepta Julia with Greek paintings and marble tablets, and placed hundreds of sculptures on fountains throughout the city. The Romans openly acknowledged the power of sculptures and paintings to enhance and define the image of a city. When Tralles in Ionia failed to coordinate artwork with building functions, Vitruvius noted, "This disregard of propriety in the interchange of statues appropriate to different places has brought the [city] State as a whole into disrepute" (7.5). Interestingly, Agrippa spoke out for the nationalization of all artwork.[52] Though this innovative proposal was never passed, it reveals a changing attitude toward art and the city. If all sculpture, reliefs, and paintings became State property, they could be programmed as a unit; competitive individual memorials would be thus superceded by a unified message enhancing the collective.

Octavian himself exploited the propagandistic properties of imported art. For example, he brought a statue of the Latin god Janus from Egypt to Rome (Pliny *HN*.36.28–9; Suet.*Aug*.22). Because *ianus* also means a door or arch, this deity was associated with good beginnings. His temple stood in

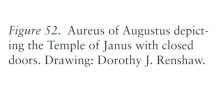

Figure 52. Aureus of Augustus depicting the Temple of Janus with closed doors. Drawing: Dorothy J. Renshaw.

the Forum Romanum below the Argiletum. Tradition dictated that the doors to this structure could be closed only when peace existed throughout Roman territory. In the late first century B.C., Vellius Paterculus wrote:

> It is strong proof of the warlike character of our state that only three times did the closing of the temple of the double-faced Janus give proof of unbroken peace: once under the kings, a second time in the consulship of the Titus Manlius . . . and a third time in the reign of [Octavian] Augustus.[53]

With great ceremony Octavian closed the doors on the Temple of Janus in 30 B.C. to celebrate formally the reintroduction of peace in Rome (fig. 52).

The closed doors of the Janus Temple aptly symbolize the role fashioned by Octavian. Of all the generals in the 40s and 30s B.C., he alone had been able to bring peace to the city on the Tiber; he alone had avenged Caesar and fought off the evil threat posed by Egypt. By 29 B.C., Octavian stood as the champion of Roman tradition and of Rome as its embodiment. Even while occupied in battles miles away, he shrewdly exploited the patronage of buildings in Rome as a means to legitimize his political inheritance from Julius Caesar, and to establish his own value as an individual triumphator and champion of Roman traditions.

Despite the number of buildings realized and vowed in the fifteen years after Caesar's murder, Rome of 29 B.C. did not appear markedly different from the city of 44 B.C. The resemblance resulted largely from the consistency in motivation for architectural patronage. The intense, ongoing political rivalry of the age provided the predominant impetus for building, with the majority of new projects celebrating the military prowess of individuals. Patrons selected sites, building types, and decorative programs to advertise particular associations, formalize rivalries, and foster competitiveness. The parade for the triple triumph of Octavian wound through an urban fabric embroidered with select, individuated flourishes. Significantly, most new projects clustered in the Campus Martius and Forum Romanum for ready viewing along the parade route. No legible urban narrative emerged. Caesar had sketched out the beginnings of an urban plan, yet few traces could be found in the extant urban fabric. The Caesarean projects completed by ambitious followers stood as isolated works valuable for the patrons' association with the deified Dictator, not for interconnections between one another.

The juxtaposition of competing buildings enriched the overall reading of the city and provided the competitive context in which Octavian formulated his attitudes toward urban alteration. Simultaneously, events conspired to clarify and expand the image of Rome. For example, the east–west contrast fostered by the Antony–Octavian rivalry provoked the Romans to define themselves and their primary city. Throughout history, periods of unrest have prompted citizens to focus on their capital or mother city as emblematic of the State. During the American Civil War, Abraham Lincoln diverted military funds to continue work on the dome of the capitol building in Washington, D.C., considering this structure to be an important symbol of national unity.[54] Admittedly, Rome was not a capital in the modern sense; the city represented a culture more than a government. Nevertheless, the internecine conflicts fought throughout the Mediterranean, along with external threats to Roman holdings, placed greater emphasis on the city as the center of the Roman world. By 29 B.C., Octavian was poised to use the image of the city as a fulcrum to leverage the Republic into an imperial state.

PHASE II, 29–17 B.C.: ROME REBORN

In the heat of August, 29 B.C., people poured into Rome to celebrate the triple triumph commemorating Octavian's victories over Dalmatia, Actium, and Egypt. The triumphator magnanimously paid all his debts, canceled those owed to him, and distributed 400 sesterces to every adult citizen. Awash with gratitude, the people of Rome participated in the festivities with pleasure, forgetting the vanquished included Roman citizens. Also without question, they accepted a slight change in the choreography of the triumphal parade. Customarily, the consuls and other magistrates met the victor outside the city, then turned and led the triumphal procession into Rome. Octavian, instead, himself walked before his coconsul and other magistrates (DioCass.51.21).

The implication of the altered ordering was clear. By putting the magistrates behind him, Octavian affirmed his own position as leader of the Roman State. Assuming this role with gusto, he spent the following months putting the state in order. He thinned the bloated Senate and increased the number of patricians.[55] As consul with Agrippa in 28 B.C., he conducted a census and performed an accompanying ceremony of purification, the *lustrum*. Octavian was listed as the *princeps senatus,* or First Senator, in the new census rolls. The following year, he underscored his faith in the Republic by nominally transferring power back to the Senate and people of Rome. In gratitude for this magnanimous act, they lavished honors upon Octavian. Included among these was a golden shield placed in the Curia to commemorate his "valor, clemency, justice and piety."[56]

Also at this time, Octavian accepted a new appellation. The choice resulted from careful consideration. Rumors circulated that Caesar's heir longed to be called "Romulus" after the city's eponymous ancestor. In the early 20s B.C., Octavian attempted to link himself with Rome's first king. He restored the Lupercal, the venerated cave on the western slope of the Palatine where Romulus was suckled, and purchased a house near the hut of Rome's founder. The name Romulus had obvious attraction for a man interested in promoting Roman heritage and the importance of Rome.[57] Ultimately, however, Octavian acknowledged the negative royal associations of the name. Instead, Suetonius records, "he accepted the title, 'Augustus,' on the ground that this was not merely a new title but a more honorable one."[58] Previously, *augustus* had appeared in religious contexts as an adjective connoting something or someone precious, sacred, and influential; the word also recalled the verb *augere,* to increase, another positive association for an ambitious individual. The gods demonstrated their approval of the new title. The night Octavian became "Augustus" the Tiber flooded the city. This prodigy affirmed for all his divine right to Rome; Dio Cassius exulted, "from this sign the soothsayers prophesied that he would rise to great heights and hold the whole city under his sway."[59]

Increasingly, the Romans began to equate the health and well being of the city with that of Augustus. When the *princeps* fell ill in 23 B.C., the populace and the city succumbed to paroxysms of anxiety. That winter floods and famine, followed by rioting, all swept through Rome as if to confirm the irrevocable link between the man and the urban environment. When Augustus recovered, the relief was palpable. The citizenry proposed offerings to his health and bestowed innumerable offices, honors, and privileges on the *princeps.*

Saved from death, Augustus was reborn. Hereafter, he cited 23 B.C. as the first year of his reign. This personal renewal mirrored the shared yearning for the restoration of the Republic. In 29 B.C., the Senate had honored Augustus with an arch inscribed with the legend *republica conservata;* other inscriptions proclaimed *respublica restituta.*[60] Modern meanings of "republic" cloud the ancient understanding of the term. To the Romans, *respublica* was not so much a specific form of government, as a descriptor for the purpose of government: namely, to provide a legitimate administrative structure, laws, and rights.[61] A return to the traditional ways of life, piety, and government helped the Romans to heal after the corruption and demoralization of the civil wars.[62] In the twelve years following his triple triumph, Augustus labored to make the renewal of the Republic manifest in the physical fabric of Rome. By rebuilding the houses of the gods and promoting responsibility for urban care, he revived the city as well as the Republic. As he grounded the State, Augustus also grounded his own power.

Rebuilding the Houses of the Gods

Few Romans active in the 20s B.C. had lived during the days of Republican tranquility, if such a period had in fact ever existed. Time had filtered away most impurities, leaving the vision of a noble, pious past as promulgated in literature, art, and stories. Augustus played to the nostalgic yearning for a return to the idealized past. Rome naturally served as both the *locus* and symbol of this nostalgia. With great fanfare, the *princeps* began to interweave the existing urban fabric with revitalized Republican threads. Foremost among these was the renewal of religious faith as represented in the city's temples and shrines.

Even before assuming the name "Augustus," Octavian had shown concern for strengthening Republican religiosity. Faced with eastern threats, in 28 B.C., he ousted Egyptian rites from within the *pomerium* of Rome.[63] Throughout the following years, he enhanced the status of various religious groups, promoted the renewal of lapsed sacred ceremonies, and encouraged the institution of rites to honor his achievements. Octavian himself belonged to several revered religious colleges. Though he longed to be Pontifex Maximus, he demonstrated reverence for Republican traditions. He patiently awaited the natural death of the man holding this high priesthood, his rival the *triumvir* Lepidus.[64] In the meantime, he collected religious distinctions. Among the honors of 27 B.C., the Senate and people voted Octavian the right to have laurel trees in front of his residence and an oak wreath above his door "to symbolize that he was always victor over his enemies and the savior of the citizens" (fig. 53).[65] Since laurel trees traditionally flanked priestly buildings, this privilege simultaneously enhanced Octavian's religious prestige.

Under the aegis of Octavian, Rome's urban fabric began to show other signs of a strong, renewed faith. At the beginning of this phase, the city still projected an air of dereliction and bankrupted piety. Ovid moaned, "where are now the temples[?] . . . tumbled down they are with the long lapse of

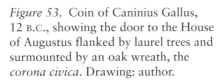

Figure 53. Coin of Caninius Gallus, 12 B.C., showing the door to the House of Augustus flanked by laurel trees and surmounted by an oak wreath, the *corona civica*. Drawing: author.

time . . . gone to wrack and ruin . . ." (*Fasti* 2.58–64). Such a condition was unacceptable. Derelict religious structures insulted the gods and incited their wrath. Horace warned:

You will pay, Romans, through no fault of yours for the sins of your ancestors, until you have restored the temples and crumbling houses of the gods, and their images marred by the black filth of incense. By humbling yourselves before the gods you rule; with the gods all things begin, and they bring all to an end; neglect of the gods had brought much evil and suffering to Italy. (Hor.*Odes* 3.6.)

In 28 B.C., Octavian ordered temples to be repaired by any surviving descendants of the original patrons; he himself assumed responsibility for the rest. In his own writing, he boasted, "In my sixth consulship [28 B.C.] I restored eighty-two temples of the gods in the city on the authority of the Senate, neglecting none that required restoration at that time."[66] With a great flourish, Augustus himself reworked the premier temple of Rome, that to Jupiter Optimus Maximus. Inside he deposited 16,000 pounds of gold, along with pearls and other precious stones (Suet.*Aug.*30).

The *princeps* urged others to follow his example. In addition, he set up his family members as alternative models. His wife Livia restored the Temple of Bona Dea on the Aventine according to Ovid so "that she might imitate her husband and follow him in everything" (*Fasti* 5.157–8). In the name of his sister Octavia, Augustus himself replaced the Porticus Metelli with a complete quadriportico surrounding the temples of Juno Regina and Jupiter Stator. Rome's citizens willingly emulated the efforts of Augustus and his family. Restoration projects associated donors with highly visible and venerated structures at a much lower cost than new construction. Generally, patrons updated existing temples by rebuilding with opulent materials, adding rich ornaments, and consolidating the surrounding spaces.

The extensive reworking of Rome's temples provided positive propaganda for all concerned. Individual donors received praise for their piety; the general populace received attractive environments for worship; the government received tangible manifestations of the renewed Republic; the city received a white mantle of marble shrines. Glistening in the sun, the city's refreshed temples overtly proclaimed a renewed faith in Rome's past and a glorious future. Contemporary literature affirmed the role of Augustus in both. Livy called him "founder and restorer of all our temples" (Livy 4.20).

The *princeps* honored humanity not only by providing refurbished shrines for worship, but by respecting the achievements of the original building patrons. Inscriptions on structures proudly advertised the largess of donors and provided a legible urban text informing all observers about Roman heritage and values. Augustus exploited donative inscriptions with great skill. When politically expedient, he maintained the name of the original donor, as with the Porticus Octavia. This structure in the southwestern Campus Martius had been erected by Gnaeus Octavius in 168 B.C. The association with the donor's name is obvious. The *princeps* claimed this project as a new construction, yet boasted, "I allowed [the portico] to be called Octavia after the name of him who had constructed an earlier one on the same site" (*ResG.*19). By not claiming renovated buildings as new undertakings Augustus honored the original donors, their heirs, and supporters. Years later Tiberius eulogized about his stepfather, "[Augustus] repaired all the public works that had suffered injury but deprived none of the original builders of the glory of their founding."[67]

Tiberius overstated his case. Augustus was not always magnanimous. If a restoration was particularly extensive, the *princeps* claimed the temple as a new project. When listing the structures he built in the *Res Gestae,* he included not only completely new works such as the Temple of Apollo, but also the renovated temples to Jupiter Feretrius, Quirinus, and Minerva (*ResG.*19). By appropriating venerated sites as his own, the *princeps* obliterated the fame of the original donors and strengthened his personal association with select buildings and urban regions. For example, after restoring a number of temples he dedicated each on the same date, September 23, his own birthday. In particular, he employed this strategy for structures erected by earlier triumphators in the area of the Circus Flaminius (Table 6).[68] Furthermore, though the *princeps* boasted he erected projects in the name of others, this generosity was equally calculated. Suetonius identified the "others" as "[Augustus'] grandsons and nephew to wit, his wife and his sister" (Suet.*Aug.*29). Thus, this beneficence was in part a sham; by promoting his family the *princeps* ultimately promoted himself. In effect, Augustus revitalized Rome's religious buildings, but at the same time imposed his own

Figure 54. Coin of Augustus showing the Temple of Jupiter Tonans on the Capitoline Hill. Photo: Fototeca Unione AAR 2976.

indelible imprint. Looking at the Temple of Magna Mater, Ovid exclaimed, "The name of the founder of the temple has not survived; now it is Augustus; formerly it was Metellus" (*Fasti* 4.347–9).

Between 29 and 17 B.C., the *princeps* had the time and money to complete the religious structures pledged during the years of civil conflicts (e.g., the temples of Apollo and Divus Julius) and those conceived earlier under Caesar (e.g., the Curia Julia and Temple of Venus Genetrix).[69] New religious constructions did not as easily fit into the program for the renewal of Republican piety. Augustus initiated only a few totally new religious projects in Rome, and then at divine urging. For example, after a near miss from a lightning bolt during the Cantabrian campaign in Spain (26/25 B.C.), the *princeps* constructed a small but opulent temple to Jupiter Tonans (Jupiter the Thunderer) on the Capitoline (fig. 54); another lightning bolt dictated construction of the temple to Apollo on the Palatine. The Senate and people of Rome showed similar restraint. In honor of the *princeps,* they voted not temples, but smaller commemorative altars, including the Ara Fortuna Redux near the Porta Capena of 19 B.C. (Suet.*Aug.*29; Pliny *HN.*36.50; *ResG.*11; DioCass.54.10; Prop.4.3.71).

Unlike the period immediately after Caesar's death, this second phase had few grand religious projects funded by triumphators. The reasons are obvious. First, there were fewer triumphs awarded (Table 1). After the successes in Spain of 25 B.C., Augustus again closed the doors to the temple to Janus, signaling peace throughout Roman territory.[70] Second, the *princeps* began to assume more and more control over triumphal building, directing victorious generals to undertake lower-profile, pragmatic projects rather than highly visible temples. The most monumental new religious building erected between 27 and 17 B.C. was the Pantheon in the Campus Martius. Donated by Agrippa in 25 B.C., a year after he had defeated Sextus Pompey, this structure was not dedicated to a deity for help in a battle. Rather, it was a paean to the *princeps*. Initially, Agrippa wished to place a statue of Augustus in the shrine and "to take the designation of the structure from his title" (DioCass.53.27). The *princeps* wisely refused to be revered as a deity in Rome. Agrippa dedicated the structure in honor of all the gods, including the deified Caesar, and placed statues of himself and Augustus in the pronaos.[71]

Among the most notable restoration projects from this phase was the temple–theater complex to Venus Victrix in the Campus Martius. Augustus had cause to let the project deteriorate. After all, the donor was Pompey the Great, rival of Caesar, and the structure was the site of the Dictator's murder. In the period after Actium, however, the *princeps* began gradually to distance himself from Caesar and his absolutist policies, while strengthening ties with figures better known for their veneration of Republican traditions. The Romans of the 20s B.C. remembered Pompey as an avid Republican, the champion of a free state. Augustus restored the temple complex, and affirmed its importance by mentioning it in association with the restoration of the temple to Jupiter Optimus Maximus (Capitolium), unequivocally the most important shrine in Rome. In the *Res Gestae*, he wrote, "I restored the Capitolium and the Theater of Pompey, both at great expense without inscribing my own name on either."[72]

In addition to providing the gods with improved temples, the *princeps* promoted ceremonies in their honor. During the decades of civil war many religious rites had been curtailed or discontinued. Augustus greatly increased the number of holidays and festivals celebrated in Rome. He revived the augury of Salus, the office of Flamen Dialis, the ceremonies of the Lupercalia, the Ludi Saeculares, and the festival of the Compitalia. In the *Fasti,* Ovid gives a full description of the festivals and sacred events for the first six months of the Augustan calendar.[73] Along with restored temples, the multiplication of ceremonies affirmed a return to normalcy after decades of civil war. Simultaneously, such activities kept the urban population preoccupied. Residents of every status occupied their free time with specific religious activities or pondering the complex iconographical programs of the city's aggrandized religious structures.

In the 30s B.C., Horace wrote, "he who takes it upon himself to look after his fellow citizens and the city, the empire and Italy and the temples of the gods, compels all the world to take an interest" (*Sat.*1.6.34–7). Augustus took this advice to heart. By 17 B.C., tangible expressions of piety filled every view of Rome. Glistening, rich materials encased dozens of restored temples; colorful imported stones and art ornamented these renewed shrines. Awareness of this achievement was widespread; coins circulated throughout the Mediterranean with depictions of the aggrandized, rebuilt temples of the great city on the Tiber (figs. 47 and 52). The healthy condition of Rome's shrines confirmed for all observers the healthy condition of the State as restored by Augustus.

Restoring Urban Responsibility

Vellius Paterculus with awe remarked of the *princeps,* "a feeling of kinship leads him to protect every famous monument."[74] Beyond the restoration of individual temples and public buildings, Augustus turned his attention to the overall care of the city. Marvelous buildings are but one part of a positive urban impression. If people show disrespect for property rights, fail to maintain streets, and ignore regular upkeep, then the physical as well as conceptual image of a city weakens. Once his own power was secure, Augustus began to turn his attention to promoting respect and a sense of responsibility for the urban environment of Rome.

In his own actions, the *princeps* demonstrated a clear veneration of places and property rights. As construction began on two large, new projects – the Forum Augustum and temple to Apollo – Augustus took great pains to emphasize that both stood on private soil not public property (*ResG.*21). When listing the *princeps'* benevolent acts, Suetonius notes, "He made his forum narrower than he had planned, because he did not venture to eject the owners of the neighboring houses" (Suet.*Aug.*56). The truncated northeastern segment of the forum has been cited as tangible evidence of this claim. In actual fact, this section bordered on a public street, not housing, yet the message is the same: traditional respect for existing urban configurations. Writing over a generation later, when the empire was well established, Suetonius was greatly impressed. He found this respect for private property to be as remarkable as the fact that Augustus "went the round of the tribes with his candidates and appealed for them in the traditional manner."[75]

By openly acknowledging the rights of individuals and venerating the time-empowered *genii locorum* of Rome, Augustus sought to promote concern for the city's physical fabric. The refurbishment of an entire cityscape requires involvement by all urban occupants. The *princeps* drew upon the deeply ingrained sense of familial honor to promote urban care. He stressed that entire families were humiliated if they did not maintain the public projects erected by their ancestors, just as all Romans were dishonored by the poor condition of the city's temples. Thus, Augustus emphasized that he personally assumed responsibility for the restoration of the Theater of Pompey because "no member of [Pompey's] family was equal to the task of restoration" (Tac.*Ann.*3.72). As a further comment on Pompey and the dangers of internecine conflict, he transformed the entire complex into a martyrium honoring both Caesar and his rival. He sealed the room where the Dictator was murdered and transferred the colossal statue of Pompey at whose feet Caesar had fallen to an arch at the grand door of the theater.[76]

For the sake of family honor, Roman patrons willingly restored high-profile public buildings. They were less inclined to expend their wealth on more pragmatic urban projects. In the 20s B.C., Rome began to function like a city again after years of being a war zone. Goods and people flowed into Rome in large numbers. Unfortunately, the city's infrastructure could not service them. The water and transportation systems were still woefully inadequate, and provisions for safety insufficient. During this phase, Augustus increasingly turned his attention to the functioning of Rome. In effect, as first citizen, he assumed responsibility for the care of the city.

Traditionally, the maintenance of the city was a loosely defined duty, the *cura urbis,* belonging to the aediles. As aedile in 33 B.C., Agrippa revitalized this charge. He assumed responsibility for reorganizing Rome's entire system for water acquisition and drainage. Such an intricate and comprehensive task could not be completed in a short time span. At the end of his aedileship, Agrippa was named perpetual curator of the water system, or *curator aquarum.*[77] An efficient administrator, he undertook numerous hydraulic projects including a notable new aqueduct. Completed in 19 B.C., the Aqua Virgo fed the extensive new facilities in the Campus Martius.

Ancient Rome was a consuming, not producing, city. Access was essential. Roads, streets, and the river had to be maintained in order to ensure the movement of comestibles, building materials, tourists, and troops. Soon after being named Augustus, the *princeps* turned his attention to Rome's transportation system "to make the approach to the city easier" (Suet. *Aug.*30). He began by initiating repairs to the great Via Flaminia north of the city. To advertise this largess, he placed statues of himself atop the arches of the bridges along the great thoroughfare (fig. 102). Highly visible, these images may have been lures to convince other patrons to undertake similar projects. Augustus found such enticements necessary, for few patrons wished to expend funds on mundane road repairs. Dio Cassius records:

[P]erceiving that the roads outside the walls had become difficult to travel as the result of neglect, he [Augustus] ordered various senators to repair the others at their own expense, and he himself looked after the Via Flaminia since he was going to lead an army out by that route. (53.22)

The obvious military importance of *viae* allowed the *princeps* to call upon all triumphators to use their *manubiae* on the repair of highways (Suet.*Aug.*30). In response, M. Valerius Messalla Corvinus, triumphator in

27 B.C., rebuilt the portion of the Via Latina nearest to Rome. Few others took up the challenge. The time-consuming, low-prestige maintenance of highways was not especially popular. Despite Augustus' efforts to promote private responsibility, Dio Cassius notes that public revenues had to be used for road repairs because "none of the senators liked to spend money upon them." Even the faithful Agrippa did not repair a road, though he took pains to justify his neglect by undertaking a different public project, the Saepta.

As a result, Augustus himself continued to underwrite the maintenance of highways around Rome. In 20 B.C., he assumed the *cura viarum*, or care of the highways in the neighborhood of Rome. To oversee the actual maintenance, he appointed a board of expraetors. Augustus commemorated the improved highway maintenance system by setting up a gilded bronze pillar in the Forum Romanum, the Milliarium Aureum, inscribed with the names of the principal cities of the empire and their distances from Rome.[78]

In the same period, the *princeps* likewise turned his attention to the other great transportation route of Rome, the Tiber River. When inundations destroyed the vital bridges connecting the left and right banks of Rome, repairs were undertaken immediately.[79] Care for the river itself remained problematic. The Tiber was a primary commercial route; daily barges approached Rome carrying goods off-loaded at the coast from seafaring ships. Augustus facilitated transportation by clearing the river bed of rubbish and removing the protruding structures narrowing its course (Suet. *Aug.*30). He may also have been responsible for new docking facilities. A mole in the northern Campus Martius dates to the late first century B.C. and was created to serve the extensive building projects of Augustus and Agrippa rising on the great northern plain. Also in this phase, large new warehouses, or *horrea*, were erected to store goods before distribution. Though not directly related to Augustan patronage, they reflect the healthiness and commercial success of the city under his tutelage.[80]

Augustus improved the fitness of Rome in other ways as well. Beyond civil conflict, the city suffered from natural disasters. Fires and floods periodically ravaged Rome (Table 2). The hydraulic improvements of Agrippa and clearing of the river by Augustus somewhat minimized flood damage. Without substantial intervention upstream, however, the city remained subject to recurring inundations.

After yet another large blaze consumed part of the city in 23 B.C., Augustus took steps to improve public fire fighting. He transferred this important responsibility from low-level officials, the *triumviri nocturni*, to the patrician curule aediles. To aid their efforts, he assigned to them a force of 600

Table 2. Major Disasters and Portents in Rome during the Augustan Age

60 B.C.	storm	22	flood
56	quake		lightning storm
54	flood	21	fire
52	fire	16	fire
	flood?	14	fire
50	fire	13	flood
49?	quake and fire	12	fire
47	quake	9	lightning storm
47	fire	7	fire
44	flood	5	flood?
43	storm		
42	lightning storm	A.D. 3	fire
40	famine	5	flood, city navigable
38	fire		for seven days
36	fire		earthquake
34	flood		famine
32	fire and storm	6	fire
31	fire		famine
29	fire	8	famine
27	flood	9	lightning storm
23	fire		locusts
	storm	12?	fire
	flood, city navigable for three days		flood
	famine	15	quake
	plague		

State slaves. Unfortunately, the aediles frequently ignored the responsibility for fighting fires, or else used it for personal gain. As aedile in the 20s B.C., the ambitious M. Egnatius Rufus won the favor of urban residents by using his own private fire brigade to extinguish fires.[81] In gratitude, the people reimbursed his expenditures and allowed him to stand for a higher office without observing the legal interval. Dio Cassius notes:

Marcus Egnatius Rufus . . . became so elated over these very honors and so contemptuous of Augustus that he issued a bulletin to the effect that he had handed the city over unimpeded and intact to his successor. All the most prominent men became indignant at this, Augustus himself most of all. (53.24)

The *princeps* did not overreact; he merely ordered the succeeding aediles to prevent fires and put out those that did occur. Nevertheless, such episodes confirmed the political importance of fire fighting in Rome and the need for careful monitoring of this necessary service.

Fire was not the only threat to city residents. During the late first century B.C., the streets were filled with danger. Suetonius records that "gangs of footpads openly went about with swords by their sides" (Suet.*Aug*.32). To address this situation, Augustus attempted to redefine the office of *praefectus urbi*. In the early days of Rome, the urban prefect was a temporary deputy acting in the name of the absent king or consuls. Augustus assigned this official an armed force and charged him to keep order in the crime ridden city. In 25 B.C., the *princeps* appointed M. Valerius Messalla Corvinus as the first *praefectus urbi* under the new arrangement. Daunted by the enormity of his task, or perhaps because he felt an armed force in Rome was contrary to Republican ideas, Corvinus resigned a few days later.[82] Rome's residents again were left vulnerable.

During the decade following his great triple triumph, Augustus attempted to rekindle the Romans' sense of propriety and responsibility along with their piety. For all Roman citizens, the city on the Tiber was both a shared environment and a shared heritage. As a result, the *princeps* could logically urge that all citizens take part in the care of Rome, much as a *paterfamilias* would urge his offspring to care for the family properties. Furthermore, involvement in the day-to-day care of the city's infrastructure deflected attention away from other, potentially incendiary activities.

Renewing a Sense of Community

Augustus kept Rome's citizens preoccupied in other ways as well. Responding to a reproach, the pantomime actor Pylades told the *princeps,* "It is in your interest Caesar [Augustus], that people should keep their thoughts on us!" (DioCass.54.17). Augustus agreed. The calendar filled not only with renewed religious ceremonies, but also with a wide range of games, theatrical performances, and races, some created specifically to celebrate the achievements of Augustus. Spectator events, such as games, ceremonies, and competitions, all are communal. By programming these activities and providing structures to house them, Augustus and his partisans not only entertained, they enhanced the feeling of community in Rome.

Augustus enjoyed bringing large crowds together for controlled, shared experiences. Suetonius tells us,

He surpassed all his predecessors in the frequency, variety, and magnificence of his public shows. . . . He gave them sometimes in all the wards [of the city] and on many stages with actors in all languages and combats of gladiators not only in the Forum or the amphitheater, but in the Circus and in the Saepta. (*Aug.*43)

The extant facilities of the Republican city could not handle all the events programmed by the *princeps*. Augustus improved Rome's existing structures, added new ones, and retrofitted others, such as the Saepta, for specific events. For the celebrations of 28 B.C. honoring the victory at Actium, he erected a temporary wooden stadium in the Campus Martius and created an artificial lake near the Tiber for a mock sea battle. After fire damaged the Circus Maximus, Augustus restored the *pulvinar* (State box).[83] When M. Claudius Marcellus organized highly successful festivities in his capacity as aedile in 23 B.C., Augustus promoted his nephew/son-in-law by sheltering the entire Forum Romanum with fluttering awnings (DioCass.53.31). Sadly, the young Marcellus died later the same year. In his honor, the *princeps* completed the theater project begun by Caesar and named it the Theater of Marcellus.

Agrippa also gave Rome several extremely popular facilities. In 25 B.C., he began the great Thermae Agrippae in the central area of the Campus Martius. These were the first large public baths of the city, replete with wondrous artworks.[84] The project included landscaped open areas for exercising and strolling, pools, and a canal (Euripus) for swimming, and several multiuse structures. The complex came into full use with the completion of the Aqua Virgo in 19 B.C. Agrippa paid all the entrance fees during his aedileship and willed the baths to the Roman people along with revenue-earning property for their upkeep (DioCass.49.43; 54.29). Nearby, the admiral created a monument commemorating his naval victories. The large Basilica Neptuni of 25 B.C., adjacent to the baths honored the sea god; the naval theme continued with another Agrippan project, the nearby Porticus Argonautarum with paintings depicting the seaborne exploits of the Argonauts. Dio Cassius praised Agrippa for beautifying the city at his own expense, yet the fame for these projects accrued equally to his father-in-law Augustus (53.27).

The residents of Rome drew strength from activities and locales tied to Republican traditions. New structures and reprogrammed places such as the Theater of Marcellus and Campus Martius gained acceptance and stature through incorporation in the burgeoning round of revitalized communal activities. As the memory of the civil wars faded, people again felt tied to the ways of their ancestors, the *mores maiorum*. Augustus enhanced this feeling by making the past visible. After seeing people in the Forum Romanum wearing dark everyday clothes, he referred to a passage in the *Aeneid* defining the early Romans by their dress, "Look, the Romans, masters of the world, people of the toga"; thereafter, the *princeps* required the toga be worn by eligible citizens at all official functions in the Forum and at the theater.[85] The sight of the billowing white garments took people back in time to the noble early days of Roman greatness. Like the ancients, they participated in communal activities and dressed in the impressive, but uncomfortable toga; like the ancients, they acknowledged one *locus* as the appropriate stage for their actions: Rome.

Creating a Capital

The restoration of the Republic, the temples of the gods, and a renewed sense of community were all predicated on the simple notion that Rome was inviolate. The city, in fact, stood as the physical representation of Roman history. Whereas Romans may have admired the broad thoroughfares of eastern cities, they did not want to remake Rome completely in their image. The power of place and power of property rights were too strong.[86] Caesar had been roundly censured when he proposed to regularize Rome's plan in emulation of Greek cities. Augustus reverentially preserved the labyrinthine streets, irregular public spaces, and mean residential facilities of Rome. From a planning standpoint, the city remained awkward, yet conceptually its form affirmed Rome's identity as capital of the Romans.

In contrast to rumors associated with both Caesar and Antony about moving the seat of government to Alexandria, every effort of Augustus reaffirmed the city on the Tiber as the center of the Roman world. No longer was Rome the premier city-state in a federation, the "first among equals." Sources began to describe Rome as the "head" of a "body" composed of the empire.[87] In the 20s B.C., the *locus* of Rome became especially important. The Milliarium Aureum affirmed this conceptualization by celebrating Rome as the starting point for highways stretching throughout the known world. Agrippa undertook the immense task of documenting the world's geography for a map displayed in the Porticus Vipsania.[88] Vitruvius explained the city's superiority as due to her placement at the center of the known world and to her felicitous climate, "Thus the divine mind has allotted to the Roman State an excellent and temperate region in order to rule the world" (Vitr.6.10–11). For the Romans of this period, Rome was not merely a city. Irrevocably linked to an energized *locus,* Rome was divinely selected as capital of the world.

The image of Rome as a capital changed the perception of public buildings in the city and their intended audience. Anxiety arose that, as Suetonius wrote,

"The city was not adorned as the renown of our empire demand" (Suet. *Aug*.28). Dio Cassius records advice Maecenas gave Augustus in 29 B.C.:

Adorn this capital with utter disregard of expense and make it magnificent with festivals of every kind. For it is fitting that we who rule over many people should surpass all men in all things, and brilliance of this sort, also, tends in a way to inspire our allies with respect for us and our enemies with terror.[89]

Maecenas next recommended that other cities should adhere to the authority of Rome and "not indulge in public buildings unnecessarily numerous or large . . . lest they exhaust themselves in futile exertions and be led by unreasonable rivalries to quarrel among themselves." Rome was to stand supreme in physical form as well as sovereignty to the rest of the Empire. As a result, works in the capital addressed far wider audiences than ever before. Patrons considered the response of outsiders (allies and foes alike) and of Romans. Reaction was not limited to the present. Writing in the late 20s B.C., Vitruvius praised the *princeps* for creating architectural projects that "correspond to the grandeur of our history, and will be a memorial to future ages" (1.pref.3).

The urban image of Rome now competed with those of other capitals in the Mediterranean. In particular, eastern cities were famous for their numerous amenities: public gardens, theaters and other entertainment structures, and libraries. The recreational center being developed in the Campus Martius can be seen as a direct rival to the Daphne of Antioch or the public adornments of Alexandria.[90] Similarly, the Theater of Marcellus could compete proudly with those at Athens and Pergamon. Reflecting culture and learning, libraries had long been viewed in the east as essential components for a capital city; Pliny records that the Kings of Alexandria and Pergamon competed in the founding of libraries (*HN*.35.10). During the 20s B.C., Rome saw the completion of facilities at the Temple of Apollo Palatinus and the Porticus Octaviae.[91]

The most remarkable structure completed in this period also reflects eastern influence: the Mausoleum of Augustus in the Campus Martius (fig. 104). Begun in 28 B.C., this tomb was enormous. The circular marble base measured over 85 meters in diameter; above rose an earthen mound approximately 45 meters in height. The mound was planted with evergreens and surmounted by a gilded statue of the *princeps*. Around the base lay a verdant garden. Contemporaries marveled at the Mausoleum's "full-fortuned opulence" and the opening of the gardens to the public.[92] In scale as well as form and amenities, the Mausoleum recalled diverse forerunners, including the kingly tombs of the Hellenistic east: the royal Lydian mounds of Anatolia, and the famous circular tomb of Alexander the Great.[93] Simultaneously, it emulated Etruscan tumuli of Italy associated with Rome's forefathers, as well as more recent examples in the Campus Martius commemorating distinguished citizens of the Republic.[94] For external observers, this great project directly signaled the wealth, leadership, and endurance of the Roman State.

Augustus began the Mausoleum when still in his thirties. He had a weak constitution and ongoing civil disruptions still threatened. The gigantic structure was to be more than a final resting place. Though a reminder of human mortality, the great tomb in the Campus Martius simultaneously represented endurance beyond human frailty. The sheer scale and solidity of construction indicated the monument would stand for centuries. Particularly at a time when no one knew Augustus would outlive his immediate heirs, the Mausoleum was a memorial to the many generations of Julii to come and to their commitment to the city of Rome.[95]

The statue of Augustus atop the Mausoleum greeted all observers approaching Rome from the north, yet during this period, the image of the capital was not shaped by the *princeps* alone. Other patrons continued to erect impressive public projects in the city. For example, L. Cornelius Balbus celebrated his African triumph of 19 B.C. by beginning a large theater in the Campus Martius. His new complex rose in direct juxtaposition with the theaters of Pompey and Marcellus. Confronted with such competition in the cityscape, the *princeps* discouraged others from seeking self-glorification through building. Instead, he continued to urge building patrons to work for the glory of the capital as a whole by funding pragmatic maintenance projects.

Augustus also called for a return to *decorum* in private works. He legitimately dealt with moral issues in his capacity as censor, a post he first held in 19 B.C.[96] Along with other provisions, he promoted antisumptuary laws to curb extravagances in dining, dress, and architecture. For example, Augustus placed a limit on building heights along street fronts. As historical justification for this restriction, he referred to a second-century, antisumptuary proposal.[97] In addition, the *princeps* himself avoided overt displays of architectural extravagance in his private projects. His house on the Palatine projected a decorous modesty in size and materials.[98] In contrast, the *domus* of Vedius Pollio on the Esquiline was extremely showy, covering an area as large as a city. Upon inheriting this extravagant estate in 15 B.C., Augustus immediately leveled the structure and replaced it with a public project, the Porticus Liviae. Ovid praised his action, "That is the way to exercise the censorship; that is the way to set an example, when the judge does himself what he warns others to do."[99]

Many Romans believed the quest for glory had ruined the Republic. Writers in the literary circle surrounding Augustus treated nobility and glory as anachronisms, and instead promoted piety and modesty. The message was clear. Everyone was to work together for the common good. Only one individual was to stand out above the others. As *princeps* and *primus inter pares,* Augustus was representative of the collective. Thus, he could undertake impressive projects such as the Mausoleum Augusti, because his fame belonged likewise to all Romans. Conversely, the renown associated with each major architectural projects in Rome gradually came to reflect back to the fame of Rome's first citizen. This conceptualization is evident in the dedication of the Saepta by Agrippa in 26 B.C.; Dio Cassius tells us that after completing this large project:

> Agrippa not only incurred no jealousy on this account, but was greatly honored both by Augustus himself and by all the rest of the people. The reason was that he consulted and cooperated with Augustus in the most humane, the most celebrated, and the most beneficial projects, and yet did not claim in the slightest degree a share in the glory of them, but used the honors . . . for the benefit of the donor [Augustus] himself and of the public. (53.23)

In effect, by championing piety and the restoration of the Republic, the *princeps* implied all environmental changes in Rome resulted from his efforts.

After celebrating the great triumph of 29 B.C., Augustus faced numerous commitments for architectural projects and even more for Rome's infrastructure. During the following decade and a half, he completed structures vowed or initiated earlier and began to address the most pressing pragmatic urban needs of Rome: repair and maintenance of religious structures, care of highways, the river, the water system, and urban safety. His calls for others to share in these urban responsibilities were not always answered. Rather than undertake mundane repairs, Rome's residents preferred to luxuriate in the renewed appearance and extensive entertainment facilities of the city on the Tiber. Before their very eyes, the cityscape was being reborn, a tangible manifestation of the restored Republic. The bustle of construction throughout Rome was exciting and uplifting (fig. 94). Urban residents proudly pointed to the sparkling new structures and redefined urban districts, and felt the city had, indeed, been transformed. Outsiders were also impressed. The extent, form, and grandeur of interventions during this period elevated Rome to a world-class city.

Perhaps the most valuable transformations from this phase were intangible. Augustus renewed a Roman sense of pride, *decorum,* and collective destiny. Happy to discard the pessimism of the recent past, the residents of Rome jettisoned personal glory in favor of piety, peace, and prosperity. All labored together for the honor of the renewed Republic. As a result, they came to accept Augustan interventions in the cityscape with the same aplomb as his rearrangements in the political power structure. In their eyes, such adjustments were a small price to pay for peace and the rebirth of Rome as a capital city.

PHASE III, 17 B.C.–A.D. 14: CONSOLIDATION

On a dark night in early summer, 17 B.C., Augustus sacrificed nine ewe-lambs and nine she-goats in a meadow by the Tiber and implored the Moirae (Fates):

I pray and beseech you to increase the power and authority of the citizens, the people of Rome, in war and peace, protect forever the name of Latium, grant for all time safety, victory, and might to the citizens, the people of Rome . . . that you may look with kindly grace on the citizens, the people of Rome, on the College of Fifteen, on me, my family and household. (*CIL* 6.32323)

The occasion was the celebration of the Ludi Saeculares. Both this prayer and the event acknowledged the restored sense of Roman destiny and the prominent place of Augustus and his family as representatives of the State. Furthermore, as an important ritual of purification and rebirth, the sacred games marked the onset of a new age.[100]

By 17 B.C., the *princeps* had been directing the State for over a decade. His policy of restoration had renewed faith in the Roman Republic and allowed time for the people and city to heal. Augustus now was ready to celebrate the achievement as his own (DioCass.54.18). He went through complex machinations to schedule the Ludi this year. Based on Etruscan precedents, these games commemorated the end of a *saeculum*, a period equivalent to the longest span of a human life, calculated at 100 years. The last event had occurred in 146 B.C.; due to the civil wars, no *Ludi* had been held in 46 B.C. The *princeps* cited new evidence that the previous games were actually in 126 B.C. and adopted a reckoning of 110 years per *saeculum*.

Augustus and Agrippa, holders of tribunician power, organized the celebrations. Day and night, large crowds moved from one venue to another. During the first two days, sacrifices on the Capitoline hill honored Jupiter and Juno Regina. The following day, attention focused on the sparkling new temple complex atop the Palatine to the south. Here Apollo and Diana received praise for interceding with Jupiter on behalf of the Roman people. Next, a well-orchestrated parade united the two hilltops. Before the Temple of Jupiter Optimus Maximus on the Capitoline, twenty-seven youths and twenty-seven maidens sang a joyous hymn specially commissioned for the event. They then moved down to the Forum and up the Palatine to stand before the Temple of Apollo Palatinus where they repeated the song "in honor of the gods who love the Seven Hills" (Hor.*Carm.Saec.*8; fig. 63).

The hymn by Horace for the Ludi Saeculares celebrated the distant past, along with the Augustan present and future. The performances honored revered Republican *loci* and anointed the new centers developed by the *princeps*. The Palatine Temple of Apollo, in existence for over a decade, assumed a stature equivalent to the long venerated Temple of Jupiter Optimus Maximus on the Capitoline. The fifty-four youths sang, "may [Apollo], if he looks with favor on the altars of the Palatine, prolong the Roman power and Latium's prosperity to cycles ever new and ages ever better!" Furthermore, the hymn acknowledged the entire city and all the blessings of the day as the handiwork of Apollo, Augustus' patron deity. In jubilation the youths prophesied, "O quickening Sun . . . ne'er mayst thou be able to view aught greater than the city of Rome!" (*Carm.Saec.*9–12, 65–8).

The great celebrations of the Ludi Saeculares left few new permanent memorials in the cityscape. Most events occurred in temporary structures or existing facilities. The one lasting display commissioned by the consuls was small: two columns, one marble and one bronze, inscribed with the full program of the games.[101] After all, major constructions were not needed. Rome of 17 B.C. had impressive buildings and an energetic, positive ambience. Augustus had crafted an attractive capital for the renewed Republic; he now began to hone this image, giving it a clear and enduring Augustan patina appropriate to the new age. The *princeps* assumed a more rigorous control over urban interventions and took steps to ensure his personal and familial imprint on the city would endure.

Redirection of Patronage

In the thirty years following the Ludi Saeculares, Rome basked in the benefits of a healthy economy and relative peace. Nevertheless, the number of new public projects declined. It was a time of consolidation. Urban undertakings were in response to disasters, not programmatic decisions. Thus, interventions in the Forum Romanum and on the Aventine Hill resulted from fires (fig. 84; Table 2).[102] Augustus himself focused on completing major projects long in progress. Other patrons followed suit, not only in emulation, but because the *princeps* restricted, or even negated, the patronage of public monuments.

The Ludi Saeculares signaled the beginning of a new, decidedly Augustan age. For this message to be clear and forceful in the cityscape, the *princeps* could no longer allow the patronage of public buildings in the capital to go undirected. This reality became painfully evident in 13 B.C. L. Cornelius Balbus returned to Rome from campaigns abroad and dedicated the theater commemorating his triumph of six years earlier. Great fanfare surrounded the event even though a flood in the Campus Martius made passage to the theater possible only by boat. The opulent new theater won rave reviews. Rome's residents marveled over four columns of precious onyx as well as the adjoining enclosed portico with a covered walkway.[103] In appreciation, the Senate allowed Balbus the privilege of the first vote. Flush with his architectural success, Balbus put on airs at the dedication ceremonies. Among other distinctions, he claimed to be the first person of foreign birth to be awarded a triumph and brazenly claimed that Augustus' imminent return from the Germany, Gaul, and Spain was due to his own efforts.[104]

Balbus' arrogance did not go unnoticed. His hubris at the dedication of a major public building once again underscored the power citizens associated with architectural patronage in Rome. Augustus responded in kind. Soon after his return to the capital, he dedicated his own theater to Marcellus, complete with four remarkable marble columns (Asc.*Scaur*.45; Dio-Cass.54.26). More importantly, the *princeps* apparently began to restrict the awarding of triumphs. In the 20s B.C., Augustus declined to celebrate two triumphs and, along with Agrippa, continued to do so in the following decades (Table 1). In the twenty years before his death only two triumphs were celebrated, both by his stepson Tiberius. In addition, Augustus restricted the patronage of gladiatorial shows and other military honors such as the awarding of the *spolia opima* (DioCass.51.24; 54.2, 17). Through these actions, he limited the number of patrons with control over *manubiae* and the accompanying traditional charge to erect monuments in Rome.

Augustus minimized his authoritative stance in the present, while applying it to past achievements. Tacitus was impressed that in the Augustan principate:

Public munificence was a custom still; nor had Augustus debarred a Taurus, a Philippus, or a Balbus from devoting the trophies of his arms or the overflow of his wealth to the greater splendor of the capital and the glory of posterity. (*Ann*.3.72; cf. Suet.*Aug*.29)

Writing in the late first century A.D. when public building in Rome was indeed restricted by the emperor, Tacitus assumed Augustus could have limited building patronage by others. In reality, the building donors in this list were all active in the 30s B.C., a time when Octavian lacked the power base to impose such restrictions. Nevertheless, he probably had some impact on their patronage as all three men mentioned were his intimates. Once he assumed virtual control over the State, the *princeps* laid claim retroactively to a wide range of projects, and to the free choice allegedly open to other patrons.

By the end of the millennium, Augustus assumed responsibility for virtually all public monuments in the capital. For example, in conjunction with the Saecular Games, Dio Cassius tells us, "[the *princeps*] commanded those who celebrated triumphs to erect out of their spoils some monument to commemorate their deeds" (54.18). In a later passage, the historian adds, "[Augustus] permitted these others to erect them [new buildings], constantly having an eye to the public good, but grudging no one the private fame attaching to these services" (56.40; cf. Vell.Pat.2.89; Suet.*Aug*.29). The architectural achievements of private patrons, however, now reflected upon the *princeps*. In 2 B.C., Augustus decreed that new triumphators should erect statues of themselves in the Forum Augustum (DioCass.55.10). The placement of these sculptures within a decidedly Augustan context implied that the triumphators' achievements were sanctioned by, if not due to, the *princeps*.

Paternal Posturing

Augustus needed an appropriate role to justify his dominance over architectural patronage in Rome. He referenced an authority figure familiar to everyone – the family head. In Roman households, the *paterfamilias* ruled supreme. As head of the extended family, he acted for the best interests of all members, often without their consultation. The *paterfamilias* cared for close relatives and properties, and especially for his own *domus* as a physical reflection of the family's status and wealth. Similarly, Augustus acted in the best interests of all Romans. By 17 B.C., he had established his benevolent caretakership of the Roman people, having provided them with peace, money, and grain (*ResG*.15). His treatment of Rome can be equated with that of a *paterfamilias* to his *domus*; in form and content, the city had to reflect the stature of the residents and their "father."

By 17 B.C., the numerous Augustan projects in Rome stood as impressive evidence of the *princeps'* paternal benevolence. The first citizen took steps to further underscore identification with the father by encouraging worship of his *genius*. The Roman *genius* was the spirit or inborn power attendant on each man; that of a *paterfamilias* was equated with the life-force of the entire family or clan under his guardianship. Each family worshiped the *genius* of the *paterfamilias* in the *lararium*, a shrine in the open atrium court of the *domus* also associated with veneration of the *lares*, tutelary gods identified with the spirits of deceased ancestors.[105] In 30 B.C., the Senate decreed that the *genius* of Augustus be included in prayers on behalf of the people and Senate of Rome, as well as in libations at banquets (DioCass.51.19.7; Hor.*Odes* 4.5.31–38). Soon after the Ludi Saeculares Augustus ensured his *genius* was evident throughout the capital. Once he became high priest or Pontifex Maximus in 12 B.C., Augustus tied the *lares* of his family with the shrines of the Lares Compitales.[106]

The Romans considered every crossroad, or *compitum,* to be charged with energy and spirits. At each urban intersection, they erected shrines dedicated to both the protective spirits known as *lares* and to Liber Pater, a deity identified with the male life-force. In the late Republic, these shrines languished after Julius Caesar abolished the related festival of the Compitalia as too incendiary (Suet.*Caes*.42). Augustus, in contrast, revived the festival and restored the shrines. Beyond simple piety, these gestures were part of a greater scheme.[107] The *princeps* not only repopulated the sacred sites with the Lares Augusti, he supplanted Liber Pater with the Genius Augusti, thereby equating his own life-force with that of the State and entire populace. The paternal references were obvious. Where members of an extended family honored the eldest male and family ancestors at their private *lararia,* Rome's residents now venerated their collective father, Augustus, and his ancestors at the shrines of the Lares Compitales found at every street corner. Ovid wrote, "In the city there are a thousand *lares,* and the *genius* of the chief, who handed them over to the public; the wards [*vici*] worship three divinities" (Ov.*Fasti* 5.145–6; fig. 55). The *princeps* further revitalized the shrines of the Lares Compitales by orchestrating seasonal embellishments. Suetonius records that in 8 B.C., "[Augustus] provided that the Lares Compitales should be crowned twice a year, with spring and summer flowers."[108]

With his presence permeating the city, Augustus logically drew comparison with Romulus. Ovid provides a persuasive description of Augustus' expanded paternal role and calls upon Romulus to yield his position as "Father of the World" or *pater orbis* (Ov.*Fasti* 2.129–44). The *princeps* himself promoted further linkage with Rome's founding father. Earlier he had lavished attention on the Lupercal precinct marking where Romulus was suckled by the she-wolf (*ResG*.19). He selected a residence atop the Palatine in part because this hill was strongly associated with Romulus. In 16 B.C., he restored the Temple of Quirinus, Romulus' divine persona, adding a portico with seventy-six columns. With hindsight, ancient authors saw the portico's form as prescient; seventy-six was the exact age of Augustus at his death, a divine affirmation of the interconnectedness between the two fathers of Rome (DioCass.54.19.4). Throughout, however, the *princeps* carefully kept his identification with Romulus loose, considering the monarchical background of Rome's founder an enduring liability.

Figure 55. Altar of the Lares Compitales depicting Augustus handing two statuettes of Lares to the *ministri compitum*. Photo: DAIR 1511.

Upon becoming Pontifex Maximus, religious dictates called for Augustus to move into the Domus Publica, a public residence in the Forum Romanum. Instead, he gave the Domus Publica to the Vestal Virgins and transferred priestly activities to his own residence on the Palatine.[109] To satisfy the requirements of his religious office, he made part of his holdings public property; on this land, the *princeps* erected an altar and shrine to Vesta, the spirit of both the communal and individual hearths. This action repeats his earlier strategy of donating a portion of his Palatine property to Apollo. Though he lessened his own private holdings on the hilltop, Augustus greatly increased his own stature. Looking at the Palatine complex, Ovid avowed, "A single *domus* holds three eternal gods."[110] As the main resident, Augustus conceptually occupied the premier domestic position of *paterfamilias*.

Every Roman house had a display of venerated ancestors in the colonnaded court of the atrium. The house on the Palatine or one of the adjacent shrines would seem logical places for Augustus as *paterfamilias* of the State to display representations of his own and Rome's ancestors. Such a *locus*, however, could generate negative associations with monarchy and the palaces of eastern kings. Augustus did set up a State display of ancestors, but in a nonresidential context. Suetonius succinctly explains that Augustus first demonstrated respect for the gods by rebuilding temples; he next, "honored the memory of the leaders who had raised the estate of the Roman people from obscurity to greatness" (*Aug*.31). Statues commemorating early heroes, politicians, kings, and other revered figures had always stood in Rome. During the Republic, the most concentrated display was on the crowded Area Capitolina before the Temple of Jupiter Optimus Maximus. Like the death masks and statues of revered ancestors in the atrium of a private home, these representations served as models to be venerated and emulated. With calculation, the *princeps* moved the sculptures from the Capitoline to the expansive Campus Martius where they probably adorned the various new Augustan projects (Suet.*Calig*.34; cf. Val.Max. 8.15).

In the center of the city, Augustus established a new, highly ordered exhibition of illustrious figures at the Forum Augustum.[111] This impressive new complex had as its focal point a temple dedicated to Mars, himself the father of Romulus and Remus. In the flanking exedras were displayed sculptures of seminal figures in the history of Rome. Niches in the south exedra held representations of Romulus and other great men from Rome's past, the *summi viri*; in the north exedra, stood statues of Augustus' own ancestors all the way back to Aeneas (figs. 51 and 96). Under each statue, an inscribed plaque listed the most significant achievements of the famous man depicted. While the curving arrangement of the sculpture recalled Greek formal analogues, the display more immediately read as an enlargement of the curved niches for sculpture in Roman homes. This effect was enhanced by the columnar screen in front of the exedras that mimicked the colonnades in residential peristyles.[112] The sculpted *summi viri* stood both as silent models of excellence encouraging emulation, and stern judges of all action, just as ancestral effigies in a *domus* atrium inspired family members and impressed clients awaiting audience. Programmed activities in the Forum Augustum interfaced directly with the elaborate sculptural program. Under the everwatchful gaze of the sculpted figures, citizens selected jurors by lot and conducted court cases, generals started out for commands abroad, the Senate discussed the granting of triumphs, victors dedicated triumphal crowns, scepters, captured military standards, and bronze statues of themselves, and foreigners negotiated.[113] In effect, the opulent Forum Augustum assumed

Figure 56. Relief believed to depict the statue group from the Temple of Mars Ultor with Venus Genetrix, Mars Ultor, and Divus Julius. Photo: Alinari/Art Resource, New York, 47176.

the position of atrium for the State, replete with representations of revered ancestors. The placement of these *summi viri* within a decidedly Augustan context implied that all the admirable figures represented – past and present – reflected glory from and to the *princeps*.

Strengthening the metaphorical link between the new forum and the *domus* atria of the *paterfamilias*, the great Forum Augustum became a center for the worship of the Lares and Genius Augusti.[114] Yearly, the Fratres Arvales, a priestly college restored by Augustus, met within the complex for elaborate ceremonies honoring both Mars, father of all Romans, and the spirits of the Augustan family.[115] In addition, the artistic program symbolically united the cults of Mars and the Genius Augusti. At the place of foremost honor within the temple stood statues of Mars Ultor along with Venus and Divus Julius, all divine ancestors of the *princeps* (fig. 56). Indeed, the very making of the Forum Augustum affirmed Augustus' concern with family responsibility since the temple avenged the murder of his stepfather

Julius Caesar. At the same time, the *princeps* demonstrated his duty to the entire State; contemporaries linked the Temple of Mars the Avenger to Caesar and to the return of the Parthian standards (Ov.*Fasti.* 5.580–90).

As much as the Ludi Saeculares, the Temple of Mars and surrounding complex celebrated the existence of a new age and Augustus as benevolent father. August 1, 2 B.C., all Rome participated in the festivities marking the dedication of the Mars temple and its surrounding complex, even though not all parts of the Forum Augustum were finished.[116] Splashy events occurred throughout the city. Water was brought to the Circus Flaminius for conflicts involving thirty-six crocodiles; at Augustus' order, workers dug a large artificial lake on the right bank measuring 1,800 by 1,200 feet for a huge mock naval battle between 3,000 men.[117] To cap the festivities, the Senate dedicated a sculpture of the *princeps* in a chariot at the center of the Forum Augustum. The inscription on the base read: "*pater patriae.*"[118]

The role of "Father of his Country" placed Augustus in an admired position of authority. The conceptualization of the city as his own *domus* justified every new project; simultaneously, it likewise could explain a benevolent nonintervention. In the last thirty years of his life, Augustus erected few major projects in Rome, yet his paternal stamp grew ever stronger. At his death in A.D. 14, the city's residents thronged to the Mausoleum. Traditionally, the gardens surrounding Roman tombs usually were accessible only to family members; as father to every Roman Augustus had opened his funerary park to all (Suet.*Aug.*100).

Dynastic Imprinting

When proclaimed *pater patriae* in 2 B.C., the *princeps* was in his sixties. As a good father, Augustus made plans for the care of his "family" (i.e., all Romans) after his death. Like Caesar before him, he had no natural son. For decades, his efforts at identifying a successor foundered and threatened to tarnish the new golden age. Marcellus, his son-in-law, nephew, and designated heir, died in 23 B.C. Agrippa and Julia produced two sons whom Augustus groomed as his successors. The great celebrations announcing the new age in 17 B.C., also marked the *princeps'* adoption of Gaius, age 3, and the newborn Lucius (DioCass.54.18). Rome's residents breathed a sigh of relief; now a clear succession was guaranteed by not one, but two youths. If Augustus died before they grew to manhood, their natural father could serve as regent; after all, Augustus had indicated Agrippa as his successor years before when ill in 23 B.C. Unfortunately, these plans came to naught. Agrippa died in March, 12 B.C., and his first two sons early in the next century.

Significantly, in the 20s B.C., Augustus did not use architectural projects in Rome to announce either Agrippa or Marcellus as possible successors, at least not during their lifetimes. In the years immediately after the battle of Actium, any extraordinary urban display proclaiming a familial succession would have belied Augustus' projected image as "first among equals" and smacked of monarchy. Furthermore, Agrippa had already erected impressive structures in his own name, and the young Marcellus presumably had a long future lifetime in which to embellish Rome. After their deaths, Augustus could appropriately demonstrate his attachment. He dedicated the impressive theater in the Forum Holitorium to Marcellus following his demise; after the death of Agrippa, he completed his work on the gigantic Diribitorium and made it public property. Augustus placed the remains of his son-in-law in the Mausoleum of Augustus, even though Agrippa had constructed his own tomb in the Campus Martius (DioCass.54.28.5, 55.8). The gesture reflected his respect for Agrippa, but also eliminated the possibility of any future competition between the burial places of the natural and adoptive fathers of Gaius and Lucius, his future heirs.

In the late teens B.C., Augustus incorporated the Mausoleum into an impressive urban ensemble. South of the great tomb a jewellike structure was under construction. The Ara Pacis flanking the Via Flaminia commemorated Augustus' victorious return to Rome from Spain and Gaul in 13 B.C.; even more significant, it may have been associated with Augustus' assumption of the high priesthood after the death of Lepidus around the same year.[119] Begun in July of 13 B.C., it was dedicated in 9 B.C. Standing one mile from the pomerial line, the altar marked the point where a magistrate's power shifted from *imperium militiae* to *imperium domi*, that is, from the external, military sphere to the more peaceful internal, urban realm.[120] Not a large structure, the Ara Pacis was remarkable for its marble, elaborate carving, and iconography. An elevated sacrificial altar formed the core, surrounded by precinct walls. The exterior surfaces were covered in detailed reliefs. Those on the side facing the highway represented Roma and Tellus, personifying the Roman people and the bounties of peace. The relief panels on the west depicted scenes relating to the origins of Rome and the Julian line. The longer figural panels to the north and south showed the procession of Romans who presumably took part in ceremonies associated with the altar (fig. 97).[121] The visually rich monument thus tied the past, present, and future of Rome to the fortunes of Augustus and his family.

While the Ara Pacis was still under construction, the *princeps* added another commemorative directly to the west. Here in 10 B.C., he set up an imported obelisk in memory of his victory over Egypt twenty years earlier. The red granite shaft stood as the gnomon of a giant sundial set upon a huge travertine pavement divided with bronze inlays (fig. 108).[122] Each day, the sun god Apollo brought the Horologium Augusti to life. The sun cast an animated, directional shadow off the gnomon, pointing to different structures associated with the Augustan family: east to the Ara Pacis with its reliefs of family members; south to the Pantheon honoring all the gods, including the Divine Julius; and north to the Mausoleum Augusti, the final resting place of the Julii. On the autumnal equinox, the shadow reached its greatest extent, stretching all the way into the Ara Pacis; the day was September 23, birthday of Augustus. In toto, the buildings linked by the sundial proclaimed the benefits of peace and the divine approbation of Augustus and all the Julian clan (Table 3).[123]

Equating the peace and health of the State with Augustus and his family, Rome's residents gladly acknowledged the young Gaius and Lucius as anointed heirs. They openly cheered when the youths received magisterial offices and other honors, even though underage. Augustus made weak gestures toward Republican propriety; according to Suetonius, "he never recommended his sons for office without adding, 'If they be worthy of it'" (Suet.*Aug.*56). Given the numerous images and dedications to the youths that began to appear throughout the city, few could deny their worthiness. After fires decimated structures in the Forum Romanum, Augustus supplanted Caesarean associations with commemorations of his heirs. He reworked the Basilica Julia, dubbing it the Basilica of Gaius and Lucius, and likewise renamed the Porticus Julia in front of the Basilica Aemilia in honor of the two boys.[124] The two projects flanked the arches to Augustus and the Temple of Divus Julius. As a result, these additions transformed the Forum Romanum into another dynastic ensemble, with the divine father surrounded by memorials to his son and grandsons (fig. 57).[125]

The *paterfamilias* incorporated Gaius and Lucius into all his urban statements. The youths appeared with other family members on the Ara Pacis. Augustus featured his heirs at the dedication of the Temple of Mars Ultor. Though he himself dedicated the great structure, Dio Cassius tells us that Augustus, "granted to Gaius and Lucius once for all the right to consecrate all such buildings [in Rome] by virtue of a kind of consular authority" (55.10.6). In fact, the *princeps* may have hastened completion of the Forum Augustum in order to coincide with Lucius' assumption of the *toga virilis*, the ceremony marking the entry of a young Roman into manhood. After 2 B.C., all patrician males followed their example and donned the toga in the Augustan complex rather than the Forum Romanum.[126] In a fragmentary passage describing various activities in the Forum Augustum, Dio Cassius wrote, "[Augustus] himself and his grandsons should go there as often as

Table 3. The Family of Augustus

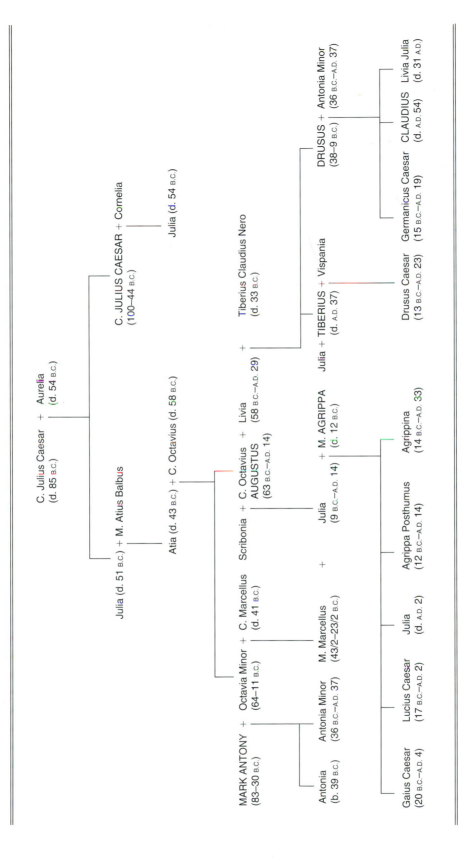

Figure 57. Reconstruction of the Temple of Divus Julius and flanking arches of Augustus. After Richter, *JDAI* 4 (1889): 157.

they wished" (DioCass.55.10.1). Although the exact meaning remains unclear, this sentence confirms the close affiliation of the *princeps* and his heirs with the new forum.

Augustus' well laid plans for his succession were not to be. Lucius died in B.C. 2, his elder brother Gaius two years later. Both were placed in the Mausoleum Augustum. Bereaved, their adoptive father replaced the large Naumachia Augusti on the right bank with a grove, the Nemus Caesarum, to honor the two youths. Augustus was left with a reluctant last choice for a successor: his stepson Tiberius, 46 years of age.[127] No major building projects or dedications in the capital celebrated the adoption. When rebuilding the Basilica Julia after a fire in A.D. 12, the aged *princeps* ordered his relatives, not Tiberius specifically, to continue the project if he should die while it was still underway (*ResG*.20).

Tiberius himself had shown little interest in the city. Like Mark Antony, he did not capitalize upon architectural patronage in Rome as a means of self-promotion. Tiberius' foremost undertaking occurred in conjunction with his German triumph in 7 B.C.: the rebuilding of the Temple of Concordia in the Forum Romanum. The same year, he also dedicated two projects honoring his mother: the Macellum Liviae (a large market on the Esquiline) and the Porticus Liviae.[128] Within the porticus, Livia herself dedicated another shrine to Concordia, perhaps hoping the deity of harmony would resolve the conflicts between her husband and son.[129] Shortly after his adoption in A.D. 4, Tiberius began to reconstruct the temple to the brothers Castor and Pollux in the Forum Romanum. On completion, he eliminated the name of the original donor and instead inscribed that of his own, highly popular sibling Drusus who had been killed in 9 B.C. In the dedication, Tiberius pointedly referred to himself as "Claudianus" to stress his recent adoption by Augustus. As a fraternal gesture, he also included Drusus' name on the Forum Temple of Concordia completed in A.D. 10.[130]

With increasing age and the death of successive heirs, Augustus became preoccupied with the endurance of his achievements. Over the years, he had redefined the urban image of Rome. In this phase, he did not need further to enhance the city's appearance. Rome was accepted as a great metropolis. Rather, the *princeps* refined the city's urban image. Fueled by the citizens' forceful longing for stability as well as his own search for immortality, he imprinted the cityscape with dynastic imagery. Existing and new monuments now created ensembles celebrating the history and future of his family. By the death of Augustus in A.D. 14, the city on the Tiber was not solely the Roman capital, it was equally the Augustan capital.

Maintaining the Augustan Urban Image

An interest in the endurance of the Augustan family line paralleled a simultaneous concern with the endurance of the Augustan city. Having transformed Republican Rome, the *princeps* knew well that an urban image is forged by more than buildings in their pristine condition at the singular moment of dedication. Because individual structures mature and age, they change in appearance and impact over time. Furthermore, individual buildings and ensembles do not stand alone; they are irrevocably tied to the symbiotic networks making up the urban infrastructure. Equally important, the memory of a city is shaped as much by the overall ambience as by the physical form; fear and insecurity can damage a city as much as a flood. After spending decades shaping an Augustan urban image, the *princeps* took steps to maintain its integrity.

During the Republic, citizens only grudgingly undertook pragmatic municipal projects and related administrative responsibilities. In the final phase of his life, Augustus emphasized issues of urban care even more than new construction. An oft-cited quotation tells how he made material changes in the cityscape to improve the image of Rome. Seen in full, the passage affirms an equal interest in the functionality and health of Rome:

Since the city was not adorned as the dignity of the empire demanded, and was exposed to flood and fire, he so beautified it that he could justly boast that he had found it built of brick and left it built in marble. He made it safe too for the future, so far as human foresight could provide for this.[131]

Augustus first dealt with urban maintenance during the 20s B.C. Notably, specific events and needs generated these early reforms. In the period following the Ludi Saeculares of 17 B.C., he expanded upon these initial forays and began to establish what would become a permanent municipal bureaucracy.

To improve Rome's great infrastructure, Augustus continued to develop curatorships. Having himself taken on the *cura viarum* in the 20s B.C., he oversaw the repair and construction of the capital's great transportation routes. Actual construction on the roads was overseen by subordinate curators appointed from among the numerous expraetors in the capital.[132] To elevate their status, the *princeps* awarded the *curatores viarum* the distinction of accompanying lictors, attendants usually assigned to magistrates. The new system apparently worked well; in 13 B.C., the *princeps* eliminated the subordinate office of *duumvirs* responsible for roads outside the city limits.[133]

The next year marked the death of Agrippa. As *curator aquarum* for life, he had developed expertise in municipal hydraulics and executed long-term projects using a team of 240 highly trained slaves. Agrippa bequeathed this force to Augustus, yet the *princeps* had neither the time nor inclination to assume the *cura aquarum* himself. Probably at his urging, the Senate in 11 B.C. passed resolutions to create a second curatorial board, the *curatelae aquarum*. This board had three members directed by a *curator aquarum* appointed for life.[134] To complete their charge, Augustus gave the board responsibility for the trained slave force. The Senate and consuls outlined the specific duties, jurisdictions, and basic policies of the board in a series of *consulta* passed in the next few years.[135]

Despite the active participation of the consuls, Senate, and people in the definition of the new water board, Augustus was clearly in control. He selected the board members and nominated the curator in charge; the Senate merely approved appointments. Similarly, though the Senate allotted the curators' working funds, the *princeps* himself continued to finance and take credit for select hydraulics projects in the capital. He maintained tight, personal control over water distribution and shrewdly passed an edict making the entire water supply of Rome dependent upon his own grants (Frontin.99, 108; *ResG*.20). The *princeps* in part masked the curators' lack of real power over the water system by the busy work of the bureaucratic office and, as with the *curatores viarum,* by the trappings of import. Frontinus explained that the *curatores aquarum:*

were allowed to wear regalia as though magistrates . . . [and] when they go outside the City in the discharge of their duties, [they] shall have two lictors, three public servants, and an architect for each of them.[136]

Two other curatorships dealing with Rome's physical form had their genesis in the late Augustan period. Suetonius mentions care of both public buildings and the channel of the Tiber in a list of new offices (*nova officia*) established by the *princeps*. Because no evidence indicates the creation of permanent curatorships, Augustus may have personally assumed these *curae* as he had done for the *cura viarum*. With his many projects in Rome, Augustus certainly fulfilled the responsibility for public works and places, though the first permanent curator charged with this duty held office under his successor.[137] The second curatorship dealt with the riverbed. Despite the earlier cleaning of the Tiber, floods repeatedly hit Rome during this late phase (Table 2). In 7 B.C., the *princeps* reworked the river banks and delineated a public flood zone. The actual board responsible for care of the river, the *curatelae alvei Tiberis* with five senatorial curators, likewise dates to the reign of Tiberius.[138]

The Augustan *curatelae* established an official and enduring bureaucracy. Each curatorial board had clearly defined tasks, adequate state funding, and a trained, permanent staff drawn from different classes. Curators held their posts for long periods, allowing them to develop expertise in their areas of responsibility, document their activities, and develop pride in their achievements. The compilation of comprehensive records for urban maintenance also stimulated pride in the office, not just in the individual. This shift in attention caused fissures in the Republican association of public works with specific patrons. Appointed by Augustus and acting as boards, the curators found their efforts enhanced the fame of Rome, or rather that of the *princeps,* instead of their own individual status.

In 8 B.C., the Senate once more renewed Augustus' *imperium,* or supreme power, for ten years.[139] Soon after, he reassessed the municipal situation; he ordered a census be taken ward by ward, and used the findings to evaluate property holdings throughout Rome and the Empire. Where the State claim over land was in dispute, he granted private citizens ownership; when necessary, Augustus restored private land to public use (*ResG*.8.3; Suet.*Aug*.32). In addition, he used the census data to support a reapportionment of Rome.

According to Republican tradition, the early king Servius Tullius (578–535 B.C.) was the first to divide Rome into regions. He identified four zones, each linked with a hilltop tribal group (fig. 58).[140] Magistrates selected by lot held responsibility for the care of each. From the beginning, the *Regiones Quattuor* did not offer comprehensive municipal coverage. The Capitoline hill stood apart as communal religious property; the Aven-

Figure 58. Four Severan Regions of Rome. Drawing: Rodica Reif.

tine hill lay outside the *pomerium* and was thus likewise beyond the jurisdiction of the four regions. Over the centuries, the city expanded far beyond
the limits of the Servian municipal apportionment, and beyond the jurisdiction of the magistrates responsible for urban care.[141] To incorporate these
omissions and provide an effective framework for municipal administration,
Augustus created fourteen new regions in 7 B.C. (fig. 59). Determination of
the regions' layout must have been based on Rome's preexisting local wards
or *vici,* numbering approximately 265.[142] Small markers, or *cippi,* defined
the fourteen Augustan regions. The number of new regions was significant.

Figure 59. XIV Augustan Regions of Rome. Drawing: Rodica Reif.

The city had long been associated with seven hills as evident from the early epithet, *Septimontium*.[143] Under the first emperor, the city of seven hills became the city of fourteen regions, *Urbs XIV Regionum*. Though never stated in antiquity, the implication is that the *princeps* doubled the size and import of the city. Seven of the new regions lay within Rome's *pomerium* and seven outside.[144]

The fourteen Augustan regions greatly improved urban administration by establishing a comprehensive and hierarchical system for urban care. Hoping to avoid favoritism, Augustus kept management under magistrates chosen by lot from among the aediles, tribunes, and praetors.[145] These higher magistrates relied on the nonelected supervisors of the individual wards to screen and refer problems. Residents in each ward nominated four *vicomagistri,* generally chosen from among resident freedmen, the *liberti.* Higher, elected officials selected the actual office holders who then served for one year.[146] Living in their respective wards, the *vicomagistri* were well-situated to assist the magistrates assigned by lot, especially since Augustus had enhanced their status in the late teens by making the *vicomagistri* responsible for the shrines honoring the Lares Compitales and his own *genius.*

In 7 B.C., Augustus further empowered the *vicomagistri* by placing them in charge of fire fighting and street maintenance.[147] Unlike the curule aediles, who previously held these responsibilities, the ward supervisors were intimately familiar with their urban districts and personally involved. Along with the added tasks, Augustus gave the *vicomagistri* visible status in the city; he allowed them to don magisterial accoutrement and be attended by lictors in their own wards on certain days (fig. 93) (DioCass.55.8). Garbed in official dress and accountable to the magistrates of the XIV Augustan regions, the ward supervisors had clear responsibilities and stature.

Unfortunately, even the hundreds of local *vicomagistri* could not handle the great conflagrations of Rome. Although given the trappings of power, the plebeian *vicomagistri* in reality lacked the clout to instigate the drastic actions necessary during a major urban fire. Above them on the chain of responsibility stood the magistrates assigned by lot to each region. Being of various ranks, these men did not necessarily work together comfortably. Furthermore, the *vici* were too numerous to organize effectively and, most obvious of all, the crew of 600 trained slaves was far too small to combat fires in the enormous capital.

In A.D. 3, a blaze consumed Augustus' own dwelling on the Palatine. After another fire three years later, the *princeps* took action. He created a new company of watchmen to fight fires and keep order at night, the *cohortes vigilum,* organized in seven divisions of 1000 freedmen, each responsible for two of the fourteen regions.[148] A tribune led each division, with an equestrian *praefectus vigilum* selected by Augustus directing the entire force. In line with their paramilitary status, the prefect and his charges donned military garb.[149] Although the *princeps* meant for the *vigiles nocturni* to serve only during the crisis of A.D. 6, they proved so useful, they became a permanent fixture in the capital. Through the long hours of the night, they patrolled the streets of Rome.[150] In addition to combatting fires, the *vigiles* supervised civilian actions, checking to be sure the residents of apartments on upper floors kept a supply of water readily available and beating those who neglected their residential fires.[151]

The arrangements of A.D. 6 gave Rome a permanent fire department with distinct social as well as functional advantages. The new offices involved citizens from different social groups. Usually, fire fighting fell to slaves, yet an armed contingent of 7,000 within the city would not be prudent. Because free-born citizens would not readily assume a task associated with slaves, Augustus turned to freedmen who both lacked such prejudice and were glad for the opportunity. Freedmen had few other options to enter civil service. Barred from the military, they must have been attracted to the civil responsibilities (and salary) of the *cohortes vigilum*.[152] For leadership roles, Augustus tapped members of the equestrian class. Like the freedmen, the *equites* were pleased to hold the new municipal offices. The position of *praefectus vigilum* gave them power and high visibility in the city.[153]

In fact, Suetonius notes that the *princeps* devised new offices specifically, "to enable more men to take part in the administration of the State" (*Aug.*37). The more men involved, the more they would care about the appearance of Rome, and the less time they would have for undesirable activities. Augustus systematically reshaped Republican extraordinary, temporary offices into a permanent municipal bureaucracy outside the *cursus honorum*. To limit the onus of mundane urban chores, he divided responsibilities among different office holders and appeased them with the trappings of power. Perhaps most significantly, he placed ongoing urban concerns in the hands of appointed, not elected, officials and himself made the most important appointments. By providing all groups with a role in urban maintenance, Augustus stabilized his broad power base and created the appearance of a well-ordered society with everyone having a place and a responsibility in the great city.

Improvements in municipal services promoted the health and beauty of Augustan Rome. Public buildings sparkled in the glow of continued care. Residents passed easily along clean and repaired streets; water flowed freely to fountains and irrigated urban landscaping. The new fire-fighting system did not end conflagrations, but limited their extent and eased the minds of all city dwellers. Municipal administrators in the magisterial trappings of office walked through Rome, visible signs of the new order. Though only subtly marked, the XIV Regions represented a comprehensive system. Being tied to the physical site and integrated with the neighborhood wards, the regions grounded all residents and helped them locate their place within the city and society.[154] Together, the revamped municipal administration, Rome's improved overall appearance, and the overt evidence of municipal officials at work all strengthened the belief that Rome and the benefits bestowed by Augustus would endure.

By assuming the *cura urbis*, the responsibility for care of the city, the *princeps* caused the infrastructure of Rome to be viewed in a new light. Previously, pragmatic tasks had provided little fame or stature and were downplayed by ancient authors. In contrast, writers from the Augustan Age celebrated the skill involved in creating and running the pragmatic networks of a large metropolis. Strabo wrote, "The Romans had the best foresight in those matters which the Greeks made but little account of, such as the construction of roads and aqueducts, and of sewers that could wash out the filth of the city into the Tiber" (5.3.8). Contemporaries now equated engineering and management skill, as much as beautiful buildings, with the greatness of a city and boasted that the Romans excelled at both. Strabo in fact continues:

[T]he early Romans made but little account of the beauty of Rome, because they were occupied with other, greater and more necessary, matters; whereas the later Romans, and particularly those of today and in my time, have not fallen short in this respect either – indeed they have filled the city with many beautiful structures.

By A.D 14, Rome stood as a capital city remarkable for her appearance and fitness. In the thirty years following the Ludi Saeculares, the city on the Tiber did not change radically in form. Rather, this phase can be characterized as one of consolidation, completion, and clarification. Residential districts retained their convoluted Republican layouts, yet materially and visually reflected the benefits of a thriving economy and comprehensive urban administration. Splendid public environments now rivaled those of other Mediterranean cities. New projects tended to be small, sparkling jewels embroidered onto an already luxurious urban fabric; each one affirmed the constancy and benevolence of Augustus. The completion of large projects planned years before imparted a sense of endurance and permanence. The paucity of new, large-scale interventions is easily explained. On a functional level, Rome already had ample impressive public works. Furthermore, with patronage effectively restricted to one family, there was no competition to stimulate architectural production. The *pater patriae* directed his efforts toward clarifying and securing the vision of a new golden age, one firmly tied to Augustus and his heirs. The bustle of construction that characterized the dynamism of the previous phase was now replaced by a sense of contentment, fulfillment, and stability.

EVALUATION

In the teens, Augustus compiled a list of his deeds accomplished known as the *Res Gestae*. At his death, the document was engraved on bronze tablets and placed before the entrance to the Mausoleum for all to see.[155] Along with military conquests, offices held, and honors received, the *princeps*

Figure 60. Diagram, three phases of Augustan building in Rome.

proudly included his building projects in Rome. Shaping the urban image of Rome was a highly political and memorable act. The Roman bond between meaning and places, and between public buildings and patrons inspired Augustus. He continuously used the built fabric of the city to convey policy. Because his goals and audience both changed over time, so did Rome's urban image. The three phases identified reflect the periodic coalescing of an urban image; just as forcefully, they attest to its constantly changing nature in response to the evolving Augustan context (fig. 60).

The disjointed image of Rome in the first phase reflects the lack of concentrated power; Octavian had not the position, financing, nor leisure to imprint a uniform message. Reflecting the political fragmentation of the day, the urban image was an agglomeration of all the individual projects in the city. In the next decade, the *princeps* restored the Republic and elevated Rome to a world capital. He embellished the entire cityscape, programming it with the same care a triumphator would give to a self-promoting manubial structure. Emboldened by his acceptance and acclamation, Augustus inaugurated a golden age in 17 B.C. He devoted the last thirty years of his life to the meticulous clarification and empowerment of an urban image directly tied to his own achievements, aspirations, and memory.

Acknowledging the Roman belief in the *genii locorum*, Augustus drew strength from association with admired locales. Through tangency, he demonstrated respect and connection. Thus, the Forum Augustum rose next to the Forum Julium and Forum Romanum. Once established, the new Augustan facilities often grew in stature until they overshadowed the Republican powers of place. Such displacement was gradual. The *princeps'* greatest advantage was time for reeducation and adjustment. Once his audience accepted one postulate, it was not as difficult to accept the next and the next, until the people of Rome found themselves embracing positions far removed from those of the Republic. Thus, over the years, Augustus transformed himself from the humble heir of Julius Caesar, to an independent building patron, to the beneficent *pater patriae* responsible for the grandeur of the entire city. As a result, by A.D. 14, the city on the Tiber displayed strong imageability. Composed of all the conceptual images formed by individual observers, and of all their various manifestations over time, this image was not singular. It evolved along with the overall Augustan program, and thus reflected different priorities at different times. And yet at the death of the *princeps,* Rome's urban image was cohesive. By associating everything positive about the city with himself, Augustus compelled all observers, from antiquity to the present, to take an interest.

CHAPTER FIVE

STRUCTURE
BUILDING
AN URBAN IMAGE

> I found Rome of clay; I leave it to you of marble.
>
> Dio Cassius 56.30

During the late first century B.C., the Greek geographer Strabo recorded the lands and cities throughout the eastern and central Mediterranean. Having visited Rome in 44–35, ca. 31, and 7 B.C., he was well familiar with the programmatic shifts that had directed urban patronage in the Augustan Age. His description of the city focuses on the tangible results:

> On passing to the old Forum, you saw one forum after another ranged along the old one, and basilicas, and temples, and saw also the Capitolium and the works of art there and those of the Palatine Hill and Livia's Portico, you would easily become oblivious to everything else outside. Such is Rome.[1]

The passage recalls the descriptions of architectural environments used by rhetoricians as mnemonic devices. The individual urban elements stand distinct, each serving as a content laden *imago*. All are interrelated. The ordering of the text implies that the Forum Romanum gains in stature by tangency to the new fora of Caesar and Augustus. Specially cited are basilicas within the old forum; the two magnificent structures both owe their grandeur to the generosity of Augustus. Too numerous to name, temples abound in the city, visible proof of the *princeps'* piety. That to Jupiter Optimus Maximus on the Capitoline is especially memorable, as much for its recent restoration as for its artwork, including a statue by Myron consecrated by Augustus. Impressive displays of art embellish the new Augustan complex dedicated to Apollo atop the Palatine; on the Esquiline, plantings enhance the large portico named after the wife of Augustus. Though seen individually, these urban *imagines* describe a primary story line: Rome is a city without compare due to the paternal efforts of Augustus.

The physical form of a city is the primary means of conveying an urban image. Augustus built dozens of projects in Rome. Observers saw these tangible architectural products first; they understood the motives for construction and iconography second. Strabo's passage affirms the familiarity of the components used by the *princeps* to shape an urban image: temples, basilicas, fora. All had established Republican acceptance. The memorability of these and other structures derived from the architects' interpretation of basic forms. In addition to subtle formal alterations to traditional building types and groupings, designers of the Augustan Age made notable changes in scale, materials, and ornament. In contrast to structures from the Republican period, those erected under Augustus transcended their individual context and content. Through careful orchestration, individual projects became recognizable as serving larger urban imperatives. The clear articulation of landmarks, nodes, paths, districts, and edges – the five urban forms isolated by Kevin Lynch – enhanced the reading of the city as a whole, creating a highly memorable urban image.

URBAN COMPONENTS AND CHARACTERISTICS

The manipulation of an extant, occupied cityscape is costly and difficult. From a strictly pragmatic side, the redirection of an urban image requires a significant number of interventions before the change becomes legible. At the same time, the city has to continue to function. The directed alterations cannot be too disruptive either in practical terms or conceptually. Julius Caesar had demonstrated the inappropriateness of Haussmannization in Rome of the late first century B.C.; citizens viewed his proposed large-scale alterations as autocratic (fig. 41).[2] Championing a return to an imagined Republican past of harmony and stability, the *princeps* avoided despotic interventions. In contrast to the excessively hybrid forms generated by the building frenzy of competitive generals and politicians in the mid-first century B.C., Augustus gave Rome sedate, conservative architecture suffused with a "cool propriety."[3] As in the political realm, he redefined the city's physical appearance gradually, from the inside out. In form, each Augustan project was immediately recognizable and justifiable within the context of late Republican architectural types. Alterations were nonthreatening, appearing either logical or inconsequential. The cumulative impact, however, was significant. Through sheer number and repetition, the subtle transformations left an enduring imprint upon the minds of all observers.

Building Forms and Types

A Roman man of substance and standing was expected to make his physical environment appropriately reflect his stature. As first man of Rome, Augustus perceived the entire city as his residence, and set about improving its appearance. His primary tool was the independent building. The *princeps* chose structures to reenforce his various programs. He confirmed the restoration of the Republic by selecting building forms and programs sanctioned by time. He affirmed his piety by strictly following religious proscriptions regarding temple restorations. In general, Augustus avoided typological innovations, even when new needs and new technologies appeared. For example, the development of an extensive bureaucracy during his lifetime was not acknowledged by new construction; imperial officials operated from residential structures surrounding his house on the Palatine.[4] Similarly, though techniques for building in concrete improved, they did not result in formal experimentation.

The architects of the Augustan Age were fortunate to live at a time when work was plentiful. The boom in building itself, however, limited typological experimentation. After the burst of new construction under Sulla earlier in the first century B.C., the intensity of building in Rome had declined for almost a generation. Thus, when a major building program was instigated under Augustus, architects responded with conservative, familiar designs. The sheer number of Augustan projects simultaneously underway also promoted conservatism. In a single year, the *princeps* boasted he restored eighty-two temples, a work load that left little opportunity for typological innovation. Temporal deadlines provided further restraints. Certain key works had to be put into service for specific events. Construction on the Theater of Marcellus was rushed to accommodate the activities of the Ludi Saeculares in 17 B.C.; the structure was not formally dedicated until over five years later. When builders could not complete the Temple of Mars Ultor by 2 B.C. to coincide with the coming of age festivities for Lucius, grandson and adopted heir of Augustus, the structure was dedicated anyway.

The density of building in Rome was also restrictive. In the first century B.C., architects in Italy achieved their most impressive results with dramatic hillside siting such as the sanctuary of Fortuna cascading down the slopes of Praeneste and that of Hercules atop a grand hillside platform at Tibur.[5] Rome offered limited opportunities for such architectural statements. The city's impressive sloping sites had long been blanketed with structures, making terraced designs possible only if accompanied by large-scale demolition.

In the late 20s B.C., Vitruvius dedicated his treatise on architecture to Augustus. Often criticized as a paean to conservatism, the text aptly reflects the businesslike atmosphere of construction in Rome at the height of the Augustan Age. Hurrying to create a visible affirmation of the restored Republic, the *princeps* selected forms with strong traditional associations and comparative ease of execution for the local work force. *De Architectura*

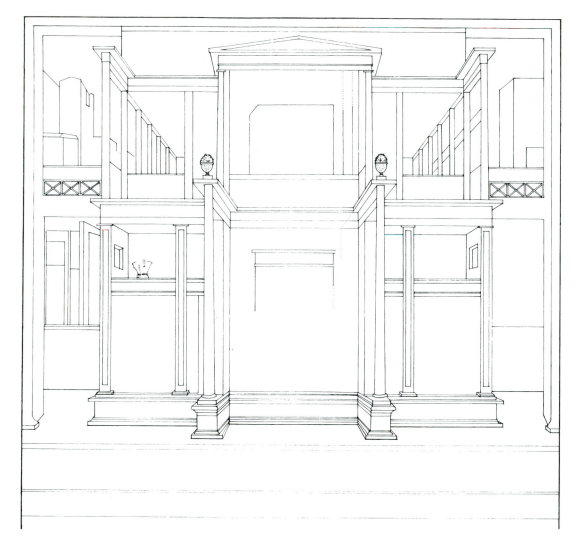

Figure 61. Drawing of architectural features shown on a wall painting from the Palatine House of Augustus. Drawing: Richard H. Abramson after Carettoni.

served as the handbook of the day.[6] Vitruvius adopted a straightforward, no nonsense approach, with lengthy descriptions of familiar building types, from temples and basilicas to fora.[7] He discussed neither theatrical hillside terracing nor the design potential of concrete.

Innovative architectural forms did appear in Augustan Rome, but not in three dimensions. Much to the chagrin of Vitruvius, contemporary wall paintings depicted fantasy architecture. Even the house of the *princeps* had colorful representations of unbuildable structures with impossibly thin column supports (fig. 61). Internal and private, these images did not directly shape the urban image, yet the potential for architectural influence existed.

Vitruvius directly linked such avant garde representations with the stature of a city. He tells the story of Apaturius at Tralles, who designed stage scenery with painted domes, porticos, and half pediments above the roof line. This showy display charmed observers, yet they were soon brought to their senses; the mathematician Licymnius came forth and declared, "If we approve in pictures what cannot justify itself in reality, we are added to those cities which, because of such faults, are esteemed slow-witted" (7.5.3). Cultivating an elevated image of Rome, Augustus allowed pictorial fantasies behind the closed doors of private homes; in the cityscape, he promoted calm reason and tradition.

Below the visible surface of the cityscape experimentation flourished. Architects explored the architectural potential of vaulting in the substructures of the theater to Marcellus and other structures, though these forms would not greatly affect Rome's appearance until the time of Nero.[8] Solid and comforting, trabeation and the external expression of the classical orders dominated the visual field. Within this vocabulary, great diversity was still possible. Architects in the first century B.C. drew upon an eclectic and varied repertoire of forms merging Greek and Latin traditions, a stylistic hybrid chauvinistically labeled by Vitruvius as the *consuetudo italica* or "Italic custom." Not only was the range of building types quite large, but within each category existed great formal variety.

Augustus set himself the difficult task of restoring all the religious structures of Rome. Formally, his options were many. In the third book of *De Architectura,* Vitruvius discusses six different configurations for the basic rectangular temple plan and explains how the permutations could multiply by varying column spacing. The *princeps* exploited them all. When restoring existing buildings, he maintained extant configurations. Thus, he preserved the original Greek peripteral layout when reworking the Temple of Quirinus. For new structures, however, he preferred Italic frontal layouts with either no rear columns (*sine postico*) or free-standing columns on the porch and engaged columns around the cella (pseudoperipteral).[9] Such frontal arrangements were best suited for sites within the tightly woven urban fabric of Rome where buildings rarely appeared as midspace objects. In the few instances where a new building could be viewed from all sides, Augustan architects selected pseudoperipteral plans that preserved a frontal emphasis, yet maintained the appearance of a surrounding portico.

The form of a Roman building, like style in sculpture, projected meaning easily read by urban observers.[10] Italic forms of course reaffirmed Augustus' restoration of the Republic. Significantly, the *princeps* chose a diastyle arrangement with widely spaced columns for his new Temple to Apollo on the Palatine.[11] Roman observers immediately read this rather retardataire config-

Figure 62. Archaizing relief depicting Nike, Apollo, Artemis, and Leto before a temple, perhaps that to Apollo on the Palatine Hill. Photo: Alinari/Art Resource, New York, # 22540; reconstruction drawing: Richard H. Abramson.

uration as a sympathetic interpretation of early buildings in Italy such as the Temple of Jupiter Optimus Maximus on the opposing Capitoline Hill. Even with an Italic form and terra-cotta ornament, the Apollo temple simultaneously conveyed Greek associations. A classicizing Augustan relief showing Leto with her children Apollo and Diana may represent this temple in the background. Seen obliquely, the porch columns give the illusion of a Greek peripteral plan, an appropriate association for Apollo (fig. 62).[12] This representation may convey the experience of the building, with its porticoed porch readily visible atop a towering podium on one of Rome's highest hills (fig. 63).

Despite the formal diversity exhibited in the first century B.C., temples were the most conservative of Roman building types. A strict canon of rites and restrictions protectively wrapped all Roman religious structures. In most cases, the sanctified plan, defined as the *templum,* could not be easily altered without special interdictions.[13] Presumably the Pontifex Maximus could approve such alterations, but Augustus did not become high priest until the late teens B.C. The sanctity of temple footprints left only the verti-

Figure 63. Model of Rome in the Age of Constantine showing the Palatine Temple of Apollo seen from the south; a portion of the Circus Maximus is visible at the lower right. Photo: Musei Capitolini after Zanker, *Images,* fig. 52.

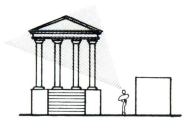

Figure 64. Diagram, urban viewing angles.

Figure 65. Relief from a Julio–Claudian altar depicting the Temple of Mars Ultor as background for a sacrifice. Among the sculptures in the pediment is a personification of the Palatine Hill in the left corner. Photo: Fototeca Unione AAR 4365.

cal dimension available for expansion. During the Augustan Age, both restorations and new temples rose to greater heights than their immediate antecedents.

The successive enlargement of buildings by competing patrons was a familiar progression in Republican Rome. Augustan architects, however, took extra pains to emphasize the vertical line of religious buildings. Formally, they enhanced the perception of height through the use of the Corinthian order and tall podia. Corinthian columns have a diameter-width-to-column-height ratio of approximately 10:1, their attenuated proportions accentuating the appearance of height. The major Augustan temples were, indeed, tall. The columns of the temple to Apollo Sosianus rose approximately 15 meters, those on the temple to Mars Ultor measured a staggering 17.7 meters.[14]

Within the crowded cityscape of Rome, observers generally viewed buildings from an acute angle. The resulting perceptual distortion accented building heights (fig. 64). The significance of the vertical emphasis is affirmed by

Figure 66. Large brass medal showing the Temple of Concordia in the Forum Romanum, ca. A.D. 11. Drawing: author.

secondary visual representations of Augustan temples. Though artists had the capability to show an undistorted elevation of a structure as if seen from an elevated angle of vision, they instead frequently attenuated buildings' proportions to maintain the same visual impact experienced by actual observers. For example, the Temple of Mars Ultor had fairly broad proportions, with eight columns across the façade (fig. 43). Nevertheless, a sculpted depiction shows the structure as tall and narrow (fig. 65). This representation is particularly interesting because the Mars temple, located at the end of the open Forum Augustum, was one of the few buildings in Rome that could be seen from sufficient distance to eliminate acute visual distortion.

Tall podia literally and conceptually added to the height of Augustan temples; most towered above their predecessors in Rome. Observers at ground level had to crane their necks upward even to see the column bases. Double podia elevated temple cellas even farther. By placing one podium atop another, Augustan architects increased the overall size of restored buildings without changing the original footprint. Similarly, vertical enhancement increased the perceived scale of new buildings without taking up increased urban space. Beyond simple vertical expansion, the experience of height derived from formal changes in the basic configuration of podia. For example, the Temple of Divus Julius was given stacked podia measuring a combined height of 6 meters.[15] In several instances, circumstances required temple stairs to be located at the sides, not the façade. With the Temple of Apollo Sosianus, a cramped site necessitated the design of a sheer podium façade with lateral stairs. Similarly, the need to preserve the altar honoring the location of Caesar's funeral pyre resulted in a niched podium wall across the front of the temple to Divus Julius, with stairs at the sides. Observers looking at these buildings faced sheer flat surfaces rising at right angles to the ground, rather than stairs receding at an angle.[16]

An obvious by-product of such developments was the acknowledgment of temple podia as important urban amenities. The sheer, frontal walls were ideal for ornamentation and advertisement. The podium supporting the Temple of Divus Julius displayed the ships beaks, or *rostra,* captured by Augustus at the battle of Actium. In addition, the highly visible, elevated podia were excellent speakers' platforms. Well situated in the Forum Romanum, the podia of the temples to Castor and Pollux, and to Divus Julius were regularly used for this purpose. In fact, the latter came to be called the *rostra aedis divi Iuli.*[17]

The shrine to Concordia restored by Tiberius in 7 B.C. did not require a high podium to dominate its surroundings. Located at the base of the slopes of the Capitoline hill, the structure looked down on the Forum Romanum. The site was proscribed by the sheer face of the hill to the rear and an important street to the front. As a result, the temple assumed an unusual configuration. The pronaos opened on the long, rather than the narrow, side of a rectangular plan (fig. 21).[18] The most remarkable features of this structure, however, were to be found in elevation. Representations on coins show unusually large windows flanking the pronaos. Like many other temples, that of Concordia Augusta contained great artworks and curiosities and was, in effect, a museum. Included among its treasures were four obsidian elephants dedicated by Augustus.[19] The large windows allowed pedestrians on the Clivus Capitolinus to see objects displayed on the interior (fig. 66).

Augustan architects consistently emphasized the façades of temples in Rome. Shrines in the Italic world had long focused on the front elevation, with less concern for lateral, rear, or oblique views. Vitruvius gives the ideal temple orientation as having the cella facing to the west in order to enhance the experience of devotees who face the structure and rising sun. He then advises architects that if this orientation was not possible the building should be placed

so that the widest possible view of the city may be had from the sanctuaries of the gods . . . [those] on the sides of public roads should be arranged so that the passersby can have a view of them and pay their devotions face to face. (4.5)

The passage is revealing on two points. First, the temple façade is valued over the whole building, with observer and structure interacting face to façade. Second, the temple façade relates to the city as a whole.

The preoccupation with façades helps explain the limited popularity of circular temples in the Augustan city. Even with entry stairs before the doorway, tholoi are decidedly unfrontal. In general, they require a broad open space to be appreciated urbanistically. In addition, they are difficult to raise in height or to enlarge. As a result, round temples do not always make a strong impression within the cityscape unless surrounded by open space (fig. 67). The *princeps* undertook repairs to existing tholoi. After the fire of 14 B.C. in the Forum Romanum, the Temple of Vesta was rebuilt; like other Augustan buildings, it received a high podium and vertical emphasis (fig. 68). With the possible exception of the small temporary structure to Mars Ultor on the Capitoline, Augustus did not erect any significant new circular structures in Rome. Perhaps the association of circular shrines with the hero Hercules, alter ego of Antony, also affected the popularity of this temple form.[20]

Augustus wanted his religious buildings to stand out from other temples in Rome. He coupled an emphasis on verticality with the appearance of massiveness. As temples grew larger, the columns were placed proportionally closer and closer. This visual tightness resulted in large part from technical reasons. Stone was the preferred material of Augustan architects; lintels of this medium could not span the same distances as wood. As a result, as buildings grew larger, the distance between columns grew proportionally narrower. The majority of new Augustan projects used a pycnostyle arrangement with a spacing of 1.5 column diameters between columns. Such a tight configuration gave Augustan projects a massiveness not found in earlier works (fig. 65).[21] The impact was immediate. Looking at the temple to Mars Ultor in the Forum Augustum, Ovid proclaimed, "the god is huge, and so is the structure" (*Fasti* 5.551–3).

Variations from the norm are always memorable. When describing the Roman house of memory, teachers of rhetoric advised their students to select *imagines* that were unusual in scale, color, or form.[22] Being atypical, diminution was as notable as gigantism. In the last phase of Augustan building, the *princeps* funded primarily small urban projects, creating an obvious contrast with the enormous temples of the second phase. Small-scale construction is understandable for works of lesser significance, yet also becomes significant when used for projects with obvious importance such as the Ara Pacis. This opulent altar enclosure measured a mere 10.6 × 11.6 meters, yet was large in significance. Its importance was further accented by proximity and programmatic association with the Mausoleum Augustum, Horologium, and Pantheon. In effect, the small project grew in stature by being part of an ensemble (figs. 105 and 108). Repetition also created identifiable cognitive groupings in the cityscape. The small shrines of the Lares Compitales gained in meaning both by direct linkage with the *princeps* and by their sheer numbers; hundreds dotted the cityscape (fig. 55).

The familiar form of Augustan religious buildings did not detract from their imageability. In fact, their impact was quite the contrary. Traditional configurations were reassuring to a citizenry buffeted by years of civil con-

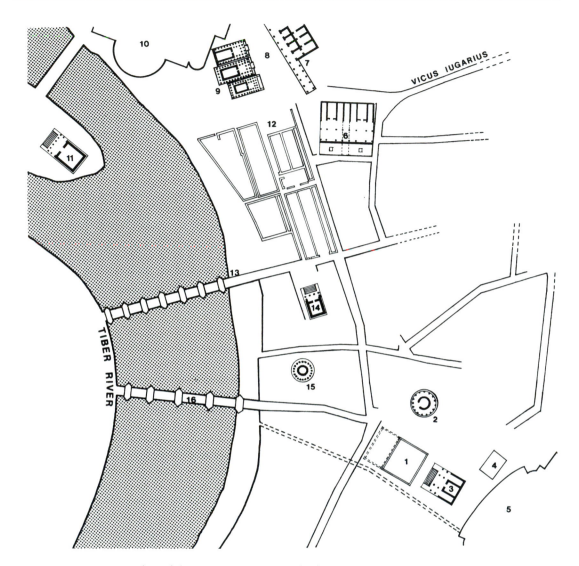

Figure 67. Plan of the Forum Boarium in the first century B.C. Drawing: Richard H. Abramson. 1: Ara Maxima Herculis; 2: Temple of Hercules Pompeianus (?); 3: Aedes Hercules Invicti (?); 4: Mithraeum; 5: Circus Maximus; 6: Temples of Fortuna and Mater Matuta (Area Sacra di Sant'Omobono); 7: Late Republican porticus; 8: Forum Holitorium; 9: Temples of Janus, Juno, Spes; 10: Theater of Marcellus; 11: Temple of Aesculapius; 12: Horrea; 13: Pons Aemilius with commemorative arch; 14: Temple of Portunus (?); 15: Temple of Hercules Victor; 16: Pons Sublicius.

flict. After the architectural novelties imposed upon the city by the competing triumphators of the 30s B.C., Rome's residents embraced the calm familiarity of Augustan temple structures. Enhancements of scale and materials and good maintenance all supported this feeling by signaling permanence and endurance.

Figure 68. Relief depicting the Temple of Vesta (heavily restored). Drawing by Richard H. Abramson.

With boastful frontality, the refurbished and new temples of Rome interacted with urban residents, each other, and the city as a whole. Rome projected an air of pious reverence for the gods. Simultaneously, the religious structures of the city conveyed the importance of a single individual; everyone was aware who stood behind the physical transformation of Rome's temples. Looking over the city, residents could join with Ovid in proclaiming, "not content with doing favors for mankind [Augustus] does them for the gods" (*Fasti* 2.62).

After devoting two books to aspects of temple design, Vitruvius followed with one covering all other public works – governmental, recreational, and functional – and another on the house. The modern categorization of Roman buildings is problematic. Terms such as "governmental," "religious," and "recreational" stand as absolutes in today's architectural typology. Clear divisions did not exist in antiquity. A building such as the Senate house, or curia, was not solely a political structure; the hall was sanctified as a *templum* and had important religious associations. Conversely, temple

complexes could also be used for Senate meetings. Theaters and other entertainment facilities sheltered religious ceremonies as well as political meetings. Given the multiuse nature of most public buildings in Rome, it is not
surprising that their layouts were not overly specialized. Both Augustus as
patron and Vitruvius as author gave short shrift to structures such as pris-
ons and treasuries with particular, limiting uses (Vitr.5.1–2). Though new
functions developed in the Augustan Age, the *princeps* conscientiously
avoided creating new building forms to house them; any new building type
would have been a tangible sign of a change, a message the "restorer of the
Republic" did not want to convey. In any event, Augustus found existing,
multipurpose building forms quite adaptable for the changing needs of the
Imperial bureaucracy.[23]

The Roman basilica is the quintessential multipurpose building. In the
form of a large colonnaded hall, the basilica's undifferentiated interior was
used for gatherings of all kinds. The two in the Forum Romanum associated
with Caesarean largess accommodated a variety of activities, from money
changing to business transactions. In particular, people thronged to these
large halls to watch court cases, boisterously taking sides in the ancient
equivalent of today's popular televised "Peoples' Court." Such activities
became even more important during the early Empire, as entertainment
replaced political action in the lives of Rome's citizens. Under the influence
of Augustus, other types of discussions formerly held in these public halls
gradually migrated to less public locations; for example, the meetings of
various governmental officials began to occur in the offices established by
the *princeps* in houses near his own (DioCass.53.16).

The Basilicas Julia and Aemilia were dominant urban structures. The
long, permeable façades defined the central area of the Forum Romanum
(fig. 69); their rich materials and elaborate decorations caught the eye of all
who visited the center of Rome. Following the lead of Caesar, Augustus
took care to maintain these great structures. Every time the basilicas suffered damage, he immediately undertook repairs and added embellishments.[24] Aware of the popularity, high use, and *imageability* of the two
basilicas, Augustus used them to promote his adopted sons Gaius and
Lucius, adding their names to both. Given such attention, it is not surprising
that these buildings were among the most memorable in Rome; in the first
century A.D., Pliny named the Basilica Aemilia as one of the most beautiful
structures in the entire world.[25]

In the Republic, Romans linked the status of a city with the appearance of
its central administrative building, the curia. Vitruvius succinctly states,
"particularly, the senate house should be constructed with special regard to
the importance of the town or city" (5.2.1). Thus, the curia of Rome had to

reflect the elevated significance of the city on the Tiber River. Caesar had acknowledged this fact by beginning a grand new structure. Augustus completed the Curia Julia and advertised the fact on coins issued soon after its dedication in 29 B.C. Numismatic representations show a tall meeting hall with colonnaded porch and pediment surmounted by a statue of Victoria, a reference to the golden statue placed inside to celebrate the defeat of Antony and Cleopatra at Actium (fig. 70).[26] As would be expected for a governmental centerpiece of the Augustan Age, this Senate building was conservative in form. In fact, Vitruvius' prescription for a generic Republican curia could be a direct description of the Julio–Augustan structure (5.2). Together, the traditional shape, propagandistic sculptural program, physical solidity, straightforwardness, and verticality of the Curia Julia visually reaffirmed the strength of the restored Republic and the physical renewal of Rome.

In the governing of the Empire, Augustus redefined Republican administrative powers. He likewise altered the associationism and application of select building types. A notable example is the honorary arch. Republican commemorative arches evolved from city gates and free-standing monuments (*fornices*) supporting sculptures.[27] Under Augustus, this building type increased in number and urban significance. During the five centuries of the Republic, the Romans erected less than half a dozen arches in Rome; during the Augustan Age, they raised at least eight.[28] Republican honorands erected arches on private initiative; in the Augustan Age, the Senate and people of Rome voted approval. Octavian personally erected the Arcus Octavii honoring his natural father, yet the Senate voted to erect the arches honoring the *princeps* himself, beginning with the Arcus Octaviani of 36 B.C. Because the commemorative now involved public discourse, terminology became important. Precisely in this period, the descriptive word *arcus* replaced *fornix*.[29] The latter term was clearly inappropriate for impressive, State-approved Augustan commemoratives. *Fornices* described vaulted spaces, including baths, cisterns, and basement spaces; as a result, the word was associated with the seamier aspects of urban life. Seneca notes, "Pleasure is lowly and servile, weak and perishable; its post and domicile are the *fornices* and taverns" (*DeVitBeat.*7.3). A different term was needed for the constructions voted by the *Senatus Populusque* to acknowledge the virtue and achievements of the first citizen.

The urban attractions of the commemorative arch are obvious. First, arches make excellent billboards. Lacking a usable interior, arches are all signage; every embellishment is acknowledged as a conveyer of meaning. Second, and related to the first, arches serve as urban markers, permanently associating particular events or achievements with specific sites. Third, being bifocal and permeable, arches simultaneously demarcate and unite

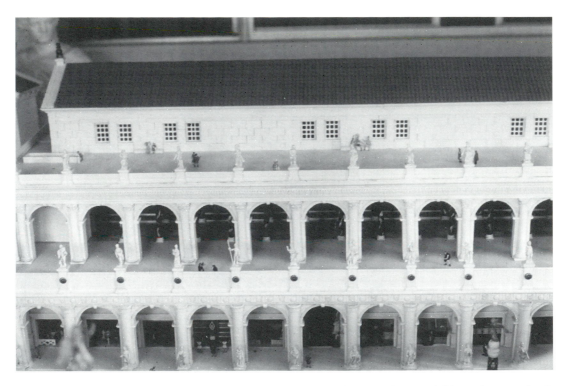

Figure 69. Reconstruction of the Basilica Aemilia. Photo: author; model by Robert Garbisch.

Figure 70. Coin of Augustus depicting the Curia Julia. Photo: Fototeca Unione AAR 2979.

Figure 71. Reconstruction of the Parthian Arch of Augustus in the Forum Romanum. After Gatti, *RendPontAcc.* 21 (1945–6), fig. 9.

distinct spaces; in effect, they are urban doorways announcing transitions in the experience of the city.

Augustus used arches with great urbanistic effect. In important locales throughout the city, arches announced the achievements of the *princeps* and his family. Thus, the Parthian arch in the Forum Romanum commemorated the return of the captured standards in 19 B.C. Atop the arch stood an impressive quadriga (military chariot). On the sides were inscribed the *fasti consulares* listing all the chief magistrates since the beginning of the Republic, and the *fasti triumphales* naming all triumphators, from Romulus onward. In content, these accoutrements powerfully conveyed the stability of the Roman State and Augustus' own place within this continuum. From a design standpoint, this work was equally notable. On either side of the large central arch were trabeated side openings embellished with engaged columns and pediments (fig. 71).[30] Placed between the temples of Divus Julius, and Castor and Pollux, this memorial acted as an internal urban doorway marking the entry into the central Forum.

Other Augustan arches likewise marked transitions from the one urban zone to another. Spanning the road up to the Palatine from the Forum, the Arcus Octavii announced the approach of the new Augustan enclave atop the hill.[31] Far north of Rome, an Augustan commemorative performed as a gateway to the entire metropolis. To celebrate the reworking of the Via Flaminia, the *princeps* erected an arch on the Pons Milvius at the intersection of the highway and the Tiber River (DioCass.53.22). Atop the structure stood a statue of the *princeps*, silently watching all who approached or left the great city on the Tiber (fig. 102). Augustus likewise restored a marble arch on the Pons Aemilius, the major approach to the city center from the west.[32]

Other members of the Augustan family also received commemorative arches. These, however, clearly did not compete with those to Augustus. In general, they stood in less important locations, were smaller in size, honored the individual only in death, and advanced Augustan imperatives.[33] For example, Drusus, the elder brother of Tiberius, defeated the Germans in the late teens B.C. The Senate and people commemorated his success with an *ovatio*, rather than a triumph, with no associated manubial monument in Rome. Drusus received a memorial arch only after his death in 9 B.C. Embellished with war trophies and marble, the Arcus Drusi stood far south of Rome, probably near the Temple of Mars Gravidus that Augustus may have restored. This shrine was the locus for ceremonies relating to war, including an equestrian cavalry parade, the *transvectio equitum*, revived by Augustus.[34]

By the late first century B.C., Romans outside the imperial family had little opportunity to have their names associated with public monuments, especially triumphal arches. This, coupled with Augustus' much touted advocacy of pragmatic urban projects, provided the incentive for magistrates to fashion ersatz commemorative arches from existing urban components. In the eastern part of Rome, the arched line of the Aquae Marcia, Tepula, and Julia crossed over the Via Tiburtina. With the addition of travertine pilasters and bucrania keystones, the single aqueduct arch marking the intersection was easily transformed into a memorial. Here the consuls of 5 B.C. proudly inscribed their names.[35] The gates of the Republican Wall likewise provided opportunities for architectural and personal aggrandizement. Though no longer of military significance, these urban gates remained important reference points in the city for both official and daily use. In the Augustan Age, the broad, triple-arched Porta Esquilina received a new surface of creamy travertine (fig. 72). In A.D. 2, the consuls inscribed their names on a gateway (Porta Trigemina?) near the Forum Boarium; those of A.D. 10 similarly embellished a gate on the Caelian (Porta Querquetula or Porta Caelimontana). Significantly, these last two gates may have also carried aqueduct lines; if so, the consuls could have justified their self-promoting projects both as the restoration of Republican public works and as pragmatic maintenance of the city's water system (fig. 73).[36]

The curved architectural form held several connotations in the cityscape. Whether viewed in the vertical or horizontal dimension, a curve is dynamic. In Republican Rome, the simple arch of the Fornix Fabianus leaping over the Sacra Via encouraged passage through. Repetitious rows of vaults animating the huge length of the Porticus Aemilius warehouse erected in the second century B.C. implied unending expansion. The tall arches of aqueducts entering the city conveyed a sense of the flowing water they carried. The overarching curves of free-standing arches evoked association with the rotating vault of the heavens. Within select Augustan temples, apses embraced cult statues, as if a commemorative arch had fallen flat around the sculpted delimiting a divine realm.[37] In the Forum Augustum, huge exedras embraced the statues of the *summi viri,* uniting them in an Augustan universe (fig. 50).

Though important architecturally and conceptually, the latter curved forms had minimal impact on the overall cityscape since they were not expressed externally. Temple apses were not evident from outside the cella; the exedrae of the Forum Augustum were largely obscured by surrounding structures. In contrast, the vaulted forms associated with select other building types were readily visible throughout Rome and helped define the urban image. The technical properties of the vaults, in particular, led to their use on structures requiring wide spans, strong support, and capillary dissipation. Such applications led to a typological association. During the late first century B.C., curving walls and arching vaults signaled a particular use: entertainment/recreation. Spying a fragment of a curved wall in the dense city, observers could be fairly sure they were near a theater, bath, stadium, or circus.

In bath complexes, vaults span large spaces and conduct moisture along their arching surfaces to the side walls or floor, thus preventing dripping. New and renovated bathing establishments graced Augustan Rome. As aedile, Agrippa maintained the 170 bathing facilities, or *balneae,* in the city with their vaulted spaces and curvilinear plans. In 25 B.C., he erected a large new public bath complex in the central Campus Martius. Though few traces remain, secondary illustrations indicate the Agrippan layout was not markedly different in form from Republican *balneae.* Rather, these baths were notable for their large size, additional amenities, and siting. Compared to the intimate spaces of earlier bath structures, that of Agrippa had grand interiors centering on a huge rotunda approximately 25 meters in diameter.

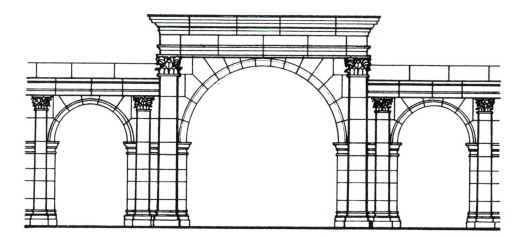

Figure 72. Reconstruction of the Porta Esquilina. Drawing: Richard H. Abramson.

Furthermore, the baths of Agrippa merged Roman forms with Greek exercise facilities by incorporating the characteristics of an open air palestra. Parklands, a canal, and a lake surrounded the main building. As a result, the term *balneum* seemed insufficient for these sprawling facilities; eventually, the great complex of Agrippa inspired a whole line of Imperial baths known as *thermae*.[38] Whereas earlier baths were usually embedded within the dense urban fabric, the Thermae Agrippae stood free within the parklands of the flat Campus Martius, the great curves of domes and vaults signaling a place of leisure and recreation.

Anxious to foster a sense of community within Rome, Augustus enlivened the city with entertainments, spectacles, and festivals. For these events, he funded well over a dozen new facilities, repaired existing recreational buildings, and adapted other projects for entertainment use. Typologically, the new Augustan structures did not reflect formal innovation or the technical ingenuity of Curio and his rotating theaters. The Theater of Marcellus adhered to the standard Republican arrangement and proportions as outlined by Vitruvius, though with added apsidal halls flanking the stage building (5.3–8). The function of these halls remains unknown, but their formal properties can be evaluated.[39] The paired curving forms facing the river echo the large arc that terminated the building on the inland side formed by the curving, stacked exterior arcades of the seating area, or *cavea*. In effect, the curves provided an animated visual metaphor for the dynamic dramas held within the theater.

The design of the Theater of Marcellus was remarkable for its efficient plan. Although smaller in diameter than the Theater of Pompey, the Augustan structure held more spectators. Measuring 150 meters in diameter, the

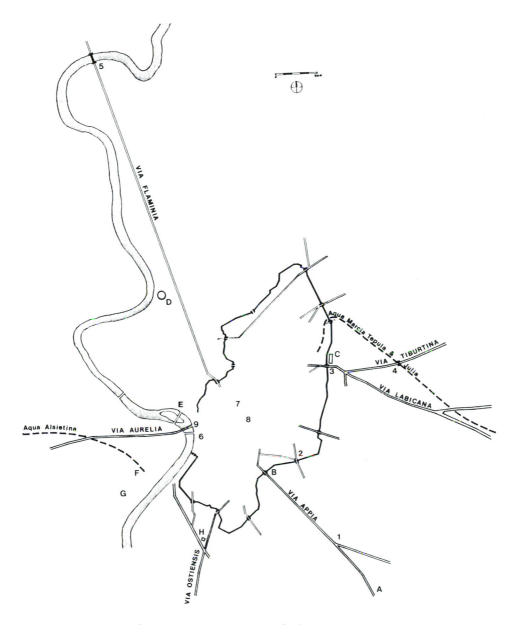

Figure 73. Location of commemorative arches and edge monuments in Augustan Rome.
Drawing: Richard H. Abramson. **Augustan Commemorative Arches**: 1: Arcus Drusi;
2: Arcus Dolabella et Silani, Porta Caelimontana (?); 3: Arcus Augusti, Porta Esquilina (later
Arcus Gallienus); 4: Arch intersection of aqueduct and Via Tiburtina (later Porta Tiburtina);
5: Arcus Augusti, Pons Mulvius on Via Flaminia; 6: Arcus Letuli et Crispini, Porta Trigemina; 7: Arcus Octaviani, Arcus Augusti, and Porticus Gaii et Lucii, Forum Romanum;
8: Arcus Octavii, Palatine; 9: Arch on the Pons Aemilius. **Select Edge Monuments**: A: Temple
of Mars Gravidus; B: Altar of Fortuna Redux; C: Macellum Liviae; D: Mausoleum of Augustus; E: Theater of Marcellus; F: Nemus Caesarum; G: Naumachia Augusti; H: Pyramid of
Cestius.

Pompeian structure had over 17,580 places, holding approximately 11,000 people, whereas that dedicated to Marcellus with a diameter of 130 meters had 20,500 *loci* equivalent to approximately 13,000 spectators. Despite this efficiency and its location closer to the city center, the Theater of Marcellus never usurped the position of Pompey's earlier complex as the premier theater of Rome. This may be due to the unusual southwest orientation of the building, a direct contradiction of the siting recommended by Vitruvius and followed for the theaters of Pompey and Balbus (Vitr.5.3.2). This axis caused the high seating of the *cavea* to cast distracting shadows on the stage during most of the day and to trap unhealthy vapors. The awkward orientation of this building may have resulted from site constrictions or the demands of urban parade routes.[40]

In addition to permanent buildings, the *princeps* erected numerous temporary theaters in Rome. Vitruvius noted, "Somebody will perhaps say that many theaters are built every year in Rome" (5.5.7). Nothing remains of these constructions put up for the Ludi Saeculares and other events. Requiring a certain amount of unencumbered land and easy access, they were generally placed on the city's edges, most notably in the Campus Martius. Although temporary theater buildings had been common in the Republic, they were not mentioned after 17 B.C., possibly because the city had three large permanent theater facilities – those of Pompey, Marcellus, and Balbus.[41]

For especially large gatherings, Rome had the great Republican Circus Maximus lying between the Palatine and Aventine Hills. Augustus conscientiously saw to its continued maintenance and aggrandizement. The capital also received its first stone amphitheater under the *princeps*. One of his most successful generals, T. Statilius Taurus, dedicated a small stone "hunting theater" in 29 B.C. Strabo groups this structure with the three stone theaters of the Campus (5.3.8). Few other references to the Amphitheater of Statilius Taurus exist to clarify its use, popularity, or siting. Since Augustus regularly included stone amphitheaters in his colonial settlements, one would expect the building type to be popular in Rome.[42] The capital city, however, always responded to different demands. Rome may have nurtured a conservative onus against permanent amphitheaters similar to that against stone theaters. Furthermore, Rome had numerous other facilities for spectator events that were larger and better located.[43]

The structures for public entertainment, like those associated with the fora, reflect the same disinterest in experimentation. Even the Thermae Agrippae were not typologically remarkable. The complex reflects a merging of existing building forms with a similar function and thus was palatable to Republican sensibilities. In one instance, however, Augustus can be associated with what appears to be an unrepublican, autocratic act. In the *Res

Gestae, he takes credit for constructing a pulvinar at the Circus Maximus (19). Originally a sacred couch for the gods, a pulvinar became a seat of distinction or an imperial box at large group events. The creation of such an isolating, dictatorial construction appears antithetical to Augustan policy. It can easily be justified. Caesar had accepted the honor of a pulvinar; Augustus as filial son completed the project initiated by his divine father.[44] To minimize any imperial associations, the *princeps* rarely watched races from the pulvinar, instead preferring to sit with his friends and freedmen. Statues of the gods, instead, occupied the box (Suet.*Aug.*45).

Caesar also had planned to introduce public libraries to Rome. In 39 B.C., C. Asinius Pollio satisfied this vision with the libraries in the Atrium Libertatis; Augustus followed suit and included a Greek and Latin collection in his monumental Palatine complex to Apollo. His sister sponsored another in the Porticus Octaviae honoring her dead son Marcellus.[45] Libraries had existed in Rome before this time, but they were private collections in the homes of wealthy patricians.[46] Vitruvius discussed the practical aspects of library construction and siting in his book on the *domus.* Unfortunately, the public libraries of the Augustan Age have left only tantalizing fragmentary remains, making determination of their exact form impossible. Logically, these structures appear to have been modeled after private libraries, with two separate chambers, one for Greek and one for Latin texts. Because these Augustan libraries stood within larger structures, they had minimal visual impact on the cityscape.

The diminution of civil strife stimulated construction of commercial and private buildings along with public monuments and amenities. As trade increased, so did the need for warehouses and market spaces. Augustus and his adherents naturally took part in these commercial ventures, though with the usual restraint demonstrated by patricians involved in business. In 7 B.C., Tiberius dedicated the Macellum Liviae just outside the restored Porta Esquilina. This market took the familiar form of a rectangular porticoed courtyard surrounded by shops of brick and *opus reticulatum.*[47] Though internalized, the Macellum Liviae garnered notice in the cityscape. A constant stream of entering and departing merchants and shoppers drew external attention to the market; once inside, the large scale of the structure (approximately 80 × 25 meters) impressed all visitors. Other commercial projects received urban notice because of placement rather than size or configuration. Agrippa erected a warehouse in the very center of Rome. The two-storied Horrea Agrippiana rose on the heavily trafficked Vicus Tuscus between the Forum Romanum and the Tiber docks.[48]

Domestic architecture in the Augustan Age underwent a schizophrenic development.[49] The emperor discouraged individuals from overt external displays of wealth in the construction of homes in Rome. Concerned with the overall appearance of his capital, he did not wish the forms, size, and ornaments of urban residences to compete for attention in the cityscape as they had during the late Republic. Wealthy patrons, of course, continued to embellish their homes, but they centered their attention on features with little urban impact. The exteriors of houses did not reveal substantial change. Most elaboration and experimentation occurred away from the eyes of city dwellers, namely, with the decorative programs on *domus* interiors and with the design of pleasure villas outside the city.[50]

Indicative of this trend is the ancient Villa Farnesina on the Right Bank dated to around 20 B.C.[51] Like the elaborate garden estates of the Pincian, this complex lay on the city's edge and was thus less constrained by urban pressures. Excavations of its eastern half have revealed a rich, progressive decorative program on the interior. Formally, the complex merged features of a country villa with those of a *domus* to create a suburban villa. The ancient Villa Farnesina was programmatically innovative, associating diverse pleasurable activities – including bathing, theatrical performances, dining, and exercising – in an enlarged, symmetrical configuration. Such experimental combining and enlarging of existing forms characterize this residential complex as the private equivalent of the Thermae Agrippae directly across the river. Within the cityscape, however, the villa's innovations were not readily evident. Few urban residents actually saw the unique combination of forms and functions evident on the interior. Externally, the complex presented shapes familiar in Rome. The large hemicycle and cascading garden terraces above the river recalled similar components evident in the city's expanding pleasure parks. Furthermore, the ancient Villa Farnesina retained a rural, almost antiurban association. Oriented to the northeast, the impressive river façade was clearly visible only from the relatively undeveloped northwestern section of the Campus Martius; viewed obliquely from the city center and from the Tiber, the structure added little to Rome's overall urban image.

Funerary architecture underwent a similar introversion. As part of the heady architectural competition in the late Republic, patrons had openly vied for attention with eye-catching tombs. Inspired by a vast Hellenistic repertoire and shaped by the individuality of patrons, these most personal of monuments took many shapes and forms.[52] The rampant competition of these years led inevitably to devaluation of meaning; in many cases, there was a clear dissonance between the imageability of a tomb and the achievements of the deceased (fig. 48). After Augustus erected his grand Mausoleum in the Campus Martius, other patrons gradually realized that self-aggrandizement through funerary architecture was both pointless and a political liability. By the later decades of the Augustan period, ostentatious tombs were replaced by burial precincts presenting blank walls toward the city, as found with internalized columbaria.

Of course, exceptions existed. Significantly, several flamboyant tombs erected in Rome during these years belonged to foreign patrons outside contemporary politics and the old aristocracy. A few individuals justified grand funerary monuments by directly associating their structures with the *princeps*. Thus, M. Lucilius Paetus modeled his tomb on the Via Salaria after the Mausoleum Augusti, though at an appropriately smaller scale.[53] C. Cestius likewise selected a building form directly in line with Augustan propaganda. Sometime before 12 B.C., he erected a large pyramid on the Via Ostiensis sheathed in sparkling white marble.[54] Clearly alluding to the Roman conquest of Egypt, the tomb stood as a billboard of Augustan achievement seen by all approaching Rome from the south.

In the public realm, Augustus drew upon the traditional repertoire of architectural forms. Such conservatism is to be expected from the man who fashioned himself as restorer of the Republic. Within these typological limitations, however, Augustus expanded applications. Changes in proportions enhanced the verticality of temples. The reenforced conceptualization of arches as gateways defined and clarified city regions. The overt proliferation of recreational structures made the visible curve an architectural sign for the function. In the private realm, the *princeps* through pressure and example discouraged competitive formal displays, forcing typological design innovations to occur on interiors, behind surrounding walls, or outside the capital city. As a result, Augustan building projects had a greater collective sense than their predecessors; all operated at the scale of the district and the entire city.

Urban Ensembles

With typological restraint as his architectural theme, Augustus explored ways to make his projects memorable without damaging their familiarity and Republican associationism. After almost seventy-five years of tumult, order and calm were the bywords of the day in Rome. The *princeps* promoted these characteristics in his architecture and urban design through the regularization and isolation of projects. The political rivalry of the late Republic had resulted in individualized structures that avoided association with other buildings both in message and planning. For example, the Republican monuments in the Forum Boarium stood in conscious competition with one another because they were erected by competing patrons; urbanistically, these memorials did not coalesce into distinct urban group-

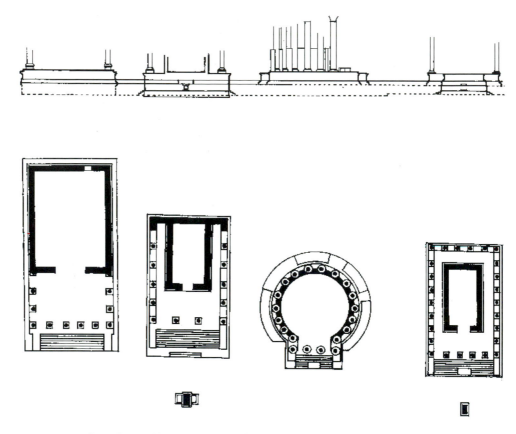

Figure 74. Plan of Republican temples in the Area Sacra of Largo Argentina. Drawing: Richard H. Abramson.

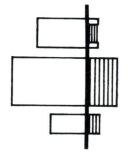

Figure 75. Diagram, alignment of temple façades.

ings (fig. 67).[55] In contrast, the projects of Augustus worked together to form ensembles projecting a sense of serenity, stability, and unity.

Urban ensembles are formed when diverse components define an urban focus perceived as affiliated. Though the buildings may be from different periods, cohesion is achieved through visual, experiential, and/or functional homogeneity. Rome always had urban ensembles. Republican architects often placed temples together to create solid groupings. The basic design concept was alignment in both the horizontal and vertical dimensions. Religious proscriptions may in part be responsible for such arrangements. For example, the four temples in the Area Sacra of Largo Argentina were erected at different times, yet all were oriented to the cardinal points and thus stood parallel to one another.[56] These temples were also tied together by a clear vertical relationship; the different architects maintained a roughly uniform height for the podia of all four structures (fig. 74).

Concern with visual effect reflects the experiential interest of Roman architects. How observers perceived buildings in the cityscape determined

Figure 76. Relief of the first century B.C. depicting a portico enclosure with plantings, altars, and two statues; from Capua. Photo: DAIR: 37.949.

placement as much as did religious restrictions.[57] Following the dictates outlined by Vitruvius, designers oriented structures to be seen from the road, and to provide a dominant view back to the city. The siting of one building therefore often determined that of nearby works, so that observers in the street would have a clear view of them all as, for example, with the three temples in the Forum Holitorium. To enhance the visual impact of temple groupings, Roman designers aligned the columnar porches, rather than the absolute frontmost edge marked by the projecting stairs (fig. 75).[58] With such an arrangement, the pediments emphasized the vertical dimension and the individuality of each structure, while the columns of the different temples appeared to march in a unified line.

Continuous rows of columns effectively shape urban ensembles. In addition to aligned temple façades, Republican architects exploited porticos. Inspired by the Greek stoa, porticos appeared in Rome by the second century B.C. (Vell.Pat.2.1). The Roman portico was a covered colonnade formed by a simple row of columns or piers with engaged columns supporting a roof; it could be trabeated or arcuated. Internally, porticos provided a roofed space for soft social uses; externally, they served as frames for various displays, backdrops for urban action, and formal edges for open spaces (fig. 76).[59]

Placed in front of disparate contiguous facades, porticos provided immediate unity and grandeur. For example, a travertine portico in the Forum Holitorium regularized the uneven base of the Capitoline hill and mirrored the aligned columns of the three opposing Republican temples.[60] Porticos could also be grouped to shape and define space. Vitruvius referred to a temple being "in" the Porticus Metelli of 147 B.C. and used the plural "portici," inferring more than one colonnade surrounding the structure.[61] In the 50s B.C., Pompey constructed a portico as an amenity to his theater; this quadriportico had four covered colonnades defining a large open court where spectators could gather before or after performances. Caesar's new forum had lateral porticos defining the open area before the Temple of Venus Genetrix. Such introverted enclosures were ideal for creating a well-defined space within a crowded cityscape and for conveying a sense of orderliness.

Augustus and his architects favored the creation of powerful ensembles in Rome. This choice was calculated. Ordered groupings helped to unite a cityscape that lacked visual cohesion. Symbolically, carefully planned ensembles projected a desired sense of cohesion, especially in comparison with the divisiveness projected by late Republican projects. Furthermore, creation of ordered urban enclosures could be seen as an homage to the Divine Caesar. Augustus' adopted father had begun to unify the Comitium area, making obvious alignments with his new forum. In addition, he popularized quadriporticos in Rome with such projects as the Forum Julium and Saepta Julia.

Designers of the Augustan Age employed both alignment and isolation in the creation of urban ensembles. For example, the great curving cavea of the theater honoring Marcellus continued the line established by the three Republican temples in the Forum Holitorium (fig. 67). The new Forum Augustum rose at a strict right angle to the Forum Julium and continued the southeastern edge established by the earlier complex (fig. 50). The Augustan arches in the Forum Romanum aligned with the Temple of Divus Julius (fig. 57). The Mausoleum Augusti with its ustrinum (crematorium) formed an ensemble based upon related function, adjacency, and a blanket of unifying landscaping.[62] In addition to alignments based on tangency, Augustus created urban ensembles based on visual and symbolic alignments. The Mausoleum and its ustrinum were visually and programmatically linked with the Horologium Augusti, Ara Pacis, and Agrippan Pantheon. This associationism was celestially reenforced on the autumnal equinox, simultaneously the birthday of Augustus, when the shadow of the Horologium's obelisk pointed to the Ara Pacis.

Equally imageable within the cityscape were urban projects based on a design strategy of isolation.[63] Although Augustus made extensive additions and alterations to Rome's urban fabric, he could not rebuild the entire city. The basic footprints of Republican temples and historical structures were inviolable; many buildings continued to project messages antithetical to the Augustan Age. In addition, much of the city's infill remained undirected and visually unappealing, with tottering houses and crumbling stucco surfaces. Thus, every new Augustan monument or ensemble was in danger of having its meaning compromised and visual impact contaminated. In response, the *princeps* favored introverted urban ensembles with open spaces and individual buildings screened from the city by surrounding porticos. Vitruvius openly stressed the importance of isolating experiences; he explained that structures within enclosures are perceived differently in part because a magnificent approach adds to their *decorum* (6.2.2; 6.5.2; 7.pref.17; cf. 1.2.6). On an urban scale, internalized complexes create islands of order and directed propaganda within the churning visual confusion of Rome.

In the Augustan capital, new introverted urban ensembles covered approximately 10 hectares (Table 4).[64] Most were projects by members of the Imperial family: Marcius Philippus, stepfather of Augustus built the Porticus Philippi; Agrippa completed the Saepta initiated by Julius Caesar; the *princeps'* sister Octavia finished the reworking of the Porticus Metelli begun by her son Marcellus, dubbing the finished work the Porticus Octaviae; Livia was associated with the Porticus and Macellum Liviae; and Augustus himself rebuilt the Porticus Octavia and erected the impressive Forum Augustum.[65] The urban impact of the numerous, large Augustan quadriporticos was dramatic and immediate. Though construction of an entire ensemble might take years, the space-defining colonnades could be erected relatively

Table 4. Approximate Areas of Some Augustan Enclosures[66]

Porticus Octavia (restored 33 B.C.)	110 × 108 m	11,880 sq. m
Porticus Philippi (ca. 29 B.C.)	63 × 104 m	6,552 sq. m
Saepta Julia (dedicated 26 B.C.)	310 × 120 m	37,200 sq. m
Porticus Octaviae (ca. 25 B.C.)	119 × 132 m	15,708 sq. m
Crypta Balbi (ca. 15 B.C.)	94 × 72 m	6,768 sq. m
Porticus Liviae (dedicated 7 B.C.)	115 × 75 m	8,625 sq. m
Macellum Liviae (dedicated 7 B.C.)	80 × 25 m	2,000 sq. m
Forum Augustum (dedicated 2 B.C.)	125 × 85 m	10,625 sq. m
		99,358 sq. m

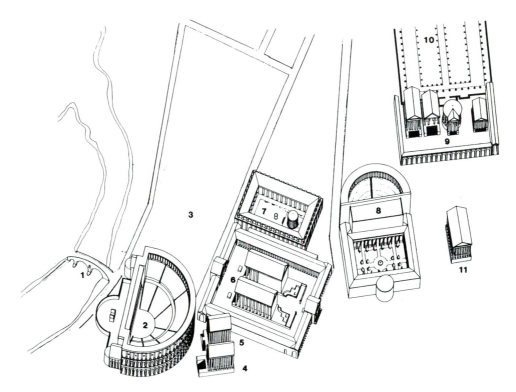

Figure 77. Reconstruction of the Southern Campus Martius in the first century B.C. Drawing: E. H. Riorden from Stambaugh, *Ancient Roman City*, courtesy Johns Hopkins University Press. 1: Pons Fabricius; 2: Theater of Marcellus; 3: Circus Flaminius; 4: Temple of Bellona (?); 5: Temple of Apollo Sosianus; 6: Porticus Octaviae surrounding the temples of Jupiter Stator and Juno Regina; 7: Porticus Philippi around Temple of Hercules Musarum; 8: Crypta and Theater of Balbus; 9: Republican Temples, Area Sacra del Largo Argentina; 10: Porticus of Pompey's theater; 11. Temple of Bellona (?).

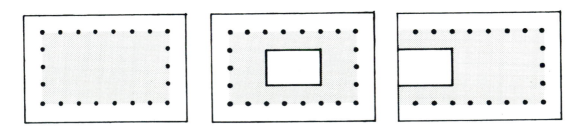

Figure 78. Diagrams of negative space in different quadriportico configurations.

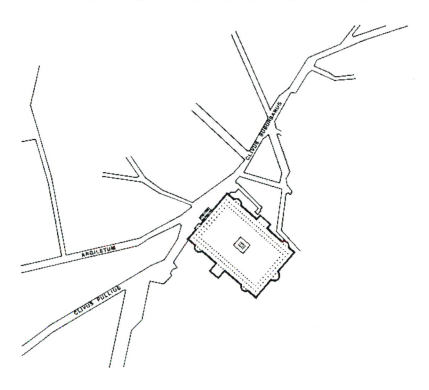

Figure 79. Plan of the Porticus Liviae and surrounding area based on the *Forma Urbis Romae*. Drawing: Richard H. Abramson.

quickly, immediately imprinting the cityscape with the project's size, form, and meaning. As a result, such complexes could be opened and even dedicated before all the construction was complete, as was the case with the Forum Augustum. Aware of the great effort required to carve large open spaces in the dense urban environment of Rome, residents considered these spaces as extravagant as huge buildings and rich materials, and just as memorable.

Externally, quadriportico enclosures presented long, regularized façades toward the city. Where they faced directly onto streets, their external columns approximated the appearance of continuous linear porticos or colonnaded streets. This effect may have been especially strong in the southern Campus Martius, where three aligned porticos – Octaviae, Philippi, and Octavia – defined a street frontage of approximately 290 meters (fig. 77).[67] Other ensembles were embedded in the tightly woven urban fabric and thus could present only a doorway to the city. On the Esquiline Hill, a broad stair opened a space between the small shops lining the Clivus Suburbanus and led up a steep incline to the Porticus Liviae. The Porticus Octaviae differentiated its entryways with projecting pedimented porches on the northeast and southwest.

Internally, Augustan quadriporticos had three basic layouts (fig. 78). The simplest had colonnades defining a rectilinear open space as with the Saepta Julia and Crypta Balbi. A second arrangement followed Greek prototypes with inward facing porticos surrounding a single free-standing structure, a configuration often used for Hellenistic ruler cults.[68] For example, at the Porticus Liviae, a double colonnade encircled a small but opulent temple to Concordia (fig. 79).[69] The third arrangement was a Roman interpretation of Greek enclosures, with a rectangular open space defined by porticos and a temple at one end of the long axis as with the Forum Julium (figs. 36 and 39).[70] The formal balance and clarity were uniquely Roman with crisply articulated negative space scaled to counterbalance the temple massing.[71] Significantly, the formal regularity of Augustan urban ensembles was relieved frequently by memorable surprises experienced only as one moved through the complex. For example, behind the double colonnades of the Porticus Liviae, observers encountered alternating curved and rectilinear niches providing variety within rigid order.

Isolated from visual contamination by other urban buildings, porticoed enclosures conveyed unadulterated propagandistic messages. Furthermore, their colonnades were ideal backdrops for sculptural display and plantings (fig. 76). Some of the most important political art in the Augustan city occurred in these environments. The complex sculptural displays of the Forum Augustum and Temple of Apollo Palatinus are the best studied examples, clearly and forcefully promoting Augustus as inheritor and savior of the Republic.[72] Yet all of the new Augustan enclosures had carefully manipulated artistic programs. To celebrate his first acknowledged triumph, Octavian rebuilt the Porticus Octavia and there proudly displayed the military standards recovered from the Illyrians (App.*Ill.*28). He further affirmed the expanding power of the Roman state, and of himself, by constructing a new portico enclosure filled with statues representing all nations, an overt counterpoint to the similar exhibition of Pompey in his theater.[73] The theme of conquest and expanding Roman power was continued in the Porticus Vipsania where a map of the world showed the extent of Roman influence (Pliny *HN*.3.17).

Other messages were less overtly political. The famous artworks displayed in Augustan enclosures demonstrated Rome's sophistication and cultural superiority. Lush plantings incorporated into ensembles improved the health of Rome's residents, revitalized the Republican reverence of nature, and acknowledged the fecundity of the Augustan state.[74] Along with artwork and landscaping, more plebeian exhibits, such as dinosaur bones and large beams, seemed calculated to draw observers into these contained environments where they would then be immersed in Augustan propaganda.[75]

As the premier urban ensemble of its day, the Forum Augustum deserves closer analysis. In form, the complex logically followed the model presented by the adjacent Forum Julium (fig. 84). Both fora allowed for multiple, and contrasting, formal readings. The basic footprint with an open central space defined by porticos and a tall temple at one end recalled Republican Italic fora, yet at the same time provoked associations with eastern models associated with divine rulers. In comparison to the loose interrelationships between buildings in the old Forum Romanum, the Fora of Caesar and Augustus conveyed a tightly controlled regularity appropriate for the new world order. For example, in both complexes, the negative space measured approximately three times the temple volume and symmetry prevailed.

The Forum Augustum introduced two formal innovations to the basic Italic forum arrangement: an enormous fire wall and parallel exedras. Behind the Temple to Mars Ultor, a rusticated tufa wall towered over 33 meters in height. The barrier was designed to halt the spread of fires from the crowded and highly flammable Subura region to the east. The huge wall also masked intrusive external views of the city, thereby keeping attention directed inward. Formally, the wall served as a neutral backdrop for the great temple. This huge, uniform vertical surface of peperino and Gabine stone was articulated with courses of travertine. These white bands moved outward from the rear temple wall, through the side porticos, and curved across the surface of the lateral exedras. If originally left visible, the white horizontal ribbons of travertine would have visually tied the various components of the Forum Augustum together into a neat package.[76]

The central open space of the Forum Augustum was dominated by orthogonal forms, from the trabeated sides porticos to the pedimented façade of the great Mars temple. All curves were excised from sight (fig. 80). As observers moved into interior spaces, this rectilinearity was counterpoised by embracing curves. Behind the porticos, pedestrians entered the two lateral exedras; within the temple itself, a vaulted nave led to an apse curving around the cult statues of Mars, Divus Julius, and Venus with Cupid.[77] Externally, however, these curves remained largely invisible in the cityscape. Surrounded by adjacent structures, the sweep of the exedras was only evident to urban observers on high vantage points.[78]

Pedestrians entering the Forum Augustum found the experience of the city immediately enriched. Approaching from the east, they moved through the dark, warrenlike streets of the Subura valley lined with residences and shops encased in stucco and tufa. Moving downhill, they came to the tower-

Figure 80. Model of the Forum Augustum showing the northwest portico and a corner of the Temple of Mars Ultor. Collection of G. Fittschen-Badura, Augsburg; 68/69/3; after Zanker, *Forum Augustum*, pl. 5.

ing gray tufa wall at the rear of the Forum Augustum and were drawn to the arched openings framed in bright white travertine. As they passed into the Augustan complex observers found that, like Dorothy entering Oz in the film classic, they experienced a dramatic change in environmental palette. The matte, earth-toned realm of the Republican cityscape was replaced by a world of glistening surfaces and bright color. Reflective marbles of every hue sparkled on most surfaces; bronze plating shone on the temple podium. The formal symmetry and openness of the Augustan forum offered a calm respite after the crowded, convoluted passageways of the Subura. Similarly, the unified, directed iconographical program presented a directed vision. Observers experienced such overt contrasts between old and new urban environments as calculated and meaningful.

Another, less permanent ensemble also transformed the image of the capital. Urban plantings formed notable groupings making Augustan Rome not only a city of marble, but one of greenery. Private houses in the city had always had kitchen gardens; sacred plantings dotted the cityscape. Inspired

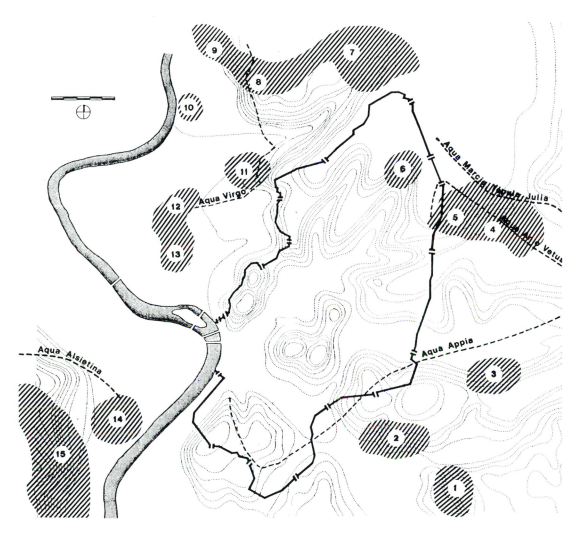

Figure 81. Aqueducts and gardens (*horti*) of Augustan Rome. Drawing: Richard H. Abramson. 1: Horti Asinii; 2: Nemus Camenae; 3: Horti Vectilii (date?); 4: Horti Maecenati; 5: Horti Lamiani and Maiani; 6: Horti Lolliani; 7: Horti Sallustiani; 8: Horti Luculliani; 9: Horti Aciliorum; 10: Mausoleum of Augustus funerary gardens; 11: Campus Agrippae; 12: Stagnum and Horti Agrippae; 13: Horti Pompeiani; 14: Nemus Caesarum; 15: Horti Caesaris.

by the splendid *paradeisoi* or garden paradises of eastern cities, the philhellenes Scipio Aemilianus and D. Junius Brutus had introduced private pleasure parks to Rome in the later part of the second century B.C.[79] Wealthy citizens created carefully designed parks, or *horti*, as overt status symbols. Thus, Pompey cultivated a large garden around his villa in the Campus Martius.[80] In physical and symbolic competition, Caesar laid out huge *horti* of his own across the river. Requiring ample space for terraces, walkways, groves, and other amenities, *horti* proliferated on the city's edges where land and water were available. By the middle of the first century B.C., private *horti* formed a loose green belt around Rome.[81] Within the city center, landscaping was more constrained. Only the most wealthy could have water brought to the hilltops not supplied by aqueducts. The valleys had more available water, but less space. Republican sources record individual plants such as the fig tree associated with Romulus and Remus, rather than extensive landscape designs.[82] Large formal planting schemes were relatively rare in public spaces, usually found in conjunction with sacred sites or quadriporticos such as the Porticus of Pompey.

Augustus sanctioned urban landscaping. He showed a personal interest in horticulture and landscape design, frequently discussing the subject. Pliny credits Gaius Matius, a friend of the *princeps*, with advancing the art of topiary, adding in another passage that from the time of Augustus onward, it was common to see trees, "clipped and made into thick walls or evenly rounded off with trim slenderness . . . to provide representations of the landscape gardener's work."[83] The *princeps* included greenery in his individual projects such as the Apollo complex on the Palatine Hill, Mausoleum of Augustus in the Campus Martius, and the Porticus Liviae on the Oppian Hill. Awarded the honor of having laurel trees before the doors of his house, he embellished many other projects with them as well. In the private realm, Augustus set an example. He preferred to sleep outdoors in a garden rather than in an opulent bed chamber, and decorated his personal properties, "not so much with handsome statues and pictures as with terraces and groves."[84] Others followed his example. Denied the possibility of triumphal monuments and other impressive public acts, and discouraged from erecting showy tombs or opulent homes, patrons turned to *horti* as a means to enhance personal status.

Augustus supplied the means as well as the incentive for the creation of urban gardens. The expansion and overhauling of the city's aqueduct system in the 30s B.C. increased the volume and distribution of water in Rome. As a result, the city burst into bloom. Numerous private *horti* enhanced the cityscape. Requiring large tracts, these parklike estates clustered on the city's edges and, in particular, on the hilltops and slopes irrigated by the new aqueduct system. In fact, private *horti* flourished along every aqueduct line (fig. 81).[85]

Equally significant, Augustus and his adherents reconceptualized urban landscaping as a public amenity in line with eastern examples.[86] All the great Hellenistic cities had impressive public parks that beautified the cityscape and provided breathing space for the urban population. For example, Antioch, headquarters of Antony during the Parthian campaign, was renowned for its expansive Daphne park; the Alexandria of Cleopatra had manicured, palatial gardens and tree-lined streets.[87] Thus, the perception evolved that a great city needed great public gardens. Again, as in other developments, Caesar led the way. In his will, he left the Horti Caesaris to the Roman people, making the sprawling park accessible to all residents of Rome (Suet.*Caes*.83). Augustus followed suit. He opened the funerary gardens around his Mausoleum to the public and developed open parklands on the right bank with a large grove, the Nemus Caesarum honoring his dead grandsons. Agrippa created a showcase of landscape architecture in the central Campus Martius connected with his baths and the private Horti Agrippae. Here were found an artificial lake (Stagnum Agrippae), the Euripus canal, and a verdant field with gardens, lawns, and trees. Like Caesar, Agrippa left these properties to the public after his death. As a result, the Campus Martius, traditionally an open public gathering place, retained its accessibility, but changed its image; the field of the war god Mars became a lush parkland.

Being fugitive, the scope and nature of plantings are difficult to document in a city such as Rome continuously occupied since antiquity.[88] Nevertheless, the impact of urban greenery should not be underestimated. Plantings visually united noncontiguous structures such as the Agrippan projects dotting the Campus Martius. In addition, *horti* themselves were formed of disparate parts melded into creative ensembles. Rome's residents thronged to the expanding public gardens to enjoy fishponds, topiary, porticos, fountains, vine-covered walkways, and sculptural displays. Inexpensive and quickly implemented in comparison to buildings, urban gardens dramatically and rapidly transformed the cityscape. One example will make the point. In the first century B.C., a forlorn remnant of the Republican fortification system remained on the Esquiline Hill, a large fosse used as a garbage and charnel pit. Augustus' cultural arbiter Maecenas filled in the fosse and laid out a wondrous park, complete with Rome's first warm-water swimming pool and a marvelous, cool garden auditorium half underground and directly on the line of the old city wall. After visiting the transformed hill, Horace breathlessly wrote, "you can [now] stroll along the [remains of the Republican city] wall in the sunshine where recently you had a grim view of white bones strewn on the ground" (*Sat*.1.8; cf. DioCass.55.7).

The greenspace within the city appealed to the eye and provided residents an escape from their crowded living and working conditions. Once inside a large urban park, it was easy to forget the teaming city outside. There, as within quadriporticos, observers found directed propaganda presented by complex artistic programs as well as by the plantings themselves with their own intricate symbolism. Collectively, urban landscaping also projected a clear message. Nature inside the city was carefully controlled and shaped by the benevolent *princeps,* as were all aspects of life.[89] Viewed as a whole, the verdant Rome of Augustus was a sophisticated city of communal recreation and repose, rather than one of war and individual competition. Given this powerful model, Romans of the Augustan Age could hardly imagine any great city devoid of urban landscaping.[90]

Order, introversion, and cohesion were the hallmarks of Augustan ensembles. These characteristics evolved in response to the contextual realities of an aging, dense city. Where open land existed, adherence to a grid imposed immediate unity among structures; in the urban center, other design solutions emerged. Through reordering, alignment, or enclosure, the *princeps* set his environments apart from their messy, unprogrammed surroundings. Observers moving through Rome's extant Republican urban fabric experienced a visual cacophony of diverse styles and forms, irregular spatial voids, and conflicting propagandas. In response, Augustan ensembles provided large, unified designs, crisply defined negative spaces, and directed propaganda. Despite the isolationist design of quadriporticos, precinct walls, and directed axes, Augustan projects enhanced the overall conception of Rome. The proliferation of plantings stressed life and abundance throughout the cityscape. Furthermore, by demonstrating the value of group design, Augustan ensembles elevated the discourse from single objects (artworks or buildings) to the level of the city.

Scale

In the Republic, the size of an architectural project reflected the donor's wealth and status. Competition was fierce, creating an escalating spiral of enlargement. The Dictator Caesar had consciously upped the ante. All his schemes were enormous. In the city center, he reworked the Basilica Aemilia and erected the new Basilica Julia; these two structures were both huge, covering a combined total of over 7,000 square meters. Nearby, he began an entirely new forum measuring approximately 12,000 square meters. To the north, he planned the Saepta Julia with a portico measuring a mile. Among his unrealized projects were the alteration of the great Tiber River and a temple to Mars, "greater than any in existence" (Suet.*Caes*.44).

Augustus fell heir to these oversized dreams. He completed Caesar's works in progress and fulfilled many projects still on the drawing table. In the Forum Augustum, the *princeps* erected a temple to Mars obviously far greater than any other in existence. The structure rose upon a podium measuring 38 × 48 meters. The octastyle form further accentuated the building's scale. Other temples in Rome had at most six columns across the front; the Temple of Mars Ultor had eight (fig. 65). Within the capital city, the Temple of Mars Ultor was second in size only to the hexastyle Temple to Jupiter Optimus Maximus, supreme deity of the Roman pantheon. With a large open area before the Temple of Mars Ultor, visitors could see the façade in all its grandeur. Viewed from just inside the western precinct wall, the lower flanking porticos forced the perspective, further accentuating the height of the temple (fig. 51). Walking the long distance to the temple podium, observers had ample time to appreciate the size of Augustus' forum, especially since the central statue forced them to move off the primary axis. Measuring approximately 125 × 85 meters, the complex was consciously larger than the adjacent Forum Julium.[91]

Many Augustan projects earned superlative adjectives, even when in comparison to Caesarean projects. South of the Saepta Julia, Agrippa began the Diribitorium for the counting of votes; Augustus completed the project and opened it with great fanfare at the time of Agrippa's funeral. Dio Cassius calls the Diribitorium "the largest building under a single roof ever constructed" (55.8). This accomplishment stood in direct superiority to Caesar, for the Dictator had not roofed the Saepta. Augustus underscored his achievement by exhibiting a timber left over from construction of the Diribitorium. People stared in amazement at the 100-foot-long beam displayed, not by coincidence, in the adjacent Saepta Julia (Cic.*Att*.4.16; Pliny *HN*.16.201).

Equally remarkable were three projects on the edges of Rome. The great Naumachia Augusti on the right bank was an artificial pool for mock naval battles and other spectacles. Gigantic in size, this artificial lake contained an island and covered an expanse larger than the combined areas of the Republican Circus Flaminius and Circus Maximus. Augustus demonstrated his pride in this tremendous undertaking by including the pool's measurements (1,800 × 1,200 Roman feet, or 536 × 357 meters) in his list of deeds accomplished (*ResG*.23). Across the river from the Naumachia rose the Mausoleum Augusti. Mountainous in size, this tomb needed no proclamation of measurements; all residents of Rome could see it exceeded every other tomb that had come before.[92] The circular monument had a diameter of 89 meters and a height of approximately 44 meters. In size alone, the structure proclaimed the status of its eternal occupant. Immediately to the south, the Horologium Augusti magnified a Roman tabletop sundial to urban scale.[93]

The simple process of agglomeration also conveyed a sense of increased scale. New urban ensembles were by nature larger than individual projects and thus implied increased significance. Just as notable, concentrations of individual Augustan projects within the cityscape created the impression of unified, large-scale urban designs. For example, the clustering of new structures in the Campus Martius created an entire district associated with Augustan largess.

Not every individual Augustan project was exceptional in size, but the majority were notably larger than their Republican predecessors and pointedly larger than the works undertaken by the rivals of the *princeps*. The Thermae Agrippae overshadowed earlier *balnea* in Rome; the Theater of Marcellus was greater in diameter than the contemporaneous Theater of Balbus; and so on. The forms were familiar, but the scale increased. The erection of ever-larger structures was fully in line with competitive Republican patronage. Following Caesar's lead, the *princeps* merely skipped several increments on the scale of progressive enlargement in order to affirm his own off-scale importance.

Vitruvius noted that the Romans equated the size of a city with the size of its forum (5.1.2). Though Rome had grown into a megalopolis, her central Forum remained small minded, constrained by existing buildings and enduring memories. Julius Caesar had acknowledged this reality by adding the new Forum Julium directly to the east. Boastful of Rome's increasing size, Augustus claimed the city in his day had so many people and so many law cases additional facilities were needed (Suet.*Aug.*29). With the construction of the Forum Augustum, Rome had a central forum composed of three distinct parts.[94] Together these magnificent spaces affirmed the greatness of the Augustan city. During the period of the triumvirate, Vergil wrote in his first *Eclogue:*

The city which they call Rome, Melioboeus, I, foolish one! thought was like this of ours . . . I knew puppies were like dogs, and kids like their dams; thus I used to compare great things with small. But this one had reared her head as high among all other cities as cypresses oft do among the bending osiers.

This passage associates the greatness of Rome with her stature as the free capital of a Republic. In the following decades, the city grew in physical size to match this political image (Dion.Hal.*AntRom.*4.13.5). Individually, the components of the Augustan city were huge. New buildings occupied more space, cast longer shadows, took longer to walk through, and filled more of observers' visual field. Simultaneously, the number of interventions in the city itself was tremendous. The home of Augustus naturally attracted people. The population rapidly expanded along with the built form; new projects pushed the edge of the roofs ever outward until the scale of Rome equalled her import.

Materials

Imageability responds to all sensory stimuli. In the late first century B.C., Cicero wrote, "the most complete pictures are formed in our minds of the things that have been conveyed to them and imprinted on them by the senses, but that the keenest of all our senses is the sense of sight" (*DeOr*.2.87.357). Beyond form and size, the eye reacts most forcefully to color and textures. The Romans, far more than urban observers today, were accustomed to reading content in hues. Given the comparatively limited palette available, these associations could be specific and powerful. The color of stripe on a garment immediately signaled social stature; the shade of fillet decorating a temple announced a specific religious meaning. Similarly, but less obviously, surface finishes reflected hierarchies according to the materials' cost, symbolism, and difficulty of procurement and craftsmanship. In particular, the Romans revered reflective surfaces as associated with expense and divinity.

Rome of the Republic was a matte city of somber natural hues with bright painted accents.[95] The primary media were mottled tufas, variegated rubble work, unglazed bricks, and stucco surface coverings, with an occasional white travertine doorway.[96] Structures with imported marbles stood out as events of great moment in the cityscape. Marbles were costly, especially during the years when civil conflict disrupted trade from quarries in the east. As a result, Republican patrons used the hard reflective stones as accents or veneers. Solid marble buildings were rare. In the Republican city, multicolored marbles elicited effluent praise and excessive condemnation. Antisumptuary laws restricted use on personal memorials such as tombs and houses, yet the value and positive associations of the hard stones ensured their application on monuments.[97] The aedile M. Scaurus, stepson of Sulla, evaded antisumptuary restrictions by importing columns of Lucullean marble for a public project: a temporary theater. A month later, work crews dragged the impressive marble pieces past the mundane terra-cotta adornments of Rome's temples and up the Palatine where they reinstalled them on Scaurus' own *domus*.[98]

The use of marble in urban architecture affirms Republican biases. The Romans believed rich materials, like large size, conveyed superior status. Authors applied the term *magnificentia* specifically to buildings of this material.[99] In reference to a Republican temple, Vitruvius wrote, "If this building had been of marble, so that besides the refinement of its art it possessed the dignity coming from magnificence and great outlay, it would be reckoned among the first and greatest of works" (7.pref.17; cf. 2.8.16). First Caesar and then his son Augustus looked at the capital and came to the same conclusion. Without a superior materiality, the urban fabric of Rome would remain second rate.

Under Julius Caesar, marble displays multiplied. One of his prefects covered an entire house in marble and the Dictator himself planned the mile-long Saepta entirely out of the hard stone. To supply these and other projects, Caesar began to work the Italian quarries of white marble at Luni

Table 5. Materials Used in a Sampling of Augustan Projects

Temple of Apollo Palatinus, dedicated 28 B.C.

Italian:	Luni marble	columns, walls
	Anio tufa	podium
	Concrete	podium
Imported:	Giallo antico	porticus columns

Basilica Aemilia, rebuilt after 14 B.C.

Italian:	Monte Verde; reused	tabernae
	Grotta oscura; reused	tabernae
	Travertine	foundations
	Concrete foundations	vaults
Imported:	Giallo antico	pavement
	Cipollino interior veneer	columns, pavement
	Porta Santa	pavement
	Pavonazzetto	columns
	Africano	columns
Unidentified white marble		exterior veneer

Forum Augustum and Temple of Mars Ultor, dedicated 2 B.C.

Italian:	Travertine	precinct wall, temple stress points
	Gabine tufa	precinct wall
	Alban tufa	precinct wall
	Peperino	temple walls
	Luni marble	temple veneer, precinct, entablature
	Bronze	stylobate facing
Imported:	Alabaster	column bases
	Cipollino	columns, pilasters
	Africano	pavement
	Giallo antico	pavement
	Pavonazzetto	pavement
	Breccia corallina	interior columns

Temple of Concordia Augusta, restored A.D. 10

Italian:	Anio tufa	podium
	Travertine	podium
	Concrete	podium
Imported:	Porta Santa	threshold
	Pavonazzetto	pavement, interior veneer
	Cipollino	interior socle
	Giallo antico	plinth, pavement
	Africano	pavement

Basilica Julia, rededicated A.D. 12

Italian:	Anio tufa; reused	walls
	Travertine	pilasters, foundations
	Grotta oscura; reused	foundations
	Concrete	foundations
Imported:	Porta Santa	pavement
	Giallo antico	pavement
	Africano	pavement
Unidentified white marble		exterior pavement, veneer

(modern Carrara). Augustus exploited the blessings of peace and prosperity to transform completely the capital's material grandeur. He improved shipping facilities at Luni and began to import stones from throughout the Empire.[100] New quarries in Egypt produced a hard stone with curls of color dubbed "Augustan"; Ovid claimed, "mountains diminish as the marble is dug from them."[101] Huge ships ferried marbles from Egypt, Greece, and Asia Minor to the harbor of Rome. From there, barges took the stones up river to docking facilities in the city proper. With dozens of projects underway in the city, the port below the Aventine could not handle all the traffic. A new mole developed farther north at the Campus Martius specifically to accommodate the large quantities of materials needed for the many Augustan projects rising on the plain.[102]

Augustus' boast that he transformed Rome from a city of clay to one of marble was not an idle one. His major monuments glistened with slick marble surfaces. Giallo antico columns cast a yellow and red glow around the portico of the Palatine temple; pavonazzetto columns graced the Basilica Aemilia; mottled Africano shone underfoot at the Basilica Julia; the Forum Augustum gleamed with over half a dozen kinds of imported stones (Table 5).[103] In most cases, Augustan architects used economical marble veneers; with a few special projects, the *princeps* ordered costly ashlar blocks. The temples of Apollo Palatinus and Jupiter Tonans as well as the Ara Pacis had walls of solid marble.[104]

Marbles offered distinct advantages to urban designers of the Augustan Age. Not widely used in the cityscape of the late first century B.C., this material immediately grabbed attention. It was colorful, shiny, and affirmed Rome architectural parity with eastern cities. Contemporary authors consistently remarked upon the use of marble when describing Augustan buildings. One characteristic stands out above all others: the reflectiveness of the stone. Vergil praised the gleaming quality of the Temple of Apollo Palatinus (*Aen.*8.720–2); Propertius referred to the yellow marble of the adjoining colonnade as golden (Prop.2.31). Amid the matte surfaces of Rome, sparkling marbles reflected simultaneously the buildings of Augustus and the patron himself. Apollo, god of light, guided the actions of the *princeps;* together they envisioned a gleaming capital city as the manifestation of a new, sparkling golden age.

The increased importation of marbles gave Rome a greater range of architectural colors beyond the brilliant white of Italian stones. With access to foreign quarries, green, red, yellow, pink, black, purple, and mottled stones appeared. Recording the contemporary situation Strabo wrote:

For at Rome are to be seen monolithic columns and great slabs of variegated marble [Brescia di Settebassi]; and with this marble the city is being adorned both at public and at private expense; and it has caused white marble to be of little worth.[105]

Thus, the material enrichment of Augustan Rome was equalled by a coloristic enhancement. The lush hues just as much as the brilliant reflections symbolized the superiority of the city.

Augustus focused his use of marble on public works. Through example, antisumptuary laws, and direct pressure, he made clear the appropriateness of opulence for State, not personal, aggrandizement, a policy that plucked the strings of Republican conservatism. In private works, Augustus avoided material opulence. Suetonius records that the house of Augustus on the Palatine had "but short colonnades with columns of Alban stone (tufa), and rooms without any marble decorations or handsome pavements" (*Aug.*72). Even the large Mausoleum Augusti was materially modest, built of concrete and reticulate faced with travertine. Following the party line, Augustan authors championed restraint in private buildings. Propertius boasted, "No marble shafts to prop my house have I" (3.2.11); Horace posed the question, "But if neither Phrygian marble nor purple brighter than the stars nor Falernian wine nor Persian nard can sooth one in distress, why should I rear aloft in modern style a hall with columns to stir envy?"[106]

Throughout the Mediterranean, marble had a long history in monumental public architecture. The gleaming materiality of eastern cities was well known and a small number of marble projects in the Republican city stood as tantalizing hints of things to come. Few patrons, Augustus included, anticipated the great difficulties involved with the material transformation of Rome. Even Vitruvius apparently did not give a second thought to construction of marble; in his treatise, he included only a short general chapter on the working of stones (2.6). With limited experience, few masons in Rome had the expertise to undertake delicate carvings or fine finish work in marble. As a result, Augustus imported artisans from the east along with building materials.[107]

The transportation of heavy blocks posed special problems within the city. Tibullus writing in the time of Augustus tells of an ambitious man, "His fancy turns to foreign marbles, and through the quaking city his column is carried by a thousand sturdy teams" (2.3). The plethora of Augustan construction projects must have clogged Rome's streets with huge wagons, especially since Caesar's *Lex Julia Municipalis* made an exception to allow the transport of materials for public buildings during daylight hours. When Scaurus moved his large columns, the contractor responsible for the city sewer required a security against possible damage. Many of the repairs to Rome's urban infrastructure during the Augustan Age may have been necessitated by the wear and tear inflicted by carts carrying weighty building materials.

In addition to marble, other media naturally continued to be used in the construction of public works. Travertine remained popular for its load-bearing capabilities, though Vitruvius warned about its tendency to split when subjected to fire. Tufas were appreciated for their perceived resistance to heat; this was the main material of the fire wall behind the Temple of Mars Ultor. During the life of Caesar, builders had discovered the advantages of concrete made from dusky-red pozzolana sand from pits near Rome. Nevertheless, little architectural experimentation resulted. Recalling past failures of other mortar mixtures, architects of the Augustan Age advised caution (Vitr.5.10.3; cf. 2.3). Used for foundations and podia, this medium had scant explicit impact on the external appearance of the city. More significant from an urban standpoint were developments in timber building. The enormous roof over the Diribitorium could have been only possible with advances in truss construction. Sadly for future generations, such expertise was not preserved. When the Diribitorium burned in A.D. 80, no one could reconstruct the roof (DioCass.55.8.4; 66.24).

In terms of the image of the city tufas, brick, rubble work, and other familiar Republican architectural materials shared a common problem. All

Figure 82. Relief from a Julio-Claudian altar depicting the Temple of Magna Mater as background for a sacrifice; Villa Medici. Photo: Fototeca Unione AAR 4366.

appear rough and weathered if not given a surface covering. The Romans were expert stucco workers. The high refinement possible with this medium was demonstrated by the Temple of Magna Mater on the Palatine. When restoring this building after a fire in A.D. 3, Augustus called for the original materials to be used, either for religious reasons or to prevent competition with his nearby marble enclave to Apollo. The rebuilt temple to Magna Mater was of tufa with a covering of stucco mixed with marble dust. Depictions of the temple prove that the finished product could readily compare with other buildings of stone in crispness of detail (fig. 82).[108] The drawback of stucco work is that it requires patience, skill, and constant maintenance to keep a reflective veneer and crisp detail. Vitruvius took great pains to explain the necessary steps in creating a stucco surface. After applying several coats, including at least three with powdered marble, he exults that the finished surface "reflects from its surface a clear image of the beholder" (7.3.11). Both the funds and skilled labor for such time-consuming work became available during the prosperous days of the Augustan Age.

In addition to sparkling stones and stuccowork, Augustan designers provided further visual excitement with metal architectural accents. A few Republican buildings boasted bronze components. For example, the Temple of Janus was sheathed completely in bronze panels in emulation of shields and M. Aemilius Lepidus decorated the Basilica Aemilia with shields in 78 B.C. (Pliny *HN*.35.13) (fig. 52). Under the *princeps,* more metal became available from mines in Alpine Ceutrones and Cordova, resulting in a slight increase in architectural usage. The restored Porticus Octavia had bronze column capitals; Agrippa included column capitals of Syracusan metal in the Pantheon.[109] Augustus also brought metal down to a pedestrian level, attaching bronze panels to the large podium of the temple to the war god in his forum. Perhaps this excessive display of metal was calculated to evoke association with the Janus temple, especially since the *princeps* had caused the doors of that temple to be closed three times signaling peace in the empire.[110]

Augustus had a unique opportunity to make a material imprint on the city of Rome. Only rarely in urban history does a city come under the sway of a single individual who has the opportunity and means to introduce a single material on an urban scale. Marble well suited the overall program of Augustus. It was solid, valuable, impressive, enduring, colorful, highly variable, and yet still familiar. The high sheen metaphorically recalled the gleaming sun god Apollo, but the polished surfaces just as forcefully reflected the image of the *princeps.*

Ornament

To help with memorization, teachers of rhetoric recommended the use of visually notable *imagines*. These could be people, plants, sculpture, or decorations. Rome in the Augustan Age filled to the brim with content-laden images. Every street corner had representations of the Lares and Genius Augusti; artworks embellished temples; municipal officers in their official garb accompanied by lictors strolled through their respective *vici*. The well-defined open spaces of the expansive new porticos all boasted artwork to help illiterate observers understand the programmed meaning of each environment.[111] In such an urban context, architectural ornament, too, conveyed a legible content.

Augustan carvers had access to a wide stylistic repertoire. The ornamentation on projects by the *princeps* ranged from the stolid embellishments of the Theater of Marcellus to the delicate carvings on the Ara Pacis (figs. 83 and 67). Eclecticism had no negative connotations. More important was the appropriateness of the style and media for the structure or complex embellished. Mixtures were readily accepted as in themselves conveying a content.

Figure 83. Theater of Marcellus, eastern façade. Fototeca Unione AAR 536.

Augustus presented his temple to Apollo Palatinus simultaneously as a reverential response to a request from the Greek god, and as an affirmation of his Latin allegiance to Rome. The complex included ivory door panels decorated with griffins and terra-cotta plaques with classicizing representations (fig. 49).[112]

The decoration on Augustan buildings was sharply carved and rich in detail. In part, such crispness and complexity was made possible by the use of marble. This hard material could take precise carving, thus emulating in stone the razor edges of first pressings from terra-cotta molds or metal work. Augustan artisans preferred a uniform depth of carving, possibly a further nod to venerated Italic terra-cotta relief work. The result was a highly coloristic effect with an even play of darks and lights conveying a sense of calmness.

Architectural ornament is not a common subject in literary descriptions, yet contemporaries of Augustus marveled at the complicated decoration of their day. For example, Propertius describes the doors on the Apollo temple as "wrought in wondrous wise" (2.31). Every major structure of the Augustan Age boasted a feast of detail, the exuberant ornament unconstrained by the limitations of a rigid canon. Pegasuses galloped amid the Corinthian capitals of the Mars temple; small insects and birds cavorted in the tendrils on the panels of the Ara Pacis.[113] The richness of carving and repertoire of forms recalled fifth-century B.C. Attic work. In fact, patrons of the Augustan Age imported Greek carvers specifically to reproduce the precision and metallic crispness of Attic architectural ornament.

The Romans had long admired Attic handiwork. They often referred to the Erectheion on the Athenian Acropolis designed by Kallimachos, the designer credited with inventing the popular Corinthian order (Vitr.4.1.10). This temple was renowned for its lush ornament, including a porch with caryatids, columns carved in the form of maidens. Pliny writing in the first century A.D. called the lavish relief work on the Erectheion "katatexitech-nic," or "frittering away one's skill upon details" (*HN*.34.92). The description could apply aptly to much of the exquisitely carved work on Augustan buildings in Rome, including the replicas of the Erectheion caryatids placed on the upper level of the lateral porticos in the Forum Augustum (fig. 80).

The complex carving on Augustan buildings created an animated play of light and shade across the surfaces. The variegated marble surfaces begged to be touched. Experientially, the ornament directly engaged observers. The intricacy of the designs drew them close, provoking viewers to puzzle out the meaning of each detail and touch the sharp edges. In effect, the attraction of ornament provided its own isolationism within the city. Observers caught up examining and touching architectural details at eye level forgot the surrounding urban fabric and entered a manipulated, Augustan realm.

The architects of the Augustan Age successfully integrated decoration into the presentation of the whole. Whereas Greek ornamentation seems complete in and of itself, that on Augustan projects is articulated as part of a greater scheme. In the Forum Augustum, the caryatids stood as replicated vertical alignments, reenforcing the syncopated rhythm of the lateral portico columns; in the Erectheion, they formed independent, three-dimensional supports on a projecting porch. The conceptualization of elements as part of a whole relates directly to the concept of *imagines*. Just as each element in an oration is tied to the central theme, so each component of a Roman building enhanced the overall design. On an urban level, the colorism of architectural surfaces and ornamentation animated the cityscape. The classicizing decorations placed Augustan projects within an enduring continuum and affirmed the supremacy of the current age.

Augustus shaped his urban image from a familiar kit of parts. The building types, materials, and ornaments of his numerous projects drew upon the strength of tradition. All were conservative, refined, and unthreatening;

nothing opposed the *mos maiorum*. In virtually every instance, however, the *princeps* and his architects pushed the existing envelope. Each urban intervention was memorable. The approach might be called "enhanced familiarity." Buildings took traditional forms, but had enlarged scale both individually and as ensembles. Richly colored, highly reflective stones expanded from mere urban accents to entire complexes, their glow dominating whole visual fields. Elaborate, coloristic architectural carvings now conveyed an intensified meaning; individual features received additional iconography, while their placement within complex programmatic displays made the parts greater because of the whole.

Visitors to any great metropolis find their senses assailed at every turn. The enhanced familiarity of Augustan urban components could have easily become lost within the morass of mundane construction. The imageability of the new urban elements resulted from an intense focus on each part. Through calculated design, Augustan temples appeared to tower over other structures; introverted ensembles closed out the rest of the city. Material attraction drew and held the eye away from the matte surfaces of the surrounding urban infill. Rich, katatexitechnic decoration channeled attention into a focused, intimate sphere, to the exclusion of the external surroundings. Furthermore, because these components belonged solely to the public realm, they gained in recognition and distinction through directed popular use. Worshiping at the temples, walking in the porticos, attending performances in the theaters, city residents focused on the activities at hand and, simultaneously, were caught up by the *publica magnificentia* of the Augustan urban components.

ORCHESTRATION

Augustus worked with notable individual components. To create a memorable and effective urban image, however, these parts had to be integrated with the existing cityscape and with each other. In the Republic, urban interventions had been individualized and thus episodic. Proximity, not conscious design, had defined interrelationships between buildings and locales. In the Augustan Age, the huge number of urban projects by one man compelled both the *princeps* as patron and all urban observers to consider interconnections. Moving through the city, Roman observers ordered their experience by drawing associations between parts. The urban design features identified by Lynch – landmarks, nodes, districts, paths, and edges – provide a useful structure for analyzing the orchestration of the Augustan urban experience in Rome (fig. 7).

Landmarks

Lynch defines a landmark as a point reference in the cityscape external to the observer. Notable components help to transform a structure into a remembered landmark, but they are not the sole determinants. A building's eye-catching materials, large-scale or unusual form only become memorable when they can be observed. Siting is therefore crucial. To perceive a building as a landmark, observers need an appropriate distance and unencumbered sight lines, whether within the overall urban context or within a localized environment. In a crowded, densely built city such as Rome, arranging clear vistas of new structures was extremely difficult. Most buildings were seen from a skewed angle and thus appeared distorted. As a result, creation of an urban landmark required the careful orchestration of how a project was perceived by observers.

In the first book of his architectural treatise, Vitruvius describes *scenographia* as the art of representing objects in perspective (1.2.2). He subsequently directed this optical interest to urban architecture, advising his contemporaries to think about the architectural distortions caused by different viewing angles:

The look of a building when seen close at hand is one thing, on a height it is another, not the same in an enclosed place, still different in the open, and in all these cases it takes much judgment to decide what is to be done. (6.2.2)

Taking such factors into account, Roman architects adopted a scenographic approach to building placement. With calculation, they sited major monuments for optimal viewing within the cityscape. By manipulating the approach, sight lines, and context skillful architects transformed individual structures into landmarks.

In the time of Augustus, Rome offered few easy opportunities for architects to create landmarks. Though the city had many dramatic hilltop sites, most had long been occupied. For example, the Temples of Jupiter Optimus Maximus and Juno Moneta rose conspicuously on the two crests of the Capitoline hill; the Temple of Magna Mater dominated the western edge of the larger Palatine Hill to the south (figs. 82 and 85). Furthermore, diverse factors constrained new public structures in the capital. Land availability, property ownership, functional requirements, religious determinants, and site-specific events all affected building form and siting. Perhaps in response to these limitations, Augustan architects and planners developed a fine sense of drama, exploiting all means to ensure memorable views of their urban projects. In particular, they favored two contrasting strategies for urban landmarks: extroversion and introversion.

As points of reference, landmarks are most powerful when seen in the broadest urban context. Extroverted sites expose landmarks to panurban views. An obvious example is the Mausoleum Augustum; rising in majesty above the flat Campus Martius, the enormous tumulus was visible for many kilometers and especially drew attention from the Via Flaminia and the Tiber River (Verg.*Aen*.6.874). Directly south, the towering obelisk of the Horologium Augusti rose in solemn isolation from a paved plaza, riveting attention from a great distance (fig. 105). As a general rule, Vitruvius recommends that temples be sited either to face west or to provide a wide urban panorama.[114] Notably, a temple with a sweeping view outward is simultaneously visible from many locations within the city and thus becomes a landmark. Such was the case with the new temple to Apollo erected by Augustus atop the southern scarp of the Palatine. According to tradition, the god himself selected the impressive site, marking it with a blazing bolt of lightning (DioCass.49.15.5). The fact that Augustus owned the property and lived on adjacent land, of course, was equally relevant. The new temple had an expansive view of the southwestern quarters of Rome and conversely was readily seen by observers sitting in the Circus Maximus, walking atop the northern Aventine, and sailing on the Tiber (fig. 73).

Although the southwestern face of the Apollo temple was widely visible from the greater urban environment, the structure did not grab the attention of observers to the northeast. Many different Augustan projects showed a similar duality, serving as landmarks in one direction, but not in another. From the east, the crowded Forum Holitorium did not allow a full view of the Theater of Marcellus. In contrast, from the west, the river allowed a panoramic vista of the theater, as if the architects followed Vitruvius' advice for religious structures: "temples that are to be built beside rivers . . . ought, as it seems, to face the river banks" (4.5.2). Observers approaching the city by barge or along the Via Aurelia saw rising high above the water the impressive exterior of the theater's scaena with apses flanking its 90-meter width. In fact, the unusual southwest/northeast orientation of the Theater of Marcellus may be due in part to these important urban viewing angles (fig. 103).

Introverted siting took an opposite tact. In places where the topography or extant urban fabric prevented viewing of a building from a distance, Augustan designers created introspective environments. The majority of Augustan architectural ensembles barred outward views and placed the primary elevation within an internalized, isolated urban space as with the Forum Augustum. This complex did not present a monumental façade to the city and could not be considered a visual landmark within the cityscape. Inside the carefully contrived forum, however, the Temple of Mars Ultor stood as a dominating landmark (fig. 51).

Urban buildings always allow multiple visual readings. The impression conveyed from a distance can be quite different from that up close. In a few instances Augustan landmarks were able to retain their status as landmarks both within an introverted context and within the greater urban setting. Such was true for the Palatine complex to Apollo. Propertius describes a containing colonnade of colorful marble "in the midst [of which] the temple with its shining marble rose up high" (2.31). In effect, the portico served the same purpose as that in the Forum Augustum: creating an insular environment to focus attention on the temple façade. Similarly, the Temple of Apollo Palatinus was a landmark both for observers in the southern part of the city and for those within the Palatine colonnade (fig. 63).

Augustus added dozens of new structures to the cityscape of Rome. A remarkably large number of these made the conceptual metamorphosis from urban building to landmark. Significantly, no one Augustan landmark took a dominant position; instead, monuments appeared throughout the capital, affirming the *princeps'* paternal benevolence for all. However, in a few notable instances, landmarks focused attention on specific urban sites by serving as the centerpieces for urban nodes.

Nodes

Whereas, a landmark is external to the observer, nodes are more interactive. Observers pass through urban nodes, and in fact are drawn irrevocably toward them. These strategic points are not singular, but made up of several individual structures or spaces that may center around a landmark. Unlike ensembles, nodes are not necessarily cohesive architectural designs, but rather concentrations of functions and meaning. They are formed by intersections of paths or by interrelated spaces or buildings associated with significant, recurring activities. An urban node may be made up of one or more ensembles, but not every ensemble becomes part of an urban node. Furthermore, because nodes rely on activities and meaning, they can shift in location within the cityscape.

The convoluted network of preexisting streets in Republican Rome precluded the development of new significant intersections. Augustus therefore enhanced existing nodes and focused on assemblages to create new nodes within his capital. By localizing his building efforts and concentrating significant urban activities, the *princeps* slowly reprogrammed the city, shifting nodes from their location within the Republican cityscape to new Augustan centers, in effect creating related but distinct urban counterpoints.

Two urban nodes had dominated Rome during the Republic. For centuries, the Forum Romanum and the southwestern Capitoline Hill were the primary focal points of the city. Though of very different character, both were areas of intensive patronage, architectural excellence, and concentrated meaning. Here ambitious citizens consistently placed enduring monuments of self-promotion; their projects automatically reached a large audience and simultaneously drew upon the potent power of each *locus*. The Forum Romanum developed in the low-lying area framed by the Capitoline, Palatine, and slopes of the plateau to the east.[115] At the convergence of several naturally defined pathways, the space evolved into a marketplace and governmental center. The Forum became the heart of Rome. Public assemblies met in the open-air Comitium, the Senate convened in the Curia, residents worshiped at the surrounding temples, and spent many hours in the central plaza socializing, admiring propagandistic sculptures, and watching important communal events such as gladiatorial games.

Though a major urban node filled with important structures and programmed events, the Republican Forum lacked architectural unity. The numerous streets entering at different angles resulted in diverse building orientations. Individual structures stood as independent units associated by closeness. Wide spaces between buildings allowed for diverse, distracting views of the surrounding urban context (fig. 13). Competition among patrons to make their structures stand out further ensured a lack of formal cohesiveness. Vitruvius described the ideal Italic fora as rectangular with unifying porticos on three sides, yet during the Republic, the most important forum in the Roman world did not follow this model.[116]

Caesar had begun to reorder the Forum Romanum. He pushed the Curia into a subservient position tangent to his new Forum Julium and established a forceful northwest/southeast axis through the Tabularium and relocated Rostra. The two huge basilicas under construction reenforced this line with an approximate symmetry. Even in death, the Dictator continued to influence the Forum's development. His siting of the Rostra Caesaris became the basis for the subsequent Rostra Augusti. Furthermore, the relocated speakers' platform inspired placement of Caesar's funeral pyre on the same axis to the southeast, thereby determining the future location of the Temple to Divus Julius (fig. 84).

Caesar laid the groundwork for the ordering of the Forum Romanum, yet credit for its realization lies with his adopted son. Augustus along with his heirs and adherents reworked virtually every building within this node. The *princeps* himself completed the temple to his divine father and the Curia Julia, and rebuilt the two basilicas whose massive forms defined the lateral edges of the central Forum, reenforcing the new axis and blocking views outward to the rest of the city.[117] Adherents of Augustus aggrandized the surrounding temples to Castor and Pollux, Saturn and Concordia, giving

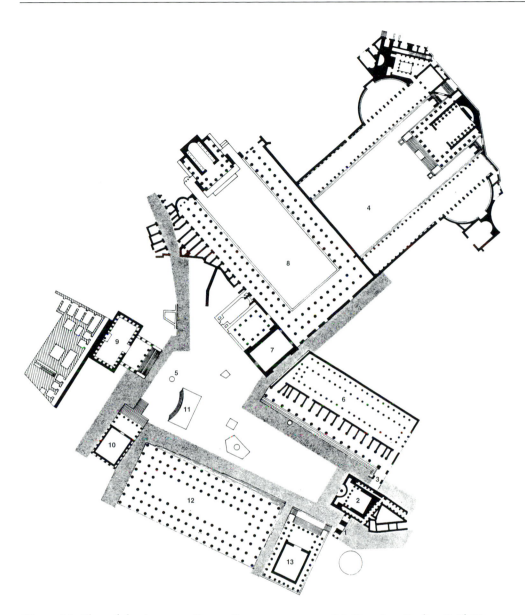

Figure 84. Plan of the Augustan Forum Romanum ca. A.D. 14. Drawing: Rodica Reif. **New Projects**: 1: Arcus Augusti (replaces Arcus Octaviani?); 2: Temple of Divus Julius; 3: Porticus Gaii et Lucii; 4: Forum Augustum; 5: Milliarium Aureum. **Restoration Projects**: 6: Basilica Aemilia; 7: Curia Julia; 8: Forum Julium with Temple of Venus Genetrix; 9: Temple of Concordia; 10: Temple of Saturn; 11: Rostra Julia; 12: Basilica Julia; 13: Temple of Castor and Pollux.

them new mantles of marble and high podia.[118] The State acknowledged the achievements of Augustus with several memorial arches as well as numerous other commemoratives.[119] The praetor peregrinus L. Naevius Surdinus laid a unifying pavement of white stone running from the Rostra downhill to the

Temple of Divus Julius; to mark this undertaking, he inscribed his name in bronze on the pavers, an explicit testament to Augustus' success in urging magistrates to undertake pragmatic projects.[120]

All these interventions brought a formal unity to the Forum Romanum. In particular, the addition of the Temple of Divus Julius and flanking commemoratives to Augustus and his heirs clarified the spatial order. This dynastic ensemble stood as the terminus of a strong northwest/southeast axis. To the sides, the repetitious façades of the opposing basilicas delimited a roughly orthogonal central space. As a result, the Augustan Forum Romanum approximated the arrangement for fora recommended by Vitruvius and represented tangentially by the adjacent Forum Julium.[121]

Although most of the Augustan projects in this node were restorations rather than new works, they crafted a new experience. The structures reworked under the *princeps* were taller and more opulent than in their Republican manifestations. Furthermore, they shared comparatively similar materials, age of reworking (i.e., newness), ornament, and style, as well as a common encoded program aggrandizing the achievements of Augustus and his family. The result was a strengthened physical and conceptual cohesiveness. From a Republican node formed at an intersection where numerous independent, powerful monuments congregated, the Forum Romanum by A.D. 14 became a unified container projecting a more directed message.[122]

Visitors to the Augustan Forum Romanum experienced a carefully choreographed environment. The subtle angling of walls and careful placement of memorials strengthened visual hierarchies and reenforced potent relationships between individual units. This manipulation is most obvious at the entry points into the node. Observers approaching from the southeast passed the gleaming marble of the renewed Regia and Temple of Vesta, symbols of Republican continuity. Soon, however, the content of the environment changed. Before them stood a marble arch commemorating the *princeps'* Parthian "victory." Urbanistically, this arch served as a doorway into the contained, redefined northwestern zone of the Forum. Passing through the arch observers stood between the high podium of the temple to the divine father of Augustus and the Temple of Castor and Pollux rebuilt by Tiberius. Immediately, their glance was drawn to a fig tree in the center of the stone-encrusted environment; this natural vertical element acted as a sight line, directing attention to the broad Rostra Augusti as it had to the earlier Rostra of Caesar. Two factors enhanced this visual axis. The northwestern ends of the lateral basilicas angled outward from one another, optically increasing the perceived width and length of the central Forum. Simultaneously, the ground rise toward the northwest placed the Rostra Augusti at a higher level; as a result, the structure dominated the visual field even though comparatively low in height. The axis terminated with the Temple of Concordia Augusta at the base of the Capitoline, above and behind the speakers' platform (fig. 37).

Other approaches to the Forum were similarly choreographed to provide a legible Augustan content. From the northwest, pedestrians entered along the Vicus Jugarius. The angled podium wall of the restored Temple of Saturn channeled views again toward the Rostra Augusti; the relative proximity of the speakers' platform allowed observers to appreciate related sculptures, including a large equestrian statue and *columna rostrata*, both surmounted by statues of Octavian, and the sparkling Milliarium Aureum commemorating the Roman highway system.[123] Beyond and at a slightly higher level, they saw the powerful vertical mass of the Curia Julia surmounted by a statue of Victoria celebrating Octavian's success at Actium. Pedestrians entering along the Clivus Argentarius found their attention drawn to the most impressive grouping of all, the Augustan dynastic set piece composed of the Temple of Divus Julius and lateral arches for the *princeps* and his heirs (fig. 57). Entering the Forum from the Argiletum on the northeast, observers again faced the fig tree, from this angle seen against the arcuated backdrop of the enlarged Basilica Julia renamed in honor of Gaius and Lucius. Turning slightly to the northwest, they saw the Rostra Augusti; beyond and above towered the Temple of Saturn, its pediment filled with Tritons trumpeting Augustan victories.

An important corollary to the imprinting of Augustan characteristics on to the Forum Romanum was the devaluing of the Republican power of place. Formally, this was achieved by focusing attention on a circumscribed portion of the Republican Forum, namely, the regularized northwestern zone loosely defined by the Clivus Capitolinus, lateral basilicas, and the Temple of Divus Julius. Outside the confines of this contained area stood formerly significant Republican structures, including the Regia, Domus Publica, and Temple of Vesta. Functionally, the Forum Romanum also lost stature. Caesar had begun the process by relocating activities from the Comitium to the Campus Martius. His magnificent new Forum Julium absorbed other public business previously accommodated in the old Forum. Following Caesar's lead, the *princeps* likewise transferred important activities away from the Forum, carefully selecting alternative Augustan venues. Senate meetings still occurred most frequently in the Curia and much public business and many ceremonies likewise continued to occur in the old Forum Romanum, affirming the alleged continuation of the Republic. Yet as decision making became associated with a person, rather than with a meeting place, the center of government conceptually shifted to whereever the *princeps* was.

As a result, the *genius loci* of the Forum Romanum subtly and slowly changed character. The strong power of the place ensured that this urban center remained a showcase of collective past achievements, but its nodal power within the cityscape declined subtly. Augustan transformations to the government and to the urban environment reprogrammed activities from largely active to largely passive. The Forum served increasingly as a museum and theater rather than governmental center. Pliny records that in the summer of 23 B.C., "from the first of August onward fixed awnings of sailcloth [hung] over the forum, so that those engaged in lawsuits might resort there under healthier conditions: what a change this was from the stern manners of Cato the ex-censor, who had expressed the view that even the forum ought to be paved with sharp pointed stones [to discourage loitering]!" (*HN*.19.23.24). Within the Forum, the *princeps* created buildings not just to house particular functions, but to entertain and educate through their form, ornament, and meaning. People came to see carefully staged events and the places where historical events had occurred, at the same time taking comfort in the confidence and continuity projected by every Augustan project. Underscoring the theatrical nature of the place, Augustus continued to hold gladiatorial games in the Forum Romanum, and required citizens to don appropriate attire before entering the space.[124] Increasingly, their stays were transitory. After admiring the museum/stage set and its Republican associationism visitors soon moved on to more vibrant, more Augustan, urban centers.

Following a shift initiated by Caesar, Augustus subtly relocated the focus of the Forum Romanum node to the northeast. Both patrons identified their new, contained foras as extensions to the old Forum Romanum rather than as confrontational alternatives.[125] Thus, Augustus could transfer the nodal center of the Forum Romanum to the Forum Augustum without explicitly denigrating the revered Republican center. He cemented this shift by embellishing his new enclosure with rich materials and famous artworks, and by programming it with both daily business, namely, the holding of courts and special events such as the granting of triumphs and yearly gathering of candidates awaiting assumption of the *toga virilis*. Pointedly, the design of the Forum Augustum promoted more select activities in contrast to some of the more popular (and rowdy) events of the old Forum. The complex followed the basic configuration recommended by Vitruvius, yet with notable alterations. In the Forum Augustum, the side porticos were surmounted by decorated attics instead of galleries, and so it could not handle numerous spectators watching gladiatorial combats or other performances in the central open space.[126] The large rectangular open area better suited large audiences passively watching action atop the high podium of the Mars temple (fig. 50).[127]

Augustus likewise subtly redirected the nodal focus of the Capitoline Hill. He paid homage to this important Republican religious focal point by renovating the existing temples of Jupiter Feretrius and Jupiter Optimus Maximus. In addition, he added another new structure to Jupiter in his guise as the Thunderer (Tonans) (fig. 54). Though small, this building drew extensive attention during the Augustan Age, including frequent visits from the *princeps*. Suetonius later grouped it with the Temple of Apollo and Forum Augustum as the most impressive public projects by Augustus.[128] The structure had walls of solid marble and a much admired sculpture by Leochares. Above all, however, the temple's great acclaim resulted from its prominent siting at the top of the road leading into the Area Capitolina. Dio Cassius explains that the people of Rome:

approached Jupiter who is called Tonans and did reverence to him, partly because of the novelty of his name and of the form of his statue, and partly because the statue had been set up by Augustus, but chiefly because it was the first [building] they encountered as they ascended the Capitol.[129]

The new, totally Augustan structure became the experiential center of this Republican urban node at the expense of the larger, more grand temple to Jupiter Optimus Maximus atop the hill. In reaction, the god complained to Augustus in a dream. As appeasement, the *princeps* proclaimed Jupiter Tonans as the watchman of Jupiter Optimus Maximus, and hung bells from the gable like those carried by night watchmen.[130] This pious, deferential act in reality must have enhanced, not minimized, the temple's attraction, the ringing bells encouraging pedestrians to dally and examine the building that provoked the jealousy of Jupiter Best and Greatest.

Augustus acknowledged the tradition-bound significance of the Capitoline Hill as a focus of display and ceremony. He reverentially conducted many rituals, often retailoring old ones or developing new ones to emphasize their association with his own programs.[131] At the same time, he began to weaken the urban significance of the entire Capitoline by transferring many vibrant activities and important objects to alternative venues. In each case, he ensured a Republican-based justification could be cited. For example, during the Republic, the Area Capitolinus was periodically cleared of commemorative statues to make room for more. The *princeps* likewise cleaned the area, but carefully reerected the important votives in the Campus Martius.[132] After becoming Pontifex Maximus, he used his authority as high priest to transfer the oracular Sibylline Books from the Temple of Jupiter Optimus Maximus to the library associated with the Temple of Apollo on the Palatine (Suet.*Aug*.29, 31). He also transferred events. Many activities associated with triumphs shifted from the Capitoline Hill down to

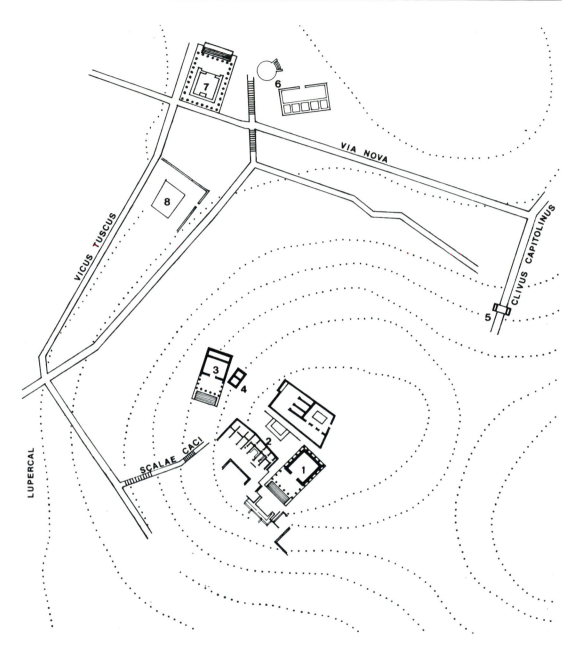

Figure 85. Plan of the Palatine Hill. Drawing: Richard H. Abramson. 1: Temple of Apollo; 2: House of Augustus; 3: Temple of Magna Mater; 4: Temple of Victoria; 5: Arcus Octavii; 6: Temple and Atrium Vestae; 7: Temple of Castor and Pollux; 8: Horrea Agrippiana.

the Forum Augustum. The Ludi Saeculares, the most important religious ceremonies in over a century, gave almost as much importance to the Augustan enclave on the Palatine as to the traditional Republican religious center on the Capitoline.

In fact, the *princeps* slowly but surely created a new urban node on the Palatine (fig. 85). Through new construction and careful reprogramming, this hill became both a viable religious alternative to the Capitoline and a nascent bureaucratic center in counterpoint to the Forum Romanum. The original power of the Palatine derived from events and structures associated with the Roman's earliest history. Atop the hill was Rome's first settlement, recalled by temples to the ancient goddesses Magna Mater and Victoria and, most poignantly, by a replica of Romulus' thatched hut. Reverently restored at least twice under Augustus, the hut was a tangible reminder that the Palatine was the residence of the city's eponymous hero; at the same time, this artifact of sticks and reeds formed a conceptual link with the Capitoline where a similar "Hut of Romulus" stood on display.[133]

Basking in the past glory of the Palatine, Augustus simultaneously imprinted the hill with his own history. He was alleged to have been born atop the Palatine; there he chose to reside.[134] His *domus* was naturally the focus of much activity. Though the *princeps* made a show of participating in meetings of the Senate down in the Curia Julia, increasingly, he ran the State from his residence on the Palatine. To accommodate the burgeoning imperial bureaucracy, he purchased unobtrusive neighboring houses. Not only did his staff members thereby have ready access to Augustus, they readily could consult the well-stocked public libraries nearby. When he became Pontifex Maximus, Augustus likewise took steps to conduct his duties on the Palatine rather than in the Forum Romanum. He made part of his own residence a *domus publica* and transferred there the altar and shrine of Vesta. By the end of his life, Augustus no longer veiled his actions with Republican propriety; he met regularly with the Senate in the Palatine libraries in close proximity to his house.[135]

Unfortunately, the exact overall external appearance of Augustus' *domus*, like most in ancient Rome, cannot be reconstructed. However, two attention-grabbing features of the structure may be discussed. State aggrandizement of private homes was an established Roman tradition as evidenced by the pediment (*fastigium*) placed on the house of Julius Caesar as a sign of honor. In particular, doorways held special importance for the Romans as transition points. The door into the house of a public figure, like the gate to a city, was a billboard avidly read by urban observers. During the Republic, certain outstanding citizens received the honor of hinging their doors to open outward into the street or hanging trophies around the entry.[136] Within the narrow streets of the Palatine Hill, the doorway into Augustus' house must have been a major attraction. It was flanked by laurel trees and surmounted by an oak crown, potent commemoratives celebrating the restoration of the Republic (fig. 53). In addition, Augustus as triumphator exercised his right to display trophies on his door. After being exiled, Ovid sends one of his books on an imagined visit to Rome. On its lonely journey, the book came upon the *princeps'* house and remarks, "While I was marveling at one thing and another, I beheld doorposts marked out from others by gleaming arms and a dwelling worthy of a god!" (*Tr.*3.1.33–4).

Viewed from a distance, the residence also stood out from other residences. Even without a pedimented roof, the House of Augustus had a notable silhouette. Suetonius records that this *domus* had a tower room used by Augustus as a private study. Although other wealthy homes may have had similar protrusions, the placement of the House of Augustus atop the lofty Palatine ensured that this particular tower was highly visible (Suet.*Aug.*72; cf. fig. 88). The skyline of the site may have been further accented by a palm tree. Suetonius records that a palm pushed through the paving stones in front of the House of Augustus. Because the palm was revered as the presager of victory, the *princeps* took this vegetal appearance as a positive sign. He transplanted the tree to his atrium and cared for it personally. The easily identifiable fronds of this tree would have drawn further attention to the Augustan residence.[137] The House of Augustus also gained stature from its immediate neighbor, the Temple of Apollo. The two structures were intimately, and obviously, connected. The temple's god, form, and iconography all promoted Augustus' achievements and programs. More tangibly, recent excavations have discovered a ramp linking the House of Augustus and the forecourt of the great Apollonian complex.

The gleaming marble temple to Apollo overtly vied with the Capitoline Temple of Jupiter Optimus Maximus for the most dramatic hilltop location in Rome. In fact, its broadly spaced columns indicate an early Italic temple format emulating, if not competing with, the Capitoline structure. Dominant in location, form, and material, the ensemble composed of the Apollo temple, porticos, and libraries became the focal point of the new Palatine urban node. People flocked to the Area Apollinis to admire the famous artworks, visit the libraries, and stroll in the gardens. Because the temple site was chosen by a bolt of lightning, Augustus could tout his new center as divinely sanctioned with little fear of recriminations for drawing attention away from Rome's earlier Republican urban centers.

Within the Augustan cityscape, the Palatine and Forum Augustum stood out as dominant urban focal points. Though not directly connected visually in the city, these two new nodes were often associated in visual representations, a clear affirmation of their elevated urban status and cognate relationship. In the Forum Augustum itself, a personification of the Palatine reclined in the pediment of the Mars temple (fig. 65).[138] The preserved reliefs from a Julio-Claudian monument locate a major sacrifice at these same Augustan

Figure 86. Relief from the Sorrento Base depicting a male figure (Aeneas or Mars?) standing before the House of Augustus identified by the *corona civica* (oak wreath) over the door. Photo: DAIR 57.1474.

nodes. The early part of the ceremony is shown taking place atop the Palatine, the site identified by representations of the Temples of Magna Mater and Victory northwest of Augustus' house. The actual bovid sacrifice is depicted occurring in front of the Temple of Mars Ultor.[139] Similarly, the famous Sorrento Base celebrates the Palatine as an Augustan urban node by representing deities associated with architectural projects undertaken by the *princeps* atop this hill. Side D depicts Cybele/Magna Mater enthroned, recalling the temple to the mother goddess completely rebuilt by Augustus. The fragmentary Side C shows the Genius of Augustus and Aeneas standing before the door to Augustus' house surmounted by the *corona civica* (fig. 86). Side A represents a procession to Vesta who took up residence within the House of Augustus, and Side B depicts Apollo whose landmark temple rose next door.[140]

The long-venerated Republican urban nodes remained significant in the cityscape and daily life of Augustan Rome, yet within a single generation, they faced competition from new and distinctive alternatives. The power of collective memory drew people in Rome to the Capitoline Hill and Forum Romanum. At the turn of the millennium architectural additions, reprogrammed activities, and careful choreography closely tied these urban nodes to the *princeps*. Nevertheless, visitors soon found themselves enticed away. The Forum Augustum beckoned with rich accoutrements, as well as court cases and other popular events. Similarly, the Palatine Hill enticed visitors from the Capitoline. Not only were the impressive Augustan structures on the Palatine clearly visible from the Capitoline, but the latter locale was imbued with allusions to the other hill, ranging from the second model of Romulus' hut to the lingering remembrance of the Sibylline Books. Secondary depictions in art and histories reaffirmed the strong *imageability* of the new Augustan urban nodes at the Forum Augustum and Palatine.

Districts

Districts are city sections with a two-dimensional extent defined by common use, appearance, and/or topographical definition.[141] Observers distinguish their locations as "at" an urban node, yet as "inside" or "outside" an urban district. For Republican Rome, districts were only loosely defined, generally based on topography. Thus, the Capitoline stood physically and conceptually apart due to its well-defined form and restrictive use as a religious center. By the late Republic, another district could be identified on the opposite hill. The limited space atop the Palatine defined a proscribed area covered with structures similar in use and form, namely, houses of the wealthy. When Augustus added a landmark, the Temple of Apollo, and developed a surrounding node, he in effect blurred the Palatine's distinction as an urban district.[142]

In general, the *princeps'* policy was to unify the city, not create distinct sectors. However, the opportunity to develop a new district in the Campus Martius was irresistible. This northern plain had well-defined limits: the river to the east and north, and hills to the east. Due to frequent flooding, the central section and riverbanks had not been developed fully during the Republic. Because much of the Campus was *ager publicus*, building was limited to such public works as temples and altars; privately owned structures were few. Only as a sign of great honor did the Senate approve the construction of private tombs on the plain. Not until late in the Republic did large-scale, permanent structures appear in the Campus Martius, most notably the Theater of Pompey complex; to the north, Caesar initiated construction of the Saepta Julia to replace a temporary enclosure.

After Caesar's death, several undertakings prepared the Campus for development. An incubator for disease, the huge pool of the Naumachia

Caesaris was covered over in 43 B.C. In the following decade, Agrippa repaired the city's drainage system and began provisions to bring potable water to the Campus. Augustus himself reworked the Tiber's banks and repaved the Via Flaminia. As a result, the Campus became a tempting *tabula rasa* begging for scripting.[143] Augustus and his supporters heeded the call, erecting over twenty buildings and restoring many others. Temporary constructions also proliferated, especially in conjunction with major events in the Augustan calendar such as the Ludi Saeculares and dedication of the Forum Augustum when wooden structures were erected to hold the hundreds of celebrants (*CIL* 6.32323; DioCass.55.10). In addition, the traditional use of the Campus as an open field near the city center was enhanced and regularized by the parklands associated with the Agrippan projects.

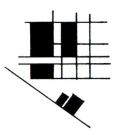

Figure 87. Diagram, urban grids.

The new additions to the Campus Martius held together visually and programmatically. The buildings displayed similar materials, style, and propaganda content. Equally significant, the majority of Augustan projects had a recreational use. Included in this pleasure zone were the Thermae Agrippae and accompanying parklands, lake, and canal; the Amphitheater of Statilius Taurus, and Theater of Balbus; even the Saepta Julia for assembly meetings was adapted for recreational use (Suet.*Aug*.43). Farther to the north, the Mausoleum of Augustus attracted people with its surrounding public park. In spite of all the new construction, the expansive Campus Martius as a whole retained the air of a park. Strabo described the activities on the plain: "The Campus . . . is of impressive size, and allows chariot-racing and other equestrian exercises to go on without interfering with the crowds of people exercising themselves with ball games, hoops, and wrestling" (5.3.8). Highly visible among the athletes were the *Juventas*, a quasi-military organization started by Augustus of young men who exercised daily in the Field of Mars.[144]

The early Republican temples in the central Campus Martius had been oriented to the cardinal points. The new Augustan buildings continued this alignment, in effect creating an ordered orthogonal plan in the heart of the plain. Standing in marked contrast to the organic arrangement of structures in the city center, this regularity further enforced the identity of the Campus as a distinct urban district (fig. 87). Looking over the Campus Martius, Strabo concludes that its monuments, amenities, and overall cohesiveness give "the impression that they are trying, as it were, to declare the rest of the city a mere accessory" (5.3.8; cf. Ov.*Pont*.1.8.33–8).

In fact, this one section of Augustan Rome became a showcase. Beyond availability of space, the Campus offered a programmatic reason for aggrandizement. Foreign ambassadors awaiting permission to cross the *pomerium* into Rome resided in the Villa Publica in the Campus Martius. When petitioning for a triumph, generals likewise waited in the Campus along with their troups and captives, often including rulers who were subsequently reinstalled in their homelands.[145] Thus, the entire district could be conceptualized as a vestibule for Rome. Visitors to the city experienced a huge district of grand marble structures laid out with Hellenistic orthogonal precision. A few Republican buildings and sculptures, notably those transferred from the Capitoline, established the venerable heritage of the city, yet the predominant message projected by this district was about Augustus and his impressive achievements. Vitruvius argued that a great house needed an impressive forecourt (Vitr.5.2). So did a great city. The Augustan Campus Martius served this purpose admirably.

Elsewhere in Rome, the creation of Augustan districts was thwarted. Not only did construction already cover every available plot, but usage was variable, with a healthy mixture of activities and classes distributed throughout the city, their interrelationships always shifting. Within the *pomerium,* formation of a distinct district would have required extensive rebuilding and reprogramming, something possible only at a high financial, social, and political cost. Furthermore, a second Augustan urban district would have detracted from the power and significance of that in the bend of the Tiber.

Paths

A path is, in essence, a memorable kinetic experience defined by the interaction of the observer with a programmed sequence of projects. Drawing on the strong association between environments and narratives articulated by rhetoricians, the Romans were predisposed to create physical as well as mental linkages between urban components connected along a path. These story lines were the collaborative result of integrating existing and new urban features. Responsible for numerous additions to the cityscape, Augustus was able to infuse select routes with legible, directed narratives read by observers moving along a continuous route. As for an orator recalling the *imagines* in a House of Memory, the direction of movement was irrelevant; the meaning of the narrative remained intact regardless of the direction taken because the relationships between content-laden images always remained the same.

The comprehensive choreography of an entire path requires either Haussmannlike intervention or a fairly undeveloped venue. The carving of a new grand avenue from the extant cityscape would have required an autocratic gesture clearly antithetical to Augustan policy. Instead, the *princeps* imprinted a new narrative on the one area of Rome with relatively limited development and a major pathway: the Campus Martius district disected on the east by the broad Via Flaminia.[146] Traveled by foreign ambassadors and triumphators, this northern pathway into Rome had special significance.

Augustan designers carefully scripted the entire linear sequence along the Via Flaminia, exploiting the roadway's high elevation as a viewing platform and narrative organizational device (fig. 103). Two urban doorways framed this path: the Augustan arch surmounting the Pons Mulvius to the north and the Porta Fontinalis in the old Republican Fortifications to the south.[147] Following the advice for mnemonic *imagines,* large and simple forms were used for monuments viewed from a distance, like the Mausoleum with its mountainlike mass.[148] Sequencing was also important. Significant Augustan structures appeared at fairly regular intervals, thereby maintaining the momentum and cohesiveness of the storyline (fig. 4; *Rhet.Her.*3.19.32). Openings between buildings or eye-directing components such as obelisks created calculated sight lines toward select monuments. Repeated images of the narrative's main character maintained the story line's continuity. Images of Augustus looked down on observers from atop an arch on the Pons Mulvius far to the north, from the height of the Mausoleum Augusti, from the Ara Pacis, from the porch of the Pantheon, and probably from many other locations as well. A wide range of artworks added by Augustus conveyed additional propaganda. For the literate, numerous inscriptions fleshed out the story.[149]

Subplots pendant to the primary narrative further enriched the story line presented along the Via Flaminia. Observers found themselves subconsciously encouraged to leave the elevated highway and investigate secondary routes. Simple devices such as the reliefs on the Ara Pacis showing a parade moving away from the Via, and enticing features including fountains, parklands, and curiosities drew people westward down into the central Campus Martius. After investigating the subplot, the majority of observers returned to the grand path and continued the narrative. By the time they climbed up the slopes of the Capitoline to the Porta Fontinalis, they were well familiar with the achievements, family, and benevolence of Augustus.

The Via Flaminia was unique in Rome for its width, straightness, and undeveloped surroundings. The convoluted, heavily built communication routes in the city center were not as conducive to comprehensive scripting nor can they be easily reconstructed.[150] One exception can be cited. The Tiber River cut a visually powerful line through the cityscape. Though unpredictable, the river was an important communication route used by barges and pleasure craft alike. Augustus had directed his personal attention to the Tiber. He cleared and widened its course, assumed the *cura riparum,* and made provisions for continual care (Suet.*Aug.*30, 37; *CIL* 6.31542). Within the city, there were two distinct routes along the river. One liquid pathway ran southward from inland locales, terminating at the Tiber Island; a second path ran upstream from the sea coast to the island.

The northern path proscribed the west limit of the Campus Martius, providing a slightly different narrative than that read from the Via Flaminia. Once again, the Pons Mulvius initiated the urban path, followed soon after by the sight of the gigantic Mausoleum Augusti.[151] Moving downstream, boat passengers encountered an urban text emphasizing the pragmatic achievements of Augustus and his adherents. In the distance, they saw the plethora of grand Augustan projects in the central Campus. Both the large number of new buildings and the docking facilities developed specifically to off-load building materials underscored the economic benefits of the Augustan peace. Sailing around the Tiber bend, observers faced a less developed portion of the Campus cut through by the glittering Euripus canal and Stagnum lake. Next, they passed under the Pons Agrippae, a forthright advertisement for the extensive practical improvements made to Rome by Augustus' son-in-law. To the east, the curving seating of the stone theaters in the Campus loomed above the structures lining the banks, calling to mind the leisure now afforded every urban resident.[152] This fluvial journey ended at the island, providing easy access to the cluster of triumphal structures in the Circus Flaminius Area.[153]

Approaching Rome from the sea coast, barge passengers read a similar urban text. Passing thriving warehouses and docks, they marveled at the variety of goods and extent of commerce during the Augustan Age. In fact, the ease of river travel itself was a testament of Augustus' paternal care for Rome. As the observers neared the city center, the sheer wall of the Aventine suddenly gave way, opening a view toward the Palatine Hill. Observers immediately saw the glistening Temple of Apollo Palatinus; in counterpoint, the Temple of Jupiter Optimus Maximus on the Capitoline likewise became visible; by standing at a greater distance its size must have appeared from this point as comparable to the smaller Apollo temple (fig. 63). As the river curved to meet the island, the Theater of Marcellus rose majestically above the Pons Aemilius restored by Augustus (*CIL* 6.878). The exterior of the scaenae frons dominated the passengers' view, a powerful monument to three generations of the imperial family: Caesar who planned the theater, Augustus who completed it, and his deceased heir Marcellus for whom it was named.

In contrast to the organic street layout within the city center, the Via Flaminia and Tiber River formed visually powerful urban lines. Both were broad, direct, and distinctive. People entering Rome along these majestic thoroughfares not only passed major monuments, they had the time and opportunity to see the structures fully. The openness of the Campus Martius, straightness of the Via Flaminia, and the wide, lowlying river allowed observers sufficient breadth of view to appreciate in full the form, size, context, and interrelationships of the glistening Augustan monuments.

Edges

The Tiber River was not only a path, but also an edge. In an urban context, edges are the lines formed at the meeting of areas with distinctly different characters. Such boundaries occur between districts, where the city ends and the countryside begins, and at the juncture of urban building and natural features including the sky. Unlike paths, edges cannot usually be traversed, but are powerful visual and conceptual boundaries. The study of urban edges requires comprehensive physical remains over large areas, a rarity for ancient cities. In particular, urban skylines are difficult to reconstruct because few buildings remain up to the roof line. Representations of Roman cities in wall paintings such as those from an Augustan villa at Boscoreale generally depict irregular upper edges with no one structure or form dominating (fig. 88). Such images, however, may be misleading in relation to the capital city, which had both a proportionally large number of major monuments and laws limiting building heights.[154]

In the early Republic, Rome had a tangible urban edge: the city wall (fig. 18). By the late first century B.C., however, the fortification circuit had long been overrun and obscured by expanding construction. Only at a few points did gates or wall segments recall the city's once distinct boundary. Other lateral urban edges lacked formal definition. The *pomerium* was an important ritual boundary, but because it was marked by simple small cippi, it had little visual impact on the cityscape. The lack of a finite urban edge created legal jurisdictional problems, but had distinct propaganda advantages. The limitless size of Rome affirmed her greatness. In the late first century B.C., numerous authors emphasized Rome's extent; Dionysius of Halicarnassus wrote:

If anyone wishes to estimate the size of Rome by looking at these suburbs he will necessarily be misled for want of a definite clue by which to determine up to what point it is still the city and where it ceases to be the city . . . giving the beholder the impression of a city stretching out indefinitely. (*Ant.Rom.*4.13–4–5)

Unending growth implied prosperity and peace, especially since the hard urban edges of ancient cities were generally militaristic in nature. In marked contrast, the Augustan city had a soft, variable edge. The green belt of *horti* and market gardens surrounding Rome served as a transitional zone between countryside and city, and like the size of the city itself emphasized the prosperity of the Augustan Age.

The strongest edge of Augustan Rome was formed by a geographical feature. The Tiber River had long been a powerful boundary defining Rome's western edge and isolating the right bank area as an insalubrious extraurban zone.[155] Augustus reworked the Tiber's banks to curb flooding and improve transportation, but did not attempt to redefine its course as had Caesar. Instead, he blurred the river's distinction as an edge by developing the right bank as a leisure zone counterpoised to the Campus Martius. On the right bank, urban residents relaxed at the public Horti Caesaris of the huge Naumachia Augusti and its surrounding park. Augustus overtly claimed the Transtiberim area as part of the city by incorporating it into his XIV Regions.

Instead of articulating a definitive urban edge, Augustus emphasized points of entry into Rome. Suetonius records that the *princeps* made "the approach to the city easier from every direction" (Suet.*Aug*.30). Furthermore, he placed explicit Augustan billboards at major entrances to Rome (fig. 73). Along the Via Flaminia, the Mulvian arch signaled the beginning of the path through the Campus Martius lined with Augustan monuments. To the west, the Via Aurelia passed by the enormous Naumachia Augusti and perhaps through the Nemus Caesarum. Travelers along the Via Appia encountered the Altar to Fortuna Redux, which celebrated Augustus's own return to Rome in 19 B.C.; it stood near the Temples of Honos and Virtus at the point where the people of Rome met with proconsuls taking their leave or returning to Rome.[156] Nearby stood the Arcus Drusi and pyramid of Cestius, the latter a clear reminder of Augustus' Egyptian conquest. Approaching Rome by river from either direction, visitors sailed by major Augustan projects.

Within the Republican urban core, Augustus followed a similar strategy. He did not create distinct linear edges between districts, regions, or nodes; rather, he used doorways or significant monuments to mark the transition from one area to another. The renewed gates in the early city wall signaled entry into the old Republican core. Because they were reached only after moving for some time along densely built streets, these portals underscored the expanded extent of the Augustan city. Passing through the gates, observers found major monuments at significant transition points. The magnificent Porticus Liviae loomed over the broad intersection where the Clivus Suburbanus split into two streets leading into the Forum (fig. 79). The Arcus Octavii marked the approach to the Palatine, and the arches flanking the Temple of Divus Julius functioned experientially as doors into the Forum Romanum. The arched openings in the eastern firewall of the Forum Augustum, carefully framed in white travertine, similarly functioned as aggrandized gateways marking the transition from one realm into another.

Hard urban edges were clearly antithetical to the Augustan image of Rome. The *princeps* did not establish visually strong urban boundaries. In

Figure 88. Wall painting of an urban scene, Boscoreale. Photo: courtesy the Metropolitan Museum of Art, Rogers Fund, 1903; 03.14.13.

fact, he took steps to weaken the role of the Tiber River as a divisive edge. Instead of linear boundaries, aggrandized entry points identified both external and internal transitions. For Augustus, the city and its intraurban divisions were not finite, but ever expanding and improving, as was his empire. Always in a state of becoming, neither was limited in time or space. The expansiveness of Rome is conveyed in a passage by Ovid, "the circuit of Rome is the circuit of the world" (*Fasti* 2.683–4).

Kevin Lynch's analysis of landmarks, nodes, districts, paths, and edges resulted from interviews of urban residents about how they perceived their physical environment. Taking the opposite tact and analyzing the tangible evidence for Lynchian elements within a Roman city reveals information about the urban perceptions of ancient residents and patrons. Residents of Rome relied on major landmarks as locators, as well as conveyors of propaganda. Public urban nodes where people frequently gathered also held special significance in a city where most residents had limited private space. Augustus responded to these urban realities by creating impressive landmarks and nodes. To maintain a purity of message, he reprogrammed Republican examples and established isolated, new Augustan alternatives. The great monetary and political cost of creating and programming districts and paths deterred Augustus from exploiting these urban ordering devices. His only examples occurred on the tabula rasa of the Campus Martius. He avoided a firm urban edge for more symbolic reasons. Although Republican cities had boasted about their city walls in writing and pictorial representations, Augustus did not wish to constrain his urban ambitions within a physical limit; his capital had no distinct edge.

A master of visual propaganda, Augustus created images of great power and familiarity such as his ubiquitous portrait (fig. 15). Despite his great expenditures on urban projects in Rome, there are no known contemporary pictorial representations of Augustan Rome. The examination of Lynchian elements within the Augustan cityscape underscores why. For the Romans, formal regularity or planning theory was less important, less memorable, than the full sensorial stimulation provided by moving through a city. Augustus acknowledged the experiential underpinnings of Roman urban design by orchestrating his urban interventions for maximum perceptual impact.

EVALUATION

When Mussolini set about remaking Rome as a Fascist capital, he set up an urban planning office to control panurban decisions and commissioned a huge model of ancient Rome for inspiration. To unify the vision of his capital, he established rules regarding materials and style.[157] Such an approach was completely unfamiliar to the Romans. Ancient urban theory focused on new cities or utopias rather than the comprehensive planning of an extant city by professionals under a single patron (Vitr.1.4–7; pref.2). Augustus reworked the administration of Rome, passed laws regarding urban functioning, and extensively reworked the city's physical fabric. Yet no evidence indicates he developed a comprehensive master plan for urban development and design, at least in the modern sense of the term.[158] He neither passed style laws nor mandated where or when new projects were undertaken. In particular, the absence of a comprehensive map or model of Rome implies a disinterest in the physical urban environment as a product of total design.[159]

Nevertheless, the *princeps'* interventions in the city were too numerous, too impressive, too similar in style and material to be viewed episodically. People spoke with awe of the *nova magnificentia* evident in Rome's physical fabric and wrote panegyrics describing the wondrous new buildings of glistening marble (Livy 1.56.2; Ov.*Pont.*1.8.33–8). By boasting he had transformed the city from clay to marble, Augustus himself inferred an underlying plan. Significantly, foresight began to be associated with urban interventions specifically during the Augustan Age. Contemporaries lavished praise on Augustus for his long-term view of urban matters. Strabo calls the enhanced beauty of the Campus Martius the result of foresight (5.3.8); Suetonius lauds the *princeps'* concern with urban safety in the future as well as the present (*Aug.*28). Vitruvius similarly implies a directed vision, "I perceived that you have built, and are now building, on a large scale. Furthermore, with respect to the future, you have such regard to public and private buildings, that they will correspond to the grandeur of our history, and will be a memorial to future ages" (1.pref.3). The implication was that such forethought had to be based on a comprehensive master plan for urban building.

In the governing the state, Augustus always took great pains to hold offices and powers with strong Republican pedigrees. He negotiated the change from Republic to Empire by consolidating these in his own hands. Similarly, he exploited Republican models for the physical aggrandizement of Rome. The *princeps* selected familiar building forms and configurations, and orchestrated them according to common experiential imperatives. The sheer number of his projects transformed Rome's urban image. Scholars have filled library shelves debating whether Augustus had a master plan for the creation of an Imperial government or responded to individual situations. A similar question arises regarding the design of Rome: Was the

Augustan city shaped by a master plan or by ad hoc decisions? At one level, the point is moot. Whether consciously or not, Augustus sparked a reconceptualization of the city's physical form as a bearer of meaning. Not just individual buildings but the entire city was a reflection of a single man's vision. By the early first century, Rome itself had become an *imagines* within the expanded *locus* of the Augustan Empire.

CHAPTER SIX

MEANING
READING
THE AUGUSTAN CITY

Never may you be able to view a city greater than Rome!

Horace, *Carmen Saeculares*, 11–12

After his stunning victory at Actium in 31 B.C., Octavian marched triumphant into the great Hellenistic capital of Alexandria. The residents girded themselves for the worst, but the general quickly calmed their fears. With great show, Octavian assured the populace, "he had no intention of holding their city to blame [for the follies of Cleopatra], first because it had been founded by Alexander, secondly because he admired its beauty and spaciousness."[1] The admiration and protection of urban beauty was not without immediate and enduring costs. To compensate his soldiers for not plundering the rich city, Octavian paid each an extra 1,000 sesterces (Dio-Cass.51.17). For the rest of his life, he continued to pay. The inspiration of eastern cities never left him; Octavian expended vast sums to transform Rome into a city even more beautiful than such renowned Hellenistic exemplars.

By the death of Augustus in A.D. 14, the prophesy articulated by Horace at the Ludi Saeculares had come true; it was difficult to "view a city greater than Rome" (*Carm.Saec.*11–12). The city was great on many levels. It was the seat of an imperial ruler who controlled a vast territory. In recognized contrast to its appearance in the late Republic, Rome was now adorned as the renown of its empire demanded. Great buildings, rich materials, and the overall size of the city all conveyed a sense of grandeur and power. On a tangible level, shared physical characteristics linked Augustan projects within the cityscape. A directed conceptual program imbued built forms with meaning and purpose, further melding them into a conceptual whole. Furthermore, various daily and exceptional activities involved people more directly with the urban environment. As a result, the experience of Augustan Rome was highly legible and highly *imageable*.

217

The reading of any urban form requires familiarity with the issues of the day. During the life of Augustus, the political message varied subtly over time, but was bolstered by the clarity and repetition of powerful themes. Continuity was paramount. Augustus stressed the continuation of the Republic, casting himself as upholder of traditional morality and beliefs. At the same time, he proffered his Age as overtly superior to the past. Romans luxuriated in the benefits of an enduring peace, renewed piety, a flourishing of the arts, security, and an underlying sense of communal destiny. The tangible counterpart was the new magnificence of their capital. All was held together conceptually through the dominant and consistent cult of personality centered on the *princeps*.

PHYSICAL UNITY

Despite his admiration for Alexandria and other eastern cities, Augustus did not impose a Hellenistic plan upon Rome. He left the existing urban fabric fairly intact, neither carving out straight new colonnaded streets nor clearing large areas for grand palaces. The *princeps* worked within Republican traditions of patronage, cultural programs, building typologies, and urban experience to create a reverential, yet magnificent, Augustan capital. During the Republic, Rome's image had been unfocused; individual buildings were impressive, but they did not work together to establish an overall identity for the city. Augustus continued this design approach by focusing on specific projects rather than an overall urban plan, yet simultaneously he forged a focused urban image by emphasizing continuity and a hierarchical structure within the cityscape.

Augustus' most tangible affirmation of the Republic's continuation was the attention he lavished on Rome. The debates about moving the center of Roman power to a more appropriate urban environment, such as Alexandria, had obvious practical advantages. Nevertheless, the *princeps* chose to remain at Rome, celebrating the city on the Tiber as the wellspring of Roman heritage. Each new urban project erected drew strength from the rich heritage of the site built up over the centuries. Simultaneously, each magnificent Augustan addition further enhanced the *genius loci* and cemented Rome's status as a capital and world-class city.

The sheer number of urban interventions by a single patron introduced temporal and topographical continuity to the physical fabric of Rome (fig. 89). With a solid power base, the *princeps* added to the cityscape over decades and made permanent provisions for ongoing care and maintenance. As a result, his beneficence seemed pervasive and without end (fig. 90). Observers mentally grouped together Augustan urban projects even though

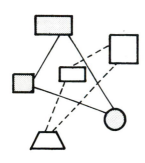

Figure 89. Diagram, coding of urban buildings by physical distinctiveness.

Figure 90. View toward the east from the Circus Flaminius, past the Porticus Octaviae and Theater of Marcellus to the Temple of Jupiter Optimus Maximus atop the Capitoline Hill, all projects associated with the *princeps*. Drawing: Richard H. Abramson.

they were dispersed over more than 500 hectares. Beyond a common iconography, these works interrelated on a physical level. Most shared notable traits: similar materials, large scale, consistent high quality of execution, and newness. For example, the prevalent use of marble set Augustan buildings apart from earlier structures and identified them as part of a group.

The majority of projects in Augustan Rome followed the *consuetudo italica* identified by Vitruvius. On an urban level, the *princeps* continued to honor Republican centers. This valuing of Republican formal traditions gave Roman audiences a sense of familiarity and endurance; for non-Roman urban observers, the respect for Republican architectural traditions affirmed the historical heritage of the Augustan State. A negative modern example demonstrates the importance of considering continuity and audience reactions when making style choices for capital cities. In the 1960s, Brazil's leaders chose a modern architectural aesthetic with highly abstract symbolism for their new capital. The design for Brasilia successfully addressed an elite world audience who identified these urban forms with optimism and progress. Internally, the response was less positive. Many Brazilians complained that the abstracted designs lacked cultural resonance or a sense of continuity.[2]

During the Republic, the major buildings in Rome were erected by different patrons, each wanting his or her project to stand distinct from all others. In the Augustan Age, Rome received dozens of projects by the same patron or his deferential supporters. The physical similarity of individual building projects went from being a liability to an asset. Furthermore, observers began to read widely distributed urban projects as interrelated. An umbrella effect resulted. Augustus' large, cohesive body of works directly shaped contemporary taste. Partisans self-consciously emulated Augustan undertakings; other patrons appeared to do so as well simply by following the fashion of the day and using the materials and craftsmen currently available. Whenever observers encountered a new structure with shining white Luni marble or classicizing reliefs, they immediately associated the work with the *princeps* regardless of the actual patron. In effect, the physical similarities and power of one patron led observers to assume that most additions to Rome from 44 B.C. to A.D. 14 were due to the intervention of Augustus.

The message is clear. When the patronage system allows, planners can foster urban unity by using high-status projects as exemplars, relying on a domino effect to create a panurban impact. A similar stylistic echoing occurred in the 1920s at Ankara. The Turkish government selected a uniform aesthetic for state buildings in the newly designated capital. The urban reverberations were comprehensive. Private patrons followed the model presented by the government and exploited the influx of European designers and styles, as well as imported masons and preferred materials. As a result, a fairly uniform aesthetic dominated the city center even in buildings not commissioned by the state.[3]

In and of itself, physical homogeneity conveys a limited or simplistic message. The *princeps* enhanced the meaning of his urban interventions by employing different structuring devices. As analyzed in the previous chapter, the cognitive ordering systems identified by Lynch provide a structure for reading any city, even one from antiquity. Augustan designers in particular favored landmarks and nodes, and to a lesser degree paths. To improve the legibility of these structuring devices, they repeatedly employed a design strategy based on physical distinctiveness.

Rome was filled with landmarks erected by important citizens seeking enduring fame. The Romans were therefore conditioned to consider single public buildings as bearers of meaning, regularly comparing the physical traits of major works to determine the value of building and patron. Following the Republican tradition of architectural one-upmanship, the *princeps* relied on the physical distinctiveness or rather the enhanced familiarity of his buildings to convey meaning. With almost every project, he aggrandized preexisting exemplars. Richer materials, larger scale, greater refinement, clarified shapes, and more cohesive formal organization characterized Augustan works, causing them to be viewed as superior to earlier projects. Distinctive in the cityscape, the landmarks created by the *princeps* became key locators used by observers moving through the city. In this realm, too, the sheer number of Augustan works was transfiguring; for the first time, observers read a homogeneous content in the structures used as point references within their cognitive maps of Rome.

Nodes also underwent a subtle transformation. During the Republic, Romans had gathered in the Forum Romanum or atop the Capitoline Hill, nodes with irregular forms and individual monuments representing diverse patrons and honorees from many centuries. Augustus introduced physical and temporal uniformity. He reprogrammed existing nodes with commemoratives of himself and his family. At the same time, he physically ordered the spaces, creating clear physical hierarchies and emphasizing formal order. Such design strategy was especially evident in the new urban foci he created atop the Palatine and at the Forum Augustum adjacent to the Forum Romanum. As a result, observers in the Augustan city began to consider urban nodes as deficit if lacking either a focused message or regular form.

In the 1970s, a similar nodal approach to urban structuring was attempted by Oakland. This California city hoped to unify a sprawling, diverse urban fabric by creating several notable, circumscribed centers. The idea was that each node would revitalize its surrounding area and create conceptual arcs allowing observers to associate dispersed urban foci. Unfortunately, the project was not successful; the proposed nodes lacked both physical and conceptual homogeneity, especially because the full program was never implemented.[4] In contrast, Augustan urban nodes were physically cohesive and complete. The successful execution of these works was an overt statement of the patron's strong and constant power base.

Even though his authority seemed boundless, Augustus avoided the extensive appropriation of urban property. As a result, he had limited opportunity to create fully programmed pathways through the city. Only where the Via Flaminia passed through the underdeveloped Campus Martius was the *princeps* able to fashion a cohesive narrative read in the content and sequencing of new structures. Less meaningful, but clearly visible in the cityscape were the elevated waterways of the expanded aqueduct system. Because these pathways could not be easily traversed, they cannot be classified as Lynchian paths, yet they too conveyed meaning.[5] In select instances,

Figure 91. Diagram, height change in aqueduct entering the city.

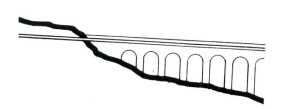

these panregional lines drew attention to areas of Augustan development. For example, the great Aqua Virgo changed its profile within the urban environment (fig. 91). Subterranean for most of its extraurban extent, this water channel rose on arches as it descended into the Campus Martius and paralleled the northern façade of the Saepta Julia. Similarly, on the right bank, the Aqua Augusta left the Janiculum on tall arches, directing the attention of travelers on the Via Aurelia toward the low-lying Naumachia Augusti and its surrounding grove (fig. 81). These forceful urban lines thus served as directional sight lines and affirmed the fecundity of the age.

The emphasis on landmarks and nodes substantiates the ways in which Romans read urban environments. Unlike modern observers who find meaning in buildings of all stripes, Roman observers tended to be selective.[6] Parallel to the mnemonic system developed by rhetoricians, they looked for memorable *imagines* located within familiar structural systems. Augustus focused on individual works related through program and status, rather than on an overall urban plan. Because projects with *dignitas* were the most memorable, he filled his list of urban interventions with temples and monuments. Rome's urban infill of commercial buildings, insulae, and factories lacked imageability and thus remained inconsequential in the shaping of an urban image.

Roman observers read meaning in the hierarchical relationships between urban *imagines*, spurring Roman designers to promote overt comparisons. The regular, internalized Augustan enclosures conveyed content both with their intrinsic characteristics – large size, symmetry, enclosure, material richness – and through contrast with less orderly Republican groupings (fig. 92). Such comparisons were generally predicated on experiential memory rather than single viewings. Thus, it was not necessary to site new projects so that they had grand approaches or could be seen at the same time as rival works. The internal formal clarity of the Porticus Liviae could be appreciated as a meaningful conscious gesture even without simultaneous viewing of irregular Republican spaces.

Figure 92. Diagram, ordered projects within disorderly fabric.

criticise this

Sharing recognizable and memorable traits, Augustan projects in Rome held together in the minds of Roman observers preconditioned to read urban parts rather than the whole. Gradually, however, the homogeneity of Augustan projects lead to a conceptualization of the entire cityscape as a conveyor of meaning. The physical aggrandizement evident in the new urban additions translated into an upgrading of the entire city, and the entire age. All recognized the change. The *princeps* restored the Republic, but left the physical realities of the rustic past far behind. Everywhere one looked, a *nova magnicentia* gleamed (Livy 1.56.2). Admiring the restored Temple of Jupiter Optimus Maximus and new Augustan complex on the Palatine Ovid gushed:

See what the Capitolium is now, and what it was: you would say they belonged to different Jupiters. . . . The Palatine whereon now Phoebus [Apollo] and our leaders are set in splendor, what was it save the pasture of oxen destined to the plough? Let ancient times delight other folk: I congratulate myself that I was not born til now (Ov.*Ars Am.*3.115–22).

For Romans at the turn of the millennium, the city on the Tiber was not only physically superior to all others, she was even greater than her own past.

PROGRAMMATIC UNITY

At the death of the *princeps* in A.D. 14, the senators of Rome vied to present appropriate commemorative honors. Among the many suggestions was a simple, but telling, proposal: "that all the period from the day of his birth until his demise be called the Augustan Age" (Suet.*Aug.*100). For an entire generation, Augustus had stood as the first man of Rome. People felt his stamp on every aspect of their lives, from the beneficial peace to the number of their offspring, from the shrines at every street corner to the *imageability* of their capital city. In large part, the legibility of Augustan Rome resulted from programmatic comprehensiveness, continuity, and sheer extent.[7]

An urban image evolves from many stimuli. A key feature of the Augustan urban image was its integration with a comprehensive social, cultural, religious, and political program. As a result, each urban intervention was reenforced by a parallel development in another area such as literature, art, or social engineering. For example, Augustan social reforms emphasizing modesty supported limitations on private architectural patronage in Rome. The *princeps* himself justified his own patronage of impressive public works as for the common good. Similarly, poetry touting a new golden age found concrete affirmation in the rich materials of Augustan buildings. Rome's residents felt grounded by the unity of thought pervading the urban environment, especially after decades of divisiveness. A comparison could be made with the unity of social and urban vision found in modern socialist utopias such as Llano del Rio designed by Alice Constance Austin.[8]

Like the creation of the new imperial state, the Augustan urban image stood on a firm Republican base. The *princeps* tapped into preexisting concepts and allusions, thereby stressing continuity. Piety, fear of the east, family values, communal destiny, and reverence for the power of places all struck a responsive chord among the residents of Rome. Once again employing a strategy of enhanced familiarity, the *princeps* exploited known Republican beliefs and images to focus the imageability of his capital. He dusted off select, recognizable Republican motifs and imbued them with new meaning by placement in directed and aggrandized Augustan contexts throughout the city. Astute urban observers thus read new meaning into familiar images; at the same time, they viewed these *imagines* as part of larger urban narratives and of a vibrant, well-established tradition.

During the Augustan Age, a whole host of sanctioned motifs served as *imagines* in the cognitive maps of ancient observers.[9] The laurel provides a clear example among many favored Augustan symbols. In the Republic, this plant was tied with transformation, victory, purification, and the god Apollo; most recently, Caesar had selected the laurel as his personal symbol of triumph (Pliny, *HN*.15.127; DioCass.43.43). Augustus further exploited the rich meaning of laurels, in particular, emphasizing the association with his patron Apollo. At least six new projects in Rome featured laurels: actual trees grew at the Temple of Divus Julius, Porticus Vipsania, Mausoleum of Augustus, and House of Augustus; carved representations appeared on the Temple of Apollo Sosianus and Ara Pacis.[10] Furthermore, the two laurels flanking Augustus' doorway were featured on thousands of newly minted coins (fig. 53). Again, an umbrella effect occurred, with observers associating an Augustan content in preexisting urban projects likewise embellished with laurels, including the Regia, Temple of Vesta, and Curiae Veteres.[11] Even the most casual of observers could draw urban connections with ease: The evergreen laurels linked the current and eternal residences of the *princeps*, while advertising his ties to Apollo, the Divine Caesar, early Republican religious centers, and, of course, victory. At the Porticus Vipsania, laurel trees evoked the memory of Augustan military successes through linkage with the general Agrippa, brother of Vipsania, and more pointedly through proximity to the world map showing pacified territories under Roman sway.

Before the time of Augustus, attempts at programming meaning into the cityscape had limited effectiveness. Either interventions were never fully realized, too scattered, or quickly superseded. In contrast, the first emperor had time to develop a program of urban imagery and let it mature. During Phase I of the Augustan period (44–29 B.C.), Octavian sought legitimacy by exploiting the motifs and urban associations with his divine father and the Republic. In Phase II (29–17 B.C.), he began to fashion a uniquely Augustan message by giving familiar urban *imagines* new meaning and shaping his own alternatives. Throughout the decades of the final phase (17 B.C.–A.D. 14), the program continued under its own force, bolstered by attempts to ensure continuity after the *princeps*' death. Despite these variations, the Augustan program was remarkably consistent, especially in contrast to the rapidly changing and competing messages imposed on Rome during the last decades of the Republic. In fact, the very durability of Augustan urban imagery gave it heightened legitimacy. Residents of the capital simultaneously looked backward at a golden past and forward to a golden future.

Continuity was also ensured by the conveyance. Augustan urban advertisements were enduring. Buildings, stone inscriptions, and even urban landscaping all have long lives, especially in comparison with the ephemeral billboards and soundbites of modern urban propagandists. Residents heavily used the new Augustan facilities, from the naumachia to the corner shrines. Once in contact with these environments, they became engrossed with the iconography and decoration. With repeated contact over the years, people living in Rome became familiar with every possible nuance of meaning.

Augustan propaganda was further strengthened by simple panurban repetition. An observer would be hard pressed to find a corner of the city without a building, artwork, or inscription honoring the *princeps*. Just as the repetition of physical traits unified the cityscape, so, too, did the repetition of Augustan propaganda. Most pervasive were depictions of the man himself. From large sculptures to the images on coins jingling in the folds of patrician togas, the visage of Augustus was all-pervasive in Rome. Hundreds of small togate representations gazed out from the crossroad altars (fig. 93); gigantic portraits towered over key urban locations, including the huge gilded figure looking down on the Via Flaminia from the Mausoleum of

Figure 93. Julio-Claudian relief from an altar showing the togate *vicomagistri* on the right and tunicate figures carrying statuettes of the lares and the Genius Augusti on the left. Photo: Archivio Fotografico Musei Vaticani XXV – 9–33.

Augustus (fig. 124).[12] Confronted over and over with the same visage, visitors did not have to ask who was *pater urbis* as well as *pater patriae.*

Despite the dominance of Augustan patronage, the urban message never became standardized or stale, in contrast to other urban environmental images shaped by powerful rulers. For example, the enclave created by the Mussolini government outside Rome for the unrealized Esposizione Universale di Roma of 1942 had a comprehensive, unified program mirrored in an unrelenting propaganda and formal conformity. The result was a sterile, oppressive, conceptually unidimensional environment.[13] In Augustan Rome, the impact of directed interventions was leavened and in fact enriched by interaction and contrast with the lively preexisting Republican urban fabric.

Furthermore, the Augustan program itself was multivalent. Interacting with a complex extant urban fabric and history, Augustan projects actively encouraged multiple interpretations. Individual projects were meant to be read in different ways by different readers at different times. Each project sparked diverse readings, depending upon the background and inclinations of the observers. For example, the Ara Pacis presented something of interest for all levels of society. The intricate iconography engaged the minds of learned observers; lively detailed representations of lizards and bugs entertained the uneducated. The new urban node on the Palatine was simultaneously interpreted as an homage to Romulus, the divine property of a foreign god, a serious center of religion, learning, and Senatorial meetings, and a place for lower-class urban residents to relax amid plantings and artwork. The conscious multivalency of Augustan works helps explain why monuments such as the Ara Pacis continue to fascinate and breed new interpretations after almost 2,000 years. It also explains the vibrancy of Rome in the Augustan Age. The city sparked many readings. Rome was the city and world, *urbs et orbis,* wellspring of an entire culture, and home to the most powerful man in the Mediterranean.

Rome had always been filled with content laden images. In the late first century B.C., the capital received a large number of interventions following a consistent program. By referencing the Republican physical context, Augustus built his urban image upon a solid base. By drawing upon the rich complexity of Augustan themes, each new urban project immediately became empowered and legitimized as part of a larger whole. The sanctioned messages pervaded daily existence and helped observers order the numerous projects in Rome erected by the first citizen and his supporters. As a result, the urban *imagines* interconnected in the minds of observers to form an urban image centered on selective narratives.

EXPERIENTIAL LEGIBILITY

In antiquity, the Romans relied on the total experience of a place, rather than words or singular images, to forge an enduring urban image. Only rarely did their pictorial or verbal representations of cities emphasize formal regularity over perception (compare figs. 2 and 88). The residents of Rome oriented themselves in the cityscape by remembering their personal experience of environments, not by referencing a regularized urban plan. The mnemonic system used by orators reflected and reenforced this kinetic, interactive conceptualization based on repeated visits to the same locales. Such an ingrained way of thinking about places helps to explain the theatrical approach to urban design and the disinterest in comprehensive, formal plans for Augustan Rome. The cityscape was an interactive stage set, where movements were carefully choreographed and tied to a legible narrative. So strong was this tradition that it lived on and helped to shape the urban expression of many future cities distributed far and wide.

Urban experience is highly variable. The mood and status of the observer, climatic conditions, and numerous other factors all affect perception. Nevertheless, a shrewd, powerful choreographer can provide some consistency by establishing set physical relationships and a uniform ambience. In Augustan Rome, the creation of new landmarks, nodes, and districts was always predicated upon consideration of their experiential impact within the preexisting Republican cityscape. Experiencing the city kinetically, usually at the relaxed pace of pedestrians, ancient observers relied on sequencing to clarify meaning. The experience of each urban environment informed the next. As people climbed the steep Clivus Capitolinus, the small Temple of Jupiter Tonans rose before and above, its significance and scale perceptually magnified. Similarly, after the dark, constricted public spaces of the Subura, observers entering the Forum Augustum found its internal formal regularity far more memorable than yet another monumental façade viewed from the street. Comparable sequential manipulations have been exploited throughout history, particularly in cultures with uniform speeds of movement and limited verbal literacy. For example, in Baroque Rome, the approach through the narrow byways of the Borgo enhanced the impact of the dynamic and gigantic Piazza San Pietro designed by Bernini.[14]

The choreographed sequencing of experiences shaped the impression of urban segments. Equally memorable for observers was the overall ambience of Augustan Rome. The city on the Tiber exuded good health, prosperity, and the promise of a glorious future. The benefits of peace, as Tacitus notes, seduced everyone (*Ann.*1.2). Certainly, life in the capital had improved during the decades of Augustan paternalism. Rome's markets displayed goods from throughout the Mediterranean; Senators gathered in the new Curia in affirmation of the restored Republic; literature and the visual arts flourished; residents relaxed in the expansive recreational facilities of the Campus Martius; armed watchmen kept the streets safe at night; jobs were plentiful, especially in the building trades.[15]

In the *Aeneid,* Vergil describes the royal city of Carthage built by Queen Dido. Looking at the many projects under construction – city gates, paved streets, temples, a harbor, fortifications – Aeneas was filled with admiration for the bustle and sense of purpose generated; with envy, he sighed to Dido, "Ah, fortunate you are, whose town is already building!" (fig. 94).[16] Such industriousness was realized in the Rome of Vergil's day. Throughout the Augustan city, new construction was a tangible sign of the State's healthy status. Programmatically, Rome's new projects promoted affirming responses. New temples fostered piety; formal porticoed enclosures encouraged refined actions; entertainment facilities diverted attention from more serious and potentially inflammatory activities.[17]

Figure 94. Dido showing Aeneas her plans for Carthage; one of six tapestry cartoons depicting the story of Dido and Aeneas by Giovanni Francesco Romanelli, ca. 1630. Courtesy of the Norton Simon Foundation.

Augustan Rome projected good health. The memorable new projects with their sparkling white marble and crisp carvings gave the city a sanitized glow.[18] Few derelict public structures marred the cityscape. Recent laws promoting solid construction and restricting tall structures served to reduce the number of building collapses. Equally important, comprehensive provisions for urban care ensured that Rome was in fact, as well as in concept, clean and safe. The city's first police and fire departments guarded the city, organized according to the new XIV Regions. Pickpockets, burglars, and robbers still operated, yet people felt a sense of increased security, especially in comparison to the late Republic when the city's streets were virtual battle-grounds.[19]

Though intangible, the healthy mood of Augustan city was extremely important in defining the Augustan urban image. The positive urban ambience complemented Rome's aggrandized urban form, and was truly panurban in scope. On a practical level, observers freed from concerns of personal safety were able to relax and read the messages projected by the renewed cityscape. Suetonius confirms the significance of a positive urban mood; he praises the *princeps'* transformation of Rome from a city from brick to marble; and his foresight in providing for the city's future (*Aug.*28).

Ancient observers did not experience the choreographed segments and positive ambience of Augustan Rome as discrete episodes. Rather, they conceptually wove such perceptions into meaningful urban narratives. Ovid provides one example of how the ancients read environments. He tells of a visit to the Forum Augustum by the war god:

Mars strong in armor looks upon the temple pediment and rejoices that unvanquished gods occupy the places of honor. At the entranceways he sees arms of all sorts from all the lands conquered by his soldier [Augustus]. On one side he sees Aeneas with his precious burden and about him the many ancestors of the Julian house; on the other, Romulus, son of Ilia, with the arms of the enemy chief he conquered with his own hand and the statues of distinguished Romans with the names of their great deeds. He gazes upon the temple and reads the name Augustus. Then the monument seems to him even greater. (Ov.*Fasti* 5.559–68; fig. 51)

The passage reveals the importance of images, verbal signage, and experiential sequencing in conveying information. It also confirms the shared knowledge base of the audience; the majority of people in Rome could identify the figures displayed and their roles in complex Roman genealogies and myths. Furthermore, the mere placement of images together in an urban environment implied an underlying storyline. The juxtaposition of Aeneas and Romulus in opposing exedrae challenged visitors to search their memories for a narrative justifying such an association.

The combining of disparate parts into a singular narrative also occurred on an urban level. Observers perceived Augustan projects as a group based on their commonalities: similar materials, form, scale, and iconography (fig. 95). In particular, the repeated images of Augustus throughout Rome triggered a cognitive search for unifying narratives. Roman artists told stories episodically. Instead of depicting every action, they relied upon seminal vignettes to stand for entire narratives, secure in the knowledge that spectators had the full narrative context in their minds. Spectators read depictions of the same individual performing different actions on a single painted panel as diachronic events in a single story (fig. 4).[20] In the cityscape of Rome, repeated depictions of the *princeps* in sculptures, paintings, and even inscriptions likewise inspired observers to find connecting story lines. Their choices were plentiful. During the Augustan Age, the narrative or epic underwent a revival, flooding the capital with stories aggrandizing the *princeps* and affirming his policies of continuity, fertility, and peace, among others. For example, Vergil's *Aeneid* reconfigures various pieces of history into a complex, continuous epic, elevating the origins of Rome and justifying the heritage and actions of Augustus.

The tight connection between environments and narratives reinforced a theatrical conceptualization of the city. Rome was the stage for important political and religious ceremonies, many revived by Augustus. In addition,

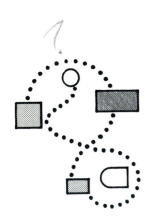

Figure 95. Diagram, experiential ordering of landmarks, nodes, and districts.

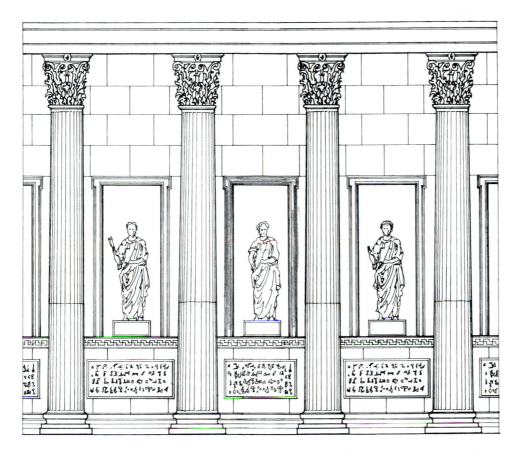

Figure 96. Reconstruction of the statue display in the exedra of the Forum Augustum showing the *summi viri* and the plaques detailing their achievements. Drawing: Richard H. Abramson.

the city's formal enclosures, carefully placed landmarks, and manipulated paths projected an air of staginess. Thus, Strabo chose a stage painting as the most apt metaphor for the Augustan Campus Martius (5.3.8). Such contrived urban environments united with stories presented in poems and epics to theatricalize life in the capital.

The daily experience of highly manipulated Augustan stage sets compelled residents to see themselves as part of a programmed existence. Observers watching trials in the exedrae of the Forum Augustum faced a curving elevation whose layered aediucla and artworks recalled the *scenae fons* of Roman theaters. In each niche stood the statue of a great man to be emulated, with his deeds carefully recorded in accompanying inscriptions (fig. 96). The existence of the trials themselves affirmed the restored security of the Augustan world. Such programmed environments reenforced the notion that each resident had a well-defined role to play. The *princeps* highlighted the effect by dictating the costumes of the urban "actors" in his capital. Suetonius records that Augustus was alarmed that people wore dark, everyday clothes in the magnificently reworked Forum Romanum; in response, "he commanded the aediles to allow no one into the Forum or its vicinity unless he had removed his cloak and wore a toga."[21]

The Augustan urban theater addressed both Romans in Rome and a larger audience. Following the lead of Caesar, the *princeps* considered world response to his capital and encouraged the citizenry to adopt a world view. Throughout the cityscape, evidence abounded. In the Porticus ad Nationes stood statues of all the nations Rome had conquered; in the Porticus Vipsania was the world map commissioned by Agrippa. In fact, the awareness of external viewers was itself a primary condition for the creation of an urban image. Once Rome was adorned as the renown of the empire demanded, all the world was compelled to take an interest. Augustus' concern with the audience's reaction never abated. On his deathbed, he quoted a line from a comedy of Menander, "Since well I've played my part, all clap your hands/ And from the stage dismiss me with applause" (Suet.*Aug*.99).

UNIFYING INVOLVEMENT

Pedestrians moving through an urban environment usually experience a city while on another mission – going to work, visiting a friend, running an errand, and so on. Augustus took steps to direct close connections between observers and Rome's physical fabric, to compel people to take an interest. He promoted the city as a shared cultural monument, encouraged personal involvement with municipal maintenance, and established recurring events tied to specific urban locales. After all, Rome was the birthplace of Roman civilization and *theatrum mundi*, the stage for all significant actions and the physical manifestation of Roman aspirations. From early in his career, Augustus promoted Rome's appearance as the result of shared traditions and collective efforts. He assiduously maintained the myth that other patrons helped shape the city's urban image. After restoring a temple, he frequently preserved the inscription of the original donor and at times claimed, not quite truthfully, that he encouraged others to undertake urban projects. The message was clear: each citizen had a stake in the city's form, appearance, and content.

The *princeps* strengthened this proprietary feeling by presenting Rome as the seat of a Roman empire. Through literature, histories, artwork, and physical aggrandizement, he promoted the city as geographically and symbolically the center of the known world. The Milliarium Aureum in the heart of Rome was merely one manifestation of this urban conceptualization; standing near the Rostra in the Forum Romanum, the bronze clad marker located other cities in relation to the capital of Augustus (cf. figs. 84 and 100).

Rome's status as a capital city facilitated the fashioning of an urban image. Capital cities are by their very nature containers of collective aspirations. Every intervention has meaning. Augustus employed traditional building components, though in an aggrandized form, and preserved the urban integrity of the preexisting cityscape. His actions honored the *genius loci* of Rome. Such reverence for Republican environments translated conceptually into reverence for the Republican state. The early designers of Washington, D.C., chose an alternative approach. Dealing with an unencumbered site, Jefferson and L'Enfant relied initially on the formal plan as much as individual architectural components to convey meaning. To give all Americans a stake in the new capital, the nation's founders named the streets after different states and assigned each state responsibility for completing one of the plazas in the master plan.[22]

To be successful, an urban image must engage and involve observers. In particular, residents should be made to feel part of the image-making process. With broad control over the state and culture, Augustus was able to supervise and channel participation in urban concerns. He encouraged Rome's residents to become involved with the cityscape. The *princeps* himself directed the patronage of major monuments, while urging others to pay homage to the capital through urban care. Using his own example and overt pressure, he compelled residents to undertake pragmatic maintenance projects and hold municipal offices. Men drawn from all social levels occupied new offices established to oversee the urban infrastructure. Freedmen enrolled as vigiles to fight fires; equites held praetorships dealing with urban safety; senators sat on boards overseeing the care of aqueducts, and so on. Specific responsibilities forged a powerful proprietary link between individuals and the city, stimulating a sense of responsibility that endured long after the term in office ended.

In contrast, for most modern cities, power over urban issues is neither centralized nor personalized. Los Angeles is a case in point; with over eighty different municipalities in the greater metropolitan area, care of the city is fractionalized and the urban image disjointed. Alienated from participation in shaping urban meaning, residents feel they have little control over or stake in their own environments. Yet when direct involvement is encouraged, as with graffiti task forces and community voting on designs for major municipal structures, the results are as positive as they were in the Augustan city.

Personal interaction with an urban environment can take many forms. Although modern cityscapes are infrequently enlivened by orchestrated ritu-

Figure 97. Southern processional relief from the Ara Pacis Augustae. The veiled figure on the left is identified as Agrippa; behind him walk members of the Imperial family. Photo: Fototeca Unione AAR 3247.

als, ancient Rome was the stage for innumerable programmed communal events. The Romans thus interacted with urban environments on a far more intimate level than do residents today. The individual places chosen for any given ritual held great significance and in fact were acknowledged actors in urban ceremonies. When Mark Antony staged a public rebuke in 44 B.C., Dio Cassius records, he carefully "selected the Forum and the Rostra that Caesar might be made ashamed by the very places" (DioCass.46.19).

With calculation, Augustus considered the interactive roles played by the urban environments he developed. He not only vitalized his new projects with carefully staged public activities, he reprogrammed many preexisting events and their associated environments to give them a decidedly Augustan slant. Revived Republican ceremonies and new Augustan rituals ran the gamut from specific ceremonies involving the patrician class, to public gatherings engaging the entire populace, including huge banquets for several thousand residents. Most effective in terms of developing an urban image were processional events incorporating several locales. The experience drew together both people and places, and disparate environments throughout the city.

As to be expected, Augustus was a prominent actor in such urban events. He appeared in all major processions either in the flesh or in effigy. Not infrequently, statues took part in urban rituals, allowing the *princeps* to appear in many guises simultaneously within a single parade. For example, a lengthy procession might have Augustus in person at its head, with the vicomagistri toward the rear carrying statuettes of the *genius Augusti* borrowed from the shrines of the Lares Compitales (fig. 92). The reliefs on the Ara Pacis memorialize the solemn processional ritual associated with a specific event with Augustus and his family as prominent participants (fig. 97). Though the ceremony represented took place at one moment in time, the connections it established reverberated for years. The reliefs continuously showed proper behavior for a communal rite, exemplified by the actions of the first citizen. Representing westward movement, the carved parade irrevocably linked the altar with the Horologium Augusti. Walking in sync with the sculpted procession to view the monument or participating in annual commemorations, Roman observers relived the event. At the same time, they identified their own progress through the city as an integral part of a choreographed, Augustan experience.

On the surface, Roman processions appear similar to modern parades, yet they differed in number and in their integration with the cityscape. A look at the Roman calendar shows the plethora of religious, triumphal, and celebratory processions that moved through the city each year (Table 6).

Figure 98. Etching by Antonio Lafréry depicting pilgrims moving between the seven churches of Christian Rome, 1575. Photo from F. Hermanin, *Die Stadt Rom im 15. und 16. Jahrhundert* (Lipsia 1911), pl. 45.

Notably, many were not mere spectator events, but required the direct participation of the citizenry who walked, prayed, danced, or ran through Rome as the program required. Furthermore, each procession followed a unique path (fig. 45). Rome did not have a single main parade street and, in any event, each ceremony drew from the power of different sites and their potent *genii*. In 17 B.C., a procession for the Ludi Saeculares began at the Augustan Temple of Apollo Palatinus and them moved down through the Forum and up to the Capitoline; each March, the Argei held rituals at the river, then passed through the city visiting twenty-seven different shrines; on the Ides of November, a procession for the plebeian games boisterously progressed from the Capitoline through the Forum to the Circus Maximus; and so on.[23]

Cumulatively, the intertwined processional routes tied residents to Rome's physical environment. In effect, these rituals compelled participants to connect urban locales kinetically, just as observers conceptually linked the related *imagines* of various sites in their minds. Medieval and Renaissance pilgrimages to Rome established similar ties between participants and revered urban locales as pilgrims moved between seven holy sites in the papal city (fig. 98).[24] The rituals drew strength from the places involved and vice versa. In contrast, modern parades too often follow routes selected for practical reasons of traffic and crowd management, not for their experiential power of place.

The Roman triumphal parade exemplifies the strong connection between processions and cityscape in Augustan Rome. A triumph was the highest attainable honor awarded a male citizen of the Republic. After a significant victory against foreign foes, a general came to Rome with his soldiers; together they waited outside the *pomerium* in the Campus Martius while the Senate deliberated about awarding a triumph. If all the criteria were satisfied, the Senate proclaimed the general *triumphator,* formally declared a holiday, and granted public resources to fund a parade and other festivities.[25]

Each general sought to outdo earlier *triumphators* in the scale and magnificence of his parade. Led by Rome's magistrates, the Republican triumphal procession included the general in his military chariot, the senators, the victorious troops, chained captives, booty displayed on floats, large paintings of battles, and exotica from the defeated land. The urban route could vary somewhat, but traditionally passed from the Campus Martius into the city through the Porta Triumphalis opened specifically for this event; it made a southern loop around the Palatine Hill and then moved along the Via Sacra through the Forum Romanum. The parade culminated atop the Capitoline Hill before the Temple of Jupiter Optimus Maximus where the Senate attended a great feast honoring the triumphator (fig. 45).[26]

January 1

Beginning of year

Day most magistrates take office

People donate gifts on the Capitoline in honor of Augustus

Caesar deified 42 B.C. and temple to him vowed; Augustus becomes *divus filius*

Triumph of L. Antonius, 41 B.C.

Triumph of L. M. Censorinus, 39 B.C.

Triumph of Tiberius, 7 B.C.; same day, Tiberius dedicates Porticus Liviae, vows Temple of Concordia Augusta and assumes second consulship

Dedication, shrine to Fortuna Augusta Stata, A.D. 12

January 7

Octavian assumes first *imperium,* 43 B.C.

January 11

Dedication, Temple of Juturna in Campus Martius, 3rd century B.C.

Closing of doors to the Temple of Janus, 29 B.C.

January 13 [IDES]

Octavian relinquishes power and restores Republic; awarded oak crown, 27 B.C.

January 14

Birth of Mark Antony 82 B.C.; later declared an unlucky day

January 16

Octavian awarded honorary title of Augustus, 27 B.C.; celebrated annually

Tiberius enters Rome triumphant after Pannonia, A.D. 9/10; postpones triumph until October 23, 12 A.D.

Rededication (formerly July 22), Temple of Concordia, A.D. 10, restored by Tiberius

January 17

Marriage of Livia and Octavian, 38 B.C.

Dedication, altar honoring the numen of Augustus, A.D. 9/5

Feriae Tiberius Caesar, ca. A.D. 5/9

January 27

Rededication (formerly July 15), Temple of Castor and Pollux, restored by Tiberius, A.D. 6

January 30

Birth of Livia, 58 B.C.

Arvals sacrifice, 38 B.C.

Supplicatio for *imperium* of Augustus

Dedication, Ara Pacis, 9 B.C.

February 5

Augustus given title *pater patriae*, 2 B.C.; made holiday by senatorial decree

Dedication, Temple of Concordia on Capitoline, 216 B.C.

February 21/22

Death of Gaius, A.D. 4

March 6

Augustus becomes Pontifex Maximus, 12 B.C.; made holiday by senatorial decree

March 15

Death of Caesar, 44 B.C.; day subsequently declared inauspicious

March 27

Caesar victorious at Alexandria, 47 B.C.

Triumph of L. C. Balbus, 19 B.C.

April 14

Augustus relieved siege of Mutina, 43 B.C.

April 16

Augustus acclaimed *imperator* for relieving Mutina, 43 B.C.

Table 6. continued

April 21

PARILIA

Foundation of Rome *(Natalis Urbis),* 753(?) B.C.

Games in honor of Caesar's victory at Munda, 45 B.C.

April 28

Statue and altar (shrine) of Vesta on the Palatine in house of Augustus dedicated, 12 B.C.; festival

Consecration of Aedes Flora, 3rd century B.C.; Augustus began restoration, Tiberius completed in A.D. 17

May 1

LARIBUS, honor Lares Compitales and Genius Augusti

May 12

Dedication, Temple of Mars Ultor, Forum Augustum, 2 B.C.

LUDI MARTIALIS from 19 B.C. onward

May 31 through June 3 LUDI SAECULARES, 17 B.C.

May 31

Augustus sacrifices to the Fates

June 1

Dedication, Temple of Mars Gradivus, 388 B.C.

Dedication, Temple of Juno Moneta, 344 B.C.

Triumph of Ap. Cl. Pulcher, 33(?) B.C.

LUDI SAECULARES: Augustus and Agrippa sacrifice cow to Juno and sow to Mother earth

June 2

LUDI SAECULARES: Augustus and Agrippa offer cakes to Apollo and Diana on Palatine

June 3

Dedication, Temple of Bellona at Circus Flaminius, ca. 296 B.C.; rebuilt by Augustus

LUDI SAECULARES: culminate on day sacred to Apollo and Diana; Agrippa and Augustus sacrifice on Palatine Hill

June 5–12

LUDI SAECULARES: games

June 9

Completion of Aqua Virgo of Agrippa, 19 B.C.

June 11

Dedication, Temple of Mater Matuta in Forum Boarium, 6th century B.C.

Dedication, Temple of Fortuna in Forum Boarium, 6th century B.C.

Dedication, Shrine to Concordia in Porticus Livia, 7 B.C.

MATRALIA

June 19

Celebration at Temple of Minerva on the Aventine; restored by Augustus, date unknown

June 22

SOLSTICE

June 26

Adoption of Tiberius by Augustus, A.D. 4, made holiday by senatorial decree

June 27

Dedication, Temple of Lares in Summa Sacra Via restored by Augustus, ca. 4 B.C.

June 29

Rededication (formerly February 17), Temple of Quirinus, restored by Augustus, 16 B.C.

June 30

Triumph of T. Statilius Taurus, 34 B.C.

Dedication, Temple of Hercules Musarum, restored by stepfather of Octavian, 29 B.C.

July 4

Consecration of Ara Pacis, 13 B.C.; on Augustus's return from Spain and Gaul

July 5

Birthday of Caesar celebrated after 42 B.C.; changed from July 13 to avoid conflict with Ludi Apollinares

POPLIFUGIA

July 6 through July 13

LUDI APOLLINARES

July 15 [IDES]

EQUITUM ROMANORUM PROBATIO, major spectacle of Augustan Age

July 20–30

LUDI VICTORIAE CAESARIS commemorate victory at Pharsalus, initiated ca. 46 B.C.

Comet appears for seven days running at funeral games honoring Caesar 44 B.C.

August 1: Important anniversary of many Augustan institutions

Dedication, Temple of Victoria on Palatine, 294 B.C.; festival

Dedication, Temple of Victoria Virgo on Palatine, 193 B.C.

Caesar victorious at Ilerda (Spain), 49 B.C.

Caesar victorious at Zela (Near East), 47 B.C.

Conquest of Alexandria by Augustus, 30 B.C.; festival

Beginning date for office of magistri vicorum and municipal Augustales

Dedication, Temple of Spes in Forum Holitorium, first Punic War; restored by Augustus after fire, 31 B.C.

Drusus founds cult of Roma and Augustus in Gaul, 12 B.C.

Cult of Lares Augusti instituted, 7 B.C.

August 3

Tiberius victorious in Illyria, A.D. 8

August 10

Consecration of Altar Ceres Mater and Ops Augusta in Vicus Jugarius, probably A.D. 7, associated with Livia

FERIAE OPIS ET CERERIS in Vicus Jugarius

August 12/13

Dedication, Temple of Venus Victrix, along with Honos, Virtus, Felicitas, and V(ictoria) in Theater of Pompey, 55/52 B.C.; complex restored by Augustus, date unknown

August 13–15

FERIAE AUGUSTALES, holiday of slaves associated with Diana

August 13 [IDES]

Dedication, Temple of Vortumnus, 3rd century B.C.; associated with triumphs

Dedication, Temple of Fortunae Equestri, 173 B.C.

Dedication, Temple of Castor and Pollux in Circus Flaminius, ca. 100 B.C.

Dedication, Temple of Hercules Victor Invictus ad Porta Trigeminam, date unknown

Dedication, Temple of Diana in Aventine restored by L. Cornificius in the 30s B.C.

Triple Triumph of Augustus, 29 B.C.; first day: celebrate success over Pannonians and Dalmatians

Dedication or rededication of Temple of Flora ad Circus Maximus, A.D. 17 (see April 28)

Table 6. continued

August 14
  Triple Triumph of Augustus, 29 B.C.; second day: Actium
August 15
  Triple Triumph of Augustus, 29 B.C.; third day: Egypt
  Triumph of L. A. Paetus, 28 B.C.
August 17
  PORTUNALIA
  Dedication, Temple of Janus in Forum Boarium, 260 B.C.; Augustus began restoration, Tiberius completed in A.D. 17
August 18
  Dedication, Temple of Divus Julius, 29 B.C.; following Augustus' triple triumph; festival
August 19
  Dedication, Temple of Venus Libitina, Esquiline, early foundation date unknown
  Dedication, Temple of Venus Obsequens at the Circus Maximus, begun 295 B.C.
  VINALIA
  Beginning of Augustus' first consulate in 43 B.C.; inauguration of his reign or *dies imperii*
  Death of Augustus, A.D. 14, age 76; *dies tristissimus*
August 20
  Death of Lucius, A.D. 2, sacrifices
August 28
  Dedication, Temple of Sol et Luna, part of Circus Maximus; maybe incorporate obelisk brought to Rome in 10 B.C.
  Dedication, Altar of Victoria in Curia, 29 B.C.; festival
September 1
  FERIAE JOVI

Dedication, Temple of Jupiter Tonans on the Capitoline, 22 B.C.
Rededication (formerly April 13), Temple of Jupiter Libertas on the Aventine, restored by Augustus, date unknown
Dedication, Temple of Juno Regina on the Aventine, restored by Augustus, date unknown
September 2
  Octavian victorious at Actium, 31 B.C.; festival
September 3
  Octavian victorious at Battle of Naulochus (Sicily), 36 B.C.; festival by senatorial decree
  Triumph of C. Sosius, 34 B.C.
September 4–19
  LUDI ROMANI honoring Jupiter Optimus Maximus; procession
September 13 [IDES]
  Dedication, Temple of Jupiter Optimus Maximus, 508 B.C.; Augustus restored
September 22–23
  Equestrians celebrate Augustus' birthday 2 days
September 23
  EQUINOX
  Birth of Augustus, 63 B.C.; public holiday, festival, and games instituted after Actium; sacrifices to Genius Augusti
  Rededication (formerly December 23), Temple of Juno Regina in Circus Flaminius, date unknown
  Rededication (formerly July 13), Temple of Apollo, restored by C. Sosius, ca. 32 B.C.
  Rededication (formerly September 5), Temple of Jupiter Stator, rebuilt by Octavia after 23 B.C.

240

Dedication, Temple of Felicitas in the Campus Martius, date unknown

Rededication (formerly May 14), Shrine of Mars at Circus Flaminius; may be site of sacrifice to Mars on this date, perhaps restored by Augustus at unknown date

Festival for Latona

September 26

Caesar's triumph ends with elephant procession, 46 B.C.

Dedication, Temple of Venus Genetrix in Forum Julium, 46 B.C.

September 28–29

Triumph of Pompey, 61 B.C.

Death of Pompey, 48 B.C.

September 29

Birth of Pompey, 106 B.C.

October 3–12

LUDI FORTUNAE REDUCIS, instituted 11 B.C.

October 9

Festival on Capitoline to Genius Populi Romani, Felicitas, and Venus Victrix; three gods of good fortune

Dedication, Temple of Apollo on the Palatine, 28 B.C.; festival and games

October 10

Celebration at Temple of Juno Moneta (maybe commemorates a restoration)

October 12

Conception (?) of Julius Caesar, 99 B.C.

Triumph of C. Norbanus Flaccus, 34 B.C.

Triumph of L. Sempronius Atratinus, 21 B.C.

Consecration of Altar of Fortuna Redux at Porta Capena to honor Augustus' return on this date in 19 B.C.; dedicated December 15

AUGUSTALIA festival honoring anniversary of Augustus' return from the East in 19 B.C.; annual after A.D. 14

October 15 [IDES]

EQUUS OCTOBER

LUDI CAPITOLINI

October 18

Octavius assumes *toga virilis*, 48 B.C.

Rededication (formerly August 17), Temple of Janus in the Forum Holitorium Portunalia; restored by Augustus and completed by Tiberius in A.D. 17

October 19

ARMISLUSTRIUM, festival to Mars involving the purification of the army

October 23

Octavian victorious at Philippi, 42 B.C.

Triumph of Tiberius, A.D. 12

November 4–17

LUDI PLEBEII

November 13 [IDES]

PLEBEIAN celebration to Jupiter

POMPA CIRCENSIS

Octavian's second *ovatio*, 36 B.C.

Dedication, Temple of Fortuna Primigenia, 3rd century B.C.

Dedication, Temple of Fortuna, 6th century B.C.; least important of three temples of Fortuna on Quirinal

November 27

Passage of Lex Titia, 43 B.C.; establishing second triumvirate of Antony, Lepidus, and Octavian

Triumph of P. Ventidius, 38 B.C.

December 1

Rededication, Temple of Neptune, restored by Cn. Domitius in 32(?) B.C.

December 10

Tribunes assume office

Table 6. continued

December 15

Dedication, Altar Fortuna Redux Porta
Capena to honor Augustus' return, 19
B.C.; consecrated October 12

CONSUALIA

December 17

Dedication, Temple of Saturn; rebuilt by
L. Munatius Plancus, 42 B.C.

December 17–23

SATURNALIA

December 22

SOLSTICE

Dedication, Temple of Lares Permarini in
Porticus Minucia, 179 B.C.

December 23

Conception (?) of Augustus, 64 B.C.

Dedication, Temple of Diana at Circus
Flaminius, 179 B.C.

Dedication, Temple of Juno Regina at
Circus Flaminius, 179 B.C.

LARENTALIA

December 29

Triumph of Planus, 43 B.C.

Triumph of Pompey, 71 B.C.

December 31

Triumph M. Aemilius Lepidus, 43 B.C.

To keep large audiences comfortable throughout the lengthy event, the organizers erected grandstands and directed the parade through spectator buildings such as theaters and circuses. The route was lined with manubial structures erected by earlier *triumphators* anxious to associate their achievements eternally with the power of this urban ritual.[27]

Huge crowds flocked to Rome to attend the magnificent triumphs given by Augustus for himself and his family members (Table 1).[28] The *princeps* maintained the outward trappings of the Republican ceremony, but redirected the message. His most blatant gesture was to reprogram the order of parade participants. Breaking with Republican tradition for his triumph of 29 B.C., Octavian placed himself, not the magistrates and senators, at the head of the procession. In addition, he accepted the great honor of wearing the purple garb and crown of a *triumphator* at other occasions, a visible manifestation of his elevated status.[29] The *princeps* made his own Forum Augustum the center of various actions linked to the triumph, including the dedications of triumphal crowns and scepters, Senatorial discussions about the granting of triumphs, and sculptural displays of past and present *triumphators*.

The location and introverted configuration of the Forum Augustum did not allow it to be incorporated into the triumphal procession itself. Similarly, the other new Augustan node high atop the Palatine remained visible from, but not accessible to, the parade. In compensation, the *princeps* imposed Augustan messages on the structures lining the triumphal route. Leaving the Campus Martius, the parade passed through the new Theater of Marcellus (cf. Josesph.*BJ*.7.113). Perhaps the structure's atypical skewed southwest/northeast alignment responded directly to the demands of the triumphal procession; this orientation made it easy for a parade to move from the Circus Flaminius, through the Augustan theater, and then into the Forum Holitorium. Entering the Forum Romanum, all triumphal parades passed under an Augustan arch. Overtly emphasizing historical continuity, the reveals of the Parthian arch were inscribed with the lists of consuls and *triumphators*. As the parade climbed the Clivus Capitolinus, the first monument visible was the marble Temple of Jupiter Tonans celebrating Octavian's Cantabrian campaign.

Augustus also manipulated the meaning of existing buildings along the triumphal route. He restored many of the structures erected by earlier *triumphators*, giving them an Augustan gloss both physically and conceptually. White marble and crisp carving associated the revamped structures with other urban projects by the *princeps*. Programmed celebrations linked select structures with events in his life. For example, several manubial temples received the same new dedication date, September 23, birthday of Augustus; the Temple of Spes in the Forum Holitorium was rededicated on first day of his eponymous month (Table 6). Tiberius likewise interrelated his buildings and triumphs; on January 1, he celebrated his victory over Germany and the dedication of the Porticus honoring his mother (Table 1). On both triumphal and dedication days, garlands and other ornaments decorated these buildings, uniting them in appearance as well as in meaning.

The dedication of a Roman temple was a moment of solemn ceremony. Augustus as high priest meticulously adhered to religious protocol and duties. In particular, he exploited building dedications as opportunities to energize and unite the city. Great fanfare surrounded the dedication of the Forum Augustum and Temple of Mars Ultor in 2 B.C. Velleius Paterculus records the *princeps* spared no expense in his quest "to fill the hearts and eyes of the Roman people with unforgettable images" (2.100.2). In the Circus Maximus, gladiators killed 260 lions; in the Forum Romanum, Augustus' grandson Agrippa Postumus participated in the rowdy Trojan Games; in the Saepta, gladiators struggled in combat; in the Circus Flaminius, hunters stalked crocodiles and other exotic beasts. Across the river, the *princeps* created the enormous Naumachia Augusti solely for this event; there 3,000 combatants on more than thirty large ships reenacted the Battle of Salamis. Important for ideological reasons, this celebration was also significant for highlighting Augustan centers in Rome and uniting residents and the entire cityscape together in a single purpose.

The *princeps* consistently enriched his architectural program in Rome by associating major buildings with the temporal topography of the Roman calendar.[30] The Romans lived closely by the official public calendar. They listened attentively to the monthly reading of the calendar on the *nones* (nine days before the *ides*) and regularly consulted permanent copies posted on temple walls. Familiarity with the calendar was essential. Not only did one need to know festival days in order to avoid offending the gods, but the entire year was categorized into days suitable for business (*dies fasti*) and days unsuitable (*dies nefasti*).[31]

In the 40s B.C., Julius Caesar had undertaken a comprehensive revision of the calendar and ensured his own aggrandizement within this important document. The Senate had proclaimed the anniversaries of Caesar's five most important victories and his day of birth as public holidays, and renamed his natal month *Julius* (Suet.*Caes*.40, 76; Plut.*Caes*.59). Augustus accepted even more honors. Eighteen new holidays celebrated secular and religious events in his life and were touted in new calendars, including a poetic version begun by Ovid.[32] All the new festivals were celebrated at Augustan buildings in Rome. A symbiotic relationship evolved with calendar events enhancing the importance of Augustan structures on a particular day, and throughout the year individual buildings sparked memories of particular events in the life of the *princeps*.

Augustus, like other Romans, celebrated his conception and birth days. Similarly, a temple had special days associated with its consecration and dedication.[33] The latter, by far the most important, became the building's *dies natalis;* this birthday was entered into the calendar and celebrated yearly by devotees. Any patron who extensively rebuilt a temple could rededicate the structure and select a new *dies natalis*. Naturally, patrons chose these dates with care, associating their projects with days celebrating important earlier events, particular deities, or annual festivals. Augustus in particular empowered his urban interventions temporally by selecting potent days for the dedication of temples. In manipulating the calendar, he employed strategies similar to those he applied to reshaping of Rome's physical environment (Table 6).

Augustus developed significant landmarks in the calendar. One means was to piggyback on existing days of import. During the Republic, generals scheduled their triumphs to coincide with former victories (March 27) or their own birthdays (September 28). Caesar held games in honor of his victory at Munda on April 21, the birthday of Rome herself. Augustus likewise associated certain structures with existing calendar dates. For example, he began his triple triumph in 29 B.C. on the Ides of August, a day sacred to Jupiter and filled with temple dedications associated with military success.

For the Temple of Apollo, he selected a birthday of October 9, the festival day honoring the Genius, or collective spirit, of the Roman people. Similarly, Livia dedicated the Temple of Concordia in her eponymous portico on June 11, the *dies natalis* for temples to several deities associated with women.

Augustus related many of his building projects in Rome to familial occurrences. Seeking an appropriate dedication date for the Ara Pacis commemorating the Augustan peace, the first emperor chose January 30, the birthday of Livia; this was simultaneously a day of supplicato for the *imperium* of Augustus. When necessary, Augustus manipulated events to fall on auspicious dates. Returning from the east in 19 B.C., he took care to arrive in Rome on October 12, conception day of his adoptive father Caesar. The cheering residents of Rome vowed a commemorative altar to Fortuna Redux, the goddess personifying the return of good fortune. The altar was later dedicated in December, yet due to the association with this specific homecoming, the consecration/conception date remained more popular. September 23 held the highest point in the temporal topography of the Augustan calendar. This day was simultaneously the autumnal equinox and Augustus' own birthday. After comprehensively rebuilding at least five select temples associated with former triumphators, the *princeps* rededicated them all on September 23. As a result, the day became the annual focus of festivals and games throughout the city, including sacrifices to the Genius Augusti.[34]

Anxious for reflected glory, Tiberius likewise tied his building projects with days important in the life of Augustus. In A.D. 9/10, he programmed his victorious entry into Rome from Pannonia to occur on the day honoring Octavian's assumption of the title "Augustus" (January 16) and chose the same date for the rededication of the Temple of Concordia in the Forum Romanum.[35] He celebrated the actual Pannonian triumph on October 23, the anniversary of Octavian's victory at Philippi. For an altar to the numen of Augustus, Tiberius picked an obvious dedication date: January 17, the wedding anniversary of Octavian and his own mother Livia.

During the Republic, dedication dates had often clustered together into nodes (August 13), with the collective celebrations of several temple birthdays enhancing the status of each individual structure. The *princeps* established his own nodes. A number of events occurred in the first half of October, including the birthday of Drusus, grandson of Livia (7th); the festival to the Genius of the Roman People (9th); the conception day of Caesar (around the 12th); the anniversary of the Dictator's Spanish triumph (date uncertain), and the great festival to Mars (18–19th) upon whom Augustus had called to aid in avenging Caesar's assassination. To these, Augustus added the dedication of the Temple to Apollo Palatinus (9th) and the consecration of the Altar of Fortuna Redux (12th), both emphasized by accompanying festivals.

On a larger scale, Augustus carefully developed the eighth and ninth months as a grand Augustan temporal district. Rather than allowing his name to be given to his natal month, a date over which he had no control, the *princeps* selected the month of his greatest attainments. *Sextilis* became *mensis Augustus* to underscore the significance of his first consulship (19th), the end of civil war (1st), and all the military victories represented by his fabulous triple triumph (13–15th).[36] The first day of the month marked celebrations for anniversaries of Caesar's victories, temples to Victoria, and Octavian's own success in Alexandria. It also became an important date for Augustan institutions, including the entry into office of the *magistri vicorum* and municipal Augustales. The 18th marked the dedication of the temple to Augustus' deified father, the divine Julius Caesar. The following month was also awash with associated events. The first day of the *mensis September* was the "birthday" of the temple to Jupiter Tonans vowed by Augustus while on campaign, as well as of the temple of Juno Regina, and the rededicated shrine to Jupiter Libertas. Several days marked Augustan victories (2nd, 3rd, 25th); the anniversary of Caesar's great quadruple triumph spanned from the 20th to the end of the month. Furthermore, the *dies natalis* of Rome's most important temple, that to Jupiter Optimus Maximus, also occurred in this month (13th), amidst the celebrations for the Ludi Romani, popular games honoring the same god. All these events, however, seemed to be mere preludes to the great celebrations on September 23, Augustus' birthday.

Legible paths also occurred in the Augustan calendar. As seen with the last example, significant urban ceremonies could be choreographed to lead up to a particular date.[37] The grand festivities for his triple triumph in 29 B.C. likewise culminated with the dedication of a temple to Augustus' divine father in the Forum Romanum. In addition, the *princeps* orchestrated larger temporal pathways. In 17 B.C., he celebrated the Ludi Saeculares after carefully manipulating the temporal accounting. The new reckoning of the *saeculum* as 110 years allowed Augustus to underscore a desired sequencing of historical events. Held in June, these festivities ended with celebrations at the restored Temple of Minerva on the Aventine, followed soon after by the summer solstice.

Augustus emphasized existing borders within the calendar, and established new entry points. The first day of the Roman calendar held great significance. It signaled a new temporal territory and the point when magistrates took office. Significantly, a large number of triumphators scheduled their parades on the days surrounding January first. Tiberius, stepson of

Augustus, celebrated a triumph on the first day of 7 B.C. and simultaneously dedicated the Porticus Liviae. On January, first Roman citizens gave thanks to Augustus' benefactions by carrying gifts up to the Capitoline. The cult of the deified Julius Caesar was also initiated on this day, an overt affirmation of Augustus' own elevation to the status of *divus filius*. Soon after the taking of Alexandria on the first day of Sextilis [August], proposals circulated to make this day a new temporal edge, marking entry into the entire year. Similar propositions called for the Roman year to start on the *princeps*' birthday. Both suggestions were implemented abroad, though not in Rome.[38]

As the Roman example shows, participatory events are a useful way to link disparate urban projects. Both recurring festivities and simultaneous episodes can bring cohesion to a city. For example, the Tuscan town of Siena has a strong urban image not only because of its preserved medieval aesthetic and compact historic core, but also because of its highly charged urbanistic events. Twice yearly, the city holds the Palio delle Contrade, a flamboyant horse race that preserves and heightens the rivalry between urban regions, while simultaneously uniting the city as a whole in a communal activity.[39] In cities today, simultaneous unifying events are often commercial in nature. When a new franchise opens, all other stores in the chain celebrate with banners and floodlights, unifying different points in the cityscape for one brief moment.

Personal interaction with a cityscape alone does not foster the creation of a clear urban image. Moving through a city, conducting daily tasks, residents learn functional patterns and relationships; they do not necessarily find a meaningful content. Augustus strengthened and unified the urban image of his capital by carefully programming how occupants interacted with the cityscape. He promoted the capital as both their home and the *locus* of renewing rituals for the city and all Romans. Furthermore, he encouraged direct participation in urban care and in panurban rituals strategically located within a recurring temporal landscape. The residents of Augustan Rome felt they had a stake in the city and her image.

LEGACY

During his lifetime, Augustus received wide acclaim for the successful aggrandizement of Rome. He clearly wanted this positive achievement to endure. The *princeps* consciously fashioned his architectural projects with an eye toward posterity, presenting them as "a memorial to future ages" (Vitr.1.pref.3). Augustan buildings were solidly constructed of durable materials; a new municipal bureaucracy provided for ongoing maintenance of the city's physical fabric; Augustan fire and police forces protected both people and buildings. Equally important, the golden age so prominently advertised in the cityscape held out the tantalizing promise that it would never end. Throughout the city, stone monuments honoring the heirs of Augustus celebrated stability and continuity. As if anxious to occupy as many minds as possible with the image of the Augustan city, the poet Propertius exhorted, "Rome in its greatness! Stranger, look your fill!" (4.1).

The image, however, was transitory. By its very nature, an urban image is always in a state of becoming. Constantly changing, it requires optimum circumstances as well as a firm hand to be created and to remain focused. In this area, as in many others, Augustus was blessed by the gods. He inherited an urban environment in which scripting was comparatively easy. The Republican cityscape was derelict, materially poor, and demoralized. As a result, every pristine building, every enrichment, every improvement in conditions became notable. After decades of bloody confrontations and danger in the streets, residents naturally praised the relative security initiated by the new municipal bureaucracy and the expansive Augustan peace. Within the preexisting Republican urban fabric, Augustan projects formed a cogent group – boastful, well-appointed, and programmatically cohesive. In large part, the perceptual unity of these works resulted from the large-scale introduction of marble into a mud-brick cityscape, a material transformation rarely possible in history. Most obvious of all, the Augustan Age was the fulcrum leveraging the Roman state, and its capital, into an Imperial realm.

Once Rome entered this realm, once the contrasts became commonalities, once grand marble buildings became familiar, the clarity of the Augustan urban image began to fade. The process was accelerated by the death of the man who directed and focused the urban image. Despite his efforts, Augustus could not prevent the urban image of Rome from evolving. After outliving a succession of anointed heirs, he was ultimately followed by his stepson Tiberius, a man of limited vision with scant interest in architecture or an urban image. Subsequent emperors attempted to impress their stamp on the city, yet few had the means, ability, or opportunities of an Augustus. Furthermore, they faced a city already aggrandized. Later, Roman emperors added to the city's visible richness, but never with the same dramatic effect as at that poignant moment when Republican Rome began to dress as an Imperial city. After the death of the *princeps,* each new impressive, formally cohesive structure erected in Rome enhanced the image of an *Imperial* city, not the image of a city tied to a specific individual or period.

Though the overall image of Augustan Rome was fugitive, certain features had an enduring impact. Synchronically, the *princeps'* projects in the city on the Tiber resonated across the Empire. During the Augustan Age, coins, other portable visual representations, and written descriptions advertised the architectural wonders of the renewed capital (fig. 54). In homage to the *princeps,* cities throughout the Empire assumed the name "Augusta" and emulated architectural projects directly associated with the first emperor.[40] For example, the citizens of Augusta Emerita in Spain modeled their new forum after the Forum Augustum, complete down to the shields of Ammon and caryatids above the side porticos (fig. 99).[41] Overall, Augustan Rome served as the incubator for what William L. MacDonald calls "Empire Imagery," the "architectural symbols without which no city or town across the empire could properly claim to be Roman."[42] Such imagery was not based solely upon individual components or motifs, but also fundamentally upon broader urban concepts. The environments of Rome so carefully scripted by Augustus further inspired an experientially and conceptually rich architecture of passage and connection in cities across the Empire.[43] Other patrons likewise attempted to craft legible urban narratives through the placement of impressive marble structures, artworks, and various amenities along the major arteries and within internalized environments.

At Rome, the interventions of Augustus affected urban developments diachronically. Many of his projects remained landmarks in the cityscape for centuries. Their strong urban presence prompted emulation. The Forum Augustum with its great exedrae served as the model for the adjacent Forum of Trajan; the Mausoleum of Augustus inspired the form of Hadrian's tomb, and so on. In many cases, the interventions of the *princeps* exerted a continuous influence on Rome's urban layout. For example, the Augustan configuration of the Forum Romanum endured with only slight modifications throughout antiquity. The new Augustan node created on the Palatine became the eponymous nucleus for Rome's great Imperial residences. Once programmed by Augustus and Agrippa, the Campus Martius continued to receive recreational buildings following the orthogonal plan formalized at the turn of the millennium. Extensively exploited by Augustus, the use of multicolored, richly carved marble became a hallmark of Roman Imperial construction.

In *Civilization and Its Discontents,* Sigmund Freud explored the memory traces within the human brain. He explains, "in mental life nothing which has once been formed can perish – that everything is somehow preserved and that in suitable circumstances (when, for instance, regression goes back far enough) it can once more be brought to light."[44] To clarify this concept, Freud selected a metaphor: the city of Rome. He asks readers to imagine the experience of the modern city with the multitudinous historical layers of occupation, building, and meaning glimpsed in tantalizing fragments within the extant urban fabric. Freud then calls upon them to imagine the city as a psychical entity, "an entity, that is to say, in which nothing that has once come into existence will have passed away and all the earlier phases of development continue to exist alongside the latest one." In this mental construct, buildings from different periods simultaneously occupy the same space, and historical sequences simultaneously recur; with a change in glance or position, the observer is able to read the form and meaning of each different era. Here Freud captures the essence of urban imagery. He conveys the strength of Rome's *genius loci* as the result of her entire history, while at the same time acknowledging urban form and experience as a mnemonic repository. An urban image forms in the minds of firsthand observers who read a cityscape as the cumulative product of all that has gone before and as a significant shaper of all that is to come. The Augustan urban image was strongest during the lifetime of the *princeps,* yet it did not completely fade. Embedded in the physical and psychical city its potent memory trace endures.

In the early years of the first millenium, the poet Ovid offended the *princeps* and was exiled to the distant shores of the Black Sea. With him he carried a focused image of the city on the Tiber. Through plaintive poems and letters, he sought to regain favor. In one, he lavishes praise upon the political achievements of Augustus, and then almost immediately describes an equally great success, the enhancement of Rome. Relying on a rhetoricians' training in creating and deciphering conceptual environments, Ovid takes the reader on a walk through the city; each step conveys the potent image-ability of Augustan Rome:

[F]rom my own house I am once again visiting the localities of the beautiful city, my mind surveying everything with eyes of its own. Now the fora, now the temples, now the theaters sheathed in marble, now every portico with its levelled ground comes before me; now the greensward of the Campus that looks towards the lovely gardens, the pools, the canals, and the water of the Virgo. (Ov.*Pont.*1.33–8)

To anyone who had visited Rome in 50 B.C., and again sixty years later a positive transformation had obviously occurred. Filled with magnificent buildings to, for, and by the *princeps,* Rome's new imperial appearance was perceived as both the achievement of one man and a memorial to his greatness. The image of the *princeps* and the city were irrevocably intertwined. The idea of Rome lay in the lap of Augustus as firmly as that of the city proposed for Alexander the Great (fig. 14). Yet, unlike the model proposed by Dinocrates, neither the form nor the name of the city literally reflected their Roman patron. Building upon the extant history of the site, drawing from the power of the place, Augustus had forged an urban image that was irrevocably Roman, yet just as irrevocably centered upon himself.

Figure 99. Reconstruction of the forum at Augusta Emerita, Spain. Drawing: Richard H. Abramson after R. Mesa.

CHAPTER SEVEN

A WALK THROUGH
AUGUSTAN ROME, A.D. 14

Rome in her greatness! Stranger look your fill!
Propertius 4.1

A low layer of mist hovers over the Campus Martius. Laborers shiver and groan as they slowly carry two large bronze tablets across the exposed paving of the Horologium Augusti. Mercifully, their goal is in sight. Before them to the north rises a large artificial mountain, the Mausoleum of Augustus. After almost an hour, the laborers enter the sheltering public gardens at the base of the mound and move toward the tomb's south-facing entrance. Here they set down their load and await the skilled workers who will do the actual installation. Though illiterate, the workers stare reverentially at the row after row of inscriptions covering the tablets. They know the content well: The text records the impressive achievements of Augustus. The list, once thought to be endless, will no longer grow. The *princeps* is dead.

All Rome mourns the death of Augustus. Far to the north of the city, two fictional figures approach the city (fig. 100). One is a young girl, the other her elderly grandfather. The old man fills the hours of their journey with stories about recent events. A few months earlier, on August 19, A.D. 14, the *princeps* died of natural causes. Already numerous stories circulate about the circumstances. The tragic event occurred at the Campanian town of Nola in the same room where Augustus' natural father had also expired. The grandfather himself had seen the great procession carrying the *princeps* back to the capital. With great ceremony, the foremost citizens of each city along the route took turns bearing the load. The cavalcade moved at night. During the hot hours of the day, the bearers placed the corpse on display in the basilicas of each successive township. Nearing Rome, the equestrians took charge and by dark conveyed Augustus' body into the city and up the Palatine hill to his residence.

Along with other patricians, the grandfather set aside his purple-bordered toga as a sign of sadness. A long meeting of the Senate debated various options for the funeral arrangements. Many senators vied to propose the most splendid commemorations. One called for the golden statue of Victoria from the Curia to lead a funeral cortege through the Porta Triumphalis in the Campus Martius accompanied by the children of leading families singing a dirge. Another suggested all citizens show reverence by exchanging their gold rings for ones of iron. As a permanent honor, another proposed that the entire lifetime of the *princeps* be designated the Augustan Age and so entered in the Calendar. Perhaps the most personal, the most "Augustan" gesture was the proposal to limit honorifics, following the *princeps'* own modesty and restrictions on excess; the attempt was futile. Extravagant commemoratives abounded. The elderly visitor silently hopes there will be no further outbursts like that which occurred only a few weeks earlier. People celebrating the Augustalia felt restrained by the extant limitations on spending. When a well-known actor refused to perform for the stipulated pay, the residents of the capital rioted rather than attend a demeaned performance unworthy of Augustus, especially because he has now become a god. Alarmed, the tribunes immediately rushed to the Curia and begged permission to spend more than the usual amount; the Senate acquiesced.[1]

With satisfaction, the grandfather recalls that ultimately the debates over the choreography of the funeral proved unnecessary. As always, Augustus provided for everything. When Drusus read aloud his will, the first roll of text contained specific instructions for the funeral (DioCass.56.33). Carefully orchestrated, the activities revealed Augustus' keen sense of theater. The funeral procession commenced from his house on the Palatine. Figures wearing wax masks or *imagines* of the *princeps'* illustrious ancestors proceeded in two distinct groups following their arrangement in the Forum Augustum and in the *Aeneid,* book 6.[2] With solemnity, the officials elected for the following year carried a body reclining upon a couch of ivory and gold with purple and gold coverings.[3] Viewed by a mournful crowd, the parade proceeded past the arch honoring the natural father of Augustus and descended into the Forum Romanum. Anxious to see the *princeps* one last time, the grandfather had maneuvered close to the old Rostra where the couch was placed on display. His efforts were in vain. The body in triumphal dress reclining on top was of wax; the corpse lay hidden inside the couch. From atop the high speakers' platform, the effigy oversaw the huge assembly of mourners. Dressed in dark clothing, Tiberius, heir to Augustus, and his son Drusus gave orations at opposing ends of the central Forum.[4] Tiberius openly equated the audience with a chorus, and himself with a

Figure 100. Diagram, walk 2.

choral leader. Together they sang the praises of Augustus in the wondrous urban stage set the great man had created.[5]

At the end of the eulogy, the officials again hoisted the elaborate funeral couch. A golden image from the Curia and another of Augustus in a triumphal chariot joined the parade. Behind these impressive images came representations of the deceased's ancestors. Included were not only the blood relatives of Augustus, but, as befitting the *Pater Patriae,* every Roman of prominence all the way back to Romulus. In effect, the funeral procession allowed all the *summi viri* of the Forum Augustum to move once again through their beloved city.[6] By senatorial decree, the cortege passed through the Porta Triumphalis and wended its way northward toward the Mausoleum of Augustus. Knowing the destination, the grandfather had hurried ahead to find a good viewing spot. At the tomb, the officials placed the body on a giant pyre. With great ceremony, first the priests marched around the funeral mound, followed by the equestrians, who tossed all the triumphal decorations they had received from Augustus upon the combustible mound. Next, the centurions paraded around the mound, then set it afire. Suddenly, an eagle flew up from the burning body. The crowd gasped, then murmured acknowledgment; the revered bird must carry the spirit of Augustus heavenward.

The patrician grandfather fondly recalls the following days as the *princeps* showered gifts upon the Romans even after his death. Augustus bequeathed forty million sesterces to the people along with other legacies to the tribes, praetorian guards, city cohorts, legionaries, and select individuals. He had ordered the disbursement be immediate. The old man had already collected his share, which was helping to finance this visit to Rome. Slaves, however, did not fare as well. Traditionally, many patrons freed slaves during the funeral commemorations of an important citizen. Fearing his great city would fill with a promiscuous rabble, Augustus specifically recommended that only a few slaves be liberated in Rome at the time of his funeral (DioCass.56.33).

Shortly following the great funeral, the Senate proclaimed Augustus a god with his own sacred rites and priests (Sodales Augustales). The widowed Livia became priestess of the cult with the honor of an accompanying lictor during the performance of her duties. Privately, Livia assuaged her grief with a closed ceremony of three days held in the Palatine residence she had shared with Augustus. As he has done many times before, the grandfather holds up Livia as a model of piety for his young granddaughter. He promises to show his young charge the shrine to the divine Augustus that Livia and her son Tiberius are erecting at the foot of the same hill. Until the new structure is complete, citizens visit the Temple of Mars Ultor in the Forum

Augustum, where they pay homage to a golden image of Augustus reclining on a couch (DioCass.56.46).

The sadness permeating the city is matched by a feeling of apprehension. Tiberius, heir to Augustus, assumed power with little opposition, yet many citizens question his capabilities. A rumor circulates that the *princeps* chose his uninspiring stepson as successor in order to have his own achievements seem more memorable by comparison (DioCass.56.45). Already urban evidence in Rome begins to support this theory. Tiberius has assumed responsibility for Augustan buildings in progress, carefully preserving the name of his adoptive father as the original donor, yet his efforts at urban aggrandizement seem half-hearted. At the urging of his mother, he has begun the temple to the Divus Augustus, but has not proposed plans for any other major structures (DioCass.57.10).

On this brisk fall day in A.D. 14, the grandfather moves slowly with his granddaughter toward the center of Rome. Wistfully, the old man recalls a walk taken with his own father over sixty years earlier. Much has changed. Then Rome was a jumbled, illegible, unimageable Republican city. With pride, the elderly patrician notes that few cities can now compare with the impressive capital on the Tiber River. Even though the two observers are several kilometers from the city center, they have ample evidence of the great metropolis to come. Nearing the city, villas increase in number and become more suburban in form (Cic.*Cat.*3.2). Large tracts of ranch and farm land give way to smaller plots of vegetables and even more valuable commodities such as roses. Most plots show careful maintenance. Shortly before crossing the Tiber River, several large highways converge. First, the Via Tiberina joins the Via Flaminia from the east; a bit farther to the southwest, the Via Claudia also joins the Flaminian highway (fig. 101). Movement slows as traffic increases. The observers pass numerous wagons leaving Rome after making deliveries at night, the only time wheeled traffic is allowed in the city without special permission. To double their pay load, carts exit filled with rubbish and human waste, the most prolific products manufactured in the capital. In the distance, the travelers already can see a brown haze marking the site of Rome, where countless cooking fires and large industrial furnaces create a smokey nimbus.

As the travelers move south, the highway rises to cross the Tiber. Though still temperamental, the great river has been partially tamed through regulation. The banks show evidence of recent cleaning and the river flows peacefully below the Pons Mulvius, erected centuries before and now meticulously maintained. Once across the bridge, the two pedestrians trod upon the left and more revered bank of the Tiber. This transition is signaled by an honorific arch atop the Pons Mulvius. This commemorative structure celebrates

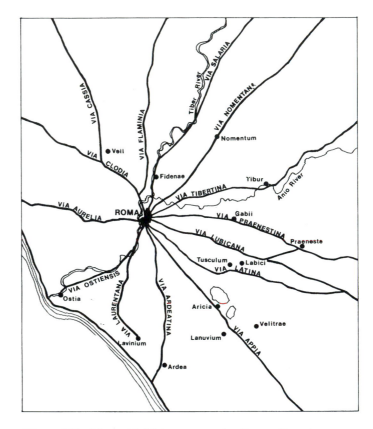

Figure 101. Map with highways entering Rome. Drawing: Richard H. Abramson.

Figure 102. Coin minted in Spain depicting Augustus in a chariot drawn by elephants atop a commemorative arch on a bridge or aqueduct, associated by some scholars with the Pons Milvius; *BMCRE* 1.75 Nr.432. Drawing: author.

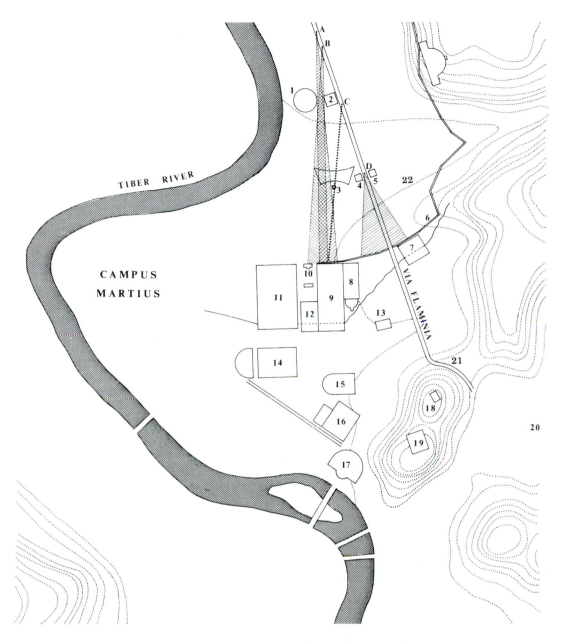

Figure 103. Map of the Campus Martius. Drawing: Rodica Reif. A: View between Mausoleum and Ustrinum to north façade of Saepta Julia; B: View between Mausoleum and Ustrinum broadening to include north elevation of Agrippan Pantheon; C: View with obelisk of Horologium as directional guide; D: Viewing angle from Ara Pacis toward Aqua Virgo; 1: Mausoleum of Augustus; 2: Ustrinum Domus Augustae; 3: Horologium Augusti; 4: Ara Pacis; 5: Ara Providentiae(?); 6: Aqua Virgo; 7: Porticus Vipsania; 8: Divorum; 9: Saepta Julia; 10: Agrippan Pantheon; 11: Stagnum and Euripus; 12: Baths of Agrippa; 13: Temple of Mars; 14: Theater of Pompey; 15: Theater of Balbus; 16: Porticus Octaviae; 17: Theater of Marcellus; 18: Temple of Juno Moneta; 19: Temple of Jupiter Optimus Maximus; 20: Forum Romanum; 21: Porta Fontinalis; 22: Campus Agrippae.

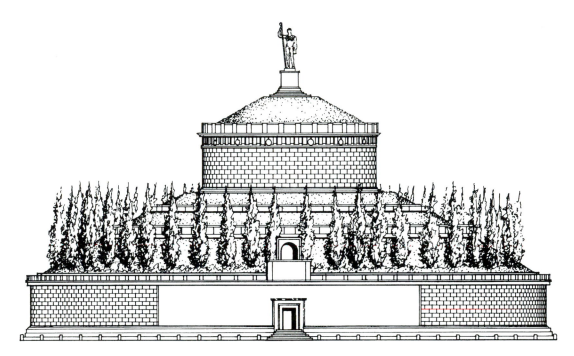

Figure 104. Reconstruction of the Mausoleum of Augustus. Drawing: Richard H. Abramson.

the repaving of the Via Flaminia by Augustus over forty years earlier. From atop the arch, a representation of the *princeps* himself benevolently looks down upon the two figures and all who approach his capital (fig. 102).[7]

Once through this symbolic doorway, the two observers face a remarkably straight stretch of highway (fig. 103). From the bridge, the Via Flaminia runs unimpeded in a direct line for three Roman miles. The highway is well maintained. In 20 B.C., Augustus himself assumed responsibility as *curator viarum* for all the *viae* leading into Rome. Eventually, he entrusted a permanent curatorial board with this charge. Along the broad expanse of the Via Flaminia, the travelers pass numerous tombs dating back to the early Republican period.[8] Funerary structures become more numerous as they draw closer and closer to the city. Constructed of rich materials and surrounded by funerary gardens in imitation of Hellenistic examples, most of these tombs show evidence of great expenditure and constant care. Sighing, the old man recalls his father's invectives against such hedonistic foreign influences and Augustus' own accepting attitude toward Greek ways.

After walking almost an hour on the left bank of the Tiber, the observers enter the plain known as the Campus Martius, bordered by the river on three sides. The old man and young girl pause as an impressive sight fills their view. A huge mound rises at a point where the highway comes close to the river (fig. 104). Surmounted by a verdant forest of evergreens, encircled by a base of sparkling white marble ashlar and a verdant public garden, the artificial mountain demands attention. The granddaughter points with excitement to the summit. Far above the morning shadows at ground level, sunlight strikes the gilded statue crowning the mound. The visual impact is powerful. The girl readily identifies the huge project as the Mausoleum of Augustus and the sculpture as a representation of the *princeps*. For many years, the tomb has dominated the northern Campus Martius, an unforgettable monument to the endurance of a single political leader. Now the structure celebrates the existence of a new god and the continuance of his line.

Directly east of the artificial mound, the pair see another relatively large project, the Ustrinum Domus Augustae, where blazing fires consumed the funeral pyres of family members to be interred in the Mausoleum Augusti. Partially planted with black poplars and surrounded by a fence of iron and white marble, this large enclosed paved area had been the staging area for grand ceremonies associated with Augustus' funeral. Situated at right angles to the Via Flaminia, the fenced *ustrinum* forms a viewing gate with the flanking Mausoleum Augusti (fig. 103, points A and B). Looking southward through this gap, the two observers see a carefully orchestrated view of the central Campus Martius. On a clear day, the two funerary constructions frame an urban stage set composed of two Agrippan projects: the original Pantheon and the short end of the Saepta voting enclosure, both dating to the 20s B.C. (fig. 105).[9]

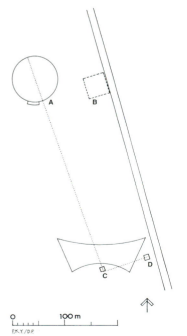

Figure 105. Plan of northern Campus Martius showing the relative locations of (A) the Mausoleum of Augustus, (B) Ustrinum Domus Augustae, (C) Horologium Augusti, and (D) Ara Pacis. Drawing: Fikret K. Yegül.

The view to the east is markedly different. To the left of the two travelers rises a tableland covered with villas and gardens. Though these luxury estates are owned by private individuals, many have become associated with the *princeps* and his family members. For example, the public park surrounding the Mausoleum Augusti merges with the private *horti* crossing the Via Flaminia and moving up the slopes to the east. Originally, the property of Pompey the Great, the *horti* came into the hands of Mark Antony. After the battle of Actium, they fell to Augustus, who retained the name of their former owner to cement his own affiliation with Pompey, regarded by many as a great Republican.[10]

In 52 B.C., the sight of opulent villas erected by competitive individuals naturally had led to discussions of political rivalry and foreign campaigns for booty. By A.D. 14, the same view sparks talk of prosperity, love of nature, and the *princeps*. The lush estates elicit comments about the fecundity and peace achieved under Augustan direction. In addition, they reveal the calculated, theatrical impression projected by the Augustan city. The grandfather quotes aloud a favorite passage from Strabo regarding the Campus Martius:

[T]he ground is covered with grass throughout the year, and the crowns of those hills that are above the river and extend as far as its bed, which present to the eye the appearance of a stage-painting – all this, I say, affords a spectacle that one can hardly draw away from. (5.3.8)

The little girl agrees as she excitedly looks from one amazing sight to another. Quickly bored by the all too familiar view of villas, she tugs the toga of her grandfather and asks about the wonders to their right. Once past the Ustrinum, the two pedestrians have a full view of the central Campus Martius. After traveling for miles through the countryside, they naturally find the active urban scene to the west far more interesting than the rather rural view to the east. The great highway emphasizes this directional preference. Ramrod straight and raised above the plain, the Via Flaminia shapes the experience of all travelers. Standing atop the highway, observers are predisposed to assume a superior stance looking down and westward. In effect, the highway acts as a viewing platform organizing the urban experience. As they move along the broad, straight line of the Via Flaminia, observers see select buildings in a prescribed sequence. Interpolating the experience, they read a clear narrative about the life and status of Augustus. Any detour from the highway requires a determined effort and is immediately perceived as ancillary.

The old man stops transfixed as he looks to the southwest. With a flourish of his woolen cape, he gestures toward a towering needle of red granite. His granddaughter listens as he identifies the foreign-looking monument. It is an obelisk brought to Rome by Augustus as a visible demonstration of his conquest of the fabled Egyptian empire.[11] What amazes the young girl, however, is the crisp shadow cast by the monolith in the morning light of autumn. From the higher position of the Via Flaminia, she can see an expansive travertine pavement directly north of the obelisk measuring approximately 160 × 75 meters. Inlaid lines of bronze describe a dovetail-shaped form associated with solar timepieces. The grandfather explains that the obelisk serves as the gnomon of a grand sundial, the Horologium Augusti (10 B.C.); on clear days, the monolith's shadow points to the bronze lines and words marking the hours of the day, months, signs of the zodiac, and seasonal winds. The solid stone needle rising approximately 30 meters in height acts as a sight line directing the observers' view once again toward the Augustan constructions in the central Campus Martius (fig. 103, point C).

To the southeast, the two travelers can now see more clearly the columnar northern façade belonging to the Pantheon. In the early 20s B.C., Agrippa attempted to glorify the Augustan family with this structure. When the *princeps* refused to be honored as a god by placement of his statue inside the building, Agrippa instead dedicated the temple to all the gods, though with special emphasis on Mars and Venus, the ancestral deities of the gens Julia. Statues of Augustus and Agrippa look northward from the pronaos; the great figure atop the Mausoleum seems to return their gaze.[12] The reciprocal sight line of the statues emphasizes the powerful visual interaction between the Augustan structures in the low-lying northern Campus Martius.

The façade of the Pantheon forms an east–west line with the northern façade of the Saepta. The latter building is huge; its short northern edge measures approximately 120 meters across. Years earlier, Julius Caesar planned this opulent enclosure to shelter tribal voting. Continued by Lepidus and completed by Agrippa, the building now serves other purposes as well. The grandfather entertains his granddaughter with a lively description of the gladiatorial combats Augustus held in the Saepta.[13] Even without the story, her attention is irresistibly drawn to the building. Arcades of a great aqueduct, the Aqua Virgo, march down from the eastern slopes and grow progressively taller; they leap over the Via Flaminia and terminate parallel to the Saepta's northern façade (fig. 103, point D; fig. 91). Scenographically, this arrangement draws the observers' eyes to the center of the Campus. In effect, the Aqua Virgo, Saepta, and Pantheon form an ensemble, confirming the identification of the vast northern Campus Martius as an Augustan enclave.

A small building opposite the Horologium Augusti clarifies the message of this district. After absorbing the dramatic impact of the sundial, the two observers turn their attention to a marble altar adjacent to the highway

Figure 106. Model of the Ara Pacis as seen from the northwest. Photo: Museo della Civiltá Romana, Rome, after Hofter, *Kaiser Augustus,* 422.

directly to the east. This is the famous Ara Pacis (fig. 106).[14] Dedicated on the birthday of Livia in 9 B.C., the enclosure commemorates the victorious return of her husband from Spain and Gaul. Twenty years later, the small altar embodies a more global message. It now celebrates the greatest gift bestowed by Augustus on the residents of Rome and the Empire: peace. The benefits of this gift are embodied by the lives of the two travelers. The grandfather's generation endured decades of war; the young girl's has known only harmony.

From a distance, the pair perceive the Ara Pacis as a comparatively small rectangular solid not dissimilar in size and form to the tombs lining the highway to the north. The exquisite, unroofed structure contrasts with the enormous scale of other Augustan projects in the northern Campus such as the Horologium and Mausoleum.[15] Nearing, they can see that the exterior walls of the surrounding enclosure are embossed with sculptural reliefs. The images call for closer scrutiny. First visible is the northern face (cf. fig. 107). The broad, lower register has exquisitely carved, stylized acanthus tendrils; the young girl points excitedly at the small creatures hidden within the leaves. On the upper register is a procession of recognizable figures. With solemnity, members of the imperial family, magistrates, and priests parade westward toward the great paved area of the Horologium. Close to life size, the human representations evoke an empathetic reaction from observers, yet their position slightly above the spectators' eye level establishes a hierarchical superiority.[16] The carved figures march westward away from the highway. This simple directional ploy encourages observers likewise to move west toward the altar's façade. Both real and carved pedestrians stroll around the altar enclosure toward the paving of the Horologium.[17]

Figure 107. Northern relief from the Ara Pacis Augustae showing senators in procession. Drawing: Fototeca Unione AAR 1042.

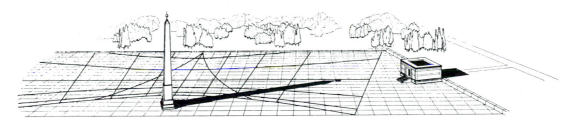

Figure 108. Reconstruction of the Horologium Augusti; bird's-eye view from the south. The shadow of the obelisk pointed toward the Ara Pacis on September 23, birthday of Augustus. Courtesy E. Buchner.

Turning the corner of the small structure, the grandfather and his young heir find themselves in the enormous travertine plaza of the Horologium Augusti. The expansive, unencumbered open space inspires movement; the inscribed texts and choreographed iconography spark contemplation. The child gleefully skips along the inlaid bronze lines humming a song; her grandfather muses over the complex scientific calibrations made by the mathematician Novius Facundus for the great sundial. Kinetic and temporal in focus, the Horologium presents different readings at different times of the day and year. On key dates, the shadow from the obelisk-gnomon visually connects the Augustan monuments of the northern Campus Martius, linking them all together programmatically and visually. In his mind, the grandfather relives the first time he saw the ensemble. Years ago, he joined a large crowd celebrating the birthday of Augustus on September 23. What excitement they all felt when the obelisk of the Horologium cast a long shadowy finger directly through the door of the Ara Pacis and onto the interior altar (fig. 108). The message was, and remains, clear: through superhuman efforts Augustus has brought peace to Rome.

In A.D. 14, the old man is subconsciously aware that every view of the Campus Martius reveals a complex iconographic program affirming the connection between Augustus, the city, and the condition of the empire. As his granddaughter spins with arms outstretched, he turns slowly and contemplates the surrounding vistas. At the southern edge of the paving stands the obelisk with its exotic and illegible hieroglyphs. On the base, the grandfather squints to read a Latin inscription proclaiming Augustus' subjugation of Cleopatra's Egypt (CIL 6.702). Whereas the lines of the Horologium paving run directly north/south, the base of this stately object parallels the Via Flaminia at several degrees off true north. Behind the obelisk, the grandfather has a clear view south, unimpeded by other Augustan buildings.[18] Southwest of the Horologium plaza, the urban text is dotted with pastoral passages. Here are grassy areas and gardens associated with Rome's first grand public bathing establishment, the Baths of Agrippa located south of the Pantheon. The grandfather shades his eyes as the morning light dances on water. An artificial pond, the Stagnum Agrippae, and an open canal, the Euripus, create an attractive vista. These human-made constructs also affirm the great effort expended by Agrippa to drain the low-lying central Campus Martius.

The autumnal mist prevents a clear view of the Tiber River to the west. Though still powerful and prone to fits of anger, the river is not so fearsome as in the grandfather's youth. Augustus cleared the bed of obstructions along the river bank and delimited a flood zone, thereby minimizing the damage caused by inundations such as that which occurred two years earlier

Figure 109. Reconstruction of the northern Campus Martius showing, from right to left, the Ara Pacis, obelisk of the Horologium Augusti, and in the distance, the Mausoleum of Augustus. Courtesy E. Buchner.

in A.D. 12. Squinting, the old man tries to see the docking facilities of the Statio Marmorum directly west of his position. In the 20s B.C., the docks accommodated enormous quantities of building materials for the great Augustan projects in the Campus Martius he and his granddaughter are now enjoying. Though construction has decreased in recent years, river traffic has not. Today, dock workers off load large quantities of wine and other goods shipped from the north.

Continuing his clockwise rotation, the patrician faces northward. The huge bulk of the Mausoleum Augusti dominates his view. Unconsciously, he faces not directly north, but slightly west. Such an orientation places him on an imaginary line parallel to the Via Flaminia, running from the obelisk of the Horologium through the center of the Mausoleum (figs. 105 and 109). Rejoining his granddaughter, the old man points toward the entry of the great tomb now visible to them for the first time.[19] Though over 300 meters away, the observers can identify two eye-catching, small obelisks only recently erected; without drawing nearer, the grandfather knows well these needles mark both the sepulcher entrance and the location for the inscribed bronze tablets being installed on this very day. The young girl solemnly listens as the old man begins to recount the *princeps'* well-known achievements. Her attention cannot span the long list; looking around, she pulls her grandfather away from his discourse back toward the more engaging Ara Pacis.

From the plaza of the Horologium Augusti, the pair see the Altar of Peace as an isolated object. The brilliant white marble of the Ara Pacis stands out against the verdant garden slopes to the east. On the altar's façade, the delicate, broad band of acanthus reliefs fills the lower register. Above, the human paraders depicted on the longer, northern exterior are replaced by representations of mythological figures. The young girl points with glee at the she-wolf and her human "cubs," Romulus and Remus, shown on the northwestern panel. Her grandfather sighs and tries once again to educate

Figure 110. Southwestern panel of the Ara Pacis depicting the sacrifice of Aeneas and the Temple of the Penates. Photo: Fototeca Unione AAR 6451.

his young companion who seems interested only in the animals, not the political and moral lessons represented by the myths. He patiently explains that this panel shows the familiar story of Romulus and Remus; the opposite relief depicts the Trojan Aeneas honoring the sacred Penates (fig. 110). Together, these scenes reenforce the close relationship between Augustus and Rome's illustrious forefathers. On the acanthus panels, swans sacred to Apollo recall the *princeps'* ties with the sun god who brought him victory at Actium. The overall structure is a paean to the fecundity, wealth, and harmony made possible by the Augustan peace.

The large travertine plaza before the Ara Pacis encourages the visitors to pause on their urban journey and assess where they have been and where they are going. Though still on the edge of the great metropolis, the pair have already become embroiled in an Augustan urban narrative. Virtually every image they have seen celebrates the life and achievements of the now-deified *princeps.* As the pair move back toward the Via Flaminia, the young girl excitedly demonstrates her knowledge of Augustus and his family. On

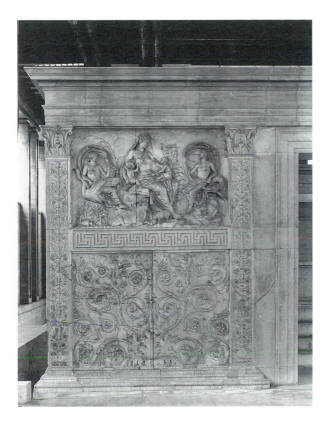

Figure 111. Southeastern panel of the Ara Pacis depicting a seated female, variously identified as Pax, Italia, Venus, Ilia, and Tellus. Photo: Fototeca Unione AAR 6450.

the southern side of the Ara Pacis, they pass a carved procession paralleling that seen on the opposite northern exterior. Moving against the direction of the parade, she can clearly see the faces of the figures. Close to the front of the monument, she identifies Augustus himself staring beyond her eastward to the obelisk. The grandfather gently corrects the child when she confuses some members of the Imperial family depicted following the image of the *princeps*. Some are too idealized even for him to recognize easily.

Stepping back up to the Via Flaminia, the young granddaughter begins to move again southward. The patrician grabs her hand and compels her northward to examine the reliefs on the eastern façade of the Ara Pacis. Here the acanthus panels flanking the eastern entrance to the enclosure are again surmounted by mythological images. The panel on the north depicts the personification of the Roman state in full armor. The child, however, is attracted to the animated southern panel. A large seated woman dominates the center flanked by wind-blown anthropomorphic depictions of fresh water and the sea. On her lap are two playful infants; at her feet a tranquil cow and lamb (fig. 111). Once again, the grandfather begins to explain the

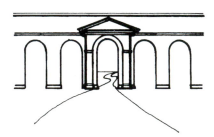

Figure 112. Diagram, aqueduct/
street intersection.

Figure 113. Marble cippus that
marked the edge of Region VII in
Augustan Rome. Photo: author.

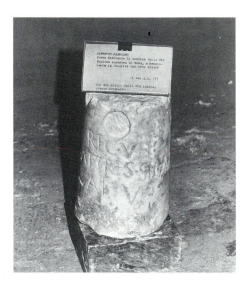

iconography. Jostled by traffic on the great highway, his voice drowned by
street noise, he terminates his lecture.[20]

The pair continue their journey. South of the Ara Pacis, the view opens
eastward across the public parkland of the Campus Agrippae.[21] Like the
Aqua Virgo, the landscaping seems to jump over the Via Flaminia and climb
the plateaus to the east. Continuing southward, the pair come even with the
façades of the Saepta and Pantheon and pass under the tall arches of the
Aqua Virgo. On the southern face of the aqueduct, a work crew busily scam-
pers up a wooden scaffolding. The sight is familiar. Following the death of
Agrippa, Augustus assigned care of aqueducts to a permanent curatorial
board. Throughout the city, water gushes from hundreds of new fountains
thoughtfully decorated by Agrippa with sculpture and rich marbles. Musing
over the efficiency of the system, the grandfather recalls the days of his
youth when the aqueducts stood in disrepair and fountains often ran dry.

Looking at his granddaughter with affection, the patrician tells a story
about the "Virgin" aqueduct. The source was discovered years earlier, when a
young girl about her age led some thirsty soldiers to a gurgling spring near the
Via Praenestina north of Rome (Frontin.1.10). Conceptually, as well as physically, the Aqua Virgo divides the relatively open northern section of the Campus Martius and the heavily developed zone to the south. Passing under the
aqueduct as it jumps over the highway, the travelers face an increasingly com-

plex urban text. They immediately sense the change. The area north of this line deserves the designation "campus" (field). North of the Aqua Virgo, the open Campus Agrippae lay on their left; south of the aqueduct stands the large Porticus Vipsania, begun by Agrippa's sister and completed by Augustus.

Sharing with Agrippa an interest in cartography, the grandfather tells his young companion about the huge world map in the Porticus Vipsania. In his younger days, he spent many hours before this great display, mentally traveling across the vast territories under the beneficent leadership of Augustus. The child at his side is more interested in projects she can actually see from their position on the Via Flaminia. Curious, she inquires about the exotic decorations on the complex to their right. Reluctantly, her grandfather explains the structure is a shrine devoted to the worship of the Egyptian gods Isis and Serapis.[22] He hastens to add that as foreign gods, they are allowed only outside the *pomerium*. The girl is confused; in her mind, the great aqueduct is like a wall defining areas outside and inside the city (fig. 112). Her elder attempts to clarify. The sacred *pomerium* describing the city edges does not relate to Rome's old Republican walls located farther south on the Via Flaminia, nor does the *pomerium* relate to the edge of urban construction. Augustus was ever conscious of this ritual boundary; he located the Ara Pacis one mile from the pomerial edge and reaffirmed the exclusion of Egyptian rites from within its confines. Carefully, the grandfather explains that Rome is now divided into fourteen regions established by Augustus to deal with administration and urban care. The young girl vainly looks in the cityscape for some overt visual indication of the XIV Regions (fig. 59). Anxious to prove his point, her grandfather searches the roadside, and triumphantly points to a small cippus identifying the Via Flaminia as the dividing line between Regions IX and VII (cf. fig. 113).

Looking westward, the child asks if the long façade running north/south behind the Egyptian temple is part of the city wall. The patrician shakes his head at her lack of familiarity with Rome, but patiently explains. It is the flank of the Saepta, measuring over 400 meters (ca. 1,400 Roman feet) in length. Adjacent stands another large structure, the Diribitorium, where votes are counted. Sharing in the expansive pride of the age, the grandfather boasts that the Diribitorium is the largest building under a single roof ever constructed. Farther west through the mist, the two travelers spy the exterior of the scenae belonging to the restored Theater of Pompey and to the smaller theater of Balbus. The latter stands out both for its opulence and for its patron. The boastful Balbus held elaborate festivities for the dedication, persevering despite threatening flood waters. Recalling the smug hubris of this patron, the grandfather muses that such architectural competition was not good for Rome. Once Augustus in his paternal wisdom assumed responsibility for the care and appearance of Rome, the city's appearance became more uniform and ordered. In fact, he notes, the entire layout of the Campus Martius reflects the wise direction of a single patron. All the new buildings follow the orientation to the cardinal points established by early Republican temples and continued by a few later structures such as Pompey's great complex. The grandfather compares such orthogonal planning to the layouts of eastern Hellenistic cities he visited in his youth. As he drones on, the young girl shakes her head. She is too short to appreciate the grid arrangement fully; her eyes and mind begin to wander.

In an attempt to recapture his granddaughter's attention, the old man recalls his own experiences in the Campus when a boy about her age. With nostalgic gusto, he tells of riding horseback across the open marshy plain, then largely unobstructed by buildings.[23] The young girl finds it hard to believe. Even he must concentrate to picture the area and himself as they once were. The intense development of the Campus Martius occurred during the 20s and teens B.C. Little has been added to the central plain since that time; its unchanging appearance over thirty years affirms the stability and endurance of the Augustan state. The repeated representation of the *princeps* himself – on the Pons Mulvius, atop the Mausoleum Augusti, in the porch of the Pantheon, and elsewhere – confirms his directed role in the creation of this urban image. Furthermore, the whole Imperial family is present to provide support. Not only do relatives take up eternal residence in the Mausoleum, they remain continually evident in the names of individual buildings, inscriptions, and various artistic representations.

As the observers continue to move southeast along the Via Flaminia, the urban image of Rome becomes more muddled. Near the base of the Mons Capitolinus, construction is denser and more varied, with structures dating from many periods. Among the jumble of residential and commercial buildings, the grandfather identifies the Villa Publica and an altar to Mars, the namesake deity of the Campus. Few other buildings stand out in the cityscape. Peering along the various side streets, the travelers catch glimpses of festooned altars to the Lares Compitales honoring the spirits of the crossroads. Twenty years ago, the *princeps* associated worship of his own *genius* and the Lares Augusti with these shrines; ever since, they have never wanted for embellishment. Local residents and especially the ward supervisors make sure the small altars always have a fresh supply of flowers, cakes, and garlands honoring Augustus.

The observers now find broad views of the city increasingly blocked by construction. In compensation, their attention is drawn forward and upward to the Capitoline. The morning sun glistens on the rich surfaces of the temple to Jupiter Optimus Maximus perched high above the plain on the southwestern promontory of the Capitoline.[24] Extensively restored by Augustus in the 20s B.C., the structure relates architecturally to the projects of the Campus Martius. Remembering its reconstruction, the grandfather uses the temple to provide a moral lesson for his young companion. Though Augustus expended great expense on the restoration of Jupiter's building, he left the original inscription intact, thereby demonstrating his great modesty and his overall concern for urban care.

For the grandfather, Augustus' paternal attitude toward the city is evident with every step. Years before, when he accompanied his own father on the same walk, danger threatened at every turn. The potholes of the unmaintained streets threatened to swallow him up as a young boy; every hill brought the threat of a runaway cart. Ruffians made passage at night impossible without a large retinue; even in daylight hours, one did not feel safe. Now he does not worry excessively about his young companion. The streets of Rome are crowded, yet easily traversed. During the daylight hours, few vehicles block traffic. The primary exceptions are the dozens of carts carrying building materials for public works and those associated with the numerous religious events. Pickpockets and other small-time thieves still roam the city, but the policing of the streets by the *cohortes urbanae* during the day and by the *vigiles* at night has at least curbed urban crime.

Grabbing his granddaughter's hand, the patrician leads her up the hill as the Via Flaminia rises and curves along the eastern slope of the Capitoline. At a high point just below the Arx, they face the Porta Fontinalis, a remnant of the old Republican city wall. Like the arch on the Pons Mulvius, the Porta serves as a threshold. Once through the opening, the broad Flaminian highway transmutes into a narrow urban street, the Clivus Argentarius, approximately half as wide (fig. 114). Commercial structures of one to two stories line its flanks, creating an urban canyon. From within the street, the travelers have only scant glimpses of the surrounding city. The patrician lifts his granddaughter up, hoping to continue her urban education with a view of the great Forum Augustum farther to the southeast, yet the jostling crowds and obstructing buildings thwart his efforts. Even the closer Forum Julium is largely invisible to the pedestrians. The grandfather knows well that the shops to their left are an integral part of Caesar's Forum, operating as a retaining wall for the grand enclosure below. A river of people moves in and out of one of the openings on the eastern side of the Clivus. Slightly wider than those to shops, this entrance way opens directly onto a stairway. Peering down the dark, roofed passage, the travelers catch a brief glimpse of the marble-clad Forum Julium. The granddaughter starts down the steep stairs but is pulled back by her elder. Together they descend the Clivus Argentarius toward the Forum Romanum.

Figure 114. View from the Forum Romanum looking northwest up the Clivus Argentarius. Photo: Fototeca Unione AAR 5900.

The urban crowd now increases. Rome has long been a magnet for peoples from all over the Mediterranean. Though much government business now centers in the Forum Julium and courts meet in the adjacent Forum Augustum, the Forum Romanum maintains its status as the city center. People of various nationalities and social classes stroll through the paved open area. Among the mob, the pair hear many different tongues. The grandfather muses that the diversity of people in Rome is much the same as in his youth, though their aims have changed. Many are tourists. They flock to the gardens, baths, and theaters of the Campus Martius or admire the monuments of Rome's noble history displayed in the three great fora of the city center. While political lobbying is still an important pursuit, commercial activities seem to have gained more predominance during the recent decades of peace. In the area of the Forum, the grandfather is constantly harangued by scruffy merchants peddling goods of every type, from every region of the empire. His granddaughter squeals with delight at the appearance of a monkey atop the back of an exotically dressed trader. The grandfather hurries her along. He does not worry for their safety moving through busy Rome, yet he does fear the city's numerous thieves who can pull a purse from one's toga without ruffling a single fold.

As the pair descends, the space before them broadens. Before them rises the flank of the Curia Julia. During the Republic, the Senatehouse was a focal point of political activity, occupying a predominant site in the central Forum. Since being moved by Julius Caesar in the 40s B.C., the structure has little visual impact on travelers entering the Forum Romanum along the Clivus Argentarius (fig. 84).[25] Their line of vision parallels the Curia's façade and terminates at the Temple of Janus. Though small in size, this structure has great meaning; under Augustus, its doors have been closed three times: an overt action signaling the existence of peace throughout the vast Roman empire. The grandfather points to the arched opening directly north of the temple. This, he tells his young granddaughter, is the portico the *princeps* added to the Basilica Aemilia to honor his own beloved grandchildren, now both dead.

Moving westward, neither observer lingers over the mournful Carcer, the Republican prison created from the early quarries (*lautumiae*) on the site. Instead, they look ahead to the southeast. Below them lies the Rostra. Atop this speakers' platform stand several eye-catching statues. The young girl is particularly taken by the golden equestrian statue of the *princeps* sparkling in the midmorning sun. Both visually and conceptually, this representation connects with a circular, relatively small monument at the northwestern corner of the Rostra. The grandfather identifies the gilt bronze marker as the Milliarium Aureum. He cannot read the inscriptions from this distance, but like most Romans, he knows them well. Erected by Augustus as *curator viarum*, the marker records the distance from Rome to all the principal cities of the empire. Beyond the Rostra looms the Basilica Julia, its clean marble blocks affirming restoration work after a recent fire. Viewed from a higher level, the repetitious openings of the Basilica Julia form a uniform, impressive backdrop along the southwestern edge of the Forum Romanum.

The Clivus now gently curves and runs atop a viaduct behind the Rostra. The two travelers feel as if they are caught in a whirlpool. Converging with the traffic from the Campus Martius are human streams flowing down the Scalae Gemoniae from the Capitoline, up from the Via Sacra from the Forum, and eastward from the docks on the Tiber. In this eddy of human forms, it is difficult to appreciate the cityscape. Before the observers rises the majestic Temple of Saturn; confined to a low level of vision, the young girl does not know it exists. Anxious to continue his heir's urban education, the grandfather leads her up the first few steps of the Temple of Concordia. From this vantage point, he points toward the Temple of Saturn, identifying it as one of the oldest in Rome. He tries to interest his granddaughter in the building's history, carefully explaining that its present form in glistening stone was the gift of L. Munatius Plancus, supporter of Augustus; she is more interested in the pediment where sculptures of tritons and horses are seen at full gallop.[26]

Turning to face the Temple of Concordia, the two have to shade their eyes as they look upward. The morning glare from the marble surfaces is harsh, and the acute angle from the porch blocks any view of the Tabularium rising behind and above. The grandfather once again launches into a history lesson, explaining that the temple, restored by Tiberius in 7 B.C., celebrates the harmony between Romans. Pushed against the base of the Capitoline, the structure extends laterally on either side of the porch (fig. 66). The granddaughter pesters the old man with questions about the artworks visible through the large windows, but his attention is drawn away by the noise and bustle of activity behind them.

Below the two travelers spreads the venerated Forum Romanum. From their elevated location on the Clivus Argentarius, they look over the top of the speakers' platform to the central Forum running northwest to southeast. Isolated sculptures and a few spots of greenery haphazardly dot the central pavement. Due to the crowds and irregular orientation of the individual monuments, few are seen clearly. For example, the bodies and shadows of people mingling in the central Forum prevent the observers from reading the inscription of L. Naevius Surdinus imbedded in the pavement. Concealment has its benefits. With relief, the grandfather notes that from their present position, his impressionable granddaughter cannot see the explicit statue of the satyr Marsyas being flayed.

The travertine paving itself dates to the extensive restorations undertaken after the fire of 14 B.C. The great orthostats cover the Caesarean level of the Forum Romanum. The grandfather recalls his youth when the Forum had been the center of extravagant entertainments as well as politics. With animation, he tells the young girl about wondrous performances put on by the Dictator when gladiators suddenly appeared as if by magic, lifted by elevators hidden underground (fig. 36). Now blocked by the Augustan pavement, the subterranean tunnels no longer function; increasingly, gladiatorial combats occur elsewhere in Rome. Nostalgically, the old patrician describes a particular event ever fresh in his memory. Musing over his lost youth, he tells his granddaughter about an awning Caesar erected to shade spectators at a performance of gladiators. In contrast to other inexpensive, temporary sun screens, Caesar's was of silk. With excitement as a young boy, he had run under the wondrous fluttering covering, following its course from the Regia, across the expanse of the Forum and up to the Capitoline.

Today, his eyes follow a reverse path. Looking down from the Clivus, the pair find their gaze channeled eastward by the great colonnaded exteriors of the two basilicas. Not parallel, these lengthy façades gradually come closer toward the east, narrowing the vista. The Temple of Divus Julius forms a visual terminus approximately 140 meters from the travelers (fig. 57). Though not as large as the adjacent temple to Castor and Pollux, nor as elaborately embellished with artwork as the Temple of Concordia, this shrine impresses by its location and form. The observers face the temple's tall base, its access stairs placed out of view on the sides. Noticing his granddaughter squinting at the shaded podium facade, the elder patrician describes the complex components. Attached to the front are the ships' beaks captured by Octavian at the battle of Actium, where he avenged the murder of his divine father. These rostra identify a secondary function; using the podium as a speakers' platform, a Senator gives a speech (fig. 115). The grandfather sighs in disappointment; the listening crowd blocks a full view of the podium. He had hoped to use the view of the circular altar marking the location of Caesar's funeral pyre as the keypoint in an excursus on the events following the death of Augustus' divine father.

Above the podium, the temple proper rises still higher on its own stylobate. The whiteness of the Corinthian marble columns is offset by the greenery in flanking planters. Arches spanning the passageways on both sides of the temple restrict views to the east (fig. 57). Completely invisible is the temple to the goddess of the hearth, Vesta; the only evidence of this venerated structure is the thin spiral of smoke rising behind the great triple arch commemorating Augustus' Parthian victory. North of the Temple of Divus Julius, the portico honoring Gaius and Lucius likewise limits views to the east. Inspired by the projects honoring three generations, the grandfather launches into a detailed lecture on Julian genealogy. Everywhere he looks

Figure 115. Coin of Hadrian with speaker on platform of the Temple of Divus Julius. After Chr. Huelsen, *Das Forum Romanum*, 1905, fig. 70.

there is support for his discourse. In A.D. 14, all the major works in the Forum owe their current magnificence to the family of Augustus. The grandfather finds it difficult to remember how the area appeared in his youth. The collection of independent Republican monuments have now been transformed into a unified ensemble, capable of rivaling the adjacent new Imperial fora in both formal and symbolic cohesion.

He remembers fondly the great festivities marking the dedication of the Forum Augustum. Visiting the enclosure for the first time, he had been awed by the variety and color of marble used in construction, the bronze plaques on the temple podium, the elaborate white marble sculpture, and other riches; sixteen years later, such materials seem commonplace in Rome. A constant flow of pedestrians moves eastward from the Republican Forum, to those named after Augustus and Caesar. Despite the physical and functional relationship with the Forum Romanum, the new enclosures do not connect visually with the old node, or with each other. Never having visited either the Forum Julium or Forum Augustum, the young girl standing in the Forum Romanum has no idea of their existence. She watches the activities in the space before her, oblivious to other centers of power and beauty in the city.

The patrician knows from past experience how easily visitors to the venerated Republican Forum succumb to its spell. Groups cluster, discussing the historical and artistic merits of various buildings and artworks; others watch the ever intriguing, ever self-conscious interaction between people from all over the Roman empire. Everyone feels on display. Despite the cold, the grandfather throws back his dull, but warm, gray cloak as they move through the Forum to reveal his white toga. To himself, he observes that the choreographed buildings and human activities in the Forum Romanum resemble a stage set. A recipient of the benefits proliferating under the *princeps,* the grandfather does not probe the significance of his own revelation. Following the years of civil war, he along with other Romans happily accepts the appearance, rather than the substance, of a restored Republic.

Shaking himself from his reverie, the patrician urges his young charge onward. They face a choice. Before the Temple of Saturn, the Clivus bifurcates. The travelers can descend southwest along the Vicus Iugarius or ascend along the Clivus Capitolinus (fig. 21). A third option opens to their right; an enclosed stairway leads from the base of the Mons Capitolinus upward through the Tabularium (fig. 26). The young girl takes one look at the dark, tunnellike stairway and shudders with fright. Despite the cold, they stay outdoors. Climbing up the steep Clivus Capitolinus, the two figures pass the Temple of Saturn on their left and a Republican portico to their right. As they near the top of the hill, they face the Temple of Jupiter Tonans. Bells hanging from the structure sway in the brisk wind and begin to ring. Remembering the stories associated with the building, the young girl asks anxiously if Jupiter Optimus Maximus is threatened. Her elder smiles at her naive belief. He reassures her that Jupiter Tonans is merely warning the great god of their approach. Panting after the difficult climb, he leads his young charge to a vacant bench in the porticos flanking the temple (fig. 54). From this vantage point, they watch the reaction of different visitors to the shrine. Some pause to admire its walls of solid marble and rich artworks; others barely give it a glance before entering the Area Capitolina.

Joining the throng, the grandfather and little girl enter the Area Capitolina. The terrace reflects a clarity of organization and content familiar from other urban areas reworked under Augustus. Years earlier, the *princeps* moved many statues of famous Romans cluttering up the space to the Campus Martius where the two travelers saw them earlier in the day. New statues honor members of the Julian clan and other important individuals directly linked to Augustus. Humbly, the two take their prayers and offerings to the greatest god and the greatest building in the Roman world. Dominating the Area Capitolina is the venerated Temple of Jupiter Optimus Maximus. The original structure was begun even before the Republic was established; in a.d. 14, the temple bears an inscription to Julius Caesar. Augustus extensively restored the huge work, but left the name of his deified father on view, gaining fame through both association and omission. Staring with open mouth at the huge temple and surrounding displays, the impressionable young girl absorbs a revisionist history of Rome.

With the short attention span of the young, the granddaughter soon tires of examining the temple. Running between the statues of the Area Capitolina, she comes dangerously close to the precipitous edge. Her grandfather grabs her sternly by the hand. Together, they look out over Augustan Rome (fig. 116). Immediately, their attention is drawn to the Palatine to the southeast. The sunlight bounces off marble structures clustered atop the hill. This is the complex honoring Augustus' patron deity, the sun god Apollo. Even a first-time visitor to the city such as the girl knows that the *princeps* resides near this sumptuous enclave. Vainly, she tries to see the famous tower associated with his *domus* or the laurels flanking his doorway. The smallish house of Augustus is not visible, yet its existence creates reverberations in the urban fabric. The buildings in the area are well-maintained and surrounded with landscaping. The connecting streets are clogged with supplicants anxious to see the *princeps,* bureaucrats trudging to work in surrounding houses, and worshipers going to pay homage at the nearby temples to different gods associated with Augustus.

The autumn sun has long since burned off the morning mist, giving the two tired figures atop the Capitoline a clear southward view of the city-

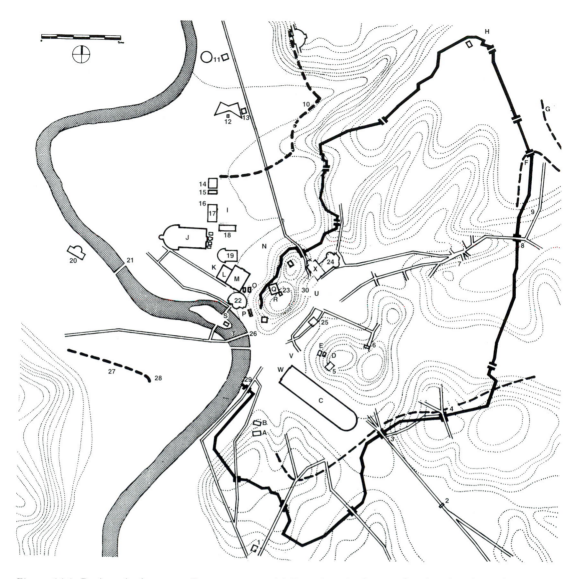

Figure 116. Projects in Augustan Rome, ca. A.D. 14. Drawing: Rodica Reif and Richard H. Abramson.
New Projects: 1: Sepulcrum C. Cestii; 2: Arcus Drusi; 3: Altar of Fortuna Redux; 4: Arcus Dolabella et Silani, Porta Caelimontana; 5: Temple of Apollo Palatinus; 6: Arcus Octavii, Palatine; 7: Porticus Liviae; 8: Arcus Augusti, Porta Esquilina (later Arcus Gallienus); 9: Macellum Liviae; 10: Aqua Virgo; 11: Mausoleum and Ustrinum of Augustus; 12: Horologium Augusti; 13: Ara Pacis; 14: Pantheon; 15: Basilica Neptuni; 16: Stagnum and Horti Agrippae; 17: Baths of Agrippa; 18: Diribitorium; 19: Crypta and Theater of Balbus; 20: Ancient villa Farnesina; 21: Pons Agrippae; 22: Theater of Marcellus; 23: Temple of Jupiter Tonans; 24: Forum Augustum and Temple of Mars Ultor; 25: Horrea Agrippiana; 26: Fornix Augusti on the Pons Aemilius; 27: Aqua Alsietina (Aqua Augusta); 28: Naumachia Augusti and Nemus Caesarum; 29: Arcus Letuli et Crispini, Porta Trigemina; 30: Forum Romanum (see fig. 16). **Restorations**: A: Temple of Diana; B: Temple of Minerva; C: Circus Maximus; D: House of Augustus; E: Temple of Magna Mater; F: Anio Vetus; G: Aqua Julia, Marcia, Tepula; H: Temple of Venus Erucina at Porta Collina; I: Saepta Julia; J: Theater of Pompey; K: Porticus Octavia; L: Porticus Philippi, Temple of Hercules Musarum; M: Porticus Octaviae, temples of Jupiter Stator and Juno Regina; N: Villa Publica;

scape. The built area seems to extend without end to the very limits of sight. Anxious to demonstrate her recently acquired expertise in reading the city, the young girl points out the Augustan projects. Within the dull, disorderly Republican urban fabric, she can easily distinguish large works with ordered plans and glistening surfaces of white marble. To affirm his own superior knowledge of the city, the grandfather explains that expansive public open spaces such as the Porticus Liviae outside their range of vision likewise signal the intervention of the *princeps*. In general, unbuilt space is a rare commodity in Rome, carved from the dense built environment only at great cost. Almost every square inch of the city is occupied. Even the city's streets and river seem full. People from across the empire clog the urban thoroughfares; barges ply the Tiber, bringing goods to the consuming urban populace. Despite the crowded conditions, the capital is filled with greenery. On the hillsides and outskirts, verdant gardens thrive, fed by the expanded aqueduct system recently upgraded by Augustus. Throughout the city, repair crews conspicuously labor to keep the built environment in good condition. The entire scene projects a positive image. The two travelers simultaneously conceptualize Rome as a mature city with a rich past; a thriving, sophisticated metropolis; and the prosperous capital of a peaceful empire. After experiencing the city first-hand, they know well the reason for Rome's orderliness, peacefulness, and prosperity. At their every step, some tangible reminder affirmed the cityscape's association with one man.

On this brisk day in A.D. 14, only a single major new public project is under construction. The grandfather points to the building site across the valley at the foot of the Palatine, behind the Basilica Julia. At this important access to the Forum Roman rises a temple to the newest god in the Roman pantheon.[27] In life, identified as *princeps, primus inter pares,* and *divus filius,* in death, Gaius Octavius has been elevated to godhead. Worship of Divus Augustus will center at the new temple, yet, in actuality, the entire city is a shrine to the deceased leader. Above the rooftops, smoke begins to gather from cooking fires for the midday meal; though hungry after their

Caption to Figure 116 (*cont.*)
O: Temple of Apollo Sosianus; P: Temple of Spes in Foro Holitorio; Q: Temple of Jupiter Optimus Maximus; R: Temple of Jupiter Feretrius; S: Pons Fabricius; T: Pons Aemilius; U: Forum Romanum: Basilica Aemilia, Basilica Julia, Temples of Vesta, Divus Julius, Concordia, Castor and Pollux; V: Lupercal; W: Temple of Ceres, Liber, and Libera; Campus Martius. **Exact Location Unknown:** Temple of Neptune; Amphitheatrum of Statilius Taurus, Campus Martius; Porticus ad Nationes; Stadium Augusti, temporary structure, Campus Martius; Porticus Vipsania, Campus Agrippae; Altar of Ceres Mater et Ops Augusta, Vicus Iugarius; Temple of Bona Dea Subsaxana, Aventine; Temple of Flora Iuxta Circum Maximum; Temple of Juno Regina, Aventine; Temple of Jupiter Libertas, Aventine; Temple of Lares, Forum Romanum; Temple of Penates, near Forum Romanum; Temple of Quirinus; Temple of Juventas; **Off Map:** Arch (Porta Tiburtina); Arcus Augusti, Pons Mulvius on Via Flaminia; Tomb of Eurysaces.

long walk, the two figures find it difficult to leave the vista before them. The grandfather silently prays to the Divine Augustus that the urban image and all that it stands for will endure during the life of his young charge. Looking admiringly one last time over the city, he acknowledges the hand of divine intervention. As they turn to leave, the patrician continues to lecture on Augustus; "the soothsayers prophesied that he would rise to great heights and hold the whole city under his sway" (DioCass.53.20).

NOTES

PREFACE

1. *Los Angeles Times,* May 16, 1991.

CHAPTER 1. INTRODUCTION: DEFINING AN URBAN IMAGE

Journal abbreviations comply with the listings in the *American Journal of Archaeology.* Abbreviations of classical works and authors follow those suggested by *The Oxford Classical Dictionary.* All translations of ancient sources are taken from the Loeb Classical Library editions, with one exception. Translations for Vitruvius are from Morgan, *Vitruvius, the Ten Books on Architecture* (New York: Dover 1960).

1. Kevin Lynch, *Image of the City* (Cambridge, MA: MIT Press 1960). Lynch's research built upon the earlier and broader consideration of the image in modern society by Kenneth Boulding who suggested the name "eikonics" to define the study of images; *The Image* (Ann Arbor: University of Michigan 1956). For a historiographic overview of image as a concept in relation to cities, see Amos Rapoport, *Human Aspects of Urban Form, Towards a Man-Environment Approach to Urban Form and Design* (Oxford: Pergamon Press 1977), 40–7.

2. Among the significant variables omitted from Lynch's study was consideration of the residents' social standing. In contrast, D. Francescato and W. Mebane evaluated class status in their interviews about the image of modern Rome; "How Citizens View Two Great Cities: Milan and Rome," in *Image and Environment, Cognitive Mapping and Spatial Behavior,* edited by R. Downs and David Stea (Chicago: Aldine Publishing 1973), 131–47.

3. D. Gebhard, "The Spanish Vocabulary in Contemporary Santa Barbara. The City as Designed Object," *Architecture California* (Sept./Oct. 1985), 20–5. Regarding the market potential of historical urban environments, see G. J. Ashworth and H. Voogd, *Selling the City: Marketing Approaches in Public Sector Urban Planning* (London: Belhaven Press 1990), 67–71, 117–19.

4. Today, increases in tourism and competition to attract businesses and residents have stimulated interest in the marketing of cities and their images. For an overview of recent research on places and place images, see Ashworth and Voogd, *Selling the City,* 77–98.

5. See Steven Marcus, "Reading the Illegible: Some Modern Representations of Urban

Experience," in *Visions of the Modern City. Essays in History, Art, and Literature,* edited by William Sharpe and Leonard Wallock (Baltimore: Johns Hopkins Press 1987), 232-56.

6. K. Hartigan, "The Poets and the Cities, Selections from the Anthology about Greek Cities," *Beitrage zu Klassischen Philologie* 87 (1979), 76–94. Sociological descriptions of Rome became more common in the late first century A.D., as represented by the writings of Martial and Juvenal. ·

7. A complete analysis of pictorial urban representations in the Roman world would greatly expand knowledge about how ancient cities were perceived and conceptualized. Individual studies, usually by medium rather than period, have been undertaken by M. I. Rostovtzeff, "Der hellenistisch-römische Architekturlandschaft," *RM* 26 (1911): 1–186; S. E. Ostrow, "Problems in the Topography of Roman Puteoli," Ph.D. dissertation, University of Michigan (1977); and G. Mansuelli, "La rappresentazione della cittá nell'arte tardo-romana e bizantina," *Corsi di cultura sull'arte ravennate e bizantina* 19 (1972): 239–44; among others.

8. For fuller discussions of Roman pictorial representations showing buildings (not cities), see Eleanor Leach, *The Rhetoric of Space, Literary and Artistic Representations of Landscape in Republican and Augustan Rome* (Princeton: Princeton University Press 1988), 261–306; and B. Bergmann, "Painted Perspectives of a Villa Visit: Landscape as Status and Metaphor," in *Roman Art in the Private Sphere,* edited by E. K. Gazda (Ann Arbor: University of Michigan Press 1991), 49–70.

9. Zanker, *Images,* 329, fig. 260.

10. O. A. W. Dilke, *Greek and Roman Maps* (Ithaca, NY: Cornell University Press 1985), 103–7; R. Ling, "A Stranger in Town: Finding the way in an Ancient City," *Greece and Rome* 37.2 (October 1990): 204–14.

11. *Adelphoe* (Harmondsworth: Penguin 1965), 573–85.

12. P. J. Holliday, "Introduction," and D. Favro, "Reading the Augustan City," both in *Narrative and Event,* 3–13, 230–4.

13. C. Geertz, "Art as a Cultural System," in *Local Knowledge* (New York: Basic Books 1983), 94–120.

14. In some cases, the experience of artwork and environments coalesced as was the case with the reading of Trajan's Column; Richard Brilliant, *Visual Narratives. Storytelling in Etruscan and Roman Art* (Ithaca, NY: Cornell University Press 1984), 90–117. For an exemplary study dealing with the experience of the Roman house and its artistic program, see B. Bergmann, "The Roman House as Memory Theater: The House of the Tragic Poet in Pompeii," *ArtB.* 76.2 (June 1994): 225–56.

15. F. A. Yates, *The Art of Memory* (Chicago: University of Chicago 1966), 1–26; Bergmann, "Roman House," 225–6; Favro, "Reading the Augustan City," 3–13, 230–50.

16. Brilliant, *Visual Narratives,* 15–20.

17. *PW* 7.1 col.1155–8; H. Kunckel, "Der Römische Genius," *RM-EH* sup.20 (1974), 10–28; Jane Nitzsche, *The Genius Figure in Antiquity and the Middle Ages* (New York: Columbia University Press 1975), 13–15. The female parallel for the male genius was a juno.

18. On the relationship of the Roman *genius urbis* and Greek *tyche,* see Chapter 3; Nitzsche, *The Genius Figure,* 13–15.

19. On the concept of cultural filters, see Rapoport, *Human Aspects,* 38–40.

20. Kent C. Bloomer and Charles W. Moore, *Body, Memory, and Architecture* (New Haven: Yale University Press 1977), 36–55; T. Higuchi, *The Visual and Spatial Structure of Landscapes,* translation by C. S. Terry (Cambridge, MA: MIT Press 1983, original edition 1975).

21. Andrew Wallace-Hadrill, "The Social Structure of the Roman House," *PBSR* 56

n.s. 43 (1988): 43–97; Bergmann, "Roman House," 225–56.

22. Steven Marcus, "Reading the Illegible, Some Modern Representations of Urban Experience," in *The Victorian City*, edited by H. J. Dyos and Michael Wolff (London: Routledge 1973), 257–74. For an experiential analysis of modern Japanese cities, see Y. Ashihara, *The Aesthetic Townscape*, translation by L. E. Riggs (Cambridge, MA: MIT Press 1983, original edition 1979). Marge Piercy provides an insightful experience of a projected feminist urban utopia in *Woman on the Edge of Time* (New York: Fawcett Crest Book 1977). Among the limited number of sources that examine the experiential image of historical cities, see Anselm L. Strauss, *Images of the American City* (New York: Free Press of Glencoe 1961).

23. Among recent exceptions are Fikret K. Yegül, "The Street Experience of Ancient Ephesus," in *Streets of the World, Critical Perspectives on Public Space*, edited by Z. Çelik, D. Favro, R. Ingersoll (Berkeley: University of California Press 1994), 95–110; C. Frugoni, *A Distant City: Images of Urban Experience in the Medieval World*, translation by William McCuaig (Princeton: Princeton University Press 1991), and C. Burroughs, *From Signs to Design. Environmental Process and Reform in Early Renaissance Rome* (Cambridge, MA: MIT Press 1990).

24. The historians Carcopino and Homo considered Rome during the entire Imperial period rather under a particular emperor; Jerome Carcopino, *La vie a Rome dans l'Antiquité* (Paris: P. U. F. 1953); Homo, *Rome impériale*.

25. In an inspiring essay, Richard Brilliant calls for researchers from all fields to share data on Rome, a move that would promote period specific studies; "Prolegomena to a Very Long Book on the City of Rome," in *In Memoriam Otto J. Brendal*, edited by L. Bonfante and H. von Heinze (Mainz: Von Zabern 1976), 255–61; see also Brunilde S. Ridgway, "The State of Research on Ancient Art," *ArtB* (March 1986): 16.

26. H. T. Rowell's incisive work on early Imperial Rome focuses on the political and social context; he does not aim to recreate an enlivened portrait of the city's physical environment; *Rome in the Augustan Age* (Norman: University of Oklahoma Press 1962).

27. Mary Taliaferro Boatwright thoroughly documents the individual building projects of Rome during the principate of Hadrian, yet does not move beyond the individual structures to consider their collective impact on the urban observer of the early second century; *Hadrian and the City of Rome* (Princeton: Princeton University Press, 1987); cf. Diane Favro, "Reading Ancient Rome," *Design Book Review* 19 (Winter 1991): 38–40.

28. For example, recent excavations in the Forum Romanum have been reworking established ideas about the form and use of this important urban space; N. Purcell, "Rediscovering the Roman Forum," *JRA* 2 (1989): 157–66. For an overview, see John R. Patterson, "Survey Article. The City of Rome: From Republic to Empire," *JRS* 82 (1992): 186–215.

29. An interdisciplinary approach focuses a fresh eye on familiar material, yet without a well-defined methodology or audience, it often satisfies few and aggravates many. The repeated calls for a truly interdisciplinary approach to urban history have, in fact, led to further divisiveness; Spiro Kostof, "Cities and Turfs," *Design Book Review* 10 (Fall 1986): 35–9; Z. Çelik and D. Favro, eds., "Methods of Urban History," special topic edition, *Journal of Architectural Education* 41:3 (Spring 1988); Z. Çelik, D. Favro, and R. Ingersoll, "Introduction," Çelik, et al., *Streets*, 1–7.

30. To date, however, examples focus on postantique cities; Richard Krautheimer,

The Rome of Alexander VII (Princeton: Princeton University Press 1985); Hilary Ballon, *The Paris of Henri IV* (New York and Cambridge, MA: Architectural History Foundation/MIT Press 1991).

31. Representative of urban perceptual studies are Grady Clay, *Close-Up: How to Read the American City* (New York: Praeger 1973), and Allan Jacobs, *Looking at Cities* (Cambridge, MA: Harvard University Press 1985).

32. For an overview of classical influences on architects in the last twenty years, see Andreas Papadakis, ed., *New Classicism* (New York: Rizzoli 1990).

33. D. Agrest, *Architecture From Without* (Cambridge, MA: MIT Press 1991); C. Boyer, *The City of Collective Memory* (Cambridge, MA: MIT Press 1994). Bergmann provides a model for the reception and representation of a Pompeian house in "Roman House," 227–32.

34. Herbert F. Crovitz, *Galton's Walk, Methods for the Analysis of Thinking, Intelligence, and Creativity* (New York: Harper & Row 1970). An interesting comparison would be between Galton's walk and the earlier peregrinations documented by Friedrich Engels in Manchester; Marcus, "Reading the Illegible."

35. Steen Eiler Rasmussen, *Experiencing Architecture* (Cambridge, MA: MIT Press 1959).

36. Lynch, *Image*, 9–10. Amos Rapoport evaluates and updates Lynch's work in *Human Aspects*, 114–18; see also M. Gottdiener and A. Lagopoulos, eds., *The City and the Sign* (New York: Columbia University Press 1986), 6–12; Alexander Tzonis and Liane Lefaivre, "Thinking in Forms as Well as Words: Kevin Lynch and the Cognitive Theory of the City," *Design Book Review* 26 (Fall 1992): 23–8.

37. *Topophilia* (Englewood Cliffs, NJ: Prentice Hall 1974). Similarly, Yoshinobu Ashihara cited diverse historical urban examples in *The Aesthetic Townscape*.

38. *Human Aspects*, 1–4.

39. D. Preziosi, *The Semiotics of the Built Environment* (Bloomington: Indiana University Press 1979). M. H. Segall, D. T. Campbell, and M. J. Herskovits referred to the color vocabulary of ancient Greece to justify research on environmental perception; *The Influence of Culture on Visual Perception* (Indianapolis: Bobbs-Merrill 1966), 38–9.

40. Christian Norberg-Schulz, *Genius loci – Towards a Phenomenology of Architecture* (New York: Rizzoli 1980), and the various authors in *L'antico come luogo della memoria,* edited by Tonino Paris (Rome: Casa del Libro 1984).

41. R. Venturi, D. Scott Brown, and S. Izenour, *Learning from Las Vegas* (Cambridge, MA: MIT Press 1977).

42. Post-Modern architects made generic references to the classical past. In contrast, architects championing Classical Romanticism in the eighteenth and early nineteenth centuries attempted to recreate classical environments. For example, Henry and Richard Hoare designed the gardens and buildings at Stourhead (1735–83) following descriptions in Vergil; *Aen.*42.

43. The experiential richness of Horton Plaza has made it a popular attraction, bursting all records for number of shoppers and their length of stay; Paul M. Sachner, "Fun City," *Architectural Record,* 174.2 (March 1986): 128–35.

44. *The Concise Townscape* (London: The Architectural Press 1961).

45. Though aimed at children, Macaulay's well-researched and wonderfully illustrated books are popular among architects. The author traces the creation and occupation of a fictional Roman urban environment in the Augustan period in *City: A Story of Roman Planning and Construction* (Boston: Houghton Mifflin 1974). In the same series, Macaulay examines other historic structures, including an Egyptian pyramid and a Gothic cathedral.

46. Educational films on historic environments have been less successful in recreat-

ing urban experience; compare, "Pompeii: Daily Life of the Ancient Romans," video production by Luigi Constantini (1989), and animated versions of Macauly's works.

47. The value of any computer model of course depends upon its accuracy. A few commercially available computer games exploit classical buildings and environments, though generally in an ahistorical manner as with the popular *Myst*, Cyan, 1994. The 1993 game *Caesar* challenges players to build a generic colonial Roman city from a kit of parts. Emphasizing components over environment, this game is of little use for the study of historic urban experience; Impressions Software, Inc., 1993.

48. The renewed interest in the experience of ancient cities is evident in recent international conferences: In 1981, the Danish Academy held a seminar entitled "Città e architettura nella Roma Imperiale"; the papers were edited by K. de Fine Licht and published as *AnalRom* Suppl. 10 (Odense: Odense University Press 1983). Two years later, the Centre national de la recherche scientifique et l'École française de Rome organized the conference "L'Urbs, Espace Urbain et Histoire, Ier siecle av. J.-C.–IIIe siecle ap. J.-C."; these presentations were edited by C. Pietri and published under the same title (Rome: École française de Rome 1987).

49. J. Rykwert, *The Idea of a Town, The Anthropology of Urban Form in Rome, Italy and the Ancient World* (London: Faber and Faber 1976).

50. J. R. Clarke, *Black-and-White Figural Mosaics* (New York: New York University Press 1979); idem, *The Houses of Roman Italy, 100 b.c.–a.d. 250, Ritual, Space and Decoration* (Berkeley: University of California Press 1991). On the experience and meaning of the Roman house see also Wallace-Hadrill, "Roman House," 43–97; L. Bek, *Towards a Paradise on Earth*, AnalRom Suppl. 9 (Rome 1980): 164–203;

Franz Jung, "Gebaute Bilder," *AntK* 27 (1984): 71–122.

51. The computer reconstructions were by artist Victoria I; Bergmann, "Roman House," 225–56.

52. P. Zanker, "Drei Stadtbilder aus dem Augusteischen Rome," in *L'Urbs, Espace urbain et histoire,* edited by C. Pietri (Rome: École française de Rome 1987), 475; D. Scagliarini Corlàita, "La situazione urbanistica degli archi onorari nella prima età imperiale," in *Studi sull'Arco Onorario Romano,* Studia Archaeologica 21 (Rome: L'Erma di Bretschneider 1979), 29; MacDonald, *Roman Empire* II, 291.

53. MacDonald, *Roman Empire* II, 5.

54. Stambaugh, *Ancient Roman City,* xv; Favro, "Reading Ancient Rome," 38–40.

55. N. Purcell, "Town in Country and Country in Town," in *Ancient Roman Villa Gardens* (Washington, DC: Dumbarton Oaks, 1987), 185–204.

56. Antonio Varone, "Le voci degli antichi: itinerario pompeiano tra pubblico e privato," in *Rediscovering Pompeii* (Rome: "L'Erma" di Bretschneider 1990), 27–41.

57. The humanity evident in the Augustan Age appeals to modern researchers awash with *fin de siecle* angst; K. Galinsky, "Recent Trends in the Interpretation of the Augustan Age," *The Augustan Age* 5 (1986): 22–36.

58. For example, both Cosimo de Medici and Mussolini selected Augustus as an exemplar; Kurt Forster, "Metaphors of Rule: Political Ideology and History in the Portraits of Cosimo I de'Medici," *Mitteilungen des Kunsthistorischen Institutes in Florenz* 15 (1971): 65–104; Spiro Kostof, "The Emperor and the Duce: The Planning of Piazzale Augusto Imperatore in Rome," in *Art and Architecture in the Service of Politics,* edited by Henry Millon and Linda Nochlin (Cambridge, MA: MIT Press 1978), 270–325.

59. Recent preoccupation with the Augustan Age is evidenced by the proceedings to several international events; "The Age of Augustus," a conference at Brown Univer-

sity, April 30–May 2, 1982, published as Winkes, *The Age of Augustus;* "Kaiser Augustus und die Verlorene Republik," an exhibition at Martin-Gropius-Bau, Berlin, June 7–August 14, 1988, published as Hofter, *Kaiser Augustus;* a series of colloquia at Brown University in spring of 1987, published as Raaflaub/Toher, *Between Republic and Empire.* For an overview of current work on Augustus, see the challenging review essay by Richard Brilliant, *ArtB* 62.2 (June 1990): 327–30; the Editors' Preface in Raaflaub/Toher, *Between Republic and Empire,* xi–xx; and Galinsky, "Recent Trends," 22–36.

60. Pierre Gros, for example, focuses on temple buildings in *Aurea Templa.* Paul Zanker considers specific buildings, not the entire city, as one of many tools used to convey Augustan propaganda in his excellent study, *The Power of Images in the Age of Augustus;* similarly, he examines three disparate urban projects, not the city, in "Drei Stadtbilder," 475–89. In a more biographical approach, Jean-Michel

Roddaz examines the role of Augustus' lieutenant Agrippa as a patron of urban projects in "Marcus Agrippa," *BEFAR* 253 (1984): 195–298. B. A. Kellum proposes to look at the artwork of the city in her forthcoming monograph, *The City Adorned: The Play of Meaning in Augustan Rome,* based upon *Sculptural Programs and Propaganda in Augustan Rome: The Temple of Apollo on the Palatine and the Forum of Augustus,* Ph.D. dissertation (Harvard University, 1981).

61. Though study of building projects in Augustan Rome has been conducted for centuries, the greatest initial strides in looking at the entire city occurred between the Wars; e.g., see F. W. Shipley, "The Building Activities of the Viri Triumphales from 44 B.C. to 14 A.D.," *MAAR* 9 (1931): 9–60; idem, *Agrippa's Building Activities in Rome, Washington University Studies, Language and Literature* 4 (1933); F. Bourne, *Public Works of the Julio-Claudians and the Flavians* (Menasha, WI: George Banta Publishing 1941).

CHAPTER 2. A WALK THROUGH REPUBLICAN ROME, 52 B.C.

1. Gaius Scribonius Curio was not particularly rich; Pliny *HN*.36.121. An enemy of Caesar, he was an optimate, elected tribune in 50 B.C.; subsequently, Caesar purchased his support with a substantial bribe; DioCass.40.60. On his rotating theater, see Pliny *HN*.36.117–20; C. Landes and J.-C. Golvin, *Amphitheatres et Gladiateurs* (Paris: Presses du CNRA 1990), 56–7.

2. The following is a fictional walk through the capital at midcentury based on the placement and configuration of buildings as known in 1990. New discoveries and interpretations may alter individual sight lines, but not the overall ambience portrayed. The aim is to approximate the experience of two individuals – one young, one old – as they move from the city center to the outskirts; these observers are kept

fairly anonymous to approximate the reactions of average pedestrians, though class status and education of course always affect interpretation. Their experience is restricted to the urban features visible from public walkways and therefore excludes most building interiors. To maintain the flow of the narrative and of the walk, each building is not fully documented; for additional information, see Platner/Ashby, *Dictionary;* Nash, *Pictorial Dictionary;* and Richardson, *New Topographical Dictionary.* These should be supplemented with individual topographical studies such as Robert E. A. Palmer, "A Roman Street Named Good," *JIES* 1.3 (1973): 370–8; "C. Verres' Legacy of Charm and Love to the City of Rome," *RendPontAcc* 51–2 (1978–80): 111–36; T. P. Wiseman, "Topography and Rhetoric. The Trial of Manlius," *Historia* 28 (1979): 32–50; "The Circus Flaminius," *BSR* 42 (1974): 3–26. Unfortunately, this manuscript was completed before I had access to the first two volumes of the excellent new *Lexicon Topographicum Urbis Romae*, edited by Eva Margareta Steinby; Vol. I: A–C (Rome: Quasar, 1993), Vol. II: D–G (Rome: Quasar, 1995).

3. In the center of Rome, the Capitoline Hill had two summits, the Arx on the north and the Capitolium on the south. Gradually, Romans applied the term Capitolium to the entire mount. The Area Capitolina was a walled precinct surrounding the Temple of Jupiter Optimus Maximus. On the Forum side, a broad platform approximately thirty meters wide lay atop retaining walls, substructures, and a leveled portion of the southern mound. Regarding the sculptures on the site, see Dio-Cass.37.9.34; 40.47; 41.14; 43.45; Pliny *HN*.34.34, 43.

4. The temple is one of the earliest and largest in Rome. Erected in the days of the kings, this structure was burned to the ground in 82 B.C. Although the temple treasure was saved, the terra-cotta statue of Jupiter and the sacred Sibylline books were destroyed; both were subsequently restored; Pliny *HN*.33; Tac.*Hist*.3.72.

5. Sulla brought marble columns from the Olympieion in Athens for his temple rebuilding. These columns are known to have been Corinthian, yet coins show the Temple of Jupiter Optimus Maximus with Doric capitals; Pliny *HN*.36.45; *B.M. Coins Rep*.1.571.4217–25. Different capitals could have been added to the Athenian columns, or those from Greece may not have been used by Catulus, who completed the restoration; Cic.*Verr*.4.69.

6. Catulus wanted to improve the temple's profile by lowering the level of the Area Capitolina, but the platform was riddled with underground passages; Val.Max.4.4; Festus *Gloss.Lat*.88; Gell.2.11.2.

7. Geese were commonly used as "watchdogs." In addition to those in the Area Capitolina, another more famous gaggle was kept on the Arx near the Temple of Juno Moneta; Livy 5.47; cf. Dion.Hal. *Ant. Rom*.13.7; Cic.*Rosc.Am*.56; Plut.*Vit.Cam.* 27; Richardson, *New Topographical Dictionary*, 31.

8. Cicero describes the hanging garrets of Rome and the rental market from the perspective of a property owner; *Leg.Agr.* 2.25.96; *Att*.13.33. Dio Cassius, among others, drew a direct connection between the large population and civil unrest in Rome; 38.3 re. 59 B.C.

9. F. Dupont, *Daily Life in Ancient Rome*, translated by Christopher Woodall (Oxford: Blackwell 1992), 151.

10. Murders occurred practically every day. As consul in 52 B.C., Pompey kept the city under guard and always moved about with a cadre of soldiers; DioCass. 40.48, 53.

11. At the funeral of the murdered Clodius, his supporters rioted and set the city ablaze as if it were his pyre; DioCass. 40.49.

12. Other hills in the capital took the name of trees, including the Collis Viminalis (osiers) and the Mons Querquetulanus (oaks).

13. In 57 B.C., rioting occurred on the Cermalus, the northern summit of the Palatine, when the tribune Clodius and a group of thugs stormed the house of the tribune Titus Annius Milo; once a counterattack began, Clodius hid in the nearby *domus* of Publius Cornelius Sulla; Cic. *Att*.4.3.

14. T. P. Wiseman, "The Temple of Victory on the Palatine," *AntJ* LXI (1981): 35–52.

15. At this event, the elephants broke down the protective iron railing of the circus and wrecked havoc among the spectators; Pliny *HN*.8.20.

16. The nobility of the first century B.C. were avid art collectors and prided themselves on their connoisseurship. While most

attention focused on portable artworks, architectural decoration was also a subject of discourse; see J. J. Pollitt, *The Art of Rome c.753 B.C.–337 A.D. Sources and Documents* (Englewood Cliffs. NJ: Prentice Hall 1966), 74–85; idem, *Art in the Hellenistic Age* (Cambridge: Cambridge University Press 1986), 159–62.

17. The Tiber River was called *flavus,* or yellow; Hor.*Carm.Saec.*1.2.13; 2.3.18.

18. Though not mentioned specifically in relation to 54 B.C., the fragile Pons Sublicius probably succumbed to this forceful flood; DioCass.39.61. This structure was revered as the site of many important events in the history of early Rome; cf. Livy 2.19; Platner/Ashby, *Dictionary,* 401–2.

19. In 45 B.C., Cicero noted: "I sometimes think of buying a suburban property on the other side of the Tiber, chiefly with this in mind – I can't think of any location which will be so much in the public eye"; *Att.*12.19.

20. The Clivus Capitolinus had a gradient of 1:8. A steep street was a *clivus* (slope), a boulevard a *platea,* a narrow alley or dead-end street an *angiportus,* and a highway a *via.* The term *vicus* actually applies to a region or neighborhood, but came to refer to the main street of the district as well; Philip W. Harsh, "Angiportum, Platea, and Vicus," *CP* 32:1 (January 1937): 44–58.

21. Erected in 174 B.C., the porticus ran along the right side of the Clivus Capitolinus as one ascends; Livy 41.27; Tac.*Hist.*3.71.

22. Ancient sources disagree about the exact founding date of the Temple of Saturn. Dates range from the mid-seventh to the early fifth century B.C. There is no record of the structure being restored before 42 B.C.

23. The Basilica Opimia was in the area, though its exact location remains uncertain. It was probably destroyed when Tiberius rebuilt the Temple of Concordia in 7 B.C.

24. Today, only the first, Doric arcade of the ancient Tabularium is standing. Removed by Michelangelo, the second Corinthian arcade cannot be securely dated; the remains appear Flavian, but may have been part of an earlier restoration.

25. Complete coverage of the buildings in the Forum is found in F. Coarelli, *Il Foro Romano, 1: periodo arcaico* (Rome: Edizioni Quasar, 1983), and *Il Foro Romano, 2: periodo repubblicano e augusteo* (Rome: Edizioni Quasar 1985). U. E. Paoli looks at the Forum in three different periods of antiquity (Republican, Early Imperial, and Late Imperial), emphasizing individual projects rather than overall appearance; *Rome, Its People, Life and Customs* (New York: David McKay 1963), 292–309.

26. The Roman comic dramatist Plautus (d. 184 B.C.), in his play *Curculio (The Parasite),* gives a lively description of the idlers in the Forum in the second century B.C.; 466–82. The shrine of Cloacina, goddess of the sewer, stood before the Basilica Aemilia.

27. Plut.*Vit.Caes.*29. The Basilica Julia replaced the wooden Basilica Sempronia. No sources record the date of construction; the building was dedicated incomplete in 46 B.C.; Hieron.*AbAbr.*1971. A confusing passage in a letter by Cicero of 54 B.C. implies L. Aemilius Paullus also acted as Caesar's agent in the construction of the Basilica Julia; *Att.*4.16.

28. Pliny notes that Caesar paid over 100,000 sesterces for the land of the Forum Julium; *HN.*36.103.

29. Juvenal provides a colorful description of the foreigners crowding Rome's streets in the first century A.D.; 3.60–72.

30. Erected in 193 B.C., the portico running from the Porta Fontinalis to the Altar of Mars in the Campus Martius provided a covered walkway for censors moving from their office and archives in the Atrium Libertatis to the area where they conducted the census; Livy 35.10.12.

31. Among the tombs along the Via Flaminia were those of the Claudii to the west and that of C. Publicius Bibulus to the east.

32. With the construction of the Aurelian wall in the third century A.D., the intramural portion of the Via Flaminia became known as the Via Lata (Broad Highway).

33. The Campus Martius covers approximately 250 hectares (600 acres), and was kept largely undeveloped during the Republic. The old Republican fortifications encompassed approximately 400 hectares (1,000 acres); Stambaugh, *Ancient Roman City*, 20.

34. Included among the revered buildings in this portion of the Campus Martius are the four early temples in the precinct known as the Area Sacra del Largo Argentina.

35. As with many monuments in the Campus Martius, the tumulus of Julia cannot be securely located; Suet.*Caes*.84.1; Dio-Cass.44.51.

36. The Horti Luculliani were laid out about 60 B.C. along the top of the tableland to the east of the Campus Martius. Here Lucullus retired, indulged his pleasures, and went mad; he died in 57/6 B.C.; Plut.*Vit.Luc*.39. The Sallustii and Caesar also had *horti* in the area. Located farther east, these gardens were probably not visible from the Via Flaminia; Pierre Grimal, *Les Jardins romains*, BEFAR 155 (Paris:

Presses Universitaires de France 1969), 128–31.

37. So many *horti* occupied the hill that within a few years, it became known as the Collis Hortulorum, or hill of the gardens (Suet.*Ner*.50). In the Late Empire, the area was renamed the Pincius Mons after the Gens Pincia.

38. The site of Scaurus' theater is not recorded, though like other temporary structures for large crowds, it probably stood in the Campus Martius; cf. Vitr.5.5.7; M. Bieber, *The History of the Greek and Roman Theater* (Princeton: Princeton University Press 1961), 168.

39. Writing a century after Scaurus erected his theater, Pliny possibly exaggerates its original appearance. When the theater was dismantled, Scaurus removed some of the marble columns to his own residence; *HN*.36.6, 114–15.

40. Despite his vast resources, Pompey borrowed money in 52 B.C.; Cic.*Fam*.6.18.3; Val.Max. 6.2.11.

41. Among the tombs visible along the northern suburban stretch of the Via Flaminia was that of the Domitii later associated with the Horti Domitiorum where Nero was later entombed; Suet.*Ner*.50; Grimal, *Jardins*, 126.

CHAPTER 3. CONTEXT: THE REPUBLICAN URBAN IMAGE

1. Livy 40.5. Demetrius, son of Philip V, took the unpopular position of favoring the Romans. To discredit him, supporters of his brother Perseus continually brought up the subject of Rome in court conversations. The Macedonians' derision of private as well as public urban projects indicates firsthand familiarity with the city. Pictorial representations of Rome's cityscape were few in the Republic, though individual buildings did appear on coins; M. J. Price and B. L. Trell, *Coins and Their Cities. Architecture on the Ancient Coins of Greece, Rome, and Palestine* (London:

V. C. Vecchi and Sons 1977), 57–65. More plentiful were written and oral descriptions. Soldiers, traders, and scholars frequented the city on the Tiber and shared their impressions; G. Gernentz, *Laudes Romae* (Rostochii: Typis Academicis Adlerianis 1918), passim.

2. T. W. Potter, *Roman Italy* (Berkeley: University of California Press 1987), 28–9.

3. *Collis* refers to high ground and frequently described both the spurs of plateaus (e.g., the Quirinalis and Viminalis) and the plateaus themselves. *Mons* defines a mountain, though the Romans applied the

term to sections of Rome's eastern plateau, including the Montes Cispius and Oppius, which together formed the Mons Esquilinus. Likewise, the Montes Aventinus and Capitolinus had attached spurs and thus were not isolated mountains. The highest points in the city were the Esquiline (54 masl.) and the Janiculum (85 masl.); Homo, *Rome imperiale*, 32–7. For convenience, the modern names of the hills will be used: Capitoline, Palatine, Caelian, and so on.

4. Tradition credits king Servius Tullius of the sixth century B.C. with formation of the first city wall. The actual remains date to two centuries later and were composed of a fosse, tufa ashlar wall, and earth-filled agger; G. Säflund, *Le mura di Roma repubblicana*. Acta Inst. Rom. Regni Sueciae II (Uppsala: Almqvist & Wiksells 1932).

5. For example, the Forum Holitorium (vegetable market) lay just outside the Porta Carmentalis of the Republican wall; Varro *Ling*.5.146.; the Forum Boarium (cattle market) was inside the fortifications next to the river; Cic.*Scaur*.23. Less smelly and messy commercial activities continued to be conducted in the Forum Romanum.

6. Among the prominent citizens who had residences on the Palatine in the first century B.C. were L. Licinius Crassus, M. Tullius Cicero and his brother Quintus, Q. Hortensius Hortalus, and Mark Antony.

7. The valley measured approximately 600 × 150 m; Platner/Ashby, *Dictionary*, 114; Livy 1.35.8.

8. The *pomerium* circumscribed an area in which no armies could gather, no dead could be buried, and no foreign cults worshiped; Varro, *Ling*.5.143; Gell.15.27.5; Richardson, *New Topographical Dictionary*, 292–6.

9. Calculations for the population of ancient Rome are based on the number of citizens enrolled on the dole; W. J. Oates, "The Population of Rome," *CP* 29 (1934): 101–16.

10. For example, in 57 B.C., the conflict between Clodius and Milo over the recall of Cicero ended in rioting throughout the entire city; DioCass.39.8; cf. 38.1.

11. Cicero's praises of Rome include: "This most fortunate and magnificent city," "No more is there anything on earth superior to our city," "[T]his beautiful city of ours"; *Cat*.3.3; *Nat.D*.3.9; *Verr*.2.5.127.

12. Cic.*Att*.1.16.11; *Quint*.2.4.5; Varro *Rust*. 1.2.2, 1.69.

13. L. Storoni Mazzolani explores the concept of Rome as a design for society in *Idea of the City in Roman Thought*, trans. S. O'Donnell (Bloomington: Indiana University Press 1972).

14. The twins Romulus and Remus were the offspring of Mars and the Vestal Virgin Rhea Silva; Livy 1.3.10. Ancient sources frequently referred to Romulus as godlike; according to Cicero, Romulus chose the location of Rome "with a wisdom more divine"; *Rep*.2.10; cf. 2.3, 5, 20; 6.11. Romulus was later subsumed by the Sabine god Quirinus.

15. Aesthetics became an acknowledged branch of philosophy only with the writings of Plotinus in the third century A.D.; Moshe Barasch, *Theories of Art, From Plato to Winkelmann* (New York: New York University Press 1985), 34–42. On theories of city planning, see E. J. Owens, *The City in the Greek and Roman World* (London: Routeledge 1991), 1–10.

16. Plato describes Atlantis; *Tim*.24. According to Aristotle, Hippodamus of Miletus aspired to be a philosopher and considered the social and political creation of an ideal community as well as "the art of laying out towns"; *Pol*.2.5–8.

17. Cf. Quint.*Inst*.12.10.1–10; Barasch, *Theories of Art*, 40–1; J. J. Pollitt, *Art in the Hellenistic Age* (Cambridge: Cambridge University Press 1986), 159–63. Regarding Greek influence on Roman planning theory, see F. Castagnoli, *Orthogonal Planning in Classical Antiquity* (Cambridge, MA: MIT Press 1971), 5-7. In a

telling passage Cicero notes, "equally fool-ish are the people who take delight in stat-ues and pictures and chased silver and Corinthian works of art and magnificent buildings"; *Paradoxa Stoicorum*, 36.

18. Vitr.1.4–6. Similarly, in the first century A.D., the rhetorician Quintilianus empha-sized planning as a criteria for greatness in urban form; *Inst.*5.10.89.

19. According to Livy, the State supplied roof tiles, granted building patrons the right to quarry stone and cut lumber where they liked as long as they agreed to complete urban structures within 1 year; 5.55.2–3.

20. Livy himself confirms in other passages that a comprehensive plan was not imposed, primarily because of pressures to preserve the power of places and property rights (6.4.6), and in any event, the destruction to Rome by the Gauls was not as complete as that to Athens by the Per-sians (5.42.1.3); Owens, *The City*, 94–5.

21. Verg.*Aen.*6.847–8, translation C. Day Lewis; cf. Frontin.1.16.

22. Erich Gruen explains the expansion of the Roman state as the result of individual cir-cumstances rather than of unbridled impe-rialism; *The Hellenistic World and the Coming of Rome*, 2 vols. (Berkeley: Uni-versity of California Press 1984), passim.

23. According to one legend, Greeks occupied the site in the twelfth century B.C. when Aeneas arrived from Troy; another credits the foundation to Romulus and his twin Remus in 753 B.C. With pride and nostal-gia, ancient authors described the early set-tlement of Rome and its ideal position; Ger-nentz, *Laudes*, 8–40; G. Lugli, *Fontes ad Topographiam Veteris Urbis Romae Perti-nentes* (Rome: Universitá di Roma 1952), 1–38. The earliest archaeological remains attest to human habitation in the fourteenth century B.C.; J. Heurgon, *The Rise of Rome* (Eng. trans., Berkeley: University of Califor-nia Press 1973), 72–5, 128–32.

24. W. V. Harris, *War and Imperialism in Republican Rome 327–70 B.C.* (Oxford: Clarendon Press 1979), 21; D. Favro,

"The Roman Forum and Roman Mem-ory," *Places* 5:1 (1988): 17–24.

25. Cic.*Fin.*5.2. On the relation between aes-thetic visualization, emotions, and reason, see E. Leach, *The Rhetoric of Space, Liter-ary and Artistic Representations of Land-scape in Republican and Augustan Rome* (Princeton: Princeton University Press 1988), 88.

26. Zanker, *Images*, 245–7. Earlier, Aristotle had equated the artist and character (*ethographos*); *Poet.*1450a23; 1448a1.

27. Patrons corrupted the symbolization of architecture by creating works inappropri-ate to their actual *auctoritas*. Zanker makes a telling comparison between the small tomb put up by the Senate to honor the consul Hirtius in 43 B.C. and the large circular structure of a well-connected, but relatively insignificant noble lady, Caecilia Metella, ca. 30 B.C.; *Images,* 15–18; 291–3; T. P. Wiseman, "*Conspicui Postes Tectaque Digna Deo:* The Public Image of Aristocratic and Imperial Houses in the Late Republic and Early Empire," in *L'Urbs, Espace urbain et histoire,* edited by C. Pietri (Rome: École française de Rome 1987), 475–89.

28. F. Gutheim, *Worthy of the Nation. The History of Planning for the National Cap-ital* (Washington, DC: Smithsonian Insti-tution 1977), 17–18, 377–8.

29. Other ancient cities could more easily be represented by a single building such as the Pharos (lighthouse) for Alexandria or the Colossus of Rhodes, both included among the seven wonders of the ancient world.

30. S.v. *PW* VII, 1, col.1155–69. The Roman *genius* was generally depicted either as a serpent, winged being, or togate youth.

31. Several different spirits represented the collective, including those for the *populi romani, res publica,* and *patria.* Only at the very end of the Republic did Roma appear as the personification of the Roman people; Ronald Mellor, "The God-dess Roma," *ANRW* 2 (1981): 954,

972–5; 1004–5; U. Knoche, "Die August-eische Ausprägung der Dea Roma," *Gymnasium* 59 (1952), 324-49; H. Kunckel, "Der Römische Genius," *RM-EH* Sup. 20 (1974): 29–40.

32. The western Greeks first personified Rome, fabricating the eponymous Rhome as founder of the city. The Greeks commonly associated a city's fortune, like that of a person, with a unique spirit, or *tyche*, generally depicted as a female wearing a mural crown (fig. 30). When eastern Greeks began to worship Roma in the early second century B.C., however, they modeled the cult after those for powerful Hellenistic rulers rather than after those honoring fortune/*tyche*; S.v. Tyche *PW* 7a.2 col. 1677; Mellor, "Roma," 956–8; Pollitt, *Hellenistic Age*, 2–3; Jane Nitzsche, *The Genius Figure in Antiquity and the Middle Ages* (New York: Columbia University Press 1975), 13–15.

33. Among the architectural elements brought to Rome in the first century were the columns for the Temple of Jupiter Optimus Maximus and the marine thiasos reliefs for the so-called Altar of Domitius Ahenobarbus; G. W. Bowersock, *Augustus and the Greek World* (Oxford: Clarendon Press 1965), 73–86; A. Kuttner, "Some New Grounds for Narrative. Marcus Antonius's Base (*The Ara Domitti Ahenobarbi*) and Republican Biographies," in Holliday, *Narrative and Event*, 198; cf. J. J. Pollitt, *The Art of Rome, c.753 B.C. –337 A.D.* (Englewood Cliffs, NJ: Prentice Hall 1966), 22–58.

34. K. Hartigan, "The Poets and the Cities, Selections from the Anthology about Greek Cities," *Beitrage zu Klassischen Philologie* 87 (1979), 76–101; MacDonald, *Roman Empire II*, 14–17, 291–2. The popularity of Asiatic architectural forms waxed and waned; J. Onians, *Art and Thought in the Hellenistic Age* (London: Thames and Hudson 1979), 143–4.

35. In the late first century B.C., Strabo vividly portrayed the garden district of Antioch; 16.2.6. Regarding Alexandria, he noted that the royal palaces constituted one-fourth or even one-third of the whole city; 17.1.8; cf. Diod.Sic.18.26.3. Cicero described Syracuse as the "loveliest of all cities . . . beautiful to behold in whatever direction it is approached"; *Verr*.2.4.117.

36. Onians examines the Hellenistic preoccupation with extremes of scale and in particular Aristotle's interest in greatness (*megethos*); *Art and Thought*, 122–33.

37. Pollitt, *Hellenistic Age*, 277, 283–4.

38. Plutarch records a relevant story. When P. Valerius Publicola, consul of 509 B.C., heard that the people of Rome disapproved of his large residence on the Velia, he immediately tore it down. In response, the citizenry "were moved to love and admiration by the man's magnanimity, but mourned, as if for a human being, for the destruction of the house's stately beauty, which their envy had provoked"; Plut.*Vit.Publ*.10.

39. Cic.*Mur*.76. Referring to the restoration of the Basilica Aemilia after the fire of 14 B.C., Tacitus in the first century A.D. noted, "public munificence was a custom still"; *Ann*.3.72.

40. Cic.*Leg.Agr*.2.23.61. A male Roman citizen was expected to complete ten annual military campaigns before he could hold political office at Rome, though exceptions were frequent; Polyb.6.19.4. The expenditure of booty (*manubiae*) on a monument in Rome was considered a duty as well as politically advantageous; Harris, *War and Imperialism*, 11–12; 257, 261–2; M. G. Morgan, "Villa Publica and Magna Mater: Two Notes on Manubial Building at the Close of the Second Century B.C.," *Klio* 55 (1973): 223; L. Pietilä-Castren, *Magnificentia publica. The Victory Monuments of the Roman Generals in the Era of the Punic Wars*, Commentationes humanarum litterarum 84 (Helsinki: Societas Scientiarum Fennica 1987), passim. The word *manubiae* is often translated as "booty," yet technically refers to the

money obtained from the sale of the spoils.

41. *Cupido gloriae* was the driving force behind many wars. Sallust, writing in the late 40s B.C., explained the quest for glory as one of the primary motivations for Roman imperialism; *Cat*.7.3–6; cf. Harris, *War and Imperialism,* 17–20, 24–27.

42. J. D. Evans, *The Art of Persuasion, Political Propaganda from Aeneas to Brutus* (Ann Arbor: University of Michigan Press 1992), 3. Custom dictated that public offices be held in ascending order of importance following the *cursus honorum,* "course of honor." In the late Republic, the usual order was military service, quaestorship, aedile, praetorship, consulship, and censorship.

43. Leo Braudy discusses Roman fame as being specifically tied to the city of Rome; *The Frenzy of Renown* (New York: Oxford University Press, 1986), 57. Similarly, D. R. Shackleton Bailey calls fame a "metropolitan commodity"; *Cicero* (New York: Duckworth 1971), 14–15.

44. Roman patrons sought status through the construction of public buildings. Such beneficence is described by the neologism *evergetism* (from patron: *evergetes*); P. Veyne, *Bread and Circuses,* translated by B. Pearce (London: Penguin Books 1990), 20–2; Zanker, *Images,* 19–22; P. Gros and G. Sauron, "Das politische Programm der öffentlichen Bauten," in Hofter, *Kaiser Augustus,* 48–50.

45. Notable exceptions were the generals Marius and Mark Antony who gained fame without erecting several significant structures in Rome.

46. As early as the XII Tables of the fifth century B.C., the Romans instituted laws against the demolition of existing buildings; D. Favro, "*Pater urbis:* Augustus as City Father of Rome," *JSAH* 51 (1992): 63–4.

47. More research needs to be done on the role of female patrons, with careful distinctions between the naming and initiation of urban projects. In addition to major urban works (Porticus and Macellum Liviae and Porticus Vipsania), women funded large funerary monuments for themselves and owned commercial property.

48. In the mid-second century B.C., Metellus Macedonicus erected one of the earliest public structures of marble in Rome; Pliny *HN*.17.6.

49. Pliny *HN*.36.110; L. Friedländer, *Roman Life and Manners Under the Early Empire* 2, translated by L. A. Magnus (New York: Dutton 1936), 185–7.

50. Calculated programs of artworks were an essential part of every Roman urban complex; Zanker, *Images,* passim. In the late Imperial period, laws forbade the eradication of donors' names from buildings erected in the Provinces: Ulpian, *Opiniones,* Book 3; *Dig*.50.10.3.

51. *Imperium* was the supreme power associated with high magisterial and military posts. In the Republic, a person vested with *imperium* could take auspices, represent the State, exercise civil and criminal jurisdiction, give punishments, issue edicts, command armed forces, and summon the Senate and Assemblies. As a sign of this power, the holder of *imperium* was always accompanied by lictors; Gros/Sauron, "Das politische Programm," 49; Adam Ziolkowski, *The Temples of Mid-Republican Rome and Their Historical and Topographical Context* (Rome: L'Erma di Bretschneider 1992), 198–201. Clodius ran into trouble in 57 B.C. when he consecrated a shrine without being commissioned to do so by order of the people or resolution of the plebs; *Att*.4.2.5.

52. Livy records that the censor M. Fulvius Nobilior contracted for the basilica in 179 B.C.; 40.51. Subsequent texts, however, refer to the structure as the Basilica Aemilia indicating the prominent role played by his co-censor M. Aemilius Lepidus. In 78 B.C., the consul M. Aemilius Lepidus decorated the building; Pliny *HN*.35.13. L. Aemilius Paullus began a

rather cursory restoration in 54 B.C., but subsequently undertook an expensive rebuilding with funding from Caesar; Cic.*Att*.4.16.8; Plut.*Vit.Caes*.29. His son L. Aemilius Lepidus Paullus finished and dedicated the structure in 34 B.C.; Dio-Cass.49.42. After 54 B.C., the structure was generally called the Basilica Paulli; Richardson, *New Topographical Dictionary*, 55. For convenience, I will refer to the building as the "Basilica Aemilia," the name most commonly used in modern literature.

53. Pliny *HN*.36.45. Significantly, Antiochus IV in the second century B.C. initially had hired the Roman architect Cossutius to oversee construction of the grand Olympieion.

54. Platner/Ashby, *Dictionary*, 506–9; Coarelli, *Roma*, 32–3. The Tabularium reflected the power of the optimates in a weak Senate, not the *res publica*; G. Charles-Picard, *Rome et les villes d'Italie, des Gracques a la mort d'Auguste* (Paris: Sociétè d'edition d'enseignment superieur 1978), 94–6.

55. Due to reworking in the Renaissance, the original height of the Tabularium and its northern elevation remain uncertain; Platner/Ashby, *Dictionary*, 507.

56. A distinction should be made between dynastic Hellenistic projects funded privately, and Roman public works funded in part with State monies; Ziolkowski, *Temples*, 193–234; D. E. Strong. "The Administration of Public Building in Rome during the Later Republic and Early Empire," *BICS* 15 (1968), 97–109.

57. On the orientation of the Forum, see E. B. Van Deman, "The Sullan Forum," *JRS* 12 (1922): 1–31.

58. Paving in the Forum Romanum is dated primarily by archaeological evidence; Blake, *Roman Construction*, 31, 140, 143–5; Platner/Ashby, *Dictionary*, 124; Van Deman, "Sullan Forum," 3–31; F. Coarelli, *Il Foro Romano, 1* (Edizioni Quasar: Rome 1983), 199–212; cf. Festus *Gloss.Lat*.416L. The main streets into the Forum were the Clivus Capitolinus raised upon arches at its lowest level, the Clivus Palatinus, Clivus Victoriae, and the Clivus Argentarius. The latter may originally have been known as the Vicus Lautumiarum after the quarries at the base of the Capitoline; Platner/Ashby, *Dictionary*, 122; Richardson, *New Topographical Dictionary*, 88.

59. The speakers' platform was named after the captured prows of ships, *rostra*, displayed on its sides; App.*BCiv*.1.97; Cic.*Phil*.9.13; Vell.Pat.2.61; DioCass. 42.18.

60. Sulla or his lieutenants built small temples to Hercules Custos at the Circus Maximus and to Hercules Sullanus on the Esquiline; Ov.*Fasti* 6.209; *Not.Reg*.V. Road repairs may have been undertaken at this time; *CIL* 6 (4,3) 1.37043; R. Coarelli, "Public Building in Rome between the Second Punic War and Sulla," *PBSR* 45 (1977): 9–23.

61. Gell.13.144; DioCass.43.50. The *pomerium* could only be enlarged by those who exalted Rome's *imperium* by adding new territory; Tac.*Ann*.12.23. M. Labrousse proposed that Sulla extended the *pomerium* to include the Fora Boarium and Olitorium; "Le Pomerium de la Rome impériale," *MEFR* 54 (1937): 168. The exact number of pomerial enlargements during the Republic are uncertain; James H. Oliver, "The Augustan Pomerium," *MAAR* 10 (1932): 147.

62. Braudy provides a succinct overview of Pompey's career and relationship to fame; he makes a distinction between Alexandrian fame as the exceptional (also the more spiritual and aesthetic) and Roman fame as defined in relation to an existing structure for recognition; *Renown*, 66–71.

63. Pompey held several positions before legally allowed. Early in his career, when supporters wished to put him forward as a member of the Senate, he declined believing greater honor would come from cele-

64. The extravagance and self-promotion of generals such as Pompey may have prompted the tribune Rullus in 63 B.C. to introduce a bill calling for war spoils to go to the decemvirs (magistrates of ten men) rather than be expended on monuments promoting individuals; Cic.*Leg.Agr.*2.23. 59–61.

65. The size and configuration of the theater at Mytilene cannot be determined exactly. The orchestra diameter was approximately 25 m and that of Pompey's theater in Rome was approximately 65 m. On the entire Pompeian theatrical complex and its comprehensive art program, see Gilles Sauron, "Le complexe pompéien du Champ de Mars: nouveauté urbanistique à finalité idéologique," in C. Pietri, ed., *L'Urbs, Espace urbain et histoire* (Rome: École française de Rome 1987), 457–73.

66. Val.Max.2.4.2; M. Bieber, *The History of the Greek and Roman Theater* (Princeton: Princeton University Press 1961), 168.

67. Tert.*De Spect.*10; Plut.*Vit.Pomp.*50.5; Cic.*Off.*2.60; Gell.10.1.7–9. Even with the temple to Venus and other shrines as justification for its existence, the stone theater of Pompey received criticism; Tac.*Ann.*14.20; Richardson, *New Topographical Dictionary*, 380.

68. Theaters were common in Italian cities under Greek sway, with the earliest appearing in Sicily; Bieber, *Theater*, 167–77; A. Boëthius, *Etruscan and Early Roman Architecture* (Harmondsworth: Penguin Books 1978), 200–6; Stambaugh, *Ancient Roman City*, 41.

69. The regionary catalogue of the third-century, the *Notitia Urbis Romae*, lists 17,580 places (*loci*) for the Theater of Pompey. The term *locus* in this context is believed to refer to one square foot, but the average spectator would require slightly more space; J. Carcopino, *Daily Life in Ancient Rome*, edited with bibliography and notes by Henry T. Rowell, translated by E. O. Lorimer (New Haven: Yale University Press 1940), 254, 358. Pliny greatly exaggerates when he writes that Pompey's theater held 40,000 spectators; *HN.*36.115.

70. The opening spectacles included the killing of 500 lions and a combat with eighteen elephants; Plut.*Vit.Pomp.*52; Dio-Cass.39.38; Cic.*Fam.*7.1. The temple was dedicated three years later; Vell.Pat.2.48.

71. Pliny *HN.*7.34; Plut.*Vit.Pomp.*50.5. With booty from his campaigns, Pompey also built a shrine to Minerva and one to Hercules Pompeianus near the Circus Maximus; Pliny *HN.*7.97; Vitr.3.3.5.

72. As with the majority of ancient gardens, the exact extent of the Horti of Pompey is difficult to determine. Asconius refers to upper and lower parts; *Mil.*37, 37, 51. P. Grimal argues persuasively that the gardens flanked both sides of the Via Flaminia and were later incorporated into the funerary monument and gardens to Augustus; *Les Jardins romains* (Paris: Presses Universitaires de France 1969), 123–6; Platner/Ashby, *Dictionary*, 270.

73. For example, the Ptolemies constructed royal grounds in Alexandria complete with palatial residential quarters, a library, tombs, a theater, and a zoo; Strab.17.1. 8–10.

74. Braudy, *Renown*, 69.

75. Caesar was quaestor in 68 B.C., aedile in 65 B.C., praetor in 62 B.C., and consul in 59 B.C. In addition, he became Pontifex Maximus in 63 B.C. Though I have separated the patronage of Caesar and Pompey, it should be stressed they were contemporaries.

76. The details of Caesar's triumphs are covered in Weinstock, *Divus Iulius*, 60–79.

77. Cic.*Milone* 41; Richardson, *New Topographical Dictionary*, 278, 340–1. Ironically, the magnificent new Julian structure continued to be called Ovile; Livy 26.22.11; Juv.6.529. Regarding the connection between Caesar's power base and his architectural projects in Rome, see

Roger B. Ulrich, "Julius Caesar and the Creation of the Forum Iulium," *AJA* 97.1 (January 1993): 74.

78. As Caesar's agent, Cicero, along with Oppius, spent huge sums buying land in the area of the Forum Romanum; *Att*.4.16.8. Pliny records Caesar spent 100 million sesterces simply for the site; Pliny *HN*.36.103. Caesar also purchased land in the area for the Basilica Julia; Anderson, *Historical Topography*, 39–43.

79. DioCass.51.22.3; App.*BCiv*.2.68–9, 102; 3.28. The change in program is supported by several factors. Archaeologists have uncovered traces of a different first scheme that was abandoned. Rome's fortification wall had been repaired only a few years before during the Social Wars; its dismantling would have been inconceivable before Pharsalus; App.*BCiv*.1.66. In addition, the construction techniques on the temple reveal evidence of haste; Ulrich, "Julius Caesar," 53–4, 56–9, 64–80; Anderson, *Historical Topography*, 43; T. Hastrup, "Forum Iulium as a Manifestation of Power," *AnalRom* 2 (1962): 45–61; Weinstock, *Divus Iulius*, 81.

80. Suet.*Caes*.39; Pliny *HN*.19.23. Dio Cassius describes the hunting theater as an amphitheater with seats all around; 43.22.

81. Rent was remitted for those who paid 2,000 sesterces or less in Rome, up to 500 sesterces in Italy; Suet.*Caes*.38; Dio-Cass.42.41; for the property owners' reaction, see Cic.*Off*.2.83; Z. Yavetz, *Plebs and Princeps* (Oxford: Clarendon Press 1969), 45.

82. As aedile, Caesar brought so many gladiators to Rome his opponents passed a bill limiting the number one could keep in the city; Suet.*Caes*.31; 10; cf. 26.

83. Cic.*Att*.4.16.8; Anderson, *Historical Topography*, 10–11. Construction of the Basilica Julia may have been undertaken in part to provide more working space for the financiers who gathered around the Temple of Saturn and its aerarium; Ulrich, "Julius Caesar," 78.

84. App.*BCiv*.2.26; Plut.*Vit.Caes*.29. Possibly the fire of 52 B.C. necessitated rebuilding; Cic.*Mil*.90. For a contrasting view on the buying of Paullus' support, see E. Gruen, *The Last Generation of the Roman Republic* (Berkeley: University of California Press 1974), 175.

85. Conceived in part as an artifice to allow the demolition of the Curia Hostilia, the Temple of Felicitas, itself may have been compromised by the subsequent Curia Julia; Richardson, *New Topographical Dictionary*, 150; Ulrich, "Julius Caesar," 72. On Caesar and Felicitas, see App.*BCiv*. 2.97.405; DioCass.43.21; Weinstock, *Divus Iulius*, 91, 113, 117. Aemilius Lepidus, Caesar's magister equitum, completed the temple along with other of the Dictator's projects; DioCass.44.52.

86. As a political gesture, Caesar entrusted the project to Pompey, but dropped the proposal when faced with the opposition of the optimates; DioCass.37.44; 43.141; Suet.*Caes*.15.

87. DioCass.43.44.6. Caesar moved into the Domus Publica when he became Pontifex Maximus in 63 B.C.; Suet.*Caes*.46. The house voted to him in 46 B.C. may have been primarily honorific, perhaps located by the Temple of Quirinus; Weinstock, *Divus Iulius*, 169–71, 277–81. The State honored certain successful generals with a gift of residential property. As a further sign of honor, a few were allowed to have the main doors of their houses open outward onto the public way; Pliny *HN*.36.112.

88. Cic.*Phil*.2.110; cf. Florus 2.13.91; Weinstock, *Divus Iulius*, 277–80. The question arises if the pediment was placed on the Domus Publica or another residence. The night before Caesar's murder, his wife dreamt that the *fastigium* toppled; Plut. *Vit.Caes*.63.

89. The seven books of *De Bello Gallico* cover the years from 58 to 52 B.C. and are written in a lucid, accessible style. The use of the third person contrasts with the writing of Cato the Censor from the second cen-

tury B.C.; Nep.*Cato* 3. Caesar demonstrated great concern with his image even in death; falling from multiple stab wounds he decorously moved to cover his body; Suet.*Caes*.82.

90. The new calendar reenforces the concept of a new age; Storoni Mazzolani, *Idea of the City*, 121–2.

91. Storoni Mazzolani, *Idea of the City*, 111, 213; Sydenham, *CRR*, nos. 1362–4 for 45–44 B.C.

92. Other epithets for Roma include "queen," "mother," and "head"; Gerentz, *Laudes Romae*, 124–35. Roma is a multifaceted personification representing simultaneously the Roman state, the Roman people, the goddess Roma, and the city; Otto Brendel, *Prolegomena to the Study of Roman Art* (New Haven: Yale University Press, reprinted 1979), 3–7; Michael Rostovtzeff, "The Roman Empire," lecture February 28, 1922, in *Urban Land Economics*, edited by Richard T. Ely (Ann Arbor: Edwards Brothers 1922), 50; Weinstock, *Divus Iulius*, 43, 52.

93. The adaptation of the Greek globe as a Roman symbol first occurred on coins of ca. 75 B.C.; Sydenham, *CRR*, 122, 130, 159; pl. 21, 752; pl. 22, 791; Gerentz, *Laudes Romae*, 124–8; E. Bréguet, "Urbi et Orbi" in *Hommages a Marcel Renard*, edited by Jacqueline Bibauw (Brussels: Latomus 1969), 140–52. The globe appears under foot of Roma, the Genius populi Romani, Jupiter, and other gods; A. Schlachter, *Der Globus* (Leipzig: Berlin 1927), 95–9. Caesar's follower, C. Vibius Pansa, issued a coin in 49 B.C. showing Roma in a similar pose; Weinstock, *Divus Iulius*, 42–3, 51–3.

94. The inscription referred to Caesar as a demigod; DioCass.43.14.6; cf. Cic.*Balb.* 28–64; Weinstock, *Divus Iulius*, 38, 45–52. Earlier Pompey included a representation of the whole world (Oikoumene) in his triumph of 61 B.C., though it is uncertain if in the form of a globe; DioCass.37.21.2.

95. Caesar traced his lineage from Venus, to the Trojan Aeneas, and ultimately to Romulus; he also claimed descent from Romulus' divine father Mars through the Alban kings, though this link was less strong. Sulla and Pompey had also drawn upon connections with Romulus; L. R. Taylor, *The Divinity of the Roman Emperor* (Middletown, CT: American Philological Association 1931), 58–9; Weinstock, *Divus Iulius*, 175–84; Evans, *Persuasion*, 91–3.

96. Caesar may also have extended Rome's *pomerium*, though sources do not agree on this point; pro: Gell.13.14.4; DioCass.43.50; con: Sen.*Dial*.13.8; Tac. *Ann.* 12.23.

97. Romulus was worshiped in divine form as the Sabine war god Quirinus. Caesar owned gardens so close to the Temple of Quirinus on the Quirinal hill they too were damaged when lightning struck the shrine in 47 B.C.; DioCass.42.26; Grimal, *Jardins*, 129.

98. Suet.*Caes*.79; DioCass.44.4; App.*BCiv.* 2. 106.442; 144.602; Weinstock, *Divus Julius*, 200–5, 270–86; Strong, "Administration," 101–2. The negative connotations of kingship may explain why Caesar made no additional architectural gestures honoring Romulus/Quirinus.

99. Significantly, in relation to Caesar's achievements Suetonius mentions care for the city before protection and extension of the Empire; Suet.*Caes*.43, 44.2.

100. Mamurra's house on the Caelian Hill had a marble veneer and solid columns of two different marbles: Carrara and greenish imported cipollino; Pliny *HN*.36.48.

101. See *De Arch*.5 and 6; Boëthius, *Early Roman Architecture*, 136–7.

102. To honor either Pompey or Caesar, or perhaps both, the people carried Julia's body to the Campus Martius for burial. Domitius opposed this action, noting that it was sacrilegious for her to be buried in the Campus without a special decree; DioCass.39.64; Plut.*Vit.Caes.*

23.4. Caesar himself was awarded the privilege of burial within the *pomerium*, though his remains were probably placed in the tumulus tomb of his daughter; DioCass.44.7, 51; Suet.*Caes*.84.

103. Appian may refer more to the function of the Persian example than to its building form; *BCiv*.2.102; Weinstock, *Divus Iulius*, 81; E. Sjöqvist, "Kaisareion," *OpRom* 1 (1954): 86–108.

104. For example, the Saepta was a new structure that replaced the wooden Ovile. Caesar so thoroughly reworked the existing Circus Maximus Pliny said it was built by the Dictator; *HN*.36.102.

105. Favro, "Roman Forum," 17–24.

106. These so-called *cuniculi* may date to the time of Sulla. On the tunnels, see G. F. Carettoni, "Le gallerie ipogee del Foro Romano e i Ludi gladiatori forensi," *BullCom* 76 (1956–8): 23–44; F. Coarelli, *Il Foro Romano, 2: periodo repubblicano e augusteo* (Rome: Edizioni Quasar 1985), 222–8; Richardson, *New Topographical Dictionary*, 173.

107. Being smaller and shorter, the earlier basilicas in the Forum had not as crisply defined the sides of the central area (fig. 13).

108. Dio Cassius explains, "the rostra, which was formerly in the center of the forum, was moved back to its present position"; 43.49; F. W. Shipley, "Concerning the Rostra of Julius Caesar," *Papers on Classical Subjects, in Memory of John Max Wulfing*, edited by F. Shipley (St. Louis: Washington University Press 1930), 88–102.

109. There were three fig trees in the Forum Romanum, all associated with famous early Romans. That before the new Rostra was self sown on the spot where Curtius had sacrificed himself for the good of Rome, a positive association for Caesar as savior of the city. Nearby, in the Comitium, stood the famous Ficus Ruminalis under which Romulus, ancestor of the Dictator, was suckled by the

she-wolf. The third fig tree stood before the Temple of Saturn; Pliny *HN*.15. 77–8; Evans, *Persuasion*, 75–8.

110. Possibly the Lapis Niger and the solitary fig tree acted as pivots angling attention north toward the planned Temple of Felicitas and new Curia Julia under construction.

111. Ulrich has argued persuasively that the Temple of Venus Genetrix emulates the Metellan phase of the Temple of Castor and Pollux in the Forum Romanum, which had lateral stairs, an octastyle configuration, and a high podium used for public proclamations. He also explores in depth the functions of the Forum's lateral rooms, mistakenly called *tabernae* or shops; "Julius Caesar," 74–5, 78–9. In a separate article, he analyses the water display located in the complex; "The Appiades Fountain of the Forum Iulium," *MdI* 93 (1986): 405–23; cf. Ov.*ArsAm*.1.81–2; 3.450–2.

112. See the view of the Forum Julium in the reconstruction by J. Buhlmann and A. Wagner, *Das Alte Rom mit dem triumphzuge kaiser Constantin's im jahre 312 n.Chr.* (Munich: F. Hanfstaengl kunstverlag 1902).

113. A comprehensive examination of Hellenistic analogs is found in Einar Gjerstad, "Die Ursprungsgeschichte der römischen Kaiserfora," *SkrRom* 10 (1944): 40–71. Caesar created similar enclosures specifically for his own worship at Alexandria and Cyrene; Sjöqvist, "Kaisareion," 86–108; Hastrup, "Forum Iulium," 54–5.

114. L. Richardson Jr. argues that colonnades did not unify the Forum Pompeianum until the first century A.D.; *Pompeii, An Architectural History* (Baltimore: Johns Hopkins University Press 1988), 261–3. On Italian fora, see J. Russell, "The Origin and Development of Republican Forums," *Phoenix* 22:4 (Winter 1968): 304–22.

115. The sculptor depicted Alexander's horse with human feet, a trait of Caesar's

favorite mount; Suet.*Caes*.61.1. Regarding other art in the Forum Julium, see Pliny *HN*.8.155; 34.18; 35.156; Anderson, *Historical Topography*, 47–8.

116. Suet.*Caes*.78. Caesar consciously manipulated or selected environments to enhance his superiority. While on campaign, he carried mosaic floors, and undoubtedly received his commanders, allies, and enemies while seated atop the tesselated platform; Suet.*Caes*.46.

117. Caesar's connection with Jupiter was reenforced by the awning running from his residence in the Forum up to the Capitoline, and by references to the general as "Jupiter Julius"; DioCass.44.6.4; Weinstock, *Divus Iulius*, 12, 305, 309. Before his death, Caesar had not outlined any major building projects on the Palatine, perhaps because the hill was primarily a residential enclave of the optimates.

118. Cic.*Att*.13.33a, July 9. Today, the law is referred to as the *Lex de urba augenda*; Zwi Yavetz, *Julius Caesar and his Public Image* (London: Thames and Hudson 1983), 159–60.

119. Cic.*Att*.13.35; July 13. The planner is described as the "namesake" of Atticus. Although that may imply he was Greek, the translation "fellow countryman [of the Greek Atticus]" is misleading.

120. Romans considered land on the right bank unhealthy and distant; Gell.19.17.1; Hor.*Sat*.1.9.18.

121. The exact route of the realigned river cannot be determined. Similarly, the precise location of the Horti Caesaris is unknown. Nevertheless, the large size of the gardens increases the possibility that Caesar intended to enhance the value of his own property through the Tiber realignment; Grimal, *Jardins*, 116–17; cf. Zanker, *Images*, 19–20; H. I. Marrou, *A History of Education in Antiquity* (New York: New American Library 1956), 278–9.

122. Caesar planned other large hydraulic projects in Italy including the draining of the Pontine marshes and Lake Fucinus; Plut.*Vit.Caes*.58; Suet.*Caes*.44.

123. Appian notes that by the end of the Civil War, the population of Rome had decreased 50%; *BCiv*.2.102.

124. DioCass.43.47; Suet.*Caes*.41; J. P. V. D. Balsdon, *Romans and Aliens* (Chapel Hill: University of North Carolina Press 1979), 14–16.

125. Suet.*Caes*.42; Cic.*Phil*.1.9.23. By making thousands homeless, the large construction projects of Caesar may have fomented social unrest in Rome.

126. Favro, "Pater Urbis," 69–71. The incomplete condition of the *Lex Julia Municipalis* at the time of passage prevents a clear understanding of Caesar's ideas for urban management. Apparently, the Dictator considered a broad range of issues, not only for Rome, but for all the Italian municipalities; M. Cary, "Notes on the Legislation of Julius Caesar," *JRS* 19 (1929): 116–19; Yavetz, *Julius Caesar*, 117–22.

127. If streets were not properly maintained, the aediles were to contract for repairs and bill the property owner. According to the *Lex Julia Municipalis*, the four magistrates known as the *quattuorviri* cleaned streets in the city, and the *duumviri* cleaned those within one mile of the capital (nos. 50–2); E. G. Hardy, *Six Roman Laws* (Oxford: Clarendon Press 1911), 152.

128. Before the *Lex Julia Municipalis*, traffic in Rome was restricted by design. For example, the surrounding portico and stairs of the Forum Julium made the central space inaccessible to wheeled traffic. In other urban spaces, entries were blocked with bollards.

129. Perhaps Caesar used his position as Pontifex Maximus to justify his actions. Ironically among the temples destroyed was one to Pietas, the personification of duty fulfilled to family and the community; Pliny *HN*.7.121.

130. Pliny *HN*.15.78. Caesar may have also caused the destruction of the Basilica Sempronia in the Forum Romanum because it was no longer mentioned after construction of the Basilica Julia.

131. Proscriptions under Caesar increased the amount of public land both inside and outside of Rome; DioCass.43.47; I. Shatzman, *Senatorial Wealth and Roman Politics* (Brussels: Latomus 1975), 350–5.

CHAPTER 4. IDENTITY: EVOLVING AUGUSTAN MOTIVES

1. The public funding of a Roman burial was a great sign of honor. As a further distinction, the aediles lifted restrictions limiting expenditure on Caesar's funeral; Cic.*Phil.* 9.16; Weinstock, *Divus Iulius,* 348–9.

2. Sulla's state-funded funeral had earlier demonstrated the difficulties of having a single urban procession. The long parade stretched on for hours before mourners reached the tomb site; App.*BCiv*.1. 106.496; Plut.*Vit.Sul*.38.3.

3. For a different periodization of the Augustan Age, see F. Coarelli, "Rom. Die Stadtplanung von Caesar bis Augustus," and Henner v. Hesberg, "Die Veränderung des Erscheinungsbildes der Stadt Rom unter Augustus," in Hofter, *Kaiser Augustus,* 68–80, 93–115.

4. Suet.*Caes*.87.

5. Suet.*Caes*.85; App.*BCiv*.2.148; Weinstock, *Divus Iulius,* 365–401. Caesar was referred to as Divus Julius as early as September, 44 B.C.; Cic.*Phil*.2.110; C. Nicolet, *Space, Geography, and Politics in the Early Roman Empire,* translated by Hélène Leclerc (Ann Arbor: University of Michigan Press 1991), 40.

6. The people of Rome reacted violently to the killing of Amatius, opposing Antony's soldiers in the Forum and burning a shop where statues of Caesar allegedly were being destroyed; App.*BCiv*.3.3.

7. DioCass.47.14. Among the hundreds who fell during the triumvirs' proscriptions was the orator Cicero who had sealed his fate with memorable speeches against Antony, the *Philippics*.

8. Taxes for the rest of Italy were reduced to a fourth for one year; DioCass.48.9.

9. F. W. Shipley, "Building Operations in Rome from the Death of Caesar to the Death of Augustus," *MAAR* 9 (1931): 45–58; H. H. Scullard, *Festivals and Ceremonies of the Roman Republic* (London: Thames and Hudson 1981), 259–79.

10. Augustus declined the triumph, but accepted the right to wear a crown and triumphal garb on January 1; DioCass. 53.26.5.

11. Scholars debate whether "triumphal honors" (*ornamenta triumphalia*) refers to an *ovatio*, also known as an "equestrian triumph" or to some other type of recognition developed in the Augustan Age; cf. DioCass.54.24.7, 33.5, 34.3; Suet.*Claud*. 1; E. Künzl, *Der römische Triumph* (Munich: C. H. Beck 1988), 100–4.

12. Tiberius was awarded an *ovatio* even though he was technically a legate fighting under Augustus' auspices. It took place before the death of Drusus, though the exact date is uncertain; DioCass. 55.2.4.

13. This interpretation is based on J. Pais, *Res Gestae Divi Augusti* (Paris: Société d'Edition Les Belles Lettres 1977), 165, 184.

14. Plancus completed the Temple of Saturn in 31 B.C., after he had reconciled with Octavian; Cic.*Phil*.5.40. The Rostra Julia stood directly east of the Saturn temple and at a lower level. In 43 B.C., the Senate honored Octavian with an equestrian statue atop the Rostra; a statue was voted Lepidus when he proclaimed fealty to the Republic; Vell.Pat.2.56.4; 2.61.2. Several statues of Caesar also stood in the area; DioCass.44.4.5; Richardson, *New Topographical Dictionary,* 336–7.

15. These statues may have included two of the four caryatids formerly used to hold

16. The only triumphal project outside the Campus and the Forum was the Temple of Diana on the Aventine renovated by L. Cornificius in the late 30s B.C. with funds from his African triumph.

17. The exact location of Statilius' amphitheater is still debated; *CIL* 2.3556; Tac.*Ann.* 3.72; DioCass.51.23.

18. DioCass.48.49. A capable general, Agrippa won many battles during the civil wars and after. He was awarded triumphs three times: in 37, 19, and 14 B.C. In each instance, he declined, directing all notoriety toward Octavian; DioCass.54.11, 24. Nevertheless, Suetonius included him among a list of triumphators and their buildings, and Agrippa apparently assumed the responsibilities of a triumphator, including the construction of public structures such as the Diribitorium, a huge structure for the counting of votes; *Aug.*29; DioCass.48.20; 49.38; 55.8.

19. Suet.*Aug.*22. According to contemporary rumors, the abolishment of debts allowed Octavian to collect good will at a time when he had little hope to collect cash; DioCass.49.15.

20. Scholars have questioned whether the coins minted in the teens B.C. depict a temporary temple to Mars erected on the Capitoline, or merely commemorate Octavian's vow; *BMCRE* 1.58 no. 315, 65–6 nos. 366–75, 114 no. 704; Zanker, *Images*, 187; Richardson, *New Topographical Dictionary*, 245–6; Weinstock, *Divus Iulius*, 131.

21. Pliny *HN.*36.26; Ahenobarbus may have restored the Temple of Neptune as a sign of fealty to Antony if, as recently speculated, the structure was reworked in the second century B.C. by the general's grandfather; Anne Kuttner, "Some New Grounds for Narrative. Marcus Antonius's Base (*The Ara Domitti Ahenobarbi*) and Republican Biographies," in Holliday, *Narrative and Event*, 198–229.

22. To be an official triumph the celebratory parade had to take place in Rome and have senatorial approval; Antony ignored both provisions; Vell.Pat.2.88.4; Plut.*Vit. Pomp.*50; DioCass.49.40.

23. F. Coarelli, *Roma Sepolta* (Rome: Armando Curcio Editore 1984), 97–8.

24. Pliny *HN.*13.53; 36.28; E. La Rocca, "Der Apollo-Sosianus-Tempel," in Hofter, *Kaiser Augustus*, 129–35.

25. Dio Cassius confuses the Porticus Octavia with the Porticus Octaviae; 49.43.8; cf. Festus *Gloss.Lat.*460; I. Shatzman, *Senatorial Wealth and Roman Politics*, Collection Latomus 142 (Brussels: Latomus 1975), 367–70.

26. The reference in the *Res Gestae* probably refers first to booty from Dalmatia and second to the treasure of the Ptolemies; 21; Shatzman, *Senatorial Wealth*, 357–77.

27. According to Nepos, the equestrian epicurean Atticus suggested Octavian undertake this project; *Att.*20.3. The rebuilding was so extensive, Octavian could claim the Temple of Jupiter Feretrius as a new structure; *ResG.*19; cf. Livy 4.20; Dion. Hal.*Ant.Rom.*2.34.

28. The *spolia opima* had been placed in the Temple of Jupiter Feretrius by A. Cornelius Cossus in 428 B.C. and M. Claudius Marcellus in 222 B.C., Livy 4.19; *CIL* 1.2:22. More recently, Caesar had been allowed to offer the *spolia opima* as an honor, not a right; DioCass.44.4.

29. Octavian took great pains to show that earlier donors of the *spolia opima* held higher offices than M. Licinius Crassus; DioCass.51.24.

30. Controversy over the Augustan arches in the Forum Romanum is currently a topic of heated debate. For an intelligent overview, see Fred Kleiner, "The Study of Roman Triumphal and Honorary Arches 50 Years after Kähler," *JRA* 2 (1989): 198–200.

31. Zanker, *Images*, 15.

32. P. C. Rossetto, *Il sepolcro del fornaio Marco Virgilio Eurisace a Porta Maggiore,*

I Monumenti romani 5 (Rome: Istituto di studi romani 1973).

33. Ovid identifies the libraries in the Atrium Libertatis as the first facilities in Rome open to the public; *Tr.*3.1.71. Like all Roman examples, these included two collections, one for Greek and another for Latin works. The libraries in the Atrium Libertatis were completed before 28 B.C., the death date of Varro who was named as the only living author included in the collection; Pliny *HN.*7.115. According to Dio Cassius, Pollio decorated the libraries with artwork from his eastern campaigns; 48.41.7.

34. Weinstock, *Divus Iulius*, 399.

35. DioCass.45.6; Pliny *HN.*35.156. Octavian sponsored a second rebuilding of the Basilica Julia after a fire and rededicated the building in A.D. 12; *ResG.*20. He also completed Caesarean projects throughout the Empire, including the new market begun by the Dictator in Athens; *IG.* 2:2 1100, 3175.

36. Caesar had planned to fill in the unhealthy Naumachia Caesaris in the Campus Martius and use the site for his new temple to Mars; Suet.*Caes.*44.2.

37. The intricate sculptural program of this complex has been analyzed by many; see Joachim Ganzert and Valentin Kockel, "Augustusforum und Mars-Ultor-Tempel," in Hofter, *Kaiser Augustus*, 149–99; B. A. Kellum, "Sculptural Programs and Propaganda in Augustan Rome: The Temple of Apollo on the Palatine and the Forum of Augustus," Ph.D. dissertation (Harvard University 1982), 106–56; Zanker, *Images*, 194–5, 209–15.

38. Antony allegedly took money from the Temple of Ops as well as other sources to help purchase the fealty of the legions; Cic.*Att.*14.14.5; 16.14.4; DioCass.45.24; Shatzman, *Senatorial Wealth*, 299–301.

39. Plut.*Vit.Ant.*54. On the use and meaning of the phrase *urbi et orbi*, see E. Bréguet, "Urbi et Orbi, Un cliché et un theme," *Hommages à Marcel Renard* (Brussels: Latomus 1969), 140–52.

40. Antony unwisely sent a dispatch to Rome boasting about this gift, known as the Donation of Alexandria; fortunately, his supporters forestalled a public reading; Plut.*Vit.Ant.*58.

41. Plut.*Vit.Ant.*4, 24, 60. According to Appian, Octavian noted that Caesar would have adopted Antony if only he had accepted kinship with Aeneas instead of Hercules; *BCiv.*3.2.16. Ironically, years later, Tiberius compared Augustus to Hercules; DioCass.56.36.

42. Prop.4.6.21, 23; Verg.*Aen.*8.678–80, 715.

43. The Romans adopted the Greek god Apollo early in their history. By the late first century B.C., he was associated with the higher developments of civilization such as elevated moral and religious principles, and healing. Aeneas was both ancestor of Caesar and an ideal hero for the Romans. He was dutiful, self-sacrificing and, in stark contrast to Anthony, had abandoned an African queen in favor of Rome; L. Storoni Mazzolani, *The Idea of the City in Roman Thought*, translated by S. O'Donnell (Bloomington: Indiana University Press 1970), 158.

44. Prop.4.6.40; Suet.*Aug.*94; DioCass.45.2–3. Underscoring the association with Apollo was a statue of the deity in the Forum Augustum allegedly bearing Octavian's features; Serv.*onVerg.Ecl.* 4.10; cf. Storoni Mazzolani, *Idea of City*, 150–2. On the feud between Antony and Octavian, see Suet.*Aug.*70; DioCass.48.39.

45. Pliny *HN.*36.36. When discussing this arch, F. Kleiner succinctly explains Octavian's calculated association with three fathers: C. Octavius, J. Caesar, and Apollo; "The Arch in Honor of C. Octavius and the Fathers of Augustus," *Historia* 37.3 (1988): 347–57.

46. Vell.Pat.2.81; DioCass.49.15.5. Suetonius interpreted the lightning strike as evidence of Apollo's own divine intervention in site

selection; *Aug*.29. As Zanker has pointed out, the physical connection between house and temple was dangerously close to Hellenistic ensembles with god and king residing together as at Pergamon and Alexandria. To downplay this monarchical association, Octavian may have selected a modest exterior for his house; *Images,* 51.

47. For a fuller account of the iconographical program, see B. A. Kellum, "Sculptural Programs and Propaganda in Augustan Rome: the Temple of Apollo on the Palatine," in Winkes, *The Age of Augustus,* 169–76.

48. Jean-Michel Roddaz, *Marcus Agrippa,* BEFAR 253 (1984), 145–6. In 21 B.C., Agrippa wed Julia, daughter of Augustus.

49. A *cura* was the responsibility for a specific project assigned by the Senate or consuls. The curator held the *cura* until completing the particular task; D. Favro, "*Pater urbis:* Augustus as city father of Rome," *JSAH* 51 (March 1992), 75–7; O. F. Robinson, *Ancient Rome, City Planning and Administration* (London: Routledge 1992), 47–58.

50. Agrippa developed aqueducts specifically to serve areas of Augustan development; Harry B. Evans, "Agrippa's Water Plan," *AJA* 86:3 (1982): 401–11. The Pons Agrippae, identifiable from a Claudian marker, may have been part of this comprehensive plan; *CIL* 31545.

51. DioCass.49.43; Pliny *HN*.36.122; Frontin.23.98. In some ways, the celebrations of 33 B.C. recalled those surrounding a triumph.

52. DioCass.53.23. The nationalization of art could be considered a logical part of the *cura urbis;* Pliny *HN*.35.26. With the artwork displayed in his library, Pollio revealed a similar aim "[to make] works of genius the property of the public"; Pliny *HN*.35.10.

53. Vell.Pat.2.38. The Temple of Janus was closed two more times under Augustus; Suet.*Aug*.22; *ResG*.13.

54. Lois Craig and the staff of the Federal Architecture Project, *The Federal Presence: Architecture, Politics, and Symbols in United States Government Buildings* (Cambridge, MA: MIT Press 1978), 134.

55. The Senate by this time had swollen to 1,000 members. Augustus reduced it to 800 and then later to 600; *ResG*.8.

56. DioCass.53.1–13. In the settlement of 27 B.C., Augustus made no specific provisions regarding the city of Rome; *ResG*.34. *Princeps senatus* was a traditional Republican title voted to Agustus. His selection of *princeps* as an unofficial title indicating his constitutional position, however, was not based upon an abbreviation of *princeps senatus,* but on Republican application of the term to one prominent statesmen; Cic.*Pis*.25, *Dom*.66, *Sest*.84; *Att*. 8.9.4. In particular, the terms *princeps/ principatus* contrasted with the more autocratic *dominus/dominatio.*

57. The astrologer Tarutius, friend of Varro, prepared a horoscope for Romulus indicating that the great king, like Augustus, had been conceived under Capricorn and born under Libra; Plut.*Rom*.12; Kenneth Scott, "The Identification of Augustus with Romulus–Quirinus," *TAPA* 56 (1925): 82–105.

58. Suet.*Aug*.7; DioCass.53.16; *ResG*.19. The name "augustus," in any event, could be linked with Romulus; the poet Ennius told how Romulus "By august omen founded the city of Rome" (*Augusto augurio postquam incluta condita Roma est;* Suet. *Aug*.7).

59. DioCass.53.21. On other prodigy associated with Augustus, see Suet.*Aug*.95.

60. *CIL* 6.873. Modern historians have often praised the *princeps* for restoring the Republic, yet authors of the first century did not record that Augustus overtly made this claim. He did, however, refer to the reinstitution of different functions and offices after the period of unrest; cf. Vell.Pat.2.89; Suet.*Aug*.28.

61. D. E. Strong, "The Administration of Public Building in Rome during the Later Republic and Early Empire," *BICS* 15 (1968): 66.

62. Zanker, *Images,* 101–2.

63. In 21 B.C., Agrippa curtailed Egyptian rites that were again invading the city; he forbade anyone to perform them even in the suburbs within one mile of the city; DioCass.53.2.4; 54.6.6.

64. The killing of the current *pontifex maximus* would have been a sacrilege. Lepidus died of natural causes in the late teens B.C.; Suet.*Aug.*31. Regarding Augustus and the position of Pontifex Maximus, see G. W. Bowersock, "The Pontificate of Augustus," in Raaflaub/Toher, *Between Republic and Empire,* 380–94.

65. DioCass.53.16; *ResG.*34. Laurels stood before the headquarters of the oldest priesthoods, at the Regia, the temple of Vesta, and the seat of the *flamines* and *pontifices;* Zanker, *Images,* 93.

66. *ResG.*20; cf. Suet.*Aug.*30.2; DioCass. 53.2; Hanz Günter Martin, "Die Templekultbilder," in Hofter, *Kaiser Augustus,* 251–60.

67. DioCass.56.40. By keeping the name of the original donor and original foundation date, Augustus may have avoided assuming the ongoing responsibility for a temple's upkeep; Duane R. Stuart, "The Reputed Influence of *Dies Natalis,*" *TAPA* 36 (1905): 57; and "Imperial Methods of Inscription on Restored Buildings: Augustus and Hadrian," *AJA* 9 (1905): 427–40. By his marriage to Livia, Augustus had two stepsons, Drusus and Tiberius.

68. Gros, *Aurea Templa,* 31–8; Scullard, *Festivals,* 188, 264. Temple dedication dates are discussed more fully in Chapter 6.

69. Tradition required the Senate to perform its duties on consecrated ground, so the Curia was sanctified as a templum.

70. Vell.Pat.2.90; *ResG.*13. Buildings associated with military victories were few in Rome during this phase. Even the arch in the Forum Romanum awarded Augustus in 19 B.C. commemorated a negotiated peace, rather than a military victory; DioCass.54.8.3. Not surprisingly, rivals of the *princeps* had little opportunity to head armies, or to have victories acknowledged.

71. The exact form and orientation of the Agrippan Pantheon are still a subject of debate; cf. M. T. Boatwright, *Hadrian and the City of Rome* (Princeton: Princeton University Press 1987), 36–7, 43–6; W. Loerke, "Georges Chedanne and the Pantheon," *Modulus* (1982): 40–55; W. L. MacDonald, *The Pantheon. Design, Meaning and Progeny* (Cambridge, MA: Harvard University Press 1976), 77–84; K. de Fine Licht, *The Rotunda in Rome. A Study of Hadrian's Pantheon* (Copenhagen: Syldendal 1968), 172–6, 191–4.

72. *ResG.*20; cf. Suet.*Aug.*31.5; Ronald Syme, *The Roman Revolution,* repr. (Oxford: Clarendon Press 1939), 50, 316–18.

73. Cf. Suet.*Aug.*31; Zanker, *Images,* 102–3.

74. Vell.Pat.2.130. For a more detailed account of Augustan provisions for municipal care, see Favro, *"Pater urbis."*

75. Suet.*Aug.*56; Anderson, *Historical Topography,* 66–7.

76. Suet.*Aug.*32.5. The hall where the murder took place was transformed into a privy at an unspecified date; DioCass.47.19.

77. Frontin.98; Roddaz, *Agrippa,* 151.

78. DioCass.53.22-23; 54.8; Pliny *HN.*3.66. Richardson associates the Milliarium Aureum with the Umbilicus Romae, which also marked the city center; *New Topographical Dictionary,* 404.

79. For example, after a flood in the late twenties B.C., the consuls restored the Pons Fabricius between the island and the left bank; DioCass.53.33; *CIL* 6:1305.

80. The warehouses from this period include the Horrea Agrippiana of the mid-twenties B.C. built by Agrippa or in his honor, and the Horrea Lolliana believed to be a project by M. Lollius, consul of 21 B.C.; G. Rickman, *Roman Granaries and Store*

Buildings (Cambridge: Cambridge University Press 1971), 89–90, 110–11, 165; *CIL* 6.31545, 9972, 10026.

81. DioCass.54.2. Ancient sources on the date of Rufus' aedileship are contradictory. Dio Cassius places it in 26 B.C.; 53.24. Velleius Paterculus records that Rufus became praetor after the aedileship, and candidate for the consulship in 19 B.C., thus making him aedile in the year 21/20 B.C.; 2.91; cf. Sen.*Clem*.1.9.6. If Dio Cassius is right, then Augustus assigned the 600 slaves to the aediles in response to the actions of Egnatius Rufus; if Velleius Paterculus is correct, Rufus made a point of not using the Augustan fire brigade. The *princeps'* absence from Rome 22–19 B.C. resulted in serious upheavals. In 19 B.C., Egnatius Rufus plotted against Augustus, was discovered, and executed.

82. Hieron.*ab Abr*.1991; Tac.*Ann*.6.11. The regular prefecture was established in A.D. 13 with L. Piso, who held office for 20 years.

83. Possibly at the same time, Augustus placed an obelisk from Heliopolis on the spina of the Circus Maximus; *ResG*.19; Pliny *HN*.36.71.

84. Pliny *HN*. 34.62; 35.26; 36.189; F. Yegül, *Baths and Bathing in Classical Antiquity* (New York and Cambridge, MA: Architectural History Foundation/MIT Press 1992), 133–7.

85. Suet.*Aug*.40, 44; Verg.*Aen*.1.282; Zanker, *Images*, 162–4. The emphasis on the toga, traditional dress of patrician Romans, was an obvious dig at Anthony, who had conspicuously donned eastern clothing; DioCass.50.25.3.

86. Zanker, *Images*, 154–5.

87. Literature abounds, with metaphorical references to Rome as *caput* and the empire as *corpus*; Livy 1.16.7; Ov.*ArsAm*. 1.15.26; Pliny *HN*.28.15, 3.38. The reconceptualization of Rome as capital is reflected contemporaneously by references to Rome's residents as distinct from the original thirty-five tribes; Nicolet, *Space*, 194–8.

88. Pliny *HN* 3.17. Vipsania Polla, sister of Agrippa, built the porticus east of the Via Flaminia in which the map was displayed; DioCass.55.8. The map and Agrippa's written geography are discussed at length in Nicolet, *Space*, 98–111; R. Moynihan, "Geographical Mythology and Roman Imperial Ideology," in Winkes, *The Age of Augustus*, 149–62.

89. These may not be the actual words of Maecenas, but those created by the author to reflect his own notions about imperial absolutism; DioCass.52.30. Compare the content with similar ideas about the propaganda value of architecture voiced by Pope Nicholas V, "the common man is innocent of literary matters and devoid of culture . . . he must be moved by some material work lest his faith fade away with the passing of time. If instead to the teaching of the scholar is added the confirmation of grandiose buildings, of monuments in a certain guise eternal . . . popular faith will be reinforced and stabilized"; quoted in S. Kostof, *A History of Architecture, Settings and Rituals* (New York: Oxford University Press 1985), 410.

90. Strabo wrote of Alexandria: "the city contains most beautiful public precincts"; 17.1.8.

91. Augustus' sister Octavia dedicated a library in the Porticus Octaviae in honor of her son Marcellus; Plut.*Vit.Marc*.30; Ov.*Tr*.1.

92. Suet.*Aug*.100; Strab.5.3.8; Prop.3.2.22. Recent scholarship proposes the statue atop the Mausoleum represented Augustus in a quadriga; John Pollini, "The Gemma Augustea: Ideology, Rhetorical Imagery, and the Creation of a Dynastic Narrative," in Holliday, *Narrative and Event*, 285, fig. 86. The gardens surrounding the tumulus may have absorbed the groves and walks of private *horti* in the area, perhaps including those belonging to

Pompey; P. Grimal, *Les Jardins romains* BEFAR 155 (Paris: Presses Universitaires de France 1969), 125, 171.

93. Scholars have long argued the symbolism and associations of the Mausoleum. The relationship to eastern royal tumuli near Troy, birthplace of Augustus' ancestors, is examined by R. Holloway, "The Tomb of Augustus and the Princes of Troy," *AJA* 70 (1966): 171–3. K. Kraft considers the relationship to the Hellenistic tomb of Antony and Cleopatra; "Der Sinn des Mausoleums des Augustus," *Historia* 16 (1967): 189–206; J.-Ch. Richard likewise explores parallels among royal tombs; "Mausoleum," *Latomus* 29 (1970): 370–88. The novelty of the monument is considered by M. Eisner, "Zur Typologie der Mausoleen des Augustus und des Hadrian," *MDAI(R)* 86 (1979): 319–24. The connection with the tomb of Alexander the Great was especially strong; D. Kienast, "Augustus und Alexander," *Gymnasium* (1969): 430–56. According to Pliny, Augustus also constructed a funeral mound for a horse, perhaps in emulation of the tomb Alexander made honoring his mount Bucephalus; Pliny *HN*.8.155.

94. For references to Etruscan tumuli, see E. Kornemann, "Octavians Romulusgrab," *Klio* 31 (1938): 81–5; cf. Zanker, *Images*, 72. Burial in the Campus Martius was granted by the Senate as a sign of honor. Here could be found tumuli honoring the daughter of Caesar and perhaps another for Sulla. Because the Mausoleum Augustum rose in the northernmost section of the flood plain, it may not have required senatorial approval.

95. DioCass.53.30.5; 54.28; 55.2.3. Because Augustus remained healthy, his relatives began to fill the Mausoleum, beginning with Marcellus, who was laid to rest while the tomb was still under construction. Gaius and Lucius, the grandsons of Augustus, may have received a separate cenotaph or memorial in Rome; DioCass.78.24.3.

96. Censors were usually elected quinquennially. Augustus held the censorship again in 11 B.C.; *ResG*.6. The *princeps* introduced various social legislation, including provisions directing marriage, childbearing, and behavior; DioCass. 53.13; 54.2, 16; 56.10.

97. Gell.2.24; cf. Tac.*Ann*.3.53–4. Augustus refers to an earlier law proposed by Rutilius Rufus regarding building heights; Suet.*Aug*.89.

98. The House of Augustus has been provisionally identified with the structure located between the Scalae Caci and Temple of Apollo. The elaborate interior wall paintings of this building would not have been readily visible to external urban observers, thus the exterior could legitimately be called "modest"; Suet.*Aug*.72. Until further evidence is uncovered, caution should be exercised and this *domus*, along with the so-called House of Livia to the north, identified as part of an Augustan enclave rather than the specific residence of the *princeps*; G. Carettoni, *Das Haus des Augustus auf dem Palatin* (Mainz am Rhein: P. Von Zabern 1983); Richardson, *New Topographical Dictionary*, 281.

99. Ov.*Fasti* 6.640–8. A similar story involves the impressive columns found in the house of Scaurus; Augustus demolished this extravagant residence at least in part, and incorporated the columns to a public use in the stage building of the theater dedicated to Marcellus; Asc. *Scaur*.45.

100. Suet.*Aug*.31; Verg.*Aen*.6.792; Vell.Pat.2. 89.4. Regarding the invocation of a restored golden age, see Peter Holliday, "Time, History and Ritual on the Ara Pacis Augustae," *ArtB* 72.4 (December 1990): 542–57; Zanker, *Images*, 167–72.

101. *CIL* 6.32323, 90–109. Some events were held in wooden stages and other temporary facilities erected in the Campus Martius. The Theater of Marcellus was

102. Fires damaged the Forum in 14 and 7 B.C. and the Aventine in 16 B.C.; DioCass.54.19, 24; 55.8.

103. Mentioned only in the late regionary catalogs, the Crypta Balbi are generally thought to describe a covered walkway associated with the theater; Richardson, *New Topographical Dictionary*, 101.

104. Pliny *HN*.36.60; DioCass.54.25; Vell. Pat.2.51; Solin.29.7.

105. Lares were identified with both ghosts of the dead and farmland deities. Over time, they became guardians of the crossroads and of the State in general; Wissowa, *Ges.Abh*.274; Ov.*Fasti* 5.129.

106. H. Kunckel, "Der Römische Genius," *RM-EH* Sup. 20 (1974): 22–8.

107. Ov.*Fasti* 5.143–7; *CIL* 6.449, 452; *ILS* 3613–21; Martin, "Templekultbilder," 258. Augustus may have chosen to promote the shrines of the crossroads in part because the guardian Lares were traditionally linked with Diana, sister of his patron Apollo; Ov.*Fasti* 5.135–45. Around 16 B.C., he also restored a shrine on the Via Sacra to the lares who served as the guardians of all Rome; *ResG*.19.

108. Suet.*Aug*.31.3; G. Niebling, "*Laribus Augustis Magistri Primi. Der Beginn des Compitalkultes der Lares und des Genius Augusti*," *Historia* (1956): 303–31. The altars would also be adorned in the fall, on the birthday of Augustus.

109. DioCass.54.27; M. Guarducci, "Enea e Vesta," *RM* 78 (1971): 102.

110. Ov.*Fasti* 4.949–54; DioCass.54.27.3; L. R. Taylor, *The Divinity of the Roman Emperor* (Middletown, CT: American Philological Association 1931), 184.

111. Ov.*Fasti* 5.563–6; Zanker, *Images*, 210–15; A. Degrassi, *Inscriptiones Italiae* 13.3 (1937): 1–36. An additional Augustan sculptural display may have been placed at the Lupercal, though the evidence is scant; *ResG*. 19; *CIL* 6.912.

112. Kellum, "Sculptural Programs," 110–12; Andrew Wallace-Hadrill, "The Social Structure of the Roman House," *PBSR* 56 n.s. 43 (1988): 43–97.

113. The cavalry commanders also celebrated yearly beside the steps of the Temple of Mars Ultor; DioCass.55.10. Regarding other activities in the Forum Augustum, including the Ludi Martiales and foreign affairs, see Anderson, *Historical Topography*, 91–6.

114. The ancestral portraits in *domus* atria were important socially and politically, as well as personally; A. N. Zadoks Josephus Jitta, *Ancestral portraiture in Rome* (Amsterdam: N.V. Noord-Hollandeche Uitgevers-Mij 1932), 32; D. and R. Rebuffat, "De Sidoine Apollinaire a la Tombe François," *Latomus* 37 (1978): 92–3. On elogia and *imagines*, see G. M. A. Hanfmann, "Observations on Roman portraiture," *Latomus* 11 (1953): 39; R. Bianchi Bandinelli, "Sulla formazione del ritratto romano," *Archeologia e Cultura* (Milan-Naples: R.Riccardi 1961), 172–88.

115. L. R. Taylor, "The Worship of Augustus in Italy," *TAPA* 51 (1920): 124–33; Anderson, *Historical Topography*, 96.

116. Ovid may have confused the temple in the Forum Augustum with a smaller and earlier temple to Mars vowed in 20 B.C. (possibly never realized), as he lists the dedication day as May 12, not August 1; *Fasti* 5.548–85.

117. DioCass.10.8; *ResG*.23. Augustus constructed a new aqueduct, the Aqua Alsietina to bring water to the huge Naumachia Augusti; Frontin.1.11.22.

118. The title was also inscribed in the porch of Augustus' house and in the Curia Julia; *ResG*.35.

119. Bowersock examines the entire period from 13–9 B.C. and convincingly argues that Lepidus died in 13 B.C. Because the Pontifex Maximus traditionally took office in March, Augustus must have

120. M. Torelli, *Typology and Structure of Roman Historical Reliefs* (Ann Arbor: University of Michigan Press 1982), 29; Mommsen *RömStaatsr.*1.65–6; 3.1035.

121. The iconography of the Ara Pacis has occupied many scholars. The procession may represent either the consecration ceremony (*constitutio*) for the altar or that when Augustus became Pontifex Maximus, or a conflation of the two. For recent interpretations and references, see Holliday, "Ara Pacis"; B. A. Kellum, "What We see and Don't See. Narrative Structure and the Ara Pacis Augustae," *Art History* 17.1 (March 1994): 26–45; and D. E. E. Kleiner, *Roman Sculpture* (New Haven: Yale University Press 1992), 90–9, 119; Bowersock, "Principate," 383–5.

122. The mathematician Novius Facundus calibrated the sundial. Unfortunately, within seventy years, this scientific marvel was rendered inaccurate, perhaps due to an earthquake; Pliny *HN.*36.73. Before the Horologium Augusti, Rome's most prominent sundials were on the temples of Quirinus and Diana; Pliny *HN.*7.213; Censorinus, *DN.*23.6. Augustus underscored the difficulty of creating this monument by putting the ship that transported the obelisk on display in dry dock at Puteoli; Pliny *HN.*36.70.

123. The primary work on the Horologium Augusti is by E. Buchner, who wrote two articles on the subject in *Römische Mitteilungen* (1976, 1980), subsequently collected into a single monograph; *Die Sonnenuhr des Augustus* (Mainz am Rhein: P. Von Zabern 1982). He argues that the project measures the time of day, sun's shadow at noon, and progress of the days of the year, and interconnects various Augustan projects temporally. My description follows Buchner's interpreta-

tion, though is tempered with the more recent analysis by M. Schutz; "Zur Sonnenuhr des Augustus auf dem Marsfeld," *Gymnasium* 97 (1990): 432–57. The latter argues that the monument is a meridian line recording the sun's movement through the zodiac, not a meridian instrument as presented by Buchner. Whereas Schutz's interpretation is persuasive, a definitive answer is impossible given the many archaeological uncertainties, including the original level and arrangement of the pavement and height of the obelisk. Furthermore, the proximity and visual interconnections between the projects in the northern Campus Martius, coupled with Augustus' interest in astrology, the concerted promotion of his birthday on the autumnal equinox, and Pliny's association of the monument with the winter solstice, all broadly support Buchner's reconstruction; Pliny *HN.*36.72–3.

124. The renaming of the Basilica Julia, however, did not gain popular acceptance. The Porticus Julia became the Porticus of Gaius and Lucius; Suet.*Aug.*29; F. Coarelli, *Il Foro Romano, 2: periodo repubblicano e augusteo* (Rome: Edizioni Quasar 1985), 174–5; Zanker, *Images,* 81–2, 117.

125. The disposition of the arches to Augustus flanking the Temple of Divus Julius are a subject of ongoing controversy. For the purpose of this study, I will follow the interpretation of S. De Maria, who locates the Parthian Arch south of the temple and the Porticus of Gaius and Lucius to the north. Fred S. Kleiner provides a thoughtful overview of current research on the subject and wisely counsels scholars to await the final publication of Elisabeth Nedergaard's work in the area; "The study of Roman triumphal and honorary arches 50 years after Kähler," *JRA* 2 (1989): 198–200; cf. E. Nedergaard, "Zur Problematik der Augustusbögen auf dem Forum

126. Romanum," in Hofter, *Kaiser Augustus*, 224–39.
126. DioCass.55.9.10; 10.6–7; Anderson, *Historical Topography*, 93–5.
127. *ResG*.23.4.43–4. After the death of Agrippa, Tiberius grudgingly divorced his wife and married the twice-widowed Julia in 11 B.C. The implication was that Tiberius would serve as regent for Gaius and Lucius until their maturity. After the youths died, Augustus adopted Tiberius along with Agrippa Postumus, the third son of Agrippa and Julia, born after his father's death.
128. A strong woman and ambitious mother, Livia may have sought visibility in the city specifically at this time in order to promote Tiberius; no buildings bear her name before the last decade of the millennium. The Porticus Liviae was a crowd pleaser, with many artworks and rarities on display; Pliny *HN*.14.11; Ov.*ArsAm*.1.71; DioCass.55.8.
129. Ov.*Fasti* 6.637–8. The goddess Concordia apparently did not intercede on behalf of Tiberius. After being passed over for succession several times, he retired to Rhodes in 6 B.C. and only returned to Rome in A.D. 2.
130. DioCass.46.25; 55.8.5, 27.4. After the death of Augustus, Tiberius included his adopted father's name in building dedications; DioCass.57.10.1.
131. Suet.*Aug*.28. In another passage, Suetonius records that Augustus undertook civic projects to improve public health, not his own popularity; *Aug*.42.
132. DioCass.54.8. Six to eight men held the praetorship each year. Only two could become consuls in the succeeding election; others served in the provinces as propraetors. Augustus held up municipal curatorships as a means for expraetors to maintain the status of office holders in Rome; Favro, "*Pater Urbis*," 61–84.
133. DioCass.54.26. Lictors were executive attendants who preceded magistrates, clearing the way and calling upon passersby to offer salutations. In certain instances, they put the magistrates' decisions into effect.
134. Frontinus, *curator aquarum* over a century later, explained that until this permanent board Rome's water system "had been managed at the option of officials, and had lacked definite control"; 99. M. Valerius Messala Corvinus succeeded Agrippa as *curator aquarum* and held office until his death in A.D. 8; he was followed by Ateius Capito in A.D. 13. The five-year gap has not been explained. Perhaps the board was run by Messala's assistant, Postumius Sulpicius, expraetor. According to the *Lex Quinctia de aquaeductibus* of 9 B.C., praetors assumed the responsibilities of the *curator aquarum* when necessary; Frontin.102, 129.
135. Frontin.97–8, 101, 106, 108, 116, 125, 127. Aediles and censors still maintained control over Rome's water distribution in relation to games; for example, they alone could give permission for the flooding of the Circus Maximus. The curule aediles assigned men in each district to care for public fountains.
136. Frontin.99–100. In the same passage, Frontinus points out there was an attempt at parity among office holders; the water commissioners received the same number of secretaries, clerks, assistants, and criers as the curators of Rome's grain supply.
137. Suetonius is the only source for the *cura operum locorumque publicorum*; *Aug*.37. Kornemann and Gordon argue for a founding date of this board after 11 B.C. when the duties of the *curatores aquarum* were defined; Frontin.100; E. Kornemann, "*Curatores aedium sacrarum et operum locorumque publicorum*," *PW* 4 (1901) 1787: 43–7; A. E. Gordon, "Quintus Veranius Consul A.D. 49," *University of California Publications in Classical*

Archaeology, II (1934–52): 257, 279; Robinson, *Ancient Rome,* 54–6.

138. Suet.*Aug.*30; *CIL* 6.1235–6, 31542; *ResG.*20. These Augustan interventions did not eliminate floods, in large part because they did not address the problem of water control upstream; nevertheless, undertakings in Rome did reduce the magnitude of damage caused to the city; DioCass.54.26, 55.22, 56.27; Tac.*Ann.* 1.76. Under Tiberius, the jurisdiction of the curators extended to Ostia; Trajan expanded the office to include care of sewers as well; *CIL* 6.1239, 31549–50; 14.192.

139. DioCass.55.6.1. In 23 B.C., Augustus' imperium as provincial governor became *maius,* greater than that of all others, and was renewed at intervals of five or ten years (18, 13, 8 B.C. and again A.D. 3 and 13); P. A. Brunt and J. M. Moore, *Res Gestae Divi Augusti* (London: Oxford University Press 1967), 12–14, 83–5.

140. Varro, *Ling.*5.45; Livy 1.43; Dionys.4. 14; L. R. Taylor, "The Four Urban Tribes and the Four Regions of Ancient Rome," *RendPontAcc* 27 (1952–4), 225–38.

141. To cover urban territory outside the Republican regions and the limits of the *pomerium,* laws were made effective "to the edge of urban construction" or "in the city of Rome and within one mile of the city"; *Lex Julia Municipalis,* nos. 20–1, 26–7, 50–1; E. G. Hardy, *Six Roman Laws* (Oxford: Clarendon 1911), 150–3; M. Voigt, "Die römischen Baugesetze," *SBLeip* 55 (1903): 175–80; Robinson, *Ancient Rome,* 5–8. Pliny used the phrase "to the edge of the roofs"; *HN.*65–6.

142. Pliny lists the number of *vici* in the Flavian age as 265; *HN.*3.66. The *Regionaries,* a fourth-century catalog of Rome's XIV regions listed 424 *vici.* Suetonius writes that Augustus "divided the area of the city into regions and wards," yet it seems unlikely he fully reordered the

hundreds of existing *vici*; *Aug.*30; Nicolet, *Space,* 195–6.

143. Suet.*Aug.*30; DioCass.55.8.7. On the Septimontium, see Varro *Ling.*5.41. The importance of multiples of seven in Roman times is explored by William Loerke, "A Rereading of the Interior Elevation of Hadrian's Rotunda," *JSAH* 49 (March 1990): 22–43.

144. Platner/Ashby, *Dictionary,* 444–5; A. Von Gerkan, "Grenzen und Grossen der vierzehn Regionen Roms," *BJb* 149 (1949): 5–65. Seven regions fell inside the *pomerium*: II, III, IV, VI, VIII, X, XI. G. Gatti argued for 7 B.C., rather than 8 B.C., as the founding date of the XIV Regions though the evidence is inconclusive; "Ara marmorea del 'vicus State matris,'" *BullCom.*34 (1906): 198–200.

145. DioCass.55.8.7; Suet.*Aug.*30; Hardy, *Six Roman Laws,* 24–6.

146. The *vicomagistri* oversaw the drains and fountains of their respective wards and provided general police supervision; *CIL* 6.445, 975.

147. DioCass.55.8.6. By giving these duties to the ward supervisors, Augustus allowed the magistrates assigned to the regions more significant responsibilities; Nicolet, *Space,* 195.

148. DioCass.55.12.3, 26; Val.Max.1.8.11; Strab.5.3.7; Suet.*Aug.*25; Paulus, *Dig.*1. 15.1. Appian put the institution of the *vigiles* in 36 B.C., but was hesitant about this early date; *BCiv.*5.122. The organization of *cohortes vigilum* paralleled a similar post in Alexandria, so the establishment of the Roman force would logically be placed after Augustus visited Egypt in the late 30s B.C.; DioCass.51.10; Strab.17.1.12; A. H. M. Jones, *The Greek City from Alexander to Justinian* (Oxford: Clarendon Press 1940), 211–12; P. K. Baillie Reynolds, *The Vigiles of Imperial Rome* (London: Oxford University Press 1926), 17–21, 24, 43–63.

149. The prefect was also called the *praefectus vigilibus*; *Dig.*47.57.1. His exact

tenure is uncertain, though no record lists any prefect as holding office longer than five years; Tac.*Ann*.1.7; 9.31. A sepulchral relief in the Vatican depicts the vigiles' standard bearer in a military tunic; *CIL* 6.2987; Reynolds, *Vigiles*, 30–2, 98.

150. The jurist Paulus specifically notes that members of this corp should wear proper shoes for patrolling; *Dig*.1.15.3. As the primary official force active after dark the *vigiles* acted as a night police and the *praefectus vigilum* as judge over a version of night court with jurisdiction in minor matters. Over time, the *vigiles* developed a comic reputation similar to the Keystone Cops. Juvenal tells us they were nicknamed "Sparteoli" after their buckets; *Schol.Iul.Sat*.14.305. Petronius pictures them chopping down a door to get at a harmless cooking fire; *Satyr*.78; Reynolds, *Vigiles*, 14–15. In A.D. 7, Augustus levied a tax on the sale of slaves in part to fund the night watchmen; DioCass.55.31.

151. Although Augustus made administrative provisions regarding fire fighting and prevention, he did not legislate for fire-retardant materials as did later emperors; cf. Tac.*Ann*.15.43. His overall success in dealing with urban fires may have inspired placement of a sculpted Vulcan, god of fire, before the Temple of Mars Ultor.

152. Augustus favored freedmen in several instances. He enrolled individual freedmen as equestrians and improved marriage laws on their behalf. Acknowledging ingrained Roman fear of arming slaves or former slaves he employed *lib-erti* as soldiers only with great reluctance. The arming of freedmen as *vigiles* was clearly notable; Suet.*Aug*.25. After the first emperor, there was a reaction against freedmen receiving too many benefits; Pliny *HN*.33.32. Nevertheless, in A.D. 24, the *Lex Visellia* granted full citizenship to freedmen who served as vigiles for six years; Ulpian, fr.3.5; Reynolds, *Vigiles*, 66–7; Zanker, *Images*, 131.

153. Though wealthy and often possessing a high social status, equestrians generally eschewed politics in favor of the commercial world. Augustus courted this group; he revived ceremonies reconfirming their position in society and appointed *equites* to the various prefectures, excluding the *praefectus urbi*; Suet.*Aug*.38–9; P. A. Brunt, "Princeps and Equites," *JRS* 73 (1983): 42–75.

154. Although numerous inscriptions refer to the *vici*, the Lares, and the *vicomagistri*, few mention the municipal regions; *CIL* 6.445, 975; Nicolet, *Space*, 196.

155. This blatantly promotional list of "deeds accomplished" paralleled the form and content of funerary *elogia* in all but one aspect: it was written by the subject himself. There were, however, precedents. In the second century B.C., the younger Tiberius Sempronius Gracchus had displayed an engraved list of his achievements in the Temple of Mater Matuta; Livy 41.28.10. Augustus wrote sections of the *Res Gestae* before A.D. 14 and its contents apparently were known, yet he may not have placed the document on permanent display before his death; Suet.*Aug*.101.4; Brunt/Moore, *Res Gestae*, 2–3

CHAPTER 5. STRUCTURE: BUILDING AN URBAN IMAGE

1. Strabo's description is not literally what could be seen from a single point in Rome, but instead is a synthetic overview of the city center; 5.3.8; cf. Pliny *HN*.36.101.

2. On behalf of Napoleon III, Baron Georges Haussmann (1809–91) oversaw major alterations to Paris in the late nineteenth century. As a result, the term "Haussman-

nization" is applied to autocratic interventions imposed upon an urban fabric.

3. MacDonald, "Empire Imagery," 137–8.

4. Suetonius recognized that although Augustus owned several residential properties on the Palatine, including the magnificent house of Q. Lutatius Catulus, not all were used for living; *Gram.*17.

5. Axel Boëthius, *Etruscan and Early Roman Architecture* (Harmondsworth: Penguin Books 1978), 166–74; MacDonald, *Roman Empire I*, 8–10.

6. I am using the term handbook in a metaphorical sense, as the exact distribution of Vitruvius' text to ancient architects and patrons was probably limited.

7. Analyses of Vitruvius are proliferating at a rapid rate. A useful compilation of essays is found in the proceedings of an international symposium held in Leiden in 1987; H. Geertman and J. J. de Jong, eds., *Munus non Ingratum, BABESCH Supplement* 2 (Leiden: Stichting Bulletin Antieke Beschaving 1989).

8. MacDonald, *Roman Empire I*, 10–46.

9. This section explores the broad impact of temple forms upon the cityscape of Rome. For an in-depth examination of the Augustan temple types, see Gros, *Aurea Templa*.

10. Anne Kuttner explores how the style of reliefs conveys meaning in "Some New Grounds for Narrative. Marcus Antonius's Base (*The Ara Domitti Ahenobarbi*) and Republican Biographies," in Holliday, *Narrative and Event*, 198. On the ornament and style of the Temple of Apollo, see B. A. Kellum, "Sculptural Programs and Propaganda in Augustan Rome: The Temple of Apollo on the Palatine," in Winkes, *The Age of Augustus*, 169–71.

11. Though Vitruvius (3.3.4) calls the Temple of Apollo diastyle, the marble building must have been closer to systyle; Gros, *Aurea Templa*, 214.

12. Compare the temple shown on the Neo-Attic relief with the Temple of Magna Mater showing columns only on the façade (fig. 62); Zanker, *Images*, 62–5. The exact plan of the Apollo temple is unknown, but may have been pseudo-peripteral.

13. *CIL* 6:576; 30837; Livy 1.55.2; Serv. *Aen.*9.446. Catulus proposed to improve the proportions of the Capitoline Temple of Jupiter Optimus Maximus by lowering the surrounding area rather than drastically altering the building; Aul.Gell.2.10.

14. For a detailed examination of the proportions of this order, see Mark Wilson Jones, "Designing the Roman Corinthian order," *JRA* 2 (1989): 35–69.

15. The lower podium of the Temple of Divus Julius measured 3.5 meters in height; the second rose 2.6 meters. The podia of Augustan temples in Rome averaged 4.9 meters in height.

16. In addition to the two temples mentioned, those to Castor and Pollux and to Venus Genetrix may also have had lateral stairs; both were extensively reworked in the Augustan period; Gros, *Aurea Templa*, 106–8, 11; I. Nielsen, "The Temple of Castor and Pollux on the Forum Romanum," *ActaArch* 59 (1988): fig. 13.

17. Among other speeches, Augustus gave the funeral oration to his sister from atop this podium; DioCass.54.35; 56.34; Roger B. Ulrich, "Julius Caesar and the Creation of the Forum Iulium," *AJA* 97.1 (January 1993): 75. Similarly, Caesar used the podium of the temple to Venus Genetrix in his forum as a speaker's platform, a fact that supports the existence of lateral stairs on the original plan; Suet.*Caes.*78.

18. Though the Temple of Concordia had a long history, it apparently assumed this distinctive configuration only in the Augustan Age; C. Gasparri, *Aedes Concordiae Augustae* (Rome: Instituto di Studi Romani 1979), 62–72. Earlier, comparable topographic constraints had resulted in a similar layout for the Temple of Vediovis inter duos lucos atop the Capitoline hill; cf. Vitr.4.8.4; Gros, *Aurea Templa*, 143–6.

19. Pliny, *HN*.35.196. On the decorative program, see B. A. Kellum, "The City Adorned: Programmatic Display at the Aedes Concordiae Augustae," in Raaflaub/Toher, *Between Republic and Empire*, 276–307; Zanker, *Images*, 111.

20. Among the tholoi in Rome dedicated to this hero were the temple to Hercules Custos near the Circus Flaminius and that to Hercules Victor in the Forum Boarium. Round buildings were also associated with Vesta; W. Altmann, *Die italischen Rundbauten* (Berlin: Weidmannsche Buchhandlung 1906). A tholos modeled on the Temple of Vesta in the Forum Romanum was dedicated to Augustus and Roma atop the Athenian Acropolis, probably around the turn of the millennium.

21. A possible exception is the Temple of Apollo Palatinus; archaizing in decoration and form, this building was systyle, with an intercolumnar spacing of two column diameters; cf. Vitr.3.3.4; Gros, *Aurea Templa*, 106, 214; Hugh Plommer, review of P. Gros, *Aurea Templa* in *JRS* 69 (1979): 216. B. A. Kellum believes the structure more closely approximated a broad, Tuscan building configuration; "Sculptural Programs," 169–70.

22. *Rhet*.3.22.35–7. On Hellenistic theories of greatness (*megethos*), see J. Onians, *Art and Thought in the Hellenistic Age* (London: Thames & Hudson 1979), 122–33.

23. One new building type did precisely satisfy the needs of the nascent imperial bureaucracy and simultaneously convey the new social structure; significantly, it did so away from the eyes of urban observers. The introverted *columbarium*-type tomb developed specifically to accept the members of the expanding imperial household. Within closed precincts, individuals' ashes were placed in niches carefully arranged to reflect social hierarchies. Thus, as Zanker has pointed out, these collective tombs represented Augustan society, with each person having an assigned place and role; *Images*, 292; Suet.*Aug*.44.

24. Augustus rebuilt the Basilica Aemilia after 14 B.C. and restored the Basilica Julia in A.D. 12; DioCass.54.24, 56.27; Heinrich Bauer, "Basilica Aemilia," in Hofter, *Kaiser Augustus*, 200–12.

25. Pliny *HN*.36.102. The Basilicas Aemilia and Julia did boast some formal innovations, yet because they occurred on the interior, not the urban exterior, they will not be explored here; A. Boëthius, *The Golden House of Nero* (Ann Arbor: University of Michigan Press 1960), 71–3; Ward-Perkins, *Roman Imperial Architecture*, 40–2.

26. DioCass.51.22. For ease of identification, the numismatic artist enlarged the entablature to accommodate an inscription; even so, an overall vertical emphasis still prevails; *BMCRE* 1.103 nos. 631–2.

27. On the complex evolution of the Roman commemorative arch, see Sandro De Maria, *Gli Archi Onorari di Roma e Dell'Italia Romana*, Bibliotheca Archaeologica 7 (Rome: L'Erma di Bretschneider Rome 1988), 31–51; Fred S. Kleiner, *The Arch of Nero in Rome. A study of the Roman Honorary Arch Before and Under Nero*, Archaeologica 52 (Rome: G. Bretschneider 1985), 13.

28. Commemorative arches were even more numerous outside of Rome. Martin Nilsson has postulated that the sudden popularity of this building type resulted both from the wish to honor Octavian and from advancements in arch design; "The Origin of the Triumphal Arch," *Svenska Instit. Rome* 2 (1932): 139; see also Marina Pensa, "Genesi e sviluppo dell'arco onorario nella documentazione numismatica," *Studi sull'arco Onorario Romano*, Studia Archaeologica 21 (Rome: L'Erma di Bretschneider 1979), 19–28; MacDonald, "Empire Imagery," 138–42. Despite the contemporary popularity of arches and their high visibility in Augustan Rome, they are not discussed by

Vitruvius. This lacuna may be explained by the fact that the majority of honorific arches appeared after Vitruvius penned his text in the 20s B.C.

29. G. Mansuelli, "Fornix e arcus," *Studi sull'Arco Onorario Romano*, Studia Archaeologica 21 (Rome: L'Erma di Bretschneider 1979), 15–17. In the A.D. 70s, Pliny mentioned "the new invention of arches," possibly in reference to the distinctly Roman origin of this building type, rather than to the newness of the form or word; *HN*.34.27; De Maria, *Archi Onorari*, 55–6; F. Kleiner, "The Study of Roman Triumphal and Honorary Arches 50 years after Kähler," *JRA* 2 (1989): 196. From a careful examination of ancient texts Wallace-Hadrill notes it is possible that *ianus* at first replaced *fornix*, only to be supplanted in turn by *arcus*; "Roman Arches and Greek Honours," *PCPS* 216 n.s. 36 (1990): 144–7.

30. Regarding the significance of pediments on arches, see Daniela Scagliarini Corlàita, "La situazione urbanistica degli archi onorari nella prima età imperiale," *Studi sull'Arco Onorario Romano*, Studia Archaeologica 21 (Rome: L'Erma di Bretschneider 1979), 30.

31. Ovid may refer to this arch when he describes "the gate of the Palatium"; *Tr.* 3.1.31.

32. *CIL* 6.878l; Richardson, *New Topographical Dictionary*, 296–7.

33. De Maria, *Archi Onorari*, 90–108.

34. Suet.*Claud*.1; De Maria, *Archi Onorari*, 272–4; F. Albertson, "An Augustan Temple Represented on a Historical Relief Dating to the Time of Claudius," *AJA* 91 (1987): 454–5; Kleiner, *Arch of Nero*, 33–4. An alternative possibility is that the Arcus Drusi was an embellishment of an aqueduct arch at the intersection of the Via Appia and the Specus Octavianus slightly to the north.

35. *CIL* 6.1244–6. Claudius later created an honorific aqueduct – arch at the intersection of the Aqua Virgo and Via Flaminia; *CIL* 6.920–3.

36. *CIL* 6.1384–5. Extensions to the Aqua Appia and the Aqua Marcia are associated with these gates, though dating remains uncertain; they may have been part of Augustus' reworking of Rome's waterworks in the late first century B.C.

37. Gros, *Aurea Templa*, 133–7.

38. Vitruvius did not use the term *thermae*; cf. 5.10–11. Dio Cassius called Agrippa's bathing complex both a *gymnasium*, a word associated with Greek palestra, and the *Laconian sudatorium*, in reference to the sweating room that formed the core of the building; 53.27.1; F. Yegül, *Baths and Bathing in Classical Antiquity* (New York and Cambridge, MA: Architectural History Foundation/MIT Press 1992), 43, 133–7.

39. The two apsidal rooms may have served as senatorial meeting halls or shrines to replace those Caesar had destroyed when clearing the site; M. Bieber, *The History of the Greek and Roman Theater* (Princeton: Princeton University Press 1961), 204, 307.

40. D. Favro "Rome. The Street Triumphant: The Urban Impact of Roman Triumphal Parades," in *Streets of the World, Critical Perspectives on Public Space*, edited by Zeynep Çelik, Diane Favro, and Richard Ingersoll (Berkeley: University of California Press 1994), 157.

41. The Theater of Balbus was a smaller, more opulent version of the Republican Theater of Pompey; Pliny *HN*.36.60.

42. Along with other Augustan colonies, that at Augusta Emerita (Merida, Spain) included a permanent amphitheater; Zanker, *Images*, 148; C. Landes and J. C. Golvin, *Amphitheatres et Gladiateurs* (Paris: Presses du CNRA 1990), 39–49.

43. Because the Amphitheater of Statilius Taurus was included among the structures damaged in the fire of A.D. 64, it probably stood east of the Via Lata, somewhat out-

44. Suetonius includes the pulvinar among the excessive honors accepted by the Dictator; *Caes*.76.

45. DioCass.53.1; Plut.*Vit.Marc*.30; *CIL* 6:2347–9; 4431–5; 5192; C. E. Boyd, *Public Libraries and Literary Culture in Ancient Rome* (Chicago: University of Chicago Press 1915), 33.

46. In the mid-first century B.C., L. Licinius Lucullus allowed visitors to his large, personal book collection housed at his garden estate on the Pincian Hill; Plut.*Vit.Luc*.42.

47. Ward-Perkins, *Imperial Architecture*, 162. Identification of the Macellum Liviae with the remains north of the Porta Esquilina is not universally accepted; Richardson, *New Topographical Dictionary*, 241.

48. Unfortunately, nothing remains of the Horrea Agrippiana's street façade. An idea of its appearance may be postulated from the treatment of the interior courtyard. Even though a Roman warehouse was not normally accessible to all urban residents, that of the Horrea Agrippiana was finely constructed with engaged travertine columns on arcaded piers similar to the exterior of the Theater of Marcellus; the street façade may have been similarly embellished.

49. This section focuses on upper-class dwellings. Few multiple housing units can be securely dated to the Augustan Age. For a discussion of attempts to localize the construction of apartment buildings (*insulae*) in Augustan Rome, see Homo, *Rome impériale*, 498; A. Boëthius, "L'insula Romana secondo Leon Homo," *Colloqui del Sodalizio II* (Rome: L'Erma 1956), 1–12.

50. The complex interior decorative programs of houses during the Augustan Age demonstrate both innovation (e.g., the development of the Third Style of wall painting) and reserve; John R. Clarke, *The Houses of Roman Italy, 100* B.C.–A.D.

side the Augustan district formed in the central Campus Martius; Richardson, *New Topographical Dictionary*, 11.

250, Ritual, Space, and Decoration (Berkeley: University of California Press 1991), 48–50, 125–46. As with urban residences, Augustus also spoke out against extravagant villas, yet because these rural residences rose far from Rome, they were less subject to Imperial pressure. Patrons expended great sums on villas and reveled in formal experimentation; Suet.*Aug*.72; Ward-Perkins, *Imperial Architecture*, 202.

51. Ownership of the ancient Villa Farnesina has been attributed to Agrippa and his profligate wife Julia, daughter of Augustus, though without substantial evidence. For a discussion of the decorative program in the Third Style and an evaluation of scholarship on the subject, see Clarke, *Houses*, 52–7. Regarding the innovative form of the ancient Villa Farnesina, see Yegül, *Baths and Bathing*, 181–3.

52. Analyzing Roman imperial tombs from a purely formal standpoint, MacDonald demonstrates their visual richness and diversity; *Roman Empire II*, 144–63. Given the unlimited possibilities for tomb forms, it is not surprising Vitruvius did not even begin to define this building type.

53. L. Lucilius Paetus erected the tumulus for himself and his sister in the late first century B.C.; it had a diameter of approximately 35 meters, compared to 89 meters for the Mausoleum of Augustus. Maecenas apparently also erected a tumulus tomb, probably near his estates on the Esquiline; Suet.*Vit.Hor*.20. This tomb form associated Maecenas both with Augustus' mausoleum and the tumuli of his own Etruscan ancestors.

54. The pyramid is 27 meters in height and approximately 21 meters square at the base. C. Cestius died before Agrippa, whom he made one of his heirs; *CIL* 6.1375. Little else is known of his life, though it is generally assumed he had some direct connection with Egypt during his career; cf. Cic.*Phil*.3.26.

55. The most comprehensive examination of this urban space is by F. Coarelli; *Il Foro Boario, dalle origini alla fine della Repubblica* (Rome: Edizioni Quasar 1988). Regarding competitive construction in this general area, see L. Pietilä-Castren, *Magnificentia publica. The Victory Monuments of the Roman Generals in the Era of the Punic Wars,* Commentationes humanarum litterarum 84 (Helsinki: Societas Scientiarum Fennica 1987).

56. Rome's earliest temples, such as the Temple of Jupiter Optimus Maximus, and those in the Area Sacra di Sant'Omobono, faced south toward the sacred Alban Hills. At the Area Sacra di Largo Argentina, the temples followed the preferred Greek orientation, looking east so the gods (cult statues) could watch the rising sun; John E. Stambaugh, "The Functions of Roman Temples," *ANRW* 2.16.1 (1978): 554–608; *idem, Ancient Roman City,* 32, 214.

57. Gros, *Aurea Templa,* 147–53.

58. If taken to an extreme, the experiential determination of architectural forms could be used to justify placement of the two northern temples in the Forum Holitorium slightly behind the earlier Temple of Spes so that their larger columns would appear compatible with those of the smaller structure.

59. Among the uses specifically associated with Roman porticos were public displays, storage, markets, strolling, and protection from the elements. They were generally located to facilitate access by visitors to theaters and temple precincts; Vitr.5.9; Richardson, *New Topographical Dictionary,* 310–11. In particular, the aediles made use of porticos or temporary colonnades to exhibit the equipment to be featured in public shows; Ulrich, "Julius Caesar," 73.

60. The Republican portico in the Forum Holitorium dates to the first century B.C. Only the southernmost bays remain, though it may have continued farther north as did its Imperial successor; Richardson, *New Topographical Dictionary,* 165.

61. Vitr.3.2.5. When a portico had more than one wing, ancient authors often referred to it in the plural, though that does not necessarily imply the structure was a quadriportico. Velleius Paterculus describes the portico erected by Quintus Metellus as surrounding the temples of Jupiter Stator and Juno Regina, though it remains uncertain if the Porticus Metelli formed a complete enclosure in the second century B.C.; 1.11.2–5. Pliny refers to the nearby portico of Gnaeus Octavius as double with bronze column capitals; it may have become a quadriportico completely surrounding the temples of Mars and Vulcanus only after later reworkings; *HN*.24.13; Richardson, *New Topographical Dictionary,* 315, 317.

62. For a full discussion of the Ustrinum Domus Augustae, see Mary T. Boatwright, "The '*Ara Ditis-Ustrinum* of Hadrian,'" *AJA* 89 (1985): 494–96. Excavations in the late eighteenth century uncovered a travertine pavement identified with the Ustrinum measuring approximately 50 sq. m. For an overview of recent debate about the location of this funerary structure, see J. R. Patterson, "Survey Article. The City of Rome: From Republic to Empire," *JRS* 82 (1992): 199.

63. For a discussion of "injunctive" (closed) versus "conjunctive" (open) ensembles, see Thure Hastrup, "Forum Iulium as a Manifestation of Power," *AnalRom* 2 (1962): 54–5.

64. For comparison, the Roman colonial city of Timgad erected in A.D. 100 originally encompassed a total area of 12.5 hectares.

65. Also erected in the Augustan Age were the Porticus ad Nationes (ca. 32 B.C., location, size, and configuration unknown), the richly appointed Porticus Apollinis linked to the Palatine temple of Apollo (28 B.C.; exact form unknown), the Porticus Argonautarum forming the west edge of the Saepta Julia (25 B.C.), a portico associated

with the rebuilding of the Temple to Quirinus (16 B.C.), the Porticus Vipsania in the Campus Agrippae (pre-7 B.C.; referred to in the singular, it cannot be the large building so identified on the east side of Via Flaminia), and the Porticus of Gaius and Lucius (2 B.C.) in the Forum Romanum; Richardson, *New Topographical Dictionary*, 310–20.

66. This list could also rightly include the Forum Julium (ca. 12,000 sq. m); though dedicated by Caesar in 46 B.C., the project was completed by Octavian who took full credit; *ResG*.19–20.

67. It remains uncertain if the plans of the Porticus Philippi and Porticus Octavia, like the Porticus Octaviae, had open colonnades on the street façade and a solid wall toward the interior or colonnades on both sides; Richardson, *New Topographical Dictionary*, 317–18.

68. This type is represented by the third-century Temple of Ptolemy III and Berenice at Hermopolis Magna in Egypt, and may have appeared in Rome by the second century B.C. with the porticos of Quintus Metellus and Gnaeus Octavius; Vitr.3.2.5; Pliny *HN*.24.13. A comprehensive examination of Hellenistic analogs is found in Einar Gjerstad, "Die Ursprungsgeschichte der römischen Kaiserfora," *SkrRom* 10 (1944): 40–71.

69. Ov.*Fasti* 6.637–8. Some scholars have argued that the central structure of the Porticus Liviae as depicted on a fragment of the third-century marble plan of Rome is in reality a fountain, not the shrine to Concordia; cf. Richardson, *New Topographical Dictionary*, 314; M. Boudreau Flory, "Livia's Shrine to Concordia and the Porticus Liviae," *Historia* 33 (1984): 309–30; also P. Zanker, "Drei Stadtbilder aus dem Augusteischen Rome," in *L'Urbs, Espace urbain et histoire,* edited by C. Pietri (Rome: École française de Rome 1987), 477–83.

70. Appian compared the enclosed Forum Julium to the "squares of the Persians";

BCiv.2.102. Yet early formal models also existed in Italy; for example, the forum at Pompeii was a rectangular open space with a 3:2 length-to-width ratio ideal for spectator events; Vitr.5.1.2; E. Sjöqvist, "Kaisareion: A Study in Architectural Iconography," *OpRom* 1 (1954): 86–108; Gjerstad, "römischen Kaiserfora," 40–72.

71. The central open area of the Forum Julium measured approximately three times the volume of the temple; the ratio was approximately the same with the Forum Augustum.

72. See Chapter Four; Kellum, "Sculptural Programs," 169–76; Zanker, *Forum Augustum,* 10–23; and Anderson, *Historical Topography,* 80–8.

73. Literary references and archaeological data for the Porticus ad Nationes are scant. Because Pliny describes a statue in front of its entrance, it was probably of the quadriporticus type; Pliny *HN*.36.39, 41. Various locations have been proposed, including several in the Campus Martius near Pompey's display; *Serv.Dan*.8.721; Richardson, *New Topographical Dictionary,* 316–17; C. Nicolet, *Space, Geography, and Politics in the Early Roman Empire,* translated by Helene Leclerc (Ann Arbor: University of Michigan Press 1991), 37–9; Coarelli, *Roma,* 290–1.

74. The Porticus Liviae was famous for art displays and a large, wine-producing vine shading the walkways; Pliny *HN*.14.11; Ov.*Ars Am*.1.71. The Forma Urbis Romae shows trees lining the interior of the Porticus Philippi. Vitruvius especially underscored the healthiness of landscaped porticoed enclosures; 5.9.5, 9.

75. An extravagant display of artworks and curiosities attracted a continuous flow of pedestrians to the Porticus Octavia; Ov.*Ars Am*.1.70; Pliny *HN*.36.15, 22, 28, 34, 35. The Saepta Julia was one of Rome's most frequented locales, famous for exhibits of famous artworks and oddities; Sen.*Ira* 2.8.1; Pliny *HN*.16.201; 36.29. Augustus apparently had a per-

sonal penchant for curiosities, including dwarves and exotic animals; Suet.*Aug*.43; Aurelius, *Epit*.1.25.

76. The exterior face of the fire wall was finely rusticated with alternating rows of all stretchers and all headers. The internal face may have been stuccoed or covered with marble veneer, yet these surface coverings could have maintained the underlying patterning.

77. The high attic above the porticos may indicate the existence of vaulted ceilings in these side passages, though as with the other curves within the complex, these would have been experienced internally; Richardson, *New Topographical Dictionary*, 161.

78. Neither the Forum Julium nor Forum Augustum has been fully excavated and thus the external urban entryways and façades cannot be analyzed.

79. The gardens of these consuls were probably located in the Campus Martius region; Cic.*Amic*.1.7, 7.25; *Rep*.1.9.

80. Richardson defines *horti* as a house resembling a villa in or near a city and argues that the term was interchangeable with *domus*; *New Topographical Dictionary*, 112, 201. Because ancient authors stress the landscaping rather than the architectural forms of *horti*, I prefer to define them as urban pleasure gardens which sometimes, but not always, included a residence. *Horti*, should not be confused that *hortus*; the latter singular term refers to a kitchen garden associated with a *domus*.

81. Ward-Perkins, *Imperial Architecture*, 202.

82. On the various fig trees in the center of Rome, see Jane DeRose Evans, *The Art of Persuasion, Political Propaganda from Aeneas to Brutus* (Ann Arbor: University of Michigan Press 1992), 75–8.

83. Pliny *HN*.12.13; 16.140. The same author remarks on the introduction of a new strain of apples developed by the consul of 23 B.C. named after Augustus; 15.47.

84. The passage on terraces and groves refers to villas rather than urban property, but

the point is the same. Augustus believed in the curative powers of fresh air and plantings; Suet.*Aug*.72, 82; cf. Pliny *Ep*.5.6.187.

85. Private owners did not always allow the public to enter their *horti*, using walls or guards to restrict use. Nevertheless, all urban residents could enjoy the sight of greenery, smell the heady fragrances of flowering plants, and hear the birds singing amid the trees.

86. Vitruvius remains conspicuously silent about large *horti*. He periodically mentions plantings in relation to the house and portico, and emphasizes the import of greenery in countering urban pollution, yet ignores urban landscaping; 5.9.5; cf. Aul.Gell.15.5.1. As an army-trained architect, he must have felt discussion of plantings belonged more properly in treatises on agriculture or private letters. Grimal identifies two broad phases of development for Roman urban gardens: first, the independent park based on eastern examples, followed in the Imperial period by the civic garden associated with public baths; P. Grimal, *Les jardins romains*, BEFAR 155 (Paris: Presses Universitaires de France 1969), 195–6.

87. The Daphne park south of Antioch had a circumference of 80 stadia; Strab.16.750. The Soma, Alexandria's main street, was lined with trees; Strab.17.793; M. L. Gothein, *A History of Garden Art* (London: J. M. Dent 1914), 73–5.

88. Most knowledge of ancient urban plantings come from Pompeii, where the volcanic preservation of root impressions has allowed researchers to identify the types and locations of urban plants; Wilhelmina F. Jashemski, *The Gardens of Pompeii* (New York: Caratzas 1978).

89. For a discussion of the meanings and presentation of plants and nature in general during the Augustan Age see Zanker, *Images*, 50, 92–3, 172–83.

90. Precisely at this time, Strabo described the buildings amid plantings along the coast-

line of Naples as resembling a great city; 5.4.8.

91. Without further excavations, the western edge of the Forum Augustum cannot be determined; if a street ran along that side, the forum would have measured approximately 115 × 85 m, making the proportions closer to those of Trajan's adjacent enclosure, which borrowed heavily from the Augustan example; Anderson, *Historical Topography*, 79–80.

92. See the size comparison of tombs for Mausolos (fourth century B.C.) and those of A. Hirtius, Augustus, and C. Metella; Zanker, *Images*, fig. 58, after J. Ganzert.

93. The Egyptians had far earlier used obelisks as the gnomons for sundials in Egypt; E. Buchner, *Die Sonnenuhr des Augustus* (Mainz am Rhein: P. Von Zabern 1982), 7. L. Papirius Cursor is credited with constructing the first sundial in Rome, located within the precinct of the temple to Quirinus; Pliny *HN* 7.213. Another early sundial graced the Temple of Diana on the Aventine; Censorinus *DN*.23.6. Tabletop models were also popular; Sharon Gibbs, *Greek and Roman Sundials* (New Haven: Yale University Press 1976).

94. Rome still had several other fora, but these were primarily commercial centers with limited political and ceremonial associations.

95. The bright colors of Roman wall paintings were generally reserved for building interiors or other protected surfaces, where they were less likely to fade; Vitr.7.3. However, structures preserved from Pompeii and elsewhere confirm that Roman buildings did boast external coloration. In addition, panel paintings were put on display in public spaces; for example, two by Apelles graced the Forum Augustum; Pliny *HN*.35.27.

96. On Roman building materials and construction techniques, see J. Adam, *La Construction romaine: materiaux et techniques* (Paris: Picard 1984).

97. For example, Cicero refers to laws limiting expenditure on monuments; if a patron spent beyond this amount, he had to pay an equal amount to the public funds, *Att*.12.35; H. Drerup, *zum Ausstatkungsluxus in der römischen Architektur, Ein formgeschichtlicher Versuch* (Münster, Wesphalia: Aschendorffsche Verlgsbuchhandlung 1957), 6–10. Pliny records that early Romans selected marble because of its strength, though he also provides ample examples of marble construction for show; *HN*.36.4–8, 45–50. On the marble trade and use in antiquity see R. Gnoli, *Marmora romana* (Rome: Ediz. dell'Elefante 1971); P. Pensabene, "Considerazioni sul trasporto di manufatti marmorei in età imperiale a Roma e in altri centri occidentali," *DialArch*. 6 (1972): 2-3; J. Ward-Perkins, "The Marble Trade and its Organization: Evidence from Nicomedia," *MAAR* 36 (1980): 325–38.

98. Pliny *HN*.36 5–7; cf. Asc.*Scaur*.45.

99. Livy 6.4.12; 41.20.8; Vell.Pat. 1.11.3; Gros, *Aurea Templa*, 50, 69.

100. The white stone from Luni is often mistaken for Greek Pentelic or Hymettian marble. A Roman colony existed at Luni by 177 B.C., though the first use of its stone in Rome occurred in approximately 48 B.C.; Pliny *HN*.36.48; Blake, *Roman Construction*, 53. Augustus resettled Luni and improved the port facilities; *CIL* 11:1330. Strabo describes the ease with which skilled shippers transported marble from Luni to Rome; 5.2.5.

101. Ov.*ArsAm*.3.125; Pliny *HN*.36.55. The stone called "Augustan" may actually have been a granite. Agrippa apparently owned quarries of crimson and white Synnadic marble in Phrygia; *CIL* 15 p.988; cf. 3:7047.

102. F. Castagnoli, "Installazioni Portuali a Roma," *MAAR* 36 (1980): 35–9; R. Lanciani, "Officina Marmoraria della regione XIII," *BullCom* XIX (1911):

23–4. Marble chips found near the mole indicate that stonecutters worked on the building blocks near the dock site; Blake, *Roman Construction,* 51.

103. L. Maddalena, "I marmi dei fori imperiali," in "*Atti dell III Congresso Nazionale di Studi Romani*" (Rome 1934), 5–10.

104. At the Apollo complex, the temple's ashlar blocks of white marble from the Italian quarries at Luni stood in refined contrast to the colorful imported stones of the adjacent portico; Serv.*Aen.*8.720; cf. Verg.*Aen.*6.69–74.

105. Strab.9.5.16. Little work has been done on color specifically in relation to ancient urban environments. For general information on the subject, see M. E. Armstrong, *Significance of Colors in Roman Ritual* (Menasha, WI: George Banta Publishing 1917); Donald Wilber, "The Role of Color in Architecture," *JSAH* 2:1 (January 1942): 17–22.

106. Hor.*Odes* 3.1.41–6; cf. Hor.*Carm.*2.18; Sen.*Ep.*89; Tib.3.3.

107. Greek artisans carved the detailed decorations on the Ara Pacis; less experienced workers executed the decorative carving on the Temple of Divus Julius; Gros, *Aurea Templa,* 57–78.

108. *ResG.*19; Blake, *Roman Construction,* 179.

109. Pliny credits the original patron of the Porticus Octavia with the bronze capitals, though they more logically belong to the Augustan restoration; *HN.*34.13. Torelli has pointed out that references to a Syracusan room in Augustus' Palatine residence may indicate the use of metalwork, rather than a tower as usually interpreted; Suet.*Aug.*72; M. Torelli, *Typology and Structure of Roman Historical Reliefs* (Ann Arbor: University of Michigan Press 1982), 32.

110. Procop.*Goth.*1.25; Blake, *Roman Construction,* 63–4.

111. For example, Augustus put large panel paintings with military themes on display in his new forum; Pliny *HN.*

35.26–8. Because the artistic programs of the Augustan city are examined by B. A. Kellum in her forthcoming book on programmatic display, this section will focus on architectural ornament.

112. Kellum, "Sculptural Programs," 172–5. Although terra-cotta work was definitely retardataire in the first century B.C., it had powerful Republican associations; Pliny *HN.*35.158.

113. Zanker, *Images,* 112. The Ara Pacis, while certainly inspired by elaborately carved Hellenistic altars such as that to Zeus at Pergamon, also recalls the small fifth-century Altar of Pity in Athens; H. Thompson, "The Altar of Pity in the Athenian Agora," *Hesperia* XXI (1952): 47.

114. Vitr.4.5.2. In an earlier passage, Vitruvius notes that in particular, the temples of the State gods, "Jupiter, Juno, and Minerva should be on the very highest point commanding a view of the greater part of the city"; 1.7.1.

115. Generally, Romans referred to the city's central node simply as "the Forum." After construction of the Forum Julium, it was sometimes called the Forum Magnum; DioCass.43.22. Vergil was the first to use the adjective "Romanum"; *Aen.*8.361. Never popular in antiquity, this descriptor is commonly used in modern sources to avoid confusion with the Imperial Fora. Sources on the Augustan Forum Romanum are prolific, including P. Zanker, *Forum Romanum: Die Neugestaltung unter Augustus,* Monumenta Artis Antiquae 5 (Tubingen: Wasmuth 1972); F. Coarelli, *Il Foro Romano 2: periodo repubblicano e augusteo* (Rome: Edizioni Quasar 1985); D. Favro, "The Roman Forum and Roman Memory," *Places* 5:1 (1988): 17–24; and Richardson, *New Topographical Dictionary,* 170–4.

116. Vitr.5.1. Recent excavations and analyses of the Forum Romanum are reshaping our picture of this node during the

Republic. Remains of a portico discovered under the Temple of Divus Julius have been tentatively identified as the Basilica Aemilia and the structure on the southern side of the Forum as the Basilica Fulvia, rebuilt later as the Basilica Paulli; E. M. Steinby, "Il lato orientale del Foro Romano," *Arctos* 21 (1987): 139–84. As a result, the Republican Forum may have been closer to Vitruvius' image of a porticoed square than previously thought, though without a dominant temple on the main axis; N. Purcell, "Rediscovering the Roman Forum," *JRA* 2 (1989): 161; Coarelli, *Il Foro Romano 2*, 59–63.

117. Stambaugh, *Ancient Roman City*, 59–62.

118. Coarelli, *Foro Romano 2*, 258–324; Zanker, *Images*, 79–82.

119. Augustus was awarded arches in the Forum Romanum after Actium (29 B.C.) and the return of the Parthian standards (19 B.C.). Two others are also associated with this node: that for the defeat of Sextus Pompey (36 B.C.; maybe never erected) and another honoring Gaius and Lucius, identified with the portion of their namesake porticus crossing from the Basilica Paulli to the Temple of Divus Julius; De Maria, *Archi Onorari*, 266–75.

120. The pavement of L. Naevius Surdinus preserved the natural gradient of the Roman Forum, which rose 2 meters from the Temple of Divus Julius to the Rostra Augusti. This paving blocked access to the underground galleries used during spectacles and was associated with a simultaneous reworking of the Lacus Curtius; Coarelli, *Il Foro Romano 2*, 225–7. C. F. Giuliani and P. Verduchi date the current level of the inscription to the Severan period; *L'Area Centrale del Foro Romano*, Universitá degli Studi di Roma La Sapienza: Il linguaggio dell'architettura romana (Florence: L. S. Olschiki 1987), 65–6.

121. Favro, "Roman Forum," 17–24; Henner v. Hesberg, "Die Veranderung des Erscheinungsbildes der Stadt Rom unter Augustus," in Hofter, *Kaiser Augustus*, 93–115.

122. For an analysis of the Forum Romanum as showplace of the Gens Julia, see Zanker, *Images*, 79–82.

123. The exact placement of the statue and column in relation to the Rostra Augusti remains uncertain; Vell.Pat.2.56.4; App. BCiv.5.130. Zanker suggests that columns decorated with the rostra captured at Actium may also have stood along this sight line; in contrast, Richardson places the *columnae rostratae* in the precinct of Apollo Palatinus, *Images*, 38, 80–1; Richardson, *New Topographical Dictionary*, 97.

124. Suet.*Aug*.40, 43. Augustus continued to hold gladiatorial events in the Forum even though other urban facilities, such as the enormous Saepta Julia, more easily accommodated large crowds.

125. Three more imperial fora were built by later emperors. Secure in their absolutist power, these patrons felt no need to justify their new enclosures as extensions of the Forum Romanum; Favro, "Forum Romanum," 20.

126. See Chapter 4. The Forum Julium may have originally had galleries above the side porticos where spectators could watch games such as those performed in 34 B.C.; DioCass.49.42.1; Anderson, *Historical Topography*, 49.

127. Court cases, the proclaimed raison d'être of the Forum Augustum, probably met in the exedral spaces behind the lateral porticos, where the absence of upper galleries diminished the noise and rowdiness of spectators. Only in one instance (A.D. 12), when floods made other facilities inoperable, was the Forum Augustum used for games; DioCass.27.4.

128. Suet.*Aug*.29; cf. Pliny *HN*.34.79, 36.50.

129. DioCass.54.4. Interestingly, Jupiter Tonans also was encountered first in Rome's temporal landscape. His temple was dedicated on September 1, that of

Jupiter Optimus Maximus on September 13. The exact location of the temple to Jupiter Tonans is still debated. It must have stood near the entrance to the Area Capitolina overlooking the Forum Romanum; the upper attic gallery depicted on coins may indicate a viewing platform; Richardson, *New Topographical Dictionary,* 226–7.

130. Suet.*Aug.*91. For a slightly different version of this story, see DioCass.54.4.3.

131. For example, to promote an increased birthrate, Augustus honored an old man and his sixty-one descendants on the Capitoline; Pliny *HN.*7.60.

132. Suet.*Calig.*34. An altar to the Gens Julia stood in the Area Capitolina, though whether erected in the Augustan Age or later remains uncertain; App.*BCiv.*1.16–17; Oros.5.9.2.

133. Regarding the hut on the Capitoline, see Vitr.2.1.5; Sen.*Controv.*2.1.5. On the continual restoration of the hut, see DioCass.48.43.4; 54.29.8; Dion.Hal.*Ant. Rom.*1.79.11. Wiseman argues that the Hut of Romulus on the Palatine was in reality the residence for the priests of Magna Mater. Augustus' association with Magna Mater was natural for she was the guardian of Aeneas and all descendants of the Julii; T. P. Wiseman, "*Conspicui Postes Tectaque Digna Deo:* The Public Image of Aristocratic and Imperial Houses in the Late Republic and Early Empire," in *L'Urbs, Espace urbain et histoire,* edited by C. Pietri (Rome: École française de Rome 1987), 401–2.

134. Augustus may have consciously avoided aggrandizing, or even securely identifying, his birthplace during his own lifetime to prevent the outright worship of the site, and himself, within the city of Rome; Suet.*Aug.*5–6; DioCass.48.43.

135. DioCass.53.1, 16. On the Augustan enclave atop the Palatine, see G. Lugli, "Le temple d'Apollon et les edifices d'Auguste sur le Palatin," *CRAI* (1950): 276–85.

136. For example, in honor of his Sabine victory in 494 B.C., the dictator M. Valerius Volusius Maximus received a house at public expense. The door opened outward as an overt indication of the occupants superiority to other citizens walking in the street; Plut.*Vit.Publ.*20.

137. One can postulate that in antiquity as today, the palm was an atypical tree in Rome, and thus quite notable. In addition, this tree was associated with other omens. When Julius Caesar spared a palm at his campsite in Spain, the tree miraculously grew at a rapid rate and overshadowed his camp just as Octavian was to overshadow Caesar's achievements; Suet.*Aug.*92, 94. Years later, during the expiation of prodigies in 39 B.C., four palms sprang up around the Temple of Magna Mater on the Palatine; DioCass.48.43.

138. Anderson, *Historical Topography,* 72.

139. These reliefs, formerly associated with the Ara Pietatis Augustae, are located in the Capitoline Museum and on the exterior of the Villa Medici. Paul Rehak has suggested they were originally part of the Ara Gentis Juliae on the Capitoline Hill and convincingly argued that the Ionic structure depicted is the Temple of Victory; "The Ionic temple relief in the Capitoline: the temple of Victory on the Palatine?" *JRA* 3 (1990): 172–86.

140. For an evaluation of various theories regarding the overall meaning of this base, see Belinda Osier Aicher, "The Sorrento Base and the Figure of Mars," *ArchNews* 15.1 (1990): 11–16; Evans, *Persuasion,* 51. A relief in the Terme Museum shows the Augustan pedimental sculptures from the Temple of Quirinus as likewise grouped topographically with Palatine deities to the left and Aventine deities to the right; R. E. A. Palmer, "Jupiter Blaze, God of the Hills, and the

Roman Topography of *CIL* VI 377," *AJA* 80.1 (Winter 1976): 55.

141. In Roman cities, particular crafts often clustered together, such as the shoemakers who gave their name to the Vicus Sandaliarius in Rome. Nevertheless, a common function was not sufficient to define an urban district in the Lynchian sense. Also necessary were distinct boundaries and a unified architecture. As a result, Rome's *vici* and XIV Regions did not form urban districts because these administrative divisions were not experienced as distinct urban areas by observers.

142. The Palatine regained its status as a district in later years when the Imperial palace and related structures covered the entire hill.

143. In the time of Sulla, some public land in the Campus Martius was sold to private parties; Oros.5.18.27. Several large suburban villas were erected, including that of Pompey adjacent to his theater. Octavian confiscated Pompey's residence along with other properties in the Campus during the proscriptions of the 40s B.C.

144. J. P. V. D. Balsdon, *Life and Leisure in Ancient Rome* (New York: McGraw-Hill 1969), 159–63.

145. Livy 30.21.12, 33.24.5; Joseph.*BJ*.7.5.4; Favro, "Street Triumphant," 152–4.

146. Near Rome, the Via Flaminia became surrounded by construction, gradually changing from a rural highway into an urban thoroughfare. Compared to the other city streets of Rome, this passageway was both straight and wide, earning the nickname of Via Lata; Richardson, *New Topographical Dictionary*, 416. The recreated walk through Augustan Rome in Chapter 7 follows this path; see also D. Favro, "Reading the Augustan City," in Holliday, *Narrative and Event*, 230–57.

147. The Porta Fontinalis was a gate in the Republican city fortifications. The remaining city walls in the area had been dismantled during the construction of the Forum Julium, yet this entry apparently remained, for it is mentioned in several imperial inscriptions; *CIL* 6.9514, 9921, 33914. Less certain is the status of the portico constructed in 193 B.C. connecting the Porta Fontinalis to the Ara Martis in the Campus; Livy 35.10.12.

148. Cicero advised rhetoricians to select mnemonic images "that are effectively and sharply outlined and distinctive, with the capacity of encountering and speedily penetrating the mind"; Cic.*De Or*.2.87.358; cf. Arist.*Rh*.3.12.5.

149. Inscriptions ranged from terse (that trumpeting the conquest of Egypt on the base of the Horologium obelisk), to lengthy (the *Res Gestae* inscribed on plaques before the Mausoleum).

150. Several urban paths hold potential for further study. These include the various approaches to Rome's new Augustan nodes, the Via Sacra through the Forum Romanum, and the elusive "covered" roads: the Via Tecta moving north from the Theater of Marcellus and that along the Via Appia.

151. Verg.*Aen*.6.874. As with the Via Flaminia, river travelers tended to look toward the built-up area of the Campus rather than the more rural perspective in the opposite direction. Views from the city back to the river were equally important; Prop.1.14.

152. The impact of these structures when viewed by pedestrians is discussed by T. P. Wiseman, who postulates the use of the Via Flaminia as a racecourse; "Strabo on the Campus Martius: 5.3.8, C235," *Liverpool Classical Monthly* 4:7 (July 1979): 130.

153. F. Coarelli, "Il Campo Marzio occidentale. Storia e topografia," *MEFRA* 89 (1977): 807–46.

154. The Boscoreale painting depicts a resort city, rather than the capital, where laws regarding building heights were enforced; F. W. Lehmann, *Roman Wall Paintings from Boscoreale* (Cambridge, MA: Archaeological Institute of America 1953). This urban image should be contrasted with the uniform skyline of the idealized city depicted on the Torlonia relief (fig. 2).

155. In the earlier Republic, crossing the Tiber symbolized going abroad, as for the March celebrations honoring Anna Perenna; F. Dupont, *Daily Life in Ancient Rome,* translated by Christopher Woodall (Oxford: Blackwell 1992), 200.

156. Paired temples to Honos and Virtus appeared at three other significant entry points; Torelli, *Typology,* 28–9.

157. Mussolini held up Augustus as his historical exemplar, uncovering and restoring Augustan monuments, yet the model of Rome created by Italo Gismondi for the Mostra Augustea della Romanità of 1937 shows the city at the time of Constantine. This apparent contradiction may have resulted from Il Duce's desire to depict the city at its apogee with all her famous ancient monuments or because documentation was lacking for a full reconstruction of Augustan city; S. Kostof, *The Third Rome,* 1870–1950, exhibition catalog (Berkeley: University); and *idem,* "The Emperor and the Duce: The Planning of Piazzale Augusto Imperatore in Rome," in *Art and Architecture in the Service of Politics,* edited by Henry Millon and Linda Nochlin (Cambridge, MA: MIT Press, 1978), 270–325.

158. Regional planning became popular in official urban schemes from the 1920s. The term "Master Plan" was popularized in planning jargon through usage by the New York Regional Plan Association; Christopher Tunnard, *The City of Man* (New York: Charles Scribner's Sons, 1953), 311.

159. In contrast, the existence of Agrippa's world map displayed in the Porticus Vipsania implies an interest in the physical layout and control of the Empire *HN*.3.17; Nicolet, *Space,* 7–8. The only preserved ancient city map of Rome is the so-called *Forma Urbis Romae* from around A.D. 200.

CHAPTER 6. MEANING: READING THE AUGUSTAN CITY

1. Plut.*Vit.Ant.*80; cf. Diod.Sic.18.26. Earlier instances of a general sparing a city because of its beauty (not to mention its economic value) imply this was a familiar trope; Cic.*Verr.*2.4.120.

2. James Holston, *The Modernist City, A Critique of Brasilia* (Chicago: University of Chicago Press 1990).

3. Michael N. Danielson, *The Politics of Rapid Urbanization: Government and Growth in Modern Turkey* (New York: Holmes & Meier 1985).

4. DeMars and Wells, and Jack T. Sidener *A Design Framework for Oakland* (Oakland: City Planning Department, June 1969), 14; Roger Rapoport, "Whimper Across the Bay," *New West* (November 17, 1980): 61–7.

5. Beneath the XIV Regions, the sewer system restored by Agrippa tied one region with another. Though the main sewers could literally be traversed by wagon, they had no impact on Rome's urban image; Pliny *HN.*36.24.

6. Modern urban observers are as likely to consider issues of security, health, and services as well as monuments when forming an urban image; G. J. Ashworth and H. Voogd, *Selling the City: Marketing Approaches in Public Sector Urban Planning* (London: Belhaven Press 1990), 65–76.

7. This section focused on characteristics of the built fabric rather than on urban artwork and inscriptions and other types of signage conveying meaning in the cityscape.

8. Dolores Hayden, *Seven American Utopias* (Cambridge, MA: MIT Press 1976), 288–317.

9. Among the motifs with an Augustan content were the oak wreath, sacral objects, the golden shield, and depictions of healthy plantings symbolizing prosperity. Associations with Augustus were also sparked by allusions to various deities and individuals, including Pax, Apollo, Romulus, Caesar, and Alexander the Great. Zanker provides a concise and rich portrayal of Augustan iconography; *Images*.

10. Laurels may have also formed part of the landscaping at the new Apollo complex on the Palatine; cf. Ov.*Ars Am.*3.389.

11. Annually, laurel branches were placed on the doorways of houses belonging to the *flamines*, including the Regia; Ov. *Fasti* 3.135–9. For a fuller discussion of this motif and further references, see B. A. Kellum, "The Construction of Landscape in Augustan Rome: The Garden Room at the Villa *ad Gallinas*," *ArtB* 76.2 (June 1994): 211–3, 219–23.

12. Unfortunately, important urban representations of Augustus have not been preserved, including the figure atop the Mausoleum, the equestrian statue in the Forum Romanum, and the quadriga in the Forum Augustum. A marble head measuring over one meter in height, now in the Vatican Cortile della Pigna, confirms the existence of colossal representations (fig. 15); Zanker, *Images*, 75–6; J. Pollini, "The Image of Augustus: Art and Ideology," forthcoming.

13. The master plan for the Esposizione Universale di Roma quarter was drawn up in 1937 and immediately approved by Il Duce; S. Kostof, *The Third Rome, 1870–1950,* exhibition catalog (Berkeley: University Art Museum 1973), 74–5; V. Testa,

"L'E.U.R.: centro direzionale e quartiere moderno alla periferia di Roma," *Studi Romani* (January–March 1970): 39–50.

14. The opening of a monumental approach to St. Peters only occurred in the Fascist era with the creation of the Via della Conciliazione in 1937, though the idea had been discussed for centuries; Kostof, *Third Rome,* 70–1.

15. M. K. and R. L. Thornton, *Julio-Claudian Building Programs: A Quantitative Study in Political Management* (Wauconda, IL: Bolchazy-Carducci Publishers 1989), 41–6.

16. Verg.*Aen.*1.418–9. Augustus ordered the rebuilding of Carthage; DioCass.52.43.

17. Roman authors on architecture do not go so far as Alberti, who claimed buildings may mold behavior, though architecture and status were clearly interrelated; D. Favro, "Was Man the Measure?" in *Architects' People,* edited by R. Ellis and D. Cuff (New York: Oxford University Press 1989), 20, 36–7. In the eighteenth century, designers believed elevating aesthetic and perceptual urban experiences would make better citizens; F. Gutheim, *Worthy of the Nation. The History of Planning for the National Capital* (Washington, DC: Smithsonian Institution 1977), 2–3.

18. On the positive and healthful associations of brightness, see C. Havelock, "Art as Communication in Ancient Greece," in *Communication in the Ancient World,* edited by E. A. Havelock and J. P. Herschbell (New York: Hastings House 1978), 97.

19. Augustus thoughtfully posted guards throughout the city on days of great entertainments to allow residents to attend the festivities without fear their homes would be robbed; Suet.*Aug.*43; M. J. McGann, "The Three Worlds of Horace's *Satires,*" in C. D. N. Costa, ed., *Horace* (London: Routledge & Kegan Paul 1973), 59–93.

20. Zanker, *Images,* 205–7; R. Brilliant, *Visual Narratives* (Ithaca, NY: Cornell University Press 1984), 53–89.

21. Suet.*Aug.*40. Augustus promoted the white toga both for its visual attraction and for its important historical associations; Verg.*Aen.*1.282. For another instance where Augustus manipulated costume for political reasons, see Suet. *Aug.*44, 98.

22. L'Enfant, designer of Washington, D.C., wrote in his manuscript plan of 1791, "The Squares . . . are proposed to be divided among the several States"; Gutheim, *Worthy of the Nation,* 35.

23. Dion.Hal.*Ant.Rom.*1.38.3; 7.70; Ov.*Fasti* 5.621; *ArsAm.*3.2.43.

24. P. Llewellyn, *Rome in the Dark Ages* (New York: Praeger), 173–98.

25. The Senate awarded the triumph based on complex criteria centered on a substantial military victory; D. Favro, "Rome. The Street Triumphant: The Urban Impact of Roman Triumphal Parades," in *Streets of the World, Critical Perspectives on Public Space,* edited by Zeynep Çelik, Diane Favro, and Richard Ingersoll (Berkeley: University of California Press 1994), pp. 152–3.

26. The Porta Triumphalis may have stood originally on Rome's pomerial line.; F. Coarelli, "La Porta Trionfale e la Via dei Trionfi," *DialArch* 2 (1968): 55–103; H. S. Versnel, *Triumphus* (Leiden: Brill), 135, 152, 394–6. For a contrasting interpretation of the Porta Triumphalis as a gate in daily use, see Richardson, *New Topographical Dictionary,* 301.

27. L. Pietilä-Castren, *Magnificentia publica. The Victory Monuments of the Roman Generals in the Era of the Punic Wars* (Helsinki: Societas Scientiarum Fennica 1987), 154–8.

28. Vell.Pat.2.89; cf. Ov.*Pont.*2.1.23. In the time of Augustus, Propertius describes lying in the arms of a paramour while gazing out an upper-story window at the banners of a passing triumphal parade; 3.4.15–18.

29. DioCass.51.20. At the death of Augustus, it was proposed his body be carried out of the city through the Porta Triumphalis as a further sign of his elevated status; Suet.*Aug.*100; DioCass.56.42.

30. The great Horologium Augusti was itself a physical reminder of Augustus' interest in time, as was the proliferation of calendars on display; A. Wallace-Hadrill, "Time for Augustus: Ovid, Augustus and the *Fasti,*" in *Homo Viator. Classical Essays for John Bramble,* edited by M. Whitby, P. Hardie, and M. Whitby (Bedminster: Bristol Classical Press 1987), 223–7; Mary Beard, "A Complex of Times: No More Sheep on Romulus' Birthday," *PSPS* 213 n.s. 23 (1987): 1–15; M. R. Salzman, *On Roman Time: The Codex-Calendar of 354 and the Rhythms of Urban Life in Late Antiquity* (Berkeley: University of California Press 1990), 6–7.

31. Astrology was also popular. During the disturbances of 33 B.C., Augustus expelled astrologers from Rome, yet he himself avidly consulted his horoscope; Suet.*Aug.* 94; DioCass.49.43. For a perceptive analysis of an Augustan sculptural display based on the zodiac, see B. A. Kellum, "The City Adorned: Programmatic Display at the *Aedes Concordiae Augustae,*" in Raaflaub/Toher, *Between Republic and Empire,* 294–6.

32. In 46 B.C., Caesar had begun restructuring the Roman calendar in order to bring the months back in alignment with the seasons; Z. Yavetz, *Julius Caesar and his Public Image* (London: Thames and Hudson 1983), 111–14. Augustus helped implement and strengthen the Julian calendar; Suet.*Aug.*31; Pliny *HN.*18.211; J. Gagé, Res Gestae Divi Augusti (Paris: Les Belles Lettres 1977), 155–85. The *princeps* also tinkered with other temporal systems, as evidenced from his machinations to justify celebrating a *saeculum* in 17 B.C.

33. D. R. Stuart, "The Reputed Influence of Dies Natalis," *TAPA* 36 (1905): 57–63; Beard, "Times," 9–10; Gros, *Aurea Templa,* 31–5. For the historiography regarding Augustus and his conception sign, the capri-

corn, see B. A. Kellum, "The City Adorned: Programmatic Display at the *Aedes Concordiae Augustae*," in Raaflaub/Toher, *Between Republic and Empire*, 385–7; Tamsyn S. Barton, *Power and Knowledge, Astrology, Physiognomics, and Medicine under the Roman Empire* (Ann Arbor: University of Michigan Press 1994), 40–1.

34. Coarelli, *Roma Sepolta,* 99–100; Gagé, *Res Gestae,* 181–2.

35. On the confusion over the date and nature of this event, see Gagé, *Res Gestae,* 165.

36. Ancient sources disagree about when Sextilis became August: either in 27 B.C., when Octavian assumed the title, or in 8 B.C., in association with the census; Censorius *Die natali* 22.16; Macrob.*Satur.* 1.12.35; Dion.Hal.*Ant.Rom.*55.6.7; cf. Livy *Per.*134. Suetonius flat out states that Augustus himself made the decision to rename the month; *Aug.*31.

37. On the orchestration of events in the calendar, see Wallace-Hadrill, "Time for Augustus," 227–8.

38. Outside Rome, Drusus founded the cult of Roma and Augustus in Gaul on August 1, 12 B.C. Dio Cassius gives the first as the *dies natalis* of the Mars temple in the Forum Augustum, though he may be in error or referring to the Mars structure on the Capitoline; Roman calendars usually place the dedication on May 12. Also questionable is Dio's statement that the censors drove a nail into the wall of the Mars temple at the close of their term, an act that should be compared with the ancient custom of marking each year with a nail in the cella wall of the Temple of Jupiter Optimus Maximus; DioCass.

55.10; 60.5.3; Dion.Hal.*Ant.Rom.* 51.19. 6; Livy 7.3.5–8; Gagé, *Res Gestae,* 157–8, 173–6; Anderson, *Historical Topography,* 93–4.

39. A. Dundes and A. Falassi, *La terra in Piazza: An Interpretation of the Palio of Siena* (Berkeley: University of California Press 1975).

40. Cities assumed the title of "Augusta" either by imperial mandate or by choice. As is often the case, the State did not sanction the wide use of the capital's name in order to keep "Roma" and her status distinct.

41. In 25 B.C., a legate of Augustus founded Augusta Emerita (Mérida) as a settlement for the veterans of the Cantabrian wars; the forum was not completed until after the dedication of the Forum Augustum in 2 B.C.; J. M. Alvarez Martinez, "El Foro de Augusta Emrita," in *Homenaje a Sáenz de Buruaga,* edited by J. Arce (Badajoz, Spain: Institucion Cultura 1982), 53–68.

42. MacDonald, "Empire Imagery," 138.

43. The urban armatures of Imperial cities are thoroughly analyzed by W. L. MacDonald, *Roman Empire II,* passim; esp. 32–110. It should be noted that the urban armatures of Roman cities were accretive, collective affairs, in stark contrast to the grand avenues imposed by other autocratic patrons, including Sixtus V and Mussolini at Rome; S. Kostof, *The City Shaped* (London: Thames and Hudson 1991), 209–74.

44. S. Freud, *Civilization and Its Discontents,* translated by J. Strachey (New York: W. W. Norton 1961), 16–20.

CHAPTER 7. A WALK THROUGH AUGUSTAN ROME, A.D. 14

1. DioCass.56.47. Instituted in 19 B.C., the Augustalia was celebrated on October 12 to mark the *princeps'* return to Rome from the east; it was proclaimed an annual festival in A.D. 14; Tac.*Ann.*1.15.3; 54.3; *ResG.*11. In an earlier passage, Dio Cas-

sius also refers to the festivities on the birthday of Augustus (September 23) as the Augustalia; 56.29.

2. J. W. Zarker, "Augustan Art and Archaeology in Vergil's *Aeneid,*" in Winkes, *The Age of Augustus,* 201.

3. Suetonius mentions forty soldiers of the praetorian guard who carried the *princeps* forth to lie in state; *Aug.*99.

4. Standing next to the funeral couch on the old Rostra, Drusus gave a short eulogy; on the opposite Rostra before the Temple of Divus Julius to the southeast, his father Tiberius gave a longer account of the *princeps'* venerable life and great attainments; DioCass.56.31; 35–41.

5. Tiberius cited several analogies for Augustus, including the hero Hercules, though he acknowledged that the achievements of the *princeps* were far greater; DioCass.53.36.

6. DioCass.56.46. Among the plethora of posthumous honors heaped upon Augustus was the provision that henceforth his image could not be carried in the funeral processions of others. The exact route of the funeral procession is unknown.

7. Unfortunately, Dio Cassius does not describe the arch or the statue in detail; 53.22.

8. On the honor associated with burial along the Via Flaminia, see Stat.*Silv.*2.1.176.

9. The area between the Mausoleum of Augustus and the Saepta may have accommodated two other tombs: the Tumulus Juliae (d. 54 B.C.) and Sepulcrum Agrippae (d. 12 B.C.); DioCass.39.64; 54.28.

10. Less is known of the hedonistic Horti Luculliani also located in this area. After the death of Lucullus, these gardens changed hands several times. By the mid-first century A.D., they were called the Horti Asiatici and became Imperial property; DioCass.55.27.3.

11. The obelisk of the Horologium Solarium Augusti is so visually powerful that it appears as an identifying attribute of the personified Campus Martius on the base of Antoninus Pius' memorial column; L. Vogel, *The Column of Antoninus Pius* (Cambridge, MA: Harvard University Press 1973), 117n.

12. The logical assumption is that the statue atop the Mausoleum faced south toward the entrance to the Mausoleum of Augustus and the city. Though the exact form of the Agrippan Pantheon remains hotly debated, it is generally agree to have faced north; cf. W. Loerke, "Georges Chedanne and the Pantheon," *Modulus* (1982): 40–55.

13. Suet.*Aug.*43; Juv.10.77–81. Romans also flocked to the Saepta to buy luxury goods; Mary T. Boatwright, *Hadrian and the City of Rome* (Princeton: Princeton University Press 1987), 36. The long flanks of the complex were known as the Porticus Argonautarum and Porticus Meleagri.

14. The Ara Pacis subsequently was mirrored across the Via Flaminia by another altar, the Ara Providentiae Augusta. Dedicated to the personification of Imperial care over the entire Roman empire, this altar stood in the Campus Agrippae perhaps as early as the reign of Tiberius; Coarelli, *Roma*, 304. Later in the Empire, the so-called Arco di Portogallo over the Via Flaminia also marked the location of the Ara Pacis; Nash, *Pictorial Dictionary*, 83–7; Niels Hannestad, *Roman Art and Imperial Policy* (Aarhus, Denmark: Jutland Archaeological Society, distrib. Aarhus University Press 1986), 206–8.

15. The pointed obelisk and moundlike Mausoleum are echoed in the forms of the famous Trylon and Perisphere for the 1939 World's Fair designed by Wallace K. Harrison.

16. The processional relief on the Ara Pacis is approximately 1.6 meters in height and the figures themselves slightly smaller than life-size.

17. The Ara Pacis has entrances on opposite sides. The U-shaped inner altar opens toward the Campus Martius, so the ceremonial approach must have been from the west.

18. Suetonius describes a purifying sacrifice (*lustrum*) at which a crowd watched an eagle circle over Augustus' head and then perch above Agrippa's name inscribed on

the Pantheon; *Aug.*97. This story confirms that the area around the Pantheon was sufficiently unencumbered to accommodate large gatherings; Boatwright, *Hadrian,* 37.

19. Because Strabo, contemporary of Augustus, did not mention the obelisks at the entrance to the Mausoleum of Augustus, they may have been erected at a later date; 5.3.8; cf. Amm.Marc.17.4.16; Boatwright, *Hadrian,* 68.

20. The old patrician may have welcomed an excuse not to explain the reliefs on this side of the monument, for as modern scholars well know, identification of the figures depicted is extremely difficult. For example, the fecund female figure may represent Tellus (Mother Earth), Venus, Ceres, or Pax.

21. Agrippa bequeathed his Campus to Augustus, who made it public property in 7 B.C.; DioCass.55.8; cf. Gell.14.5.1.

22. In 43 B.C., the Senate voted approval for a temple to Serapis and Isis, though there is no evidence that it was built immediately; DioCass.47.15.4. Augustus made provisions for Egyptian temples, yet he did not allow the rites to be celebrated inside the *pomerium;* ibid., 53.2.4. The Augustan temple to the Egyptian gods probably stood on the same extrapomerial location as the later shrine (Iseum Campense) located east of the Saepta; G. Gatti, "Topografia dell'Iseo Campense," *Rend-PontAcc* 20 (1943–4): 117–63. The Augustan Campus boasted other Egyptiana, including several obelisks and pyramidal tombs; Coarelli, *Roma,* 88–91; P. Lambrechts, *Augustus en de Egyptische Goodsdient* (Brussels: Awlsk 1956), 33–4.

23. The Campus Martius' historical association with exercise continued under Augustus. For example, youthful Roman athletes focused their exercises around the Horologium; F. Coarelli, *Roma sepolta* (Rome: Armando Curcio Editore 1984),

90. Among the many celebrations held in the Campus were the Circensian games of 28 B.C. and the Ludi Saeculares of 17 B.C., as well as various funerary ceremonies; DioCass.53.1; *CIL* 6.3232375; cf. Strab.5.3.8; Boatwright, *Hadrian,* 225–6.

24. The Temple of Juno Moneta on the Arx of the Capitoline hill was aligned with the Via Flaminia, yet few late Republican or Augustan sources refer to the structure; Ov.*Fasti.*6.183. It may have declined in importance with the transferral of the mint at the end of the first century; Richardson, *New Topographical Dictionary,* 215.

25. Pedestrians entering the Forum on the Clivus Argentarius faced the large northwestern wall of the Curia Julia; it is tempting to hypothesize that paintings were displayed here as they had been earlier on the walls of the Curia Hostilia; Pliny *HN* 35.22. From the Vicus Iugarius on the opposite side of the Forum Romanum, the view of the Curia was encumbered by intervening buildings.

26. L. Munatius Plancus restored the temple in 42 B.C. when consul and supporter of Mark Antony. A decade later, he changed allegiances and went over to the side of Octavian; in 27 B.C., he subsequently proposed Octavian adopt the title "Augustus." By the time of the fictional walk through Rome, few would remember his early anti-Octavian affiliations.

27. The Temple of Divus Augustus, also known as the *templum novum,* was begun by Tiberius, probably in conjunction with his mother. The ancient sources are confused as to who finished and dedicated the temple; Suet.*Tib.*47; *Calig.*21. What seems obvious is that Tiberius did not rush to complete the temple honoring his resented stepfather. Until extensive excavations are conducted in the area behind the Basilica Julia, the exact location of this temple will likewise remain uncertain.

ABBREVIATIONS

Anderson, *Historical Topography*	James Anderson Jr. *The Historical Topography of the Imperial Fora.* Coll.Lat. 182. Brussels: Latomus 1984.
Blake, *Roman Construction*	M. E. Blake. *Ancient Roman Construction in Italy from the Prehistoric Period to Augustus.* Washington, DC: American Philosophical Society 1947.
Coarelli, *Roma*	F. Coarelli. *Roma Guide archeologiche Laterza.* Rome: Laterza and Figli 1980.
Gagé, *Res Gestae*	J. Gagé. *Res Gestae Divi Augusti.* Paris: Les Belles Lettres 1977.
Gros, *Aurea Templa*	P. Gros. *Aurea Templa: Recherches sur l'architecture religieuse de Rome à l'époque d'Auguste.* Rome: École Française de Rome 1976.
Hofter, *Kaiser Augustus*	M. Hofter. *Kaiser augustus und die verlorene Republik.* Mainz: P. von Zabern 1988.
Holliday, *Narrative and Event*	P. Holliday. *Narrative and Event in Ancient Art.* New York: Cambridge University Press 1993.
Homo, *Rome impériale*	Léon Homo. *Rome impériale et l'urbanisme dans l'antiquité,* 2nd ed. Paris: Éditions Albin Michel 1971.
MacDonald, "Empire Imagery"	W. L. MacDonald. "Empire Imagery in Augustan Architecture." In *The Age of Augustus,* edited by Rolf Winkes, Archaeologia Transatlantica 5 (Louvain-la-Neuve, Belgium: Art and Archaeology Publications 1985), 137–48.
MacDonald, *Roman Empire I*	W. L. MacDonald. *The Architecture of the Roman Empire, Volume I: Introductory Study,* 2nd ed. New Haven: Yale University Press 1982.
MacDonald, *Roman Empire II*	W. L. MacDonald. *The Architecture of the Roman Empire, Volume II: An Urban Appraisal.* New Haven: Yale University Press 1986.
Nash, *Pictorial Dictionary*	E. Nash. *Pictorial Dictionary of Ancient Rome,* 2nd rev. ed., 2 vols. New York: Praeger 1968.
Platner/Ashby, *Dictionary*	S. B. Platner and T. Ashby. *A Topographical Dictionary of Ancient Rome,* 2 vols. Oxford: Clarendon Press 1929.

Raaflaub/Toher, *Between Republic and Empire* — Kurt Raaflaub and Mark Toher, eds. *Between Republic and Empire, Interpretations of Augustus and his Principate*. Berkeley: University of California Press 1990.

Richardson, *New Topographical Dictionary* — Lawrence Richardson Jr. *A New Topographical Dictionary of Ancient Rome*. Baltimore: Johns Hopkins University Press 1992.

Stambaugh, *Ancient Roman City* — John E. Stambaugh. *The Ancient Roman City*. Baltimore: Johns Hopkins University Press 1988.

Ward-Perkins, *Imperial Architecture* — John Ward-Perkins. *Roman Imperial Architecture*. Harmondsworth: Penguin Books 1981.

Weinstock, *Divus Iulius* — S. Weinstock. *Divus Iulius*. Oxford: Clarendon Press 1971.

Winkes, *The Age of Augustus* — Rolf Winkes, ed. *The Age of Augustus*. Louvain-La-Neuve: Art and Archaeology Publications 1985.

Zanker, *Images* — P. Zanker. *The Power of Images in the Age of Augustus*. Ann Arbor: University of Michigan Press 1988.

BIBLIOGRAPHY

Abbreviations follow the *AJA* format, supplemented by those of the *Oxford Classical Dictionary*.

Adam, Jean Pierre. *La Construction romaine: materiaux et techniques*. Paris: Picard 1984.

Albertson, F. "An Augustan Temple Represented on a Historical Relief Dating to the Time of Claudius." *AJA* 91 (1987): 441–58.

Balsdon, J. P. V. D. *Life and Leisure in Ancient Rome*. New York: McGraw-Hill 1969.
  Romans and Aliens. Chapel Hill: University of North Carolina Press 1979.

Barasch, Moshe. *Theories of Art, From Plato to Winkelmann*. New York: New York University Press 1985.

Bergmann, B. "The Roman House as Memory Theater: The House of the Tragic Poet in Pompeii." *ArtB* 76.2 (June 1994): 225–56.

Bieber, M. *The History of the Greek and Roman Theater*. Princeton: Princeton University Press 1961.

Bloomer, Kent C., and Charles W. Moore, *Body, Memory, and Architecture*. New Haven: Yale University Press 1977.

Blumenfield, Hans. "Scale in Civic Design." *Town Planning Review* 24.1 (April 1953): 35–46.

Boatwright, Mary T. *Hadrian and the City of Rome*. Princeton: Princeton University Press 1987.

Bodei-Giglioni, G. *Lavori pubblici e occupazione nell'antichità classica*. Bologna: Patron 1974.

Boëthius, Axel. *Etruscan and Early Roman Architecture*. Harmondsworth: Penguin Books 1978.
  The Golden House of Nero. Ann Arbor: University of Michigan Press 1960.
  "L'insula romana secondo Léon Homo." *Colloqui del Sodalizio* II. Rome: L'Erma 1956, 1–12.

Bourne, F. C. *The Public Works of the Julio Claudians and Flavians*. Princeton: George Banta Publishing 1946.

Bowersock, G. W. *Augustus and the Greek World*. Oxford: Clarendon Press 1965.
  "The Pontificate of Augustus." In Raaflaub/Toher, *Between Republic and Empire*, 380–94.

333

Boyd, C. E. *Public Libraries and Literary Culture in Ancient Rome*. Chicago: University of Chicago Press 1915.

Braudy, Leo. *The Frenzy of Renown*. New York: Oxford University Press, 1986.

Bréguet, E. "Urbi et orbi, Un cliché et un theme." In *Hommages à Marcel Renard*, edited by Jacqueline Bibauw. Brussels: Latomus 1969, 140–52.

Brendel, Otto. *Prolegomena to the Study of Roman Art*. New Haven: Yale University Press, reprinted 1979.

Brilliant, Richard. *Visual Narratives. Storytelling in Etruscan and Roman Art*. Ithaca, NY: Cornell University Press 1984.

Brown, Frank. "Roman Architecture." *College Art Journal* 17.2 (1958): 105–14.

Roman Architecture. New York: Braziller 1965.

Brunt, P. A. "Princeps and Equites." *JRS* 73 (1983): 42–75.

Brunt, P. A., and J. M. Moore. *Res Gestae Divi Augusti*. London: Oxford University Press 1967.

Buchner, Edmund. *Die Sonnenuhr des Augustus*. Mainz am Rhein: Von Zabern 1982.

Carcopino, J. *Daily Life in Ancient Rome*. Edited with bibliography and notes by Henry T. Rowell; translated by E. O. Lorimer. New Haven: Yale University Press 1940.

Carettoni, G. *Das Haus des Augustus auf dem Palatin*. Mainz am Rhein: Von Zabern 1983.

Castagnoli, F. "Il Campo Marzio nell'antichità." *MemLinc* 8.1 (1945): 93–193.

Topografia e urbanistica di Roma antica. Bologna: L. Cappelli 1969.

Clarke, John R. *The Houses of Roman Italy, 100 B.C.–A.D. 250, Ritual, Space, and Decoration*. Berkeley: University of California Press 1991.

Clay, Grady. *Close-Up: How to Read the American City*. New York: Praeger 1973.

Coarelli, F. "Il Campo Marzio occidentale. Storia e topografia." *MEFRA* 89 (1977): 807–46.

Il Foro Romano, 1: periodo arcaico. Rome: Edizioni Quasar 1983.

Il Foro Romano, 2: periodo repubblicano e augusteo. Rome: Edizioni Quasar 1985.

"Organizzazione urbanistica della Roma augustea." In *Roma repubblicana dal 270 a.C. all'età augustea*, edited by F. Coarelli et al. Roma: Quasar 1987, 7–16.

"Public Building in Rome between the Second Punic War and Sulla," *PBSR* 45 (1977): 1–23.

"Rom. Die Stadtplanung von Caesar bis Augustus." In *Kaiser augustus und die verlorene Republik*, edited by M. Hofter. Mainz am Rhein: Von Zabern 1988, 68–80.

Roma sepolta. Rome: Armando Curcio Editore 1984.

Coarelli, F, et al., eds. *Roma repubblicana dal 270 a.C. all'età augustea*. Roma: Quasar 1987.

Corlàita, D. Scagliarini. "La situazione urbanistica degli archi onorari nella prima età imperiale." In *Studi sull'Arco Onorario Romano*. Studia Archaeologica 21. Rome: L'Erma di Bretschneider 1979, 29–72.

Cullen, Gordon. *The Concise Townscape*. London: Architectural Press 1961.

de Fine Licht, K., ed. *Città e architettura nella Roma Imperiale. Atti del seminario del 27 ottobre 1981 (AnalRom Suppl. 10, Odense University Press 1983)*.

De Maria, Sandro. *Gli Archi Onorari di Roma e Dell'Italia Romana*. Bibliotheca Archaeologica 7. Rome: L'Erma di Bretschneider 1988.

Drerup, H. "Architektur als Symbol." *Gymnasium* 73 (1966): 181–96.

zum Ausstattungsluxus in der römischen Architektur, Ein formgeschichtlicher Versuch. Munster, Wesphalia: Aschendorffsche Verlgsbuchhandlung 1957.

"Bildraum und Realraum in der römischen Architektur." *RömMitt* 66 (1959): 147–74.

Dudley, Donald. *Urbs Roma, A Source Book of Classical Texts on the City and Its Monuments.* Aberdeen: Phaidon, 1967.

Dupont, Florence. *Daily Life in Ancient Rome.* Translated by Christopher Woodall. Oxford: Blackwell 1992.

Earl, Donald. *The Age of Augustus.* New York: Crown Publishers 1968.

Evans, Jane DeRose. *The Art of Persuasion, Political Propaganda from Aeneas to Brutus.* Ann Arbor: University of Michigan Press 1992.

Favro, Diane. "*Pater urbis*: Augustus as City Father of Rome." *JSAH* 51 (1992): 61–84.

"Reading the Augustan City." In *Narrative and Event in Ancient Art,* edited by Peter Holliday. New York: Cambridge University Press 1993, 230–57.

"The Roman Forum and Roman Memory." *Places* 5:1 (1988): 17–24.

"Rome. The Street Triumphant: The Urban Impact of Roman Triumphal Parades." In *Streets of the World, Critical Perspectives on Public Space,* edited by Zeynep Çelik, Diane Favro, and Richard Ingersoll. Berkeley: University of California Press 1994, 151–64.

"Was Man the Measure?" In *Architects' People,* edited by R. Ellis and D. Cuff. New York: Oxford University Press 1989, 15–43.

Frank, T. *Roman Buildings of the Republic. An attempt to date them from their materials.* PAAR III. Rome: American Academy in Rome 1924.

Friedländer, Ludwig. *Roman Life and Manners under the Early Empire.* Translated by L. A. Magnus. New York: E. P. Dutton 1928–36.

Geertman, H., and J. J. de Jong, eds. *Munus non Ingratum, BABesch Supplement* 2. Leiden: Stichting Bulletin Antieke Beschaving 1989.

Gernentz, G. *Laudes Romae.* Rostochii: Typis Academicis Adlerianis 1918.

Giulani, C. F., and P. Verduchi. *L'Area Centrale del Foro Romano.* Università degli Studi di Roma La Sapienza: Il linguaggio dell'architettura romana I. Florence: Leo S. Olschiki 1987.

Gjerstad, Einar. "Die Ursprungsgeschichte der römischen Kaiserfora." *Acta Inst. Rom. Regni Sueciae* 10 (1944): 40–71.

Göthein, M. L. *A History of Garden Art.* London: J. M. Dent 1914.

Grimal, P. *Les Jardins romains.* BEFAR 155. Paris: Presses Universitaires de France 1969.

Gros, P. *Architecture et sociétè.* Collection de l'École Française de Rome 66. Rome: École Française de Rome 1983.

Aurea Templa: Recherches sur l'architecture religieuse de Rome à l'époque d'Auguste. Bibliothèque des Ecoles Françaises d'Athènes et de Rome. Fasc. 231. Rome: Ecole française de Rome 1976.

Gros, P., and Gilles Sauron. "Das politische Programm de öffentlichen Bauten." In Hofter, *Kaiser Augustus,* 48–50.

Giuliani, C. F. "Il Foro romano in età augustea." In *Roma repubblicana dal 270 A.C. all'età augustea,* edited by F. Coarelli et al. Roma: Quasar 1987, 23–8.

Hannestad, Niels. *Roman Art and Imperial Policy.* Aarhus: Jutland Archaeological Society, distrib. Aarhus University Press 1986.

Hanson, J. A. *Roman Theater-Temples.* Princeton: Princeton University Press 1959.

Harris, William V. *War and Imperialism in Republican Rome 327-70 B.C.* Oxford: Clarendon Press 1979.

Hastrup, Thure. "Forum Iulium as a Manifestation of Power." *AnalRom.* 2 (1962): 45–61.

Havelock, Christine. "Art as Communication in Ancient Greece." In *Communication Arts in the Ancient World,* edited by Eric A. Havelock and Jackson P. Hershbell. New York: Hastings House 1978, 95–118.

Haverfield, F. *Ancient Town-Planning.* Oxford: Clarendon Press 1913.

Holliday, Peter. "Time, History and Ritual on the Ara Pacis Augustae." *ArtB* 72.4 (December 1990): 542–57.

Holloway, R. R. "The Tomb of Augustus and the Princes of Troy." *AJA* 79 (1966): 171–3.

Johnson, J. R. "Augustan Propaganda." Ph.D. diss., University of California, Los Angeles, 1976.

Jones, A. H. M. *The Greek City from Alexander to Justinian.* Oxford: Clarendon Press 1940.

Jones, Mark Wilson. "Designing the Roman Corinthian order." *JRA* 2 (1989): 35–69.

Jordon, H., and C. Hülsen. *Topographia der Stadt Röm im Althertum.* 2 vols. Berlin: Weidmannsche Buchhandlung 1871–1907.

Kellum, B. A. *The City Adorned: The Play of Meaning in Augustan Rome.* Princeton University Press, forthcoming.

   "The City Adorned: Programmatic Display at the *Aedes Concordiae Augustae*." In Raaflaub/Toher, *Between Republic and Empire,* 276–307.

   "The Construction of Landscape in Augustan Rome: The Garden Room at the Villa *ad Gallinas*." *ArtB* 76.2 (June 1994): 211–24.

   "Sculptural Programs and Propaganda in Augustan Rome: The Temple of Apollo on the Palatine and the Forum of Augustus." Ph.D. dissertation, Harvard University, Cambridge, 1982.

   "Sculptural Programs and Propaganda in Augustan Rome: the Temple of Apollo on the Palatine." In Winkes, *The Age of Augustus,* 169–76.

   "What We see and Don't See. Narrative Structure and the Ara Pacis Augustae." *Art History* 17.1 (March 1994): 26–45.

Kleiner, D. E. E. "The Great Friezes of the Ara Pacis Augustae. Greek Sources, Roman Derivatives, and Augustan Social Policy." *MEFR* xc (1978): 753–85.

   Roman Sculpture. New Haven: Yale University Press 1992.

Kleiner, Fred S. "The Arch in Honor of C. Octavius and the Fathers of Augustus." *Historia* 37.3 (1988): 347–57.

   The Arch of Nero in Rome. A Study of the Roman Honorary Arch before and under Nero. Archaeologica 52. Rome: G. Bretschneider 1985.

   "The study of Roman triumphal and honorary arches 50 years after Kaehler." *JRA* 2 (1989): 195–206.

Kraft, K. "Der Sinn des Mausoleums des Augustus." *Historia* 16 (1967): 189–206.

Kuttner, Anne. "Some New Grounds for Narrative. Marcus Antonius's Base (*The Ara Domitti Ahenobarbi*) and Republican Biographies." In *Narrative and Event in Ancient Art,* edited by Peter Holliday. New York: Cambridge University Press 1993, 198–229.

Kyrieleis, H. "Zur Vorgeschichte der Kaiserfora." In *Hellenismus in Mittelitalien. Kolloquium in Göttingen vom 5. bis 9. Juni 1974,* edited by P. Zanker. Göttingen Vandenhoeck und Ruprecht 1976, 431–8.

Labrousse, Michel. "Le Pomerium de la Rome impériale." *MEFR* 54 (1937): 165–99.

Lanciani, R. *Ruins and Excavations of Ancient Rome*. New York and Boston: Houghton Mifflin 1897.

Leach, E. *The Rhetoric of Space, Literary and Artistic Representations of Landscape in Republican and Augustan Rome*. Princeton: Princeton University Press 1988.

Lugli, G. *Fontes ad topographiam veteris urbis Romae pertinentes*. Rome: Università di Roma 1952.

"Le temple d'Apollon et les édifices d'Auguste sur le Palatin." *CRAI* (1950): 276–85.

Roma antica: il centro monumentale. Rome: G. Bardi editore 1946.

Lynch, Kevin. *The Image of the City*. Cambridge, MA: MIT Press 1960.

Mellor, Ronald. "The Goddess Roma." *ANRW* 2 (1981): 954–1030.

Mierse, W. "Augustan Building Programs in the Western Provinces." In Raaflaub/Toher, *Between Republic and Empire*, 308–33.

Millar, F. *The Emperor in the Roman World*. Ithaca, NY: Cornell University Press 1977.

Millar, F., and E. Segal, eds. *Caesar Augustus. Seven Aspects*. Oxford: Oxford University Press 1984.

Moynihan, R. "Geographical Mythology and Roman Imperial Ideology." In Winkes, *The Age of Augustus*, 149–62.

Muratori, S. *Operante Storia Urbana di Roma*. Rome: Instituto Poligrafico dello Stato P.V. 1963.

Nedergaard, Elisabeth. "Zur Problematik der Augustusbögen auf dem Forum Romanum." In *Kaiser augustus und die verlorene Republik*, edited by M. Hofter. Mainz am Rhein: Von Zabern 1988, pp. 224-239.

Nicolet, Claude. *Space, Geography, and Politics in the Early Roman Empire*. Translated by Hélène Leclerc. Ann Arbor: University of Michigan Press 1991.

Norberg-Schulz, Christian. *Genius Loci: Towards a Phenomenology of Architecture*. New York: Rizzoli 1980.

Ogilvie, R. M. *The Romans and Their Gods in the Age of Augustus*. New York: W. W. Norton 1969.

Olinder, B. *Porticus Octavia in Circo Flaminio. Topographical Studies in the Campus Region of Rome*. Svenska Institutet Skriften 8.ii. Rome: P. Aastroems Foerlag 1974.

Oliver, James H. "The Augustan Pomerium." *MAAR* 10 (1932): 145–82.

Onians, J. *Art and Thought in the Hellenistic Age*. London: Thames and Hudson 1979.

Owens, E. J. *The City in the Greek and Roman World*. London: Routeledge 1991.

Pais, Jean. *Res Gestae Divi Augusti*. Paris: Société d'Edition Les Belles Lettres 1977.

Palmer, R. E. A. "C. Verres' Legacy of Charm and Love to the City of Rome." *Rend-PontAcc* 51–2 (1978–80): 111–36.

"Jupiter Blaze, God of the Hills, and the Roman Topography of *CIL* VI 377." *AJA* 80.1 (Winter 1976): 43–56.

Roman Religion and Roman Empire. Philadelphia: University of Pennsylvania Press 1974.

"A Roman Street Named Good." *JIES* 1.3 (1973): 368–78.

Paoli, Ugo Enrico. *Rome, Its People, Life and Customs*. New York: David McKay 1963.

Pape, M. *Griechische Kunstwerke aus Kriegsbeute und ihre öffentliche Aufstellung in Rom: von der Eroberung von Syrakus bis augusteische Zeit*. Ph.D. dissertation, University of Hamburg, 1975.

Patterson, John R. "Survey Article. The City of Rome: From Republic to Empire." *JRS* 82 (1992): 186–215.

Payne, Robert. *The Roman Triumph*. London: Robert Hale 1962.

Picard, G. Ch. *Rome et les villes d'Italie, des Gracques à la mort d'Auguste.* Paris: Société d'édition d'enseignement supérieur 1978.

Pietri, C., ed. *L'Urbs, Espace urbain et histoire.* Rome: École française de Rome 1987.

Pollini, J. "The Gemma Augustea: Ideology, Rhetorical Imagery, and the Creation of a Dynastic Narrative." In *Narrative and Event,* edited by Peter Holliday. New York: Cambridge University Press 1993, 258–98.

Pollitt, J. J. *Art in the Hellenistic Age.* Cambridge: Cambridge University Press 1986.

Price, Martin J., and Bluma L. Trell. *Coins and Their Cities: Architecture on the Ancient Coins of Greece, Rome, and Palestine.* Detroit: Wayne State University Press 1977.

Purcell, Nicholas. "Rediscovering the Roman Forum." *JRA* 2 (1989): 157–66.

"Town in Country and Country in Town." In *Ancient Roman Villa Gardens,* edited by E. B. MacDougall. Dumbarton Oaks Colloquium on the History of Landscape Architecture 10. Washington, DC: Dumbarton Oaks, 185–203.

Rasmussen, S. E. *Experiencing Architecture.* Cambridge, MA: MIT Press 1977.

Richmond, I. A. "Commemorative Arches and City Gates in the Augustan Age." *JRS* 23 (1933): 149–74.

Robinson, O. F. *Ancient Rome, City Planning and Administration.* London: Routledge 1992.

Roddaz, Jean-Michel. *Marcus Agrippa.* BEFAR 253. Paris: Presses Universitaires de France 1984.

Rossetto, P. Ciancio. *Il sepolcro del fornaio Marco Virgilio Eurisace a Porta Maggiore.* I Monumenti romani 5. Rome: Istituto di studi romani 1973.

Rowell, H. T. *Rome in the Augustan Age.* Norman: University of Oklahoma Press 1962.

Scagnetti, F., and G. Grande. *Roma Urbs Imperatorum Aetate.* Rome: Staderini 1979.

Scullard, H. H. *Festivals and Ceremonies of the Roman Republic.* London: Thames and Hudson 1981.

Settis, S. "Die Ara Pacis." In Hofter, *Kaiser Augustus,* 400–26.

Shatzman, I. *Senatorial Wealth and Roman Politics.* Collection Latomus 142. Brussels: Latomus 1975.

Shipley, F. W. *Agrippa's Building Activities in Rome.* St. Louis: Washington University Press 1933.

"Building Operations in Rome from the Death of Caesar to the Death of Augustus." *MAAR* 9 (1931): 7–60.

Sjöqvist, E. "Kaisareion: A Study in Architectural Iconography," *OpRom* 1 (1954): 86–108.

Stambaugh, John E. "The Functions of Roman Temples." *ANRW* 2.16.1 (1978): 554–608.

Storoni Mazzolani, L. *The Idea of the City in Roman Thought.* Translated by S. O'Donnell. Bloomington: Indiana University Press 1970.

Strong, D. E. "The Administration of Public Building in Rome during the Later Republic and Early Empire." *BICS* 15 (1968): 97–109.

"Some observations on early Roman Corinthian." *JRS* 53 (1963): 73–84.

"The Temple of Castor in the Forum Romanum." *PBSR* 30 (1962): 1–30.

Stuart, D. R. "The Reputed Influence of Dies Natalis." *TAPA* 36 (1905): 52–63.

Syme, Ronald. *The Roman Revolution,* repr. Oxford: Clarendon Press 1939.

Tamm, Birgitta. *Auditorium and Palatium.* Stockholm Studies in Classical Archaeology 2. Stockholm: Almqvist and Wiksells 1963.

Taylor, Lily Ross. *The Divinity of the Roman Emperor*. Middletown, CT: American Philological Association 1931.

"The Worship of Augustus in Italy." *TAPA* 51 (1920): 124–33.

Thornton, M. K., and R. L. Thornton. *Julio-Claudian Building Programs: A Quantitative Study in Political Management*. Wauconda, IL: Bolchazy-Carducci Publishers 1989.

Torelli, Mario. *Typology and Structure of Roman Historical Reliefs*. Ann Arbor: University of Michigan Press 1982.

Tuan, Yi-Fu. *Topophilia*. Englewood Cliffs, NJ: Prentice Hall 1974.

Ulrich, Roger B. "Julius Caesar and the Creation of the Forum Iulium." *AJA* 97.1 (January 1993): 49–80.

Veyne, Paul. *Bread and Circuses*. Translated by Brian Pearce. London: Penguin Books 1990.

Voigt, M. "Die römischen Baugesetze." *SBLeip* 55 (1903): 175–98.

von Hesberg, Henner. "Die Veranderung des Erscheinungsbildes der Stadt Rom unter Augustus." In *Kaiser augustus und die verlorene Republik*, edited by M. Hofter. Mainz am Rhein: Von Zabern 1988, 93–115.

Wallace-Hadrill, Andrew. "Roman Arches and Greek Honours." *PCPS* 216 n.s. 36 (1990): 143–81.

"The Social Structure of the Roman House." *BSR* 56 n.s. 43 (1988): 43–97.

"Time for Augustus: Ovid, Augustus and the *Fasti*." In *Homo Viator. Classical Essays for John Bramble*, edited by M. Whitby, P. Hardie, and M. Whitby. Bedminster: Bristol Classical Press 1987, 221–30.

Wiseman, T. P. *Catullus and His World: A Reappraisal*. Cambridge: Cambridge University Press 1985.

"The Circus Flaminius." *PBSR* 42 (1974): 3–26.

"*Conspicui Postes Tectaque Digna Deo*: The Public Image of Aristocratic and Imperial Houses in the Late Republic and Early Empire." In *L'Urbs, Espace urbain et histoire*, edited by C. Pietri. Rome: École française de Rome, 1987, 475–89.

"Strabo on the Campus Martius: 5.3.8, C235." *Liverpool Classical Monthly*. 4:7 (July 1979): 129–34.

"The Temple of Victory on the Palatine." *AntJ* LXI (1981): 35–52.

"Topography and Rhetoric. The Trial of Manlius." *Historia* 28 (1979): 32–50.

"The Two Worlds of Titus Lucretius." *Cinna the Poet and Other Roman Essays*. Leicester: Leicester University Press 1974, 11–43.

Wiseman, T. P., ed. *Roman Political Life 90 B.C.–A.D. 69*. Exeter: University of Exeter 1985.

Yates, Frances. *The Art of Memory*. Chicago: University of Chicago Press 1966.

Yavetz, Z. *Julius Caesar and his Public Image*. London: Thames and Hudson 1983.

Plebs and Princeps. Oxford: Clarendon Press 1969.

Yegül, Fikret. *Baths and Bathing in Classical Antiquity*. New York and Cambridge, MA: Architectural History Foundation/MIT Press 1992.

Zanker, Paul. "Der Apollontempel auf dem Palatin. Ausstattung und politische Sinnbezüge nach der Schlacht von Actium." In *Città e architettura nella Roma Imperiale. Atti del seminario del 27 ottobre 1981*, edited by K. de Fine Licht. *AnalRom* Suppl. 10, Odense University Press 1983, 21–40.

"Drei Stadtbilder aus dem Augusteischen Rome." In *L'Urbs, Espace urbain et histoire*, edited by C. Pietri. Rome: École française de Rome 1987, 475–89.

Forum Augustum. Tübingen: Ernst Wasmuth Verlag 1972.

Forum Romanum: Die Neugestaltung unter Augustus. Monumenta Artis Antiquae 5. Tübingen: Wasmuth 1972.

"Über die Werkstätten augusteischer Laren altäre und damit zusammenhängende Probleme der Interpretation." *BullCom* 82 (1970–1): 147–155.

Zarker, J. W. "Augustan Art and Archaeology in Vergil's Aeneid." In Winkes, *The Age of Augustus,* 197–208.

Ziolkowski, Adam. *The Temples of Mid-Republican Rome and Their Historical and Topographical Context.* Rome: L'Erma di Bretschneider 1992.

INDEX